THE
AMBASSADOR

ALSO BY
SUSAN RONALD

Condé Nast:
The Man and His Empire—A Biography

A Dangerous Woman:
American Beauty, Noted Philanthropist, Nazi
Collaborator—The Life of Florence Gould

Hitler's Art Thief:
Hildebrand Gurlitt, the Nazis, and the Looting of Europe's
Treasures

Shakespeare's Daughter (A Novel)

Heretic Queen:
Queen Elizabeth I and the Wars of Religion

The Pirate Queen:
Queen Elizabeth I, Her Pirate Adventurers, and the Dawn
of Empire

The Sancy Blood Diamond:
Power, Greed, and the Cursed History of One of the World's
Most Coveted Gems

France:
The Crossroads of Europe

THE
AMBASSADOR

JOSEPH P. KENNEDY
AT THE
COURT OF ST. JAMES'S
1938–1940

SUSAN RONALD

ST. MARTIN'S PRESS
NEW YORK

First published in the United States by St. Martin's Press,
an imprint of St. Martin's Publishing Group

THE AMBASSADOR. Copyright © 2021 by Susan Ronald.
All rights reserved. Printed in the United States of America.
For information, address St. Martin's Publishing Group,
120 Broadway, New York, NY 10271.

www.stmartins.com

Library of Congress Cataloging-in-Publication Data

Names: Ronald, Susan, author.
Title: The ambassador : Joseph P. Kennedy at the Court of St. James's
    1938–1940 / Susan Ronald.
Other titles: Joseph P. Kennedy at the Court of St. James's 1938-1940
Description: First edition. | New York : St. Martin's Press, 2021. |
    Includes bibliographical references and index.
Identifiers: LCCN 2021006975 | ISBN 9781250238726
    (hardcover) | ISBN 9781250238733 (ebook)
Subjects: LCSH: Kennedy, Joseph P. (Joseph Patrick), 1888–1969. |
    Ambassadors—United States—Biography. | World War,
    1939–1945—Diplomatic history. | United States—Foreign
    relations—1933–1945. | Great Britain—Foreign relations—
    1936–1945. | Kennedy, Joseph P. (Joseph Patrick), 1888–1969—
    Political and social views. | United States—Foreign relations—
    Great Britain. | Great Britain—Foreign relations—United States.
Classification: LCC E748.K376 R65 2021 | DDC 973.9092 [B]—
    dc23
LC record available at https://lccn.loc.gov/2021006975

Our books may be purchased in bulk for promotional,
educational, or business use. Please contact your local bookseller or
the Macmillan Corporate and Premium Sales Department
at 1-800-221-7945, extension 5442, or by email
at MacmillanSpecialMarkets@macmillan.com.

First Edition: 2021

10 9 8 7 6 5 4 3 2 1

For Doug
Always

CONTENTS

JOSEPH PATRICK KENNEDY
FAMILY TREE

Joseph Patrick Kennedy
(1888–1969)
m.
Rose Fitzgerald Kennedy
(1890–1995)

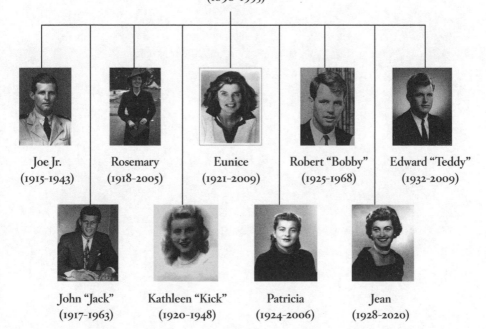

Joe Jr.
(1915–1943)

Rosemary
(1918–2005)

Eunice
(1921–2009)

Robert "Bobby"
(1925–1968)

Edward "Teddy"
(1932–2009)

John "Jack"
(1917–1963)

Kathleen "Kick"
(1920–1948)

Patricia
(1924–2006)

Jean
(1928–2020)

NOTE ON NAMES
AND SPELLING

During the 1930s and 1940s many Europeans and Americans, including Joe Kennedy, incorrectly referred to the United Kingdom of Great Britain and Northern Ireland as "England." I refer to the country as "Great Britain" herein, as it is more in accordance with modern sensitivities. During Joe Kennedy's tenure as American ambassador to the Court of St. James's in London from February 18, 1938, until January 11, 1941, the British Empire and Dominions still encompassed two-fifths of the world's land surface, making it the largest empire ever known. Following World War II, mapmakers enjoyed a heyday renaming and recoloring maps and globes as the British, Italian, French, and Dutch empires were all dissolved, and countries often changed their names. Cities and smaller places, too, like airports, also had different names. I refer to all these entities in the names of the period herein. The term "MP" stands for Member of Parliament and is shortened after the first mention. Any quotations in English are spelled either in American English or British English depending on the original source. I have not corrected the grammar or typographical errors in the Kennedy or other letters, but have where necessary clarified the text [in square brackets].

The first task of an ambassador is to faithfully interpret the views of his own Government to the Government to which he is accredited . . . the second is to explain, no less accurately, the views and standpoint of the Government of the country in which he is stationed to the Government of his own country . . .

—SIR NEVILE HENDERSON,
BRITISH AMBASSADOR TO BERLIN 1937–1939,
FAILURE OF A MISSION

THE
AMBASSADOR

PROLOGUE

O n the same day Adolf Hitler traveled south to the French border with Spain for talks with Generalissimo Francisco Franco, U.S. Ambassador Joseph Patrick Kennedy bid his farewells to senior members of his team at the American embassy in London. As staffers shuffled out of the ambassador's office, some were dabbing tears from their eyes while others sported half-hidden sly smiles. Despite their differences of opinion about the ambassador, each one recognized that it was the end of a turbulent era of American diplomacy in Europe. In his two years and seven months in England, Joe Kennedy had been taken to the people's hearts, then widely loathed. From the outset, he was feared and deemed insufferable by both the White House and the State Department.

When Kennedy stepped out onto Grosvenor Square for the last time, the ever-present international newshounds barked: *What will you do now, Mr. Ambassador?* Kennedy—standing ramrod tall in his homburg and overcoat, perhaps some pounds thinner than his normal svelte self— merely smiled. The press generally remarked that old Joe wore a somber, even sullen face. Some mistook it as regret at being recalled "for consultation" by President Franklin D. Roosevelt. But this was no recall. And there were scores of people who knew it. Joe Kennedy was going home to put FDR out of a job.

Predictably, photographers begged the ambassador to turn this way and that. Jim Seymour, one of Kennedy's stalwart Hollywood friends, was asked to shake his boss's hand one last time for the cameras. Flanked on his right by his most private Mister Fix-It, "London Jack" Kennedy, the ambassador obeyed, seething. Minutes earlier, Kennedy's press handler, Harvey Klemmer, had given him a final warning: "For Heaven's sake, do not say anything before you see Roosevelt at the White House, for if you do, it will mean, politically, gravely damaging things."[1] So Joe hung onto his quick Irish temper and thought of his sons' futures.

Then the throng unexpectedly parted, making way for the giant figure of Prince Monolulu—the feted horse-racing tipster wearing his ostrich-feathered crown, black and gold waistcoat, multicolored silk trousers, and matching frock coat. Monolulu bellowed in a deep, honey-coated voice his famous strapline, *"I have a horse."* The photographers snapped away while Monolulu whispered to Kennedy the name of his favorite Thoroughbred running that day. Of course the ambassador had made use of Monolulu's tips during his leisure time at the races with England's ruling elite. So, Joe gave Monolulu a smile, not quite hiding his irritability.[2] When, at last, Kennedy turned away from the embassy, he also left behind the pinnacle of his public service career.

Joe Kennedy was both bitter and aggrieved. Everything had changed since his arrival in Great Britain on March 1, 1938. Former Prime Minister Neville Chamberlain, Kennedy's great friend, was dying. Winston Churchill, whom Kennedy never trusted, had become prime minister on May 10, 1940. Joe had made acres of friends in high places. Then he lost the esteem of all but a select few. The ambassador had a long memory, particularly when it came to grudges, and would never forgive Churchill, who in Joe's opinion had laid *his* military blunder in Norway that April at Chamberlain's feet. Just the same, as Kennedy was driven south to Bournemouth in thickening fog to catch his clipper flight home, he never thought that the brickbats hurled at him by the British predated Churchill's rise by over a year. Undoubtedly, the shots that stung the most came from the big guns of the White House and the U.S. State Department.[3]

BY OCTOBER 1940, Kennedy's outrage was aimed at the two-term Democratic President Franklin D. Roosevelt, for how shabbily the president had treated his ambassador to the Court of St. James's. Joe was determined to wreak his revenge on the president's bid for a third term in just ten days' time by urging everyone to vote for the Republican candidate, Wendell Willkie. Months earlier, Joe had told Clare Boothe Luce—his lover and the wife of publisher Henry R. Luce of *Time, Fortune,* and *Life*—what he planned to do. While Clare smoothed his ruffled brow, Joe might have forgotten that she was a die-hard Republican and could have had an ulterior motive in fueling his flames of indignation against the president.

And yet, Kennedy's wife, Rose, had written to her husband a few weeks earlier that she wanted to tell Roosevelt she would "guarantee to chloroform you [Joe] until after the election."[4] This is the true story of Joe Kennedy's rise to the pinnacle of his public service career as U.S. Ambassador to the Court of St. James's in London and his fall from grace.

PART I

THE WINTERS
OF OUR
DISCONTENT

Why, I, in this weak piping time of peace,
Have no delight to pass away the time,
Unless to spy my shadow in the sun . . .

—WILLIAM SHAKESPEARE, *THE TRAGEDY OF RICHARD III*,
ACT I, SCENE I

THE PRESIDENT'S MAN

---

*"Hatred" is the only word that properly defines the attitude
toward Roosevelt of thousands of men and women
among the more fortunate.*

—JOSEPH P. KENNEDY,
I'M FOR ROOSEVELT, 1936

Joseph Patrick Kennedy was sworn in as U.S. Ambassador to the Court of St. James's in London on February 18, 1938. His appointment was the belated reward for backing President Franklin D. Roosevelt in his successful reelection campaign of 1936. As thanks for his efforts in the 1932 election, Kennedy became the first ever Chairman of the Securities and Exchange Commission (SEC) from June 30, 1934, to September 23, 1935, and the first Chairman of the Federal Maritime Commission from April 14, 1937, to February 19, 1938.

Then, as now, America's ambassadors were an uneven mix of high net worth individuals—like Kennedy—and career diplomats. Often they were at loggerheads with one another, but the State Department pay scale for ambassadors was meager. Having ambassadors who could entertain lavishly in places like London, Paris, and Rome was deemed to be worth the potential friction. Since Kennedy did not have the skill set of a career diplomat, his legacy would depend entirely on what he made of his time in office during one of the most difficult periods in world history.

So, who was Joe Kennedy?

A second-generation American of Irish descent, Joe was born on September 6, 1888, in the predominantly immigrant quarter of East Boston, or Noddle's Island, as it was then known. Kennedy grew up cocky, confident, and devoutly Catholic. He would always claim that his father, Patrick Joseph "P.J." Kennedy, had been excluded from politics because he was an Irish Catholic. Yet Kennedy's Irish Catholic father-in-law, the Democrat John F. "Honey Fitz" Fitzgerald, had served in the Massachusetts state senate and in the U.S. House of Representatives, and was twice the city's beloved mayor.

In truth, P. J. Kennedy was a saloonkeeper of considerable influence, who preferred the "I scratch your back, you scratch mine" machinations of behind-the-scenes ward politics, like Frank Skeffington, the Edwin O'Connor character in the 1956 bestseller *The Last Hurrah.** Local politics promoted respect in the community—even if the methods employed by the neighborhood bosses were often illegal. Daily, P.J. and men like him doled out heaps of food for the starving, treats for orphans, whisky for a dying man, and much more. Ward bosses were the trusted shadow government, and often the only men who helped the immigrant poor, all in exchange for their votes. Poverty-stricken young men of intellectual promise were saved by politics, and men like P.J. and Honey Fitz were prime examples. Back then, local politics preferred street wisdom to a college degree.[1]

P.J. was expert at getting rich off his own largesse. As the boss of East Boston's Ward Two, he passed his philosophy of life on to Joe: nothing is given to you on a plate; you have to give a little to get a lot.[2] P.J.'s Ward Two political endeavors raised him to the middle class; which, in turn, enabled him to pay for Joe to receive his education at the expensive and prestigious—albeit Protestant—Boston Latin School and Harvard University. Joe's grades in these institutions were, at best, mediocre.

At Harvard, social acceptance outweighed the significance of good grades. Joe won his varsity letter in the last baseball game of the season against Yale as a bench substitute. Although he struck out at bat, he did

---

* O'Connor's most memorable and impressive character—the charming, humane, and underhanded Frank Skeffington—was broadly modeled on both Rose Kennedy's father, Honey Fitz, and Fitzgerald's implacable ward enemy, James Michael Curley.

end the game by tagging the Yale runner. Pocketing the winning ball, which by rights belonged to the Harvard team captain, Kennedy ran off the field with his captain in hot pursuit.[3] Joe had his father's lust for wealth and advancement—but lacked P.J.'s soul.

Most remembered for his larger-than-life personality, and always eager to press his case for social advancement, Kennedy was rough—perhaps a rough diamond. His peers often recalled his profanity, toothy smile, quick wit, quicker temper, ready charm with the girls, brawling, and dedicated organizational skills in his "not-to-be-denied pursuit of wealth."[4] Odd jobs abounded in Joe's youth, as P.J.'s obsession with status and money were ingrained in his son; just as Joe's own obsessions would be visited upon his children. They would not be outsiders like he was.

Shortsighted since a young man, wearing his horn-rimmed round glasses long before they were fashionable, Kennedy was farsighted when it came to making money. Back then, banking was still a time-honored profession, and an attractive one to a young man lusting after riches. So, with help from P.J. and his friends, Joe became a bank examiner. Not only was he paid handsomely, but his raw intelligence taught him how the whole monetary system worked.

When the tiny Columbia Trust Company in East Boston (in which P.J. held a majority interest) looked as if it might be gobbled up by a larger competitor, P.J. sent out the call to his henchmen for cash. Joe got his old Harvard classmates to back him to become "the youngest bank president in the nation" at Columbia Trust, too.[5] Some may not have liked the cocky young Kennedy, but all recognized a born money-spinner when they saw one and hopped on board.

FROM HIS YOUNGEST days, Joe longed to be an "insider" at the top man's table. That meant marrying up the social ladder. And so Honey Fitz's eldest daughter and college girl, Rose Fitzgerald, became the object of his affections. Rose was two years younger than Joe, and he had been courting her since his junior year at Harvard. It was only when Joe became America's youngest bank president at age twenty-five that the mutual dislike between Honey Fitz and P.J. melted. The wedding took place on October 7, 1914. Joe would always address his father-in-law when writing as "Mr. Mayor."

Within the year, Joseph Patrick Kennedy Jr. was born. Both grand-fathers cooed and smiled over the baby's crib, and Honey Fitz announced that he would be the first Catholic president of the United States. From that moment, Joe set his heart on making the name Kennedy as important to Americans as that other Boston name: Adams. Attaining that dream would be at the heart of Kennedy's relationship—not only with Roosevelt, but also with his sons.

YEARS AFTER ROOSEVELT'S death, in Kennedy's unpublished *Diplomatic Memoir,* he laid claim to a nodding acquaintance with young FDR as assistant secretary of the navy in 1917. Back then, Kennedy was the new assistant manager at Bethlehem Steel's Fore River Shipyard. In essence, Joe said he lost a skirmish to FDR when he was forced to release two battle-ships to the Argentinean government despite their failure to pay for them. The truth was far more damaging. Kennedy, married and father of two sons,* had avoided the draft of 1917 by taking the "reserved occupation" job at Fore River—a job which came his way with the help of his father-in-law, Honey Fitz. Fore River's general manager had met Joe at Fitzgerald's behest at a downtown Boston hotel, and agreed to hire Kennedy because "he was impressed with the young man's personal style."

What made Joe's appointment so unusual is that no one prior—or afterward—had reached a management position at Fore River without a strong background in shipbuilding.[6] Due to promotions and rapid changes in management caused by the Great War, however, Kennedy was left briefly in charge of the shipyard in October 1918, after a mere month on the job. Fore River was, according to Assistant Secretary Roosevelt, one of the most important shipyards due to its expertise in building destroyers, submarines, the largest battleships, merchant ships, and any class of cruiser.[7]

Within days of Kennedy taking over as "acting general manager," five hundred machinists went out on strike. They had been promised equal pay to the Boston Naval Shipyard by management, but after a month's delay, their pay packets remained unchanged. An employees' strike during wartime could prove fatal to American troops and the war effort. But

---

* Joe Jr. was born on July 25, 1915. John Fitzgerald was born on May 29, 1917.

Kennedy's stance was that if such a promise had been made, no one had informed him—and he was not prepared to ask the bosses at Bethlehem, either. His arrogance in ordering the skilled workmen to resume their jobs so angered the others that *all* the yard's machinists walked out. They "were joined by about 3,500 of the 9,000 workers," idling over half the shipyard. Kennedy had made a blunder that eventually took the chairman of Bethlehem Steel, Charles M. Schwab, and Roosevelt to iron out personally. Thereafter, Joe was demoted to less onerous tasks and left the shipyard shortly after the November 1918 armistice.[8] Years later, Roosevelt may not have recalled that it was Kennedy who had created the furor at Fore River. Then again, he may have chosen to ignore the incident in light of Kennedy's influence and wealth.

AFTER THE WAR and a short stint with Hayden, Stone stockbrokers in Boston, Kennedy judged his horizons had become "too big" for the city's closed Protestant Brahmin community. Possessed of an active mind, Kennedy bored easily and needed a larger stage for his talents. So, by the mid-1920s, he headed for New York and Wall Street with his young family. There he made his first multimillion-dollar fortune and bought a mansion in Bronxville, just under seventeen miles north of New York City. Kennedy then proudly set up million-dollar trust funds for each of his children. Never accepted by veteran Wall Streeters, Joe had gained a reputation as a "shrewd market speculator." He became used to the fact that he drew strong opinions, and always defended his actions as legal.

IN 1927, KENNEDY eyed up Hollywood, where he would make millions more as a producer and wheeler-dealer. Cobbling together a syndicate of his powerful Boston friends including Guy W. Currier and Louis E. Kirstein,* Kennedy raised the money to buy a loss-making British-owned company, Film Booking Offices of America, known as FBO, for a million dollars. Essentially a film distribution company, FBO was failing primarily because its British owners could not obtain affordable finance.[9] The

---

* Currier was a distinguished, wealthy, and influential Massachusetts lawyer and politician. Kirstein was the owner of Filene's, Boston's premier department store, a philanthropist, and a leader of American Jewry.

Kennedy consortium was poised to take advantage of the introduction of "talkies" that year and watched the money roll in.

Hollywood undoubtedly raised Joe's public profile to "celebrity businessman" status. The films he financed opened with the screen credit "JOSEPH P. KENNEDY PRESENTS."[10] Even so, his films were not memorable—like his *Galloping Thunder* and *The Little Buckaroo* (released in 1927 and 1928). What mattered were profits, and Kennedy cashed in, just as motion pictures became America's greatest world export.

At the first of many lunches with Hollywood's then most famous female star, Gloria Swanson, she recalled Joe's breaking into "peals of laughter" and how he began "whacking his thigh" so "unabashedly, so unaffectedly, that I [Gloria] started laughing too." She said that his expressive hands—unused to hard work—and the way he talked with them were his most remarkable feature. Most others thought it was his strong Boston accent.[11] Within weeks, Kennedy would become Swanson's business manager and lover. Uncharacteristically, Joe saw the tremendous scope for Hollywood as a sure thing, telling Swanson, "The Cabots and the Lodges," referring to his Boston Yankee nemeses, "wouldn't be caught dead at the pictures, or let their children go. And that's why their servants know more about what's going on in the world than they do. The working class gets smarter every day, thanks to radio and the pictures."[12]

WHILE KENNEDY WAS making a bigger name for himself in Hollywood, Franklin Delano Roosevelt, then serving on the Democratic National Committee's Executive Committee for the 1928 presidential campaign, wrote to him.[13] Roosevelt was deeply concerned by the anti-Catholic bombast and the rhetoric of those working against the repeal of the Eighteenth Amendment and asked Kennedy for a contribution.[*] The Republican candidate, Herbert Hoover, repeatedly damned the Democratic (and Catholic) four-term governor Al Smith of New York as a "Yankee wet." In fact, it was one of the nastiest presidential campaigns ever fought. Back then, being a Roman Catholic was as disabling to a candidate as being Black, Irish, Italian, or Jewish. Hoover's tactics upset

---

[*] The Eighteenth Amendment, also known as the Volstead Act, was repealed on December 5, 1933, after the state of Utah became the thirty-sixth state to vote for repeal.

Catholics and other Americans like Roosevelt, who were dumbfounded by the nation's bigotry.* The able Democrat Smith was widely smeared with claims that any Catholic was unable to act as a loyal American, since Catholics had a *prior* allegiance to the Vatican. That campaign, for all its ills, became a significant watershed and the beginning of a certain political understanding between Kennedy and Roosevelt.

BY 1931, KENNEDY'S FBO had acquired a controlling interest in Radio-Keith-Orpheum Corporation (RKO), one of the big five studios of Hollywood's Golden Age. Joe was in the process of taking over Pathé while also running Gloria Swanson's production company. Among the loyal employees who helped manage Gloria Productions for him was Edward E. "Eddie" Moore, Honey Fitz's former secretary. Moore would become Joe's closest business confidant and friend throughout his career.

Although Hollywood offered unprecedented and exciting opportunities, it was a dangerous place for a family man. Publicly, Kennedy espoused Catholic values but could never turn away from a pretty face or shapely leg. Then, too, Miss Swanson's on-screen steamy image was precisely what Joe loved. His affair with her was not the first or last time Joe strayed. Rose, heavily pregnant with their second daughter, Kathleen, ran back to her parents in 1920 when she suspected Joe was unfaithful. A woman's first duty was to her family, Honey Fitz told her after she spent two weeks sulking in her bedroom, and ordered Rose to go home.† And so Rose

---

* Roosevelt wrote a "Dear Sir" letter to Kennedy during the 1928 campaign, to which Kennedy replied he would help. That campaign was punctuated with violence and racism. The Ku Klux Klan took it upon itself to disseminate an anti-Catholic hate mail crusade to its 5 million registered supporters right up to election day, all with Hoover's knowledge. Protestants in Florida were told that their marriages would be dissolved and their children made illegitimate if Smith was elected. Even the newly completed Holland Tunnel between Manhattan and New Jersey was implicated in some weird Catholic plot as the secret tunnel between Rome and Washington. (*Sources:* Rory McVeigh, Daniel J. Myers, and David Sikkink, "Corn, Klansmen, and Coolidge: Structure and Framing in Social Movements." *Social Forces* 83, no. 2 (2004): 653–90; http://www.jstor.org.ezproxy2.londonlibrary.co.uk/stable/3598343; https://campaignstops.blogs.nytimes.com/2011/12/10/when-a-catholic-terrified-the-heartland/.)

† She hadn't appreciated that her father, too, was noted for his adulterous affairs and had forsaken his political career when his liaison with a woman called "Toodles" was about to be revealed.

returned to her unfaithful husband, two infant sons, Joe Jr. and John Fitzgerald, called Jack, and daughter Rose Marie, known as Rosemary, who had special needs.

In 1929, at the height of Joe's affair with Gloria, their first talking picture, *The Trespasser,* premiered in London. Rose, now a mother of eight children, never let her suspicions get the better of her again. The same could not be said of Gloria's third husband, Henri de La Falaise, Marquis de La Coudraye. When he joined the Kennedys in London, *he* could not escape the reality that his wife captivated Joe.[14] Then, two months later, Hollywood gossip columnist Hedda Hopper reported that "Rose's doting father, John F. 'Honey Fitz' Fitzgerald, the former powerful mayor of Boston and a leading political boss, had taken certain steps to restore his philandering son-in-law to the family fold."[15]

Those steps became clear when one of Joe's employees, Ted O'Leary, drove Gloria to a hotel to see "an important person" and "friend of the Kennedys." A bespectacled man in his seventies greeted her, dressed in his cardinal red silk steeped in the pungent smell of incense. After a short but polite chat, Boston's Cardinal William Henry O'Connell—the same man who had married Rose and Joe—told Gloria flatly that her relationship with Kennedy was "an occasion of sin" each time she saw him. Swanson replied curtly that the cardinal was talking to the wrong person and left. Afterward, she asked O'Leary who had put the cardinal up to his saintly mission and he replied that "it was Cardinal O'Connell who contacted me."[16]

Just the same, Kennedy remained Swanson's lover and business manager. Even the artistic and financial disaster of *Queen Kelly*—that unwatchable, never-released film directed by Erich von Stroheim—did not separate them. Gloria later said the movie was "only fit to be viewed in a museum" and would certainly be killed by the censors at Will Hays's office.* During this fiasco, Kennedy's beloved father, P.J., became seriously ill. Urged repeatedly by Swanson to come to Hollywood to sort things

---

* Will H. Hays was the former postmaster general of the United States who was the president of the Motion Picture Association of America (MPAA) from 1922 to 1945. The MPAA set the Motion Picture Production Code for morality guidelines for studios and what could and could not be seen on-screen from 1934 to 1968. In Gloria's August 3, 1971, interview on *The Dick Cavett Show,* she claimed rather disingenuously that *What a Widow!* repaid "the bankers most all" of the debt on *Queen Kelly.*

out, Kennedy was on the West Coast when P.J. finally died. On hearing the news, Joe shut down the set of *Queen Kelly* and headed back east.[17] He never forgave himself for abandoning his father's deathbed. Gloria Productions was left with *Queen Kelly*'s $800,000 debt. Their last film together, *What a Widow!,* was also a flop. Kennedy gave the playwright a bonus of a new Cadillac for devising the witty title and inexplicably charged it to Gloria's personal account. So, Swanson asked him about the "bookkeeping error." In a silent, livid rage, Joe simply left the room. Gloria never saw or heard from him again.

With a similar silent alacrity, Kennedy extricated himself unscathed from the financial debacle of Swanson's production company. Then he made several million more on the merger of Pathé with RKO. After that, Joe announced that he would return to Wall Street in association with Elisha Walker, the millionaire chairman of the Transamerica Corporation.[18]

THE GREAT CRASH of 1929 molded Kennedy's political ideals into the single and urgent purpose of saving capitalism. He had become a millionaire in the era when the symbol for the U.S. dollar was still written with two vertical bars through the *S.* Those who worked with Kennedy knew that he saw the world only within that narrow perspective. Nonetheless, Joe was just the kind of man Roosevelt needed for his planned recovery of the American economy, dubbed the New Deal.

Kennedy began his public service career in 1932 as an avid supporter of New York governor Franklin D. Roosevelt for president. His backing did not come from any love for Roosevelt or even the New Deal as much as a deep-rooted fear that America's freewheeling capitalist system would be obliterated by a communist revolution. The huge social and economic displacement caused by the Great Depression and the subsequent rise of communist and socialist ideologies in the United States terrified him. To his mind, "Big Business" and the "rugged individualists" of the twenties had not embraced the stark reality that they had to change their wicked ways or capitalism would perish. Roosevelt's plans to introduce workmen's compensation, Social Security, aid to farmers, electricity for the masses, and a raft of other new government benefits to put America back to work through his New Deal were a small price to pay to avert the coming cataclysm in Joe's eyes.

Roosevelt's historic win in 1932 against the incumbent Herbert Hoover was down to the promise of the New Deal. The president-elect had many active supporters to thank, including Joe Kennedy. Few had his flair and the skin-deep affability of a fast-moving entrepreneur with the eye and bite of a predator. Joe charmed the most unlikely benefactors and grabbed ahold of their unwilling dollars for Roosevelt's campaign. Like any self-promoting celebrity businessman, he was good at handling the press and had become friends with the biggest publisher of them all, William Randolph Hearst. Given the reforms that Roosevelt believed were necessary to save the American capitalist system, having a successful Wall Streeter and Hollywood financier expressing the need for economic reform was essential. Joe worked tirelessly, raising money for FDR—often getting wealthy Republicans demanding anonymity to contribute. Most crucially, Kennedy mobilized his friendship with Hearst and his Pathé News connections, too.[19]*

That said, Roosevelt closed his eyes to Kennedy's playing the lone hand of an entrepreneur. Joe was not then—nor would he ever be—a team player. Shortly after Roosevelt secured the Democratic nomination for president, Roy Howard, publisher of the Scripps-Howard newspapers, met with Joe to hear more about the candidate. Kennedy "is quite frank in his very low estimate of Roosevelt's ability. . . . Kennedy expects to fly to whatever port Roosevelt is in for the night, to be present at the evening conferences because he knew that if he were not present, the other men . . . would 'unmake' Roosevelt's mind on some of the points which Kennedy had made it up for Roosevelt," Howard said. He was astounded at Kennedy's frankness and his "understanding of Roosevelt's immaturity, vacillation, and general weak-kneed character." Howard added, Kennedy "is, I believe, enjoying his Warwick role" of kingmaker.[20]

But a kingmaker always has his price. Kennedy calculated the contributions, goodwill, and contacts he had mobilized to back the president-elect, making it known he lusted after the post of secretary of the treasury.

---

* Kennedy had met Hearst and his mistress, actress Marion Davies, during his Hollywood days, when Hearst was also actively producing motion pictures. Hearst had not been supporting Roosevelt in 1932, and many believe that it was Kennedy's intervention that changed his mind to back Roosevelt.

But when Roosevelt's preliminary lists for his cabinet began to circulate, Kennedy's name was not there.

Kennedy's wrath was palpable. His sums made Joe believe he was owed Roosevelt's lasting friendship. It never occurred to him that the president-elect might have gotten wind of his disloyalty from Howard and others, and that Roosevelt's friendship was not for sale. Kennedy "is hurt because I have not seen him," the president lamented to Harold Ickes, the secretary of the interior. Roosevelt grumbled that Joe had to be sent for "every few days" to know he was loved. "The trouble with Kennedy," Roosevelt confided to his friend and secretary of the treasury Henry Morgenthau Jr., "is you always have to hold his hand."[21] As New York's governor, Roosevelt became highly adept at depriving overeager allies of the honors they believed were their appropriate recompense.

But Kennedy would not be placated, as New Dealer Raymond Moley* found when he visited Joe at his Palm Beach home afterward. His "excoriation of Roosevelt" and "criticisms of the President-elect, who according to Kennedy, had no program—and what ideas he had were unworthy of note" stunned Moley. Shocked, too, by the "hundreds of dollars in telephone calls to provide an exchange of abuse of Roosevelt" with Hearst, Moley was certain that the publisher must have wondered why he had supported Roosevelt to the nomination.[22]

Despite Kennedy's persistence, Roosevelt ignored him throughout 1933.† Down but not defeated, Joe returned to Wall Street, masterminding a pool trading in shares of Libbey-Owens-Ford and spreading the word that the glass manufacturer was tooling up to produce liquor bottles. He knew that prohibition would be repealed. With his insider's knowledge, Kennedy sold short and made yet another fortune.

ALWAYS A FIERCE competitor, Joe did not give up. That summer, he invited the president's eldest son, James, called Jimmy, to spend time at the

---

* Raymond Moley was an original New Deal economist and adviser to Roosevelt. He later became one of the New Deal's most bitter foes.

† An elderly uncle of Rose's, James Fitzgerald, was appointed to the federal alcohol tax office in Boston. It would be a tremendous convenience for Joe's new liquor business, Somerset Importers.

Kennedy home at Hyannis Port. Jimmy, also a Harvard graduate, had run his father's Massachusetts headquarters during the election and hoped to settle in Boston earning a living from his new insurance business. After listening to Jimmy's hopes for the future, Kennedy told him that the steadfast Republican, Henry Ford, still had twenty-six of his thirty-two Ford Motor Company assembly plants mothballed since 1929. But the outspoken elderly car manufacturer now wanted to make his peace with the president. All it would take—Joe reliably told Jimmy—was for FDR to inquire after old man Ford's health.

So, Jimmy told his father. The president was aware that Ford's son, Edsel, had donated money to Roosevelt's health retreat at Warm Springs, Georgia.* Roosevelt mulled over Kennedy's proposition with his secretary, Marguerite "Missy" LeHand. "The big thing here is a hundred thousand men going back to work" and not Jimmy's picking up the car company's workmen's compensation insurance business, Roosevelt concluded. FDR sent the warm telegram as suggested to Ford, and the assembly plants began to roll once again. Years later, Jimmy said he never got a look-in for the insurance business, but he was grateful to Joe for trying.

Next, Kennedy invited Jimmy and his wife, Betsey, to join him on a trip to Great Britain in the fall of 1933. It was widely believed prohibition would end before the year was out, and Kennedy promised Jimmy they could make a killing in the renewed liquor trade. Though others vied for the exclusive rights to import liquor from the British Distillers Company, with its near monopoly on aged Scotch, no other competitor had Kennedy's braggadocio to negotiate while standing next to the president's eldest son. Britain's leading distillery men were thrilled to meet Jimmy, and it was readily agreed to give the young Roosevelt the insurance contract for fire risk on the eventual imports to the United States. Kennedy probably never realized he had put the president in an awkward position. Directly involving Jimmy in a deal that depended on

---

* Roosevelt was stricken with what doctors believed to be polio at age thirty-nine in 1921. His symptoms, however, were more akin to Guillain-Barré syndrome, an autoimmune neuropathy that was not considered by his doctors. Roosevelt founded the rehabilitation center at Warm Springs, Georgia. He went to great lengths to hide his disability on-camera, yet it was widely known, respected, and part of his image.

the repeal of prohibition *before* it had become a fact was perhaps good business. It was certainly bad politics.*

Early in December, just after the Eighteenth Amendment was rescinded, Kennedy's company, Somerset Importers, was officially awarded the contracts to import Haig & Haig and Dewar's Scotch whisky. Somerset was also named the distributor of Gordon's gin and secondary liquor brands imported in bulk. In its first year, the company imported some 130,000 cases of Scotch and cleared $536,000 net of costs. Paul Murphy, who headed up Kennedy's New York City office at 30 Rockefeller Plaza, estimated Somerset's profits would rise to "approximately $560,000 to $600,000."[23] In 1934, Kennedy set up nine additional trusts for his unborn grandchildren to shelter his profits from tax. These trusts came in handy during the lean ambassadorial years in London.[24]

ROOSEVELT HAD SEEN that Kennedy tired of any new challenge after a few years. Aware that it was safer to have Joe inside the presidential tent as he approached the midterms, he offered Kennedy the position of Chairman of the new Securities and Exchange Commission (SEC)—so it was said by citing the "it takes a thief to catch a thief" thesis. Roy Howard's *Washington News* published an editorial pleading with the president not to "with impunity administer such a slap in the face to his most loyal and effective supporters as that reported to be contemplated in the appointment of Joseph P. Kennedy." Although James M. Landis and Benjamin V. Cohen had drafted the initial Securities Act of 1933, Kennedy proved a wise choice for the enactment of the more important Securities Exchange Act of 1934, intended to combat fraud in the trading of securities.[25]

---

* Kennedy had ready access to alcohol during prohibition through his British and Canadian sources and did indeed provide alcohol to his Harvard reunion at this time. That said, he was careful not to be involved in the delivery or sale of the bootleg product personally. In *Joseph P. Kennedy: The Mogul, the Mob, the Statesman, and the Making of an American Myth* (New York: John Wiley, 2003, 95–96), Ted Schwarz writes that Kennedy made contacts with "men such as Al Capone" who handled the deliveries of the liquor throughout the United States on his behalf. As Capone was too clever to be apprehended on bootlegging or murder charges, the government could arrest and convict him only on lesser tax evasion charges. Kennedy's dealings with Capone remain unproven.

When Moley summoned Kennedy to the White House, he asked Joe if there was "anything in your career in business" that could "injure the President." If so, "this was the time to spill it." This was no Gloria Swanson asking about a bookkeeping error. So, with a liberal dash of profanity, Kennedy "defied anyone to question his dedication to the public interest or to point to a single shady act in his life."[26] Moley recalled that after an unrepeatable string of swearwords, Kennedy said he would deliver "an administration of the SEC that would be a credit to the country, the President, himself, and his family—clear down to the ninth child."[27]

Kennedy remained at the helm of the SEC from June 30, 1934, until September 23, 1935—delivering his letter of resignation on September 6 to the president citing "personal reasons" for leaving the post. Twelve-hour days and six-day weeks often challenged his health, meaning his delicate gastrointestinal system, he said.* Administration of the Securities Act of 1933 and the Securities Exchange Act of 1934 became Kennedy's legacy and had been broadly successful. According to the Associated Press, Kennedy was the "now-smiling, now-explosive" administrator, who had weighed in on Washington politics as its "Wolf of Wall Street."[28] Everyone wondered what he would do next.

---

* The Kennedys never revealed what was wrong with Joe Kennedy's digestive system.

2

AN IMPERFECT FAMILY PORTRAIT

Family is the first essential cell of human society.
—POPE JOHN XXIII

Kennedy still deemed himself part of Roosevelt's administration, writing "as you know, Mrs. Kennedy and I plan to go abroad with the children the latter part of the month and it seems wiser for me to terminate my official relations prior to leaving."[1] In reply, the president asked if Joe would be willing to act as his unofficial observer while in Europe: "I wish you would do a trouble shooting job and find out for me just what the threat to peace amounts to," Kennedy wrote in his *Diplomatic Memoir*.[2] Just the same, given Joe's lack of international political expertise, it is more likely that Roosevelt wanted Kennedy to turn his financial wizardry to resolving the outstanding European war debt from 1918, worth billions of dollars.

FDR saw this as a great opportunity to test out how well Joe would perform internationally. It suited the president, too, for his talks to be unofficial in nature. Secretary of the Treasury Henry Morgenthau had been singularly unsuccessful in obtaining any repayment of the war debt, and Roosevelt did not want Morgenthau to think he had lost confidence in him. From the president's perspective, it was good that Joe planned to travel with the Kennedy clan, who would act as legitimate cover for such a delicate mission, too.

Roosevelt gave Kennedy personal letters of introduction to the American ambassadors in Paris, London, the Hague, Berlin, and Rome. Alexander Noyes, financial editor of *The New York Times,* and Arthur Krock, who represented the paper as its Washington bureau chief, wrote to their correspondents in the same cities, too. They arranged for Kennedy to meet Geoffrey Dawson, editor of *The Times* of London, and Robert Brand of the investment bank Lazard Brothers.[3]* Kennedy obtained access to Winston Churchill through Bernard Baruch, another Roosevelt adviser and Churchill's investment expert in the United States for over ten years.[4] Churchill had been out of the government since 1929 due to his perceived adventurism; and from 1933 for his anti–Nazi rhetoric. Even so, Churchill had personal knowledge of why the war debt had not been paid.

New York's bishop Francis Spellman jumped at the chance to help, too. Spellman had been sent by Boston's Cardinal O'Connell to study at the Pontifical North American College in Rome for seven years as a young man. He knew the ins and outs of the Vatican and was a valued adviser on the state of Catholicism in America. Caring and wise, Spellman moved in important circles and was a canny businessman for the Church. As Rose Kennedy's confessor and a close family friend, he had been guiding Joe, too, in national and religious matters. Spellman's letter to Count Enrico Galeazzi, at the time the Vatican archaeologist and close personal friend of Cardinal Eugenio Pacelli, then secretary of state of the Holy See, speaks well of the Kennedy family.† Spellman unrestrainedly praised Joe as a "good Catholic who has done much to help our nation and our religion." Calling Kennedy a "dear friend," Spellman told Galeazzi that Joe was "the President's personal and confidential envoy," and asked that he be given "every benefit" of Galeazzi's expert advice.

---

* *The Times* of London was owned by John Jacob Astor V, younger brother of Waldorf Astor, owner of *The Observer.* Robert Brand was married to Nancy Astor's sister, Phyllis Langhorne.

† Spellman was made a cardinal in 1939 by Pacelli, as Pope Pius XII.

Spellman emphasized his hope that the Count would be of "assistance in any manner possible."[5]

LATER, ROOSEVELT DISCOVERED that Kathleen and Jack were the only Kennedy children to accompany their parents to Europe. Kathleen, aged fifteen and always known as Kick in the family, was deemed "old enough to get something out of a year of schooling abroad"—in a suitable French convent. Since "Jack had graduated in reasonably good standing from Choate," Joe and Rose agreed, he, too, should be exposed to European culture and history. Neither parent saw that they had passed over Rosemary, and that their eldest daughter would see her rightful place had been usurped by Kick. Today it is believed that Rosemary, who was born at the height of the Spanish flu epidemic on September 13, 1918, suffered from a lack of oxygen during childbirth, making her "slow." By the time of the 1935 voyage, Joe and Rose understood that Rosemary suffered from mild to moderate intellectual mental retardation—until the 1950s superstitiously believed to be a punishment against the parents for some unknown sin.

Joe decreed that Jack, aged eighteen, should follow in Joe Jr.'s footsteps for a year's study at the London School of Economics with the socialist ideologue of the Labour Party, Professor Harold Laski.[6] Given that Joe feared any outbreak of left-wing violence against the established social order, the motive for sending his sons to study under Professor Laski seems to have been to groom them for public service, in order to combat a socialist world of the future. It was a big step, since Jack had been a relentlessly sickly but uncomplaining child with a propensity to mysterious illnesses and fevers, involving prolonged periods of convalescence.* Jack was fascinated by history, and history books were frequently stacked by his sickbed.

Joe had fretted over Jack's health since the boy had contracted scarlet fever as a three-year-old and had been given the last rites. Joe often recalled the priest's praying over the deathly ill child. He had rarely left his son's side, praying as well. Deeply distressed—it was the first time Joe

---

* Jack would be diagnosed with the endocrine disorder Addison's disease in 1947. Although the illness was treated secretly, the diagnosis was not revealed until long after his death.

had experienced "very serious sickness in my family"—Joe offered half of his entire wealth to the Catholic Church if Jack's life could be saved.*

And saved Jack was. Once he was out of danger and safely returned home from his three-month convalescence in Maine, Joe moved the family to an imposing colonial-style home with curving bay windows and a broad veranda that hugged the entire ground floor. There were fourteen rooms with nearly an acre of land. Then, too, there was a new Rolls-Royce parked in the garage. The house was registered solely in Rose's name. With the bulk of his cash fortune spent improving their social standing, Joe stood by his word and gave half of *his* remaining wealth, some $3,500, to the Church.[7] Kennedy wore his heart in his wallet and lived for his children.

Rose adored the house and ignored that Joe always had some pretty young girl on his arm. Mistresses and one-night stands would come and go by the busload, but she had learned her lesson and asked her husband no questions. Instead, she turned her mothering into an "enterprise." She concentrated on clothing the children, so every button was properly sewn on, every outfit well-tailored and laundry fresh. An army of governesses, housekeepers, cooks, and a secretary made the house run smoothly. Rose did little in the way of "diaper changing" but recalled how in the winter diapers "froze stiff and then had to be thawed." She remembered "all those radiators, sizzling away, draped in white."[8] Missing from Rose's reminiscences are examples of motherly love for any of her children or mentions of her incessant travels without her family.

Paradoxically for a devout woman, Rose adored shopping for luxury possessions. She kept up with her Catholic social circle and her presidency at the charitable organization Ace of Clubs, which she co-founded in 1911. The club was dedicated to its membership of socially elite college-educated Catholic ladies, with frequent talks and events geared to self-improvement. At home, Rose insisted on good manners at all times but was often sorely let down by her rowdy fledglings.[9]

IT WAS JOE who created the family dynamic. He had ingrained in all the children that Kennedys were not tattletales. Kennedys were winners.

---

* Joe's younger brother, Francis, born in 1891, died when he was only a year old.

Kennedys stuck together—always—to the point of being aggressive about it. Not one of the younger eight children ever dared to take the place of—or infringe on—the rights of an older one, except in the case of Rosemary. Joe Jr. often took his father's place as disciplinarian when Joe traveled or was at work. Frequently Rose was away, too, much to the annoyance of Jack as a youngster. In truth, the children thought it was normal that their parents should spend as much as three hundred days a year apart from each other. As an adult Jack described his mother as "terribly religious. She was a little removed and still is, which I think is the only way to survive when you have nine children."[10]

In her own way, Rose accepted that Joe was a serial philanderer. To think anything else would insinuate that she was a stupid woman—which she was not. Her 1920 epiphany about Joe's infidelities taught her that she would have to create her own world within the family unit. Outwardly she was always supportive. While we will never know what she really felt, evidently she needed a corner of her life to call her own. Joe—whether at home or traveling—remained the "boss." When Kennedy went to Hollywood, she enrolled Joe Jr. and Jack at boarding school and placed Rosemary in a Catholic institution. Coping with the boys at home in Bronxville and Rosemary's learning difficulties was beyond her endurance. Extensive travel alone or with friends became Rose's primary coping mechanism. She never visited her children at boarding school or Rosemary when institutionalized. Her religion remained her most important buttress against any recurring doubts and personal vanity.

Then, too, Rose may have found the easy relationship Joe had with his children hurtful. It was Joe who ran the family circus. It was Joe who made them "close-knit" and "mutually supporting." It was Joe who laid down the law, and Joe who picked up the pieces. Joe was called "Daddy" by the girls and "Dad" by the boys. Rose was always "Mother." He dictated family togetherness, and many said he ran his family like a tribal chieftain.[11] Rose shriveled into the background, a distant figure.

IN 1935, WITH Jack and Kick aboard the *Normandie,* Joe confessed he was concerned that as the elder children grew into adulthood and encountered influences over which *he* had no control, they would grow apart. This anxiety manifested itself in an impromptu encounter with

Lawrence Fisher, who happened to be stretched out on an adjacent deck chair. Fisher was one of the famous "body by Fisher" brothers of General Motors fame, so Joe quickly sent for Jack. With his "hair tossed, and necktie askew from playing in a game of deck tennis, Joe greeted Jack with the words 'I want you to meet Mr. Lawrence Fisher, one of the famous Fisher Body family. I wanted you to see what success brothers have who stick together.'"[12]

Had Joe heard that Jack referred to young Joe as a bit of a bully? Or had some family friend told Kennedy the truth: all the younger siblings loved but feared Joe Jr. and his propensity to cruelty?[13] Jack, always a mischievous and lively child, would never have told his father outright. Besides, in elementary school, Jack always bet his marbles—the currency of his youth—on Joe's winning every brawl. Pride in being a Kennedy seemingly won out over everything else. Just the same, Joe wanted the brothers to stay close. Paradoxically, he also wanted Jack to attend a different Ivy League university than Joe Jr., who was already studying at Harvard. By giving Jack a splash of European culture and smattering of a diplomatic education, Kennedy hoped it would help his second son feel his older brother's equal.

AFTER THE *NORMANDIE* docked at Le Havre, each of the four Kennedys assumed their roles as designated by Joe. Rose shepherded Kick to the convent school at Neuilly just outside Paris before spending a few weeks replenishing her designer wardrobe. Paris, always the home of fashion, was where all women of wealth and social standing went to clothe themselves.

For Joe and Jack, Paris held different pleasures. Jack shadowed his father on his visits to the American ambassador Jesse Straus and to meet French financiers. With business out of the way, it would have been entirely in keeping for Joe to further Jack's "education" by introducing his sexually hyperactive son to the ways of every diplomat's favorite Parisian brothel, Le Sphinx. But neither Kennedy came to look at its lavish Egyptian decor or read its promotional brochures written by the novelist Henry Miller.[14] For the Kennedy men, Paris always meant hedonism and sex.

3

THE PRESIDENTIAL ENVOY

. . . the topsy-turvy political situation prevailing in
Europe . . . had an Alice-in-Wonderland quality.

—JOSEPH P. KENNEDY,
DIPLOMATIC MEMOIR

America's ambassador in London, Robert Worth Bingham, set up un-official meetings for Kennedy with Sir Montagu Norman, Chairman of the Bank of England; Neville Chamberlain, Lord Chancellor of the Treasury; and several top investment bankers. Kennedy told them he was informally exploring the financial position of Great Britain to repay its war debt.

Of all the contacts Kennedy made, his meeting with Chamberlain was especially important. As a long-standing government minister of several departments since 1923, Chamberlain understood the workings of the British Empire extremely well. Even so, Kennedy could not know that Chamberlain held anti-American prejudices or would become prime minister within two years. Despite Chamberlain's later reputation for appeasement, his was the loudest voice in the Baldwin cabinet demanding that Britain rearm when Hitler came to power in 1933. Chamberlain actively encouraged building a large air force, one "so powerful as to render success in attack [against Britain] too doubtful to be worthwhile."[1] Prime Minister Stanley Baldwin, however, disliked the notion of rearmament, claiming that it would be an unpopular measure with the public.

Baldwin, like most, was blind to the threat the Nazis posed to peace. He believed in laissez-faire and chose to ignore advice and intelligence. Hitler's belligerency, including the June 1934 murders of his political rivals and the September 1935 Nuremberg Race Laws against the Jews, were mere internal matters for him. Baldwin reflected the opinions of Britain's ruling elite, many of whom believed fascism was the cure for communism. Early in the summer of 1935, there was "much gossip about the Prince of Wales' alleged Nazi leanings" when he praised the Nazi regime to a large delegation of British ex-servicemen visiting Germany.[2] Their benign view of fascism was shared by Kennedy, his friends, international financiers, and a significant number of powerful people in the United States, too. Communists were the real enemy because they opposed the capitalist system, the rights of the individual, and all religious worship.[3]*

KENNEDY KNEW THAT Chamberlain was the man behind the 1932 conversion of Britain's £4 billion Great War debt to government gilts.[4]† With a general election looming in five weeks, Kennedy hoped to catch Chamberlain and others in a more pliable mood for their discussions. Instead, he was shocked by the Lord Chancellor's reaction to the international situation in general, and toward the United States in particular.

Like many Britons, Chamberlain believed that America's first foray onto the multinational diplomatic scene with the Treaty of Versailles was an unmitigated disaster. President Woodrow Wilson's "Fourteen Points" and agreement to allow a vengeful Georges Clemenceau of France to occupy the presidency in the negotiations proved disastrous. The impossible

---

*   That March, Baldwin sent Foreign Secretary Sir John Simon and his Lord Privy Seal, Anthony Eden, to Berlin in a show of solidarity when Hitler announced rearmament in a deliberate flouting of the Treaty of Versailles.

†   Chamberlain converted the war loan to government gilts in 1932 at a lower interest rate to save money. The remaining war debt of £1.9 billion for fighting World War I was finally paid off in 2015 by Chancellor of the Exchequer George Osborne, who also took advantage of lower interest rates (*Source:* https://www.gov.uk/government/news/chancellor-to-repay-the-nations-first-world-war-debt).

THE PRESIDENTIAL ENVOY ✦ 25

peace shunned the stark truth that the Allies imposed terms that were unacceptable to the Germans—like dividing the country by the Polish Corridor and making the Germans acknowledge the sole blame for the war. When the Germans demurred, the Allies enforced their terms by blockade, compelling the Germans to sign.

Nonetheless, the treaty included the laudable but failed concept of the League of Nations, for which President Wilson was awarded the 1919 Nobel Prize for Peace as its leading architect. When the United States Senate vetoed plans to join the League, the organization was doomed to fail.* Japan's exit from the League, followed hotly by Hitler's Germany in 1934—and the absence of the Soviet Union until that same year—crippled any peaceful solutions the League wished to impose. The League simply lacked credibility and teeth in the age of the rise of the European dictators.

And so Chamberlain took Kennedy through the outcome of the Great War from a British perspective. The U.S. insistence on toppling the European monarchies, along with the French desire for dismemberment of the Austro-Hungarian Empire, saw the formation of thirteen little states (called the Little Entente) whose peace would be "guaranteed" by the French. The British outcry that such pledges were impossible went unheeded. France's strategy was to surround Germany with French vassal states.† Chamberlain was sympathetic to Germany's viewpoint and recited Lloyd George's famous statement to Kennedy: "I cannot conceive . . . any greater cause of future war than that the German people . . . should be surrounded by a mob of small States, many of them consisting of peoples who have never previously set up a stable government for themselves, but each of them containing large masses of Germans."⁵ And so in 1935, Britain found itself at a crossroads: rearm or appease. Then, too, since Mussolini's army had just marched into Abyssinia on October 3,

---

* Germany was excluded from the League of Nations until September 1926.

† France was invaded shortly after German unification in the Franco-Prussian War of 1870–71, as well as during the Great War of 1914–18. Understandably, from a French perspective, the Little Entente was designed to prevent this happening again.

Chamberlain advised that the time was not ripe for repayment of the war debt.*

KENNEDY'S MEETING WITH Winston Churchill at the sixty-year-old's home, Chartwell, with its breathtaking views over the peaceful Kent countryside, was equally unsettling. Churchill agreed with Chamberlain's assessment that President Wilson, despite his good intentions, had done much to damage the future security of Europe. What could the French and Americans have been thinking to hive off millions of Germans into an assortment of new European countries? From 1933, Churchill voiced his defiance against the rise of Nazism, urging again and again that redressing the outrageous injustices against Germany must be "one of the greatest practical objectives of European peace-seeking diplomacy."

The January 1935 Saar plebiscite, in which residents voted overwhelmingly to return to Germany from France, was proof that Germans did not want to be divided from their homeland. The Treaty of Versailles had outlawed any unification (Anschluss) between Austria and Germany, too, Churchill told Kennedy. When Hermann Göring, Hitler's number two and Germany's *reichsmarschall,* announced his new German Luftwaffe in March 1935, Churchill's fears of an aerial war and how one could defend against it mushroomed into a terrifying reality. The Luftwaffe was, of course, in direct contravention of the Treaty of Versailles, but what did that matter now?

Churchill called the first half of the decade "the Locust Years," referring to the Bible and "the years that the locust hath eaten."† The period had been gobbled up by financial worries and the Depression, and not enough time and energy had been spent on righting the wrongs of Versailles. Now the entire world watched as a dangerous despot plotted and planned to do the job for them by force. Millions of Germans lived in countries that were not their own, and Hitler made sure that Germany still smarted from the stigmas forced upon it by the Allies. Yet Baldwin

---

* Abyssinia is now called Ethiopia. According to Kennedy's *Diplomatic Memoir,* he heard about the invasion afterward, which is not possible, as all the newspapers and government offices discussed the invasion during his visit.

† In the King James Bible: Joel 2:25.

steadfastly refused to listen, since Churchill's message would not win votes in October 1935.[6]

Kennedy's meetings with John Maynard Keynes and other men who formulated British economic policy fared no better. Although Joe and Rose both later claimed that he had "got the better" of Keynes in an argument about economics, Kennedy made no headway on repayment of the war debt. Sir Montagu Norman gave Kennedy a salutary lesson in world economics and finance, leading Joe to call him "the smartest banker I ever met."[7] Norman had advocated direct government reorganization of industry in early 1930, and the worse aspects of the worldwide depression had been averted in Britain.[8]

AT KENNEDY'S NEXT stop, Berlin, Ambassador William Dodd tried to open Joe's eyes to the dangers posed by the Nazis. Roosevelt did not tell Kennedy that Dodd despaired of American isolationism. Kennedy must have felt Dodd was mad when he said: "There is a feverish arming and drilling of 1,500,000 men, all of whom are taught every day to believe that continental Europe must be subordinated to them." Dodd was an academic who was fluent in German and had sent out warnings to the State Department, stating categorically that "the German authorities are preparing for a great continental struggle. There is ample evidence. It is only a question of time."[9]

Kennedy had hoped Dodd would introduce him to the Nazi elite, especially to the German economics minister, Hjalmar Schacht. As a novice to the international scene, Joe had come to believe he could charm both Hitler and Göring. However, he hadn't appreciated that Dodd was persona non grata with the Nazis and isolated from most diplomatic discourse.* Joe came away depressed at Dodd's attitude and appointment to such a significant post. And yet, despite Dodd's warnings, the most unusual aspect of Kennedy's Berlin trip was that he did not notice the obvious Nazi militarization.[10] Instead, Joe came away believing more

---

* Dodd tried to appease Hitler on the "Jewish question" and paid the price. He was also ill-qualified for the job of canny ambassador, pitted as he was against State Department insiders on the "home team" and the Nazis on the "away" side. For more on Dodd's dilemma, read Erik Larson's magnificent *In the Garden of Beasts: Love, Terror, and an American Family in Hitler's Berlin.*

strongly than ever that German fascism was a necessary step to combat the spread of socialism and communism.[11]

IN ROME, THE seasoned diplomat Samuel Breckinridge Long greeted Kennedy with more bad news. He could not arrange a meeting with Benito Mussolini or his foreign minister and son-in-law, Count Galeazzo Ciano, as they were busy with the Abyssinian war. During the Wilson years, Long was an assistant secretary of state; his specialty had been Asian affairs. He hoped to educate Kennedy to Japan's threat to U.S. security, and how past international tensions like the invasion of Manchuria in China by 10,400 Japanese troops in September 1931 was the first significant test of the failed Treaty of Versailles and the untested League of Nations.* With Joe, it was always the economic—and not the political or military—reasoning that he understood best. Then, as later, he agreed with the sentiments voiced in *The Philadelphia Record* that "the American people do not give a hoot in a rain barrel who controls North China."[12]

As disappointing as his meeting with Long had been, Kennedy finally had some success with the Vatican, thanks to Bishop Spellman in New York. Count Enrico Galeazzi opened the doors to Italian society and financiers. Most significantly, Kennedy's time with Galeazzi blossomed into a lifelong friendship. The Count freely gave Joe his first insider's peek at the vast and complex Vatican network and its secretary of state, Cardinal Eugenio Pacelli.

Pacelli occupied the highest administrative post in the Holy See. His real strength was as the Vatican's "glittering diplomat" who negotiated a series of concordats stretching from Italy to Rumania, Yugoslavia, Austria, and Germany between the years 1933 and 1935. These agreements were intended to protect *all* Catholics in Europe against the coming fascist storm. They also accumulated vast power back to the Vatican from local and regional church authorities—a power that had been lost in the years since Bismarck and Garibaldi led their respective countries to unification.

---

* The Japanese thumbed their nose at the League's talk of sanctions in February 1933 and demands to withdraw from Manchuria. Tokyo responded by bombing the British commercial capital in the Far East, Shanghai, some 700 miles to the south of their occupied territory. Japan quit the League shortly thereafter, and Germany followed in October 1933, ostensibly because the European powers did not want to agree to military parity.

That spring, while preaching to 250,000 worshipers at Lourdes in France, Pacelli spoke out: "These ideologues [the Nazis] are in fact only miserable plagiarizers who dress up ancient errors in new tinsel," referring to the unremitting abuses against Catholics and the Nazis' anti-Semitism. "It matters little whether they rally round the flag of social revolution or are possessed of the superstition of race and blood."[13]

Whether Kennedy had asked to be presented to Cardinal Pacelli, who was resting in Switzerland, remains something of a mystery. That said, Joe's plan *did* include travel to Switzerland after Rome. Was he summoned there, or had he asked to meet the man who had been dubbed as the likely future pope? Irrespective of his original intention, his trip was curtailed by yet another of Jack's emergency hospitalizations, and he rushed to his son's bedside in London, peppering Jack's doctors in the United States with cables for advice. After a mere month at London School of Economics, Jack had to be withdrawn from his studies. Again, no one understood the cause, except that it might be a recurrence of agranulocytosis, a debilitating condition involving a lack of neutrophils (a type of white blood cell) to combat infection. Even the Mayo Clinic had no idea what ailed the young man. Jack wrote in his self-deprecating, stiff-upper-lip way to his good friend, K. LeMoyne "Lem" Billings at Princeton, "I am once more baffling the doctors. I am a 'most amazing case.'"[14]

4

THE IMPORTANCE OF BEING CATHOLIC

Will no one rid me of this turbulent priest?
—Henry II of England,
referring to Thomas à Becket, 1170

Kennedy's report about the "Alice-in-Wonderland" European political scene was delayed due to Jack's poor health. With the help of
Herbert Bayard Swope,* Joe was able to squeeze a recovering Jack into
Princeton University that November—where Jack's good friend Lem
Billings from Choate could alert Kennedy if things went wrong. In Joe's
thank-you note to Ambassador Robert Worth Bingham, written shortly
after their return to the United States on November 11, 1935, he says,
however, "Jack is far from being a well boy and as a result I am afraid my
time for the next six months will be devoted to trying to help him regain
his health with little or not time for business and politics."[1]

Although Jack had been accepted at Princeton, his remaining there
would depend on his health. "I had a nice talk with Doctor Raycourt

---

* Swope was a three-time recipient of the Pulitzer Prize for Reporting and spent most
of his career at Joseph Pulitzer's *New York World,* which provided significant support for the
Democratic Party. In 1917, Swope won his first Pulitzer for his series of articles "Inside the
German Empire" and could have been of great help to Kennedy in writing an in-depth
report.

[the university doctor at Princeton]. He is very much interested in your case and we have decided to go along on the proposition as outlined by Doctor Murphy [who had treated Jack at Peter Bent Brigham Hospital in Boston] and see how you get along until Thanksgiving."[2] It was not a suggestion, but an order.

JOE SETTLED JACK in at Princeton, then spent the night at the White House as Roosevelt's guest to deliver his report verbally. He had performed his task admirably, and most certainly delivered the hard messages from the British to FDR. Even so, their remarks were not for general consumption and the press, so Roosevelt and Kennedy agreed on what should be said instead. The next day Joe held an informal press conference which was reported as a "special" to *The New York Times*.

The headline was DECLARES EUROPE LIKES OUR POLICIES—KENNEDY REPORTS TO PRESIDENT THAT HIGH CONFIDENCE IS HELD IN OUR RECOVERY. Kennedy was quoted as saying that "foreign experts" looked to "us as being in a position of success and security, as compared with major European nations." He explained that monetary stabilization was something for the future and left out all the criticisms he had heard about the United States. He "based this view on an observation made by Neville Chamberlain . . . that monetary stabilization could only follow economic stabilization, and second, a prevalent belief in France that stabilization of the franc in relation to other currencies could come only after that country had settled the problem raised by possibly necessary devaluation."[3] It was no accident that Kennedy quoted Chamberlain. He genuinely liked the former industrialist turned politician.

A FEW DAYS later, Kennedy flew from Washington to Palm Beach. "On December 3, James Roosevelt joined Kennedy, Eddie Moore, and 'London Jack' Kennedy at Joe's Palm Beach home on Ocean Boulevard."[4] London Jack, RKO's European publicist, knew his way around the back corridors of the European media. Joe used him from time to time as his eyes and ears overseas. Arthur Krock of *The New York Times* joined the team shortly before Christmas. Although they had assembled to enjoy the sun, sea, and Joe's hospitality, they were there for a more serious purpose, too.

Kennedy was working toward proper presidential recognition that Christmas. With the 1936 election looming large, he made it his brief to deliver the business and Catholic vote for Roosevelt. Surely this time, if he was successful, Kennedy would be appointed as Secretary of the Treasury. During the next two months he labored over his political endorsement for Roosevelt—with the ample help of friends like his former SEC colleague, friend, and lawyer John J. Burns; Arthur Krock; and lawyer James M. Landis.*

STILL, IT *WAS* Christmas, and Joe prided himself on being a good father. Jack had been withdrawn from Princeton after nearly a month's stay at Peter Bent Brigham Hospital in Boston. Jack spent the Christmas holidays in Palm Beach with his own friends, but was unceremoniously redispatched back to the Boston hospital for two months more of tests in January. Demanding to know what *exactly* was wrong with Jack, Joe was angry when all the tests again proved inconclusive. By the end of February 1936, the baffled doctors released Jack back into his father's care in Palm Beach. Joe and Krock were hard at work on his campaign pamphlet *I'm for Roosevelt,* and suddenly there was little time to devote to his sickly son. It was Krock who suggested that Jack work on a ranch in the dry heat of Arizona at a friend's place. Reluctantly, Jack agreed. By May, the sickly eighteen-year-old returned hale and hearty, and told his father that he wanted to go to Harvard to join his brother.[5]

Rose's memory of Jack's illness is passed down as if from some faraway place. She did not enjoy being around Joe and his "golfing buddies," as she called the team. Often the children did not know where she was. Kick wrote to her mother that February: "I hope this letter reaches you in Florida as you seem to jump around like a frog between N.Y. and Florida—one minute in New York the next in Florida."[6]

It seems surprising that Joe did not fret over Kick—the favorite Kennedy daughter—still at her convent school in an increasingly hostile

---

* Although a highly intelligent, talented academician and lawyer, if a somewhat humorless soul, Landis would become Joe Kennedy's wordsmith not only for the campaign pamphlet *I'm for Roosevelt* (1936) but also his *Diplomatic Memoir* (1948) and the credited coauthor of Kennedy's *The Surrender of King Leopold,* published in 1950.

Europe. On January 7, 1936, Mussolini told the German ambassador in Rome, Ulrich von Hassell, that he would not object to Austria becoming a de facto satellite of Hitler's Reich. Then, too, there was rising violence in Spain. The February 1936 elections saw the left win by a narrow majority, compounding the country's instability. On February 29, America's Second Neutrality Act came into effect to link aid to repayment of the war debt and to strengthening its embargo provisions. On March 7, Hitler extended his sovereignty over the Rhineland.* Unbelievably, neither Great Britain nor France made any objection.

Kick's April 15, 1936 letter to "Dearest Dad" was written from the Hôtel Metropole et Ville in Naples. Chatting about her time in Rome, she said that the convent where they were staying "is perfectly beautiful" and that there were nine English girls from the same order staying there from Switzerland. She wrote how she "Tried to get Mr Galeazzi but had quite a time trying to understand the Italian, French and English all at the same time of his maid." It was a thrill for the sixteen-year-old to see St. Peter's, but as she couldn't speak to Galeazzi, she was not allowed to go to the mass in the Sistine Chapel on Holy Thursday when Pope Pius XI officiated.

Her disappointment was short-lived. The next day Galeazzi saw Kick, and she effused: "He is one of the most charming men I have ever met— The nuns know him at school as he has done a great deal for different Americans who have been here—He got me three tickets for the Mass on the Sistine Chapel Good Friday said by the Pope by calling the Vatican that night."[7]

Kick's star ascended even further with her accompanying friend and chaperone when they were ushered through the private apartments of Cardinal Pacelli into the Sistine Chapel. "After it was over we had quite a time getting out as no one understood and the Swiss guards speak only German—We had a little man in black velvet shorts running around for us—When we arrived as guests of Cardinal Pacelli, who is the Secretary of State in the Vatican there was plenty of excitement."[8] Kick couldn't have known that her father was already in contact with Galeazzi for

* The result of the French parliamentary elections in May 1936 saw the rise of the left coalition, the Popular Front, with Léon Blum as prime minister.

another extremely important mission, which—in part—had to do with reelecting Roosevelt.

THE CATHOLIC VOTE was important to Roosevelt, particularly as the popular Catholic radio personality Father Charles E. Coughlin was giving the president a good tongue-lashing. When Coughlin took to the national airwaves back in June 1930 with his richly mellow reassuring voice on Station WJR Detroit, his ingratiating charm begged his listeners to wrap their arms around their radios and listen to his own brand of "Fireside Chat." Coughlin had thrown his considerable weight behind the 1932 Roosevelt campaign with a push from Kennedy. Yet, as the New Deal took shape and Louisiana's Senator Huey Long attracted the priest's admiration—along with Benito Mussolini—Coughlin turned like a rabid dog on Roosevelt and the Democrats. Nothing stopped his poisonous and repeated condemnations. Not even Long's assassination in 1935. That's when Coughlin announced his "apolitical" National Union for Social Justice platform and whipped up a frenzy of support. Incensed Americans—Jews, Protestants, Catholics, and others—ran to Father Coughlin's defense, since he stood up for America's poor. They flocked in droves to become members of his People's Lobby, in part funding Coughlin's programs and increasing his radio hookup from twenty-nine to thirty-five stations.[9]

That's when August T. Gausebeck, Reichsmarschall Göring's banker in America, approached the turbulent priest. If Coughlin took off the gloves and plainly said what he meant, Gausebeck would fund any shortfalls the good father might experience—in untraceable donations of five to ten dollars. Thanks to the Nazis, Coughlin was freed from any financial worries and attacked the president without restraint. Roosevelt knew about the Nazi funding but remained silent—even with Kennedy—as he feared a backlash which would favor the radio priest.[10]

"Joe was fascinated by Coughlin's talent on the radio," James Roosevelt remembered. "He recognized it as demagoguery but reveled in what the priest could accomplish. He was intrigued by Coughlin's use of power." Joe, plain-speaking as ever, often called Coughlin a "jackass" to his face when discussing politics, and Coughlin laughed good-naturedly. Nonetheless, the radio priest still lambasted Roosevelt's "means and methods closely allied with socialism and communism to rectify our economic ills."[11] Roosevelt was a "great betrayer and a liar," according to Coughlin. By early 1936, the remnants of Huey Long's Share Our Wealth movement joined him.* The only person who could silence this "turbulent priest" was his bishop, and Bishop Michael James Gallagher of Detroit wasn't lifting a finger. It was time for Kennedy to step in.

KENNEDY'S JOB WAS to keep the errant priest inside the presidential tent, so he turned to Bishop Francis Spellman for help. After all, Pacelli had recently consecrated Spellman in Rome as bishop-elect and often used him as his personal translator.[12] For Pacelli and Galeazzi, Spellman was the best choice of behind-the-scenes operator, given their close bond of trust.

Spellman noted all matters of importance in his diary. For example, his November 7, 1933, entry began: "Had letter from Mr. Galeazzi saying that Pope wished him to tell James Roosevelt to ask his father to request some guarantee for freedom of religion in Russia before recognition. Sent letter to Apostolic Delegate." Three days later, he wrote that the United States recognized Russia. "Mr. Galeazzi . . . [who] will never appear in history did much to get President Roosevelt to insist that American citizens at least should worship God as they wished in Russia."[13] Spellman was well aware that both the Vatican's 1929 Lateran Treaty with Mussolini and the July 1933 *Reichskonkordat* with Hitler stipulated that the Holy See would not meddle in politics.†

Kennedy had Spellman ask Pacelli to visit the United States in 1936 and to conspicuously visit the president at Hyde Park. Surely that would be a counterweight to Detroit's Father Coughlin? And it *was* Spellman, not his superior, Boston's Cardinal O'Connell, who arranged everything. Spellman wrote to Galeazzi in Rome with his suggestions, which

---

* Long's program of Share Our Wealth proposed limiting annual income to $1 million and inheritance to just over $5 million.

† The Lateran Treaty saw the Vatican give up its temporal role in the former Papal States and other areas, leaving it in sole charge of Vatican City (108.7 acres) and with territorial rights to several churches, buildings in Rome, and the papal summer palace at Castel Gandolfo on Lake Albano, in exchange for a much-needed $85 million (circa $1.7 billion in 2020).

incorporated Kennedy's advice that Pacelli should visit Roosevelt. Galeazzi replied that the Cardinal Secretary agreed to Spellman's suggestions. It was both Kennedy's and Roosevelt's fondest hope that Pacelli would denounce Father Coughlin for his labeling the president an "upstart dictator" in the White House.[14]

WHILE CARDINAL PACELLI and his entourage journeyed to New York on the *Conte di Savoia* in late September 1936, Joe's magnum opus *I'm for Roosevelt* was published. Roosevelt was so thrilled with the pamphlet that he thanked Joe declaring, "I'm for Kennedy." The gist of the booklet was that the New Deal was necessary and that Americans should ask "whether we should intelligently regulate our social life as to assure the maintenance of a democracy or should smash our regulatory machine and thus pave the way for dictatorship." Although it was a glowing endorsement of Roosevelt's policies—and successfully insulated smaller business owners and newer businesses from Wall Street and Big Business—Roosevelt silently took note that Kennedy had protested in the pamphlet that he held "no political ambitions for myself or my children."[15]

Next, Kennedy proposed that he should take to the airwaves. Joe had a charisma that he was sure would radiate across American radio sets. It would raise his profile within the Democratic Party, too. When Steve Early, Roosevelt's press secretary, gave Kennedy the go-ahead for three radio programs—subject to White House clearance and a few suggestions from the president—it was Kennedy, not Pacelli, who became the president's Catholic voice. Roosevelt wanted Joe to underline how Big Business and Wall Street had played a dangerous game with American democracy. "The country is not going to revert to complete freedom for business where such freedom results in over-speculation, overproduction, tax avoidance through the corporate process," Roosevelt warned. Nor would it allow "stock watering" or "price fixing."[16]

Talking on the radio was the most exhilarating part of the 1936 campaign for Kennedy. He loved calling Wall Streeters "the few stuffed shirts who had lost their silk hats." During Cardinal Pacelli's visit, Joe longed to lock horns with Father Coughlin, too. The radio priest continually vilified the president, calling him "Franklin Double-Crossing Roosevelt" and the "great betrayer." Joe, however, was Coughlin's "shining star among the dim knights of the Administration." Kennedy attacked "the efforts made for low, practical purposes to confuse a Christian program of social justice with a Godless program of Communism," but thanked Coughlin, nonetheless, for "all the kind things you are saying about me."[17]

Just the same, Kennedy never took his eye off the visiting cardinal. When arrangements for the Italians to fly westward fell through, it was Kennedy who hired another private aircraft and pilot. Toward the end of October, Joe was exhausted, but not too tired to write to his friend Senator James Byrnes, "Well, boy—win, lose or draw—after Tuesday, one Joseph Patrick Kennedy retires from the political ring forever and a day."

On Saturday, October 24, a dog-tired Bishop Spellman jotted in his diary: "Joe Kennedy arranged for President to invite Cardinal to lunch with him at Hyde Park on November 5th and so told me, but I said to have Cardinal invited directly and through neither of us."[18] A meeting was arranged in Kennedy's 30 Rockefeller Plaza offices with Spellman and Galeazzi to discuss the matter. Initially, Joe was unhappy that the cardinal would not meet with Roosevelt until election day had passed. After a heated discussion, Joe eventually took charge of all arrangements as Galeazzi wished. Kennedy's administrative skills impressed him. "Tall, elegant, gentlemanly," Galeazzi remembered later, Kennedy "could be as gentle and kind as a gallant knight or as violent and cross as a general at war."[19] Sometimes the change could be as rapid as the flick of a light switch.

Roosevelt's team had campaigned hard and won the greatest presidential landslide in American history to date. The Republican candidate, Alf Landon, carried only two states—Vermont and Maine. For all Coughlin's rhetoric, his candidate polled fewer than a million votes. A celebration was in order, and so Cardinal Pacelli accepted the reelected Roosevelt's invitation to luncheon.

Two days later, Joseph and Rose Kennedy joined the Pacelli entourage, which included the cardinal, Bishop Spellman, Bishop Stephen J. Donahue representing Cardinal Hayes of New York, and Mr. Galeazzi aboard a special train bound for Hyde Park. Eleanor Roosevelt did not attend, preempted by her charming but domineering mother-in-law, Mrs. Sara Delano Roosevelt. The president's son James was also there. Bishop Spellman wrote: "There is one American recollection that is etched in my memory as actually having taken place which, before the Presidency of Franklin Delano Roosevelt, would have been considered fantastic." Spellman added: "I can see in my mind's eye as clearly as if it were yesterday, His Eminence and President Roosevelt talking alone near the fire place at the far end of the great living room in the President's home at Hyde Park. . . . This was a great day for America and a great day for Catholic America."[20]

Did Pacelli and Roosevelt discuss Father Coughlin? Absolutely. On his return to the Vatican, the cardinal launched an investigation into the radio priest's possible abuses from his pulpit. Certainly, too, Pacelli made his wishes known to have an American ambassador appointed to the Holy See. To his mind, it would strengthen his position against the dictators and open the lines of communication directly to the U.S. State Department. That request led on to discussions about Mussolini and Hitler, where Pacelli's circumspection rang alarm bells with Roosevelt.

Naturally, the president was anxious to understand how the man who negotiated the only agreements signed by both dictators felt about them as men of their word. By November 1936, Pacelli could not hide his anger with Hitler for the continued persecution of Catholics and priests in Germany. He may have warned Roosevelt, too, that Mussolini was an unpredictable weather vane in a storm. To move Italy's allegiance away from Hitler would require more sacrifices than either Great Britain or France could easily stomach. As to Il Duce's ability to sway the führer from his chosen course, Pacelli's eminently sensible reply was to shrug his shoulders and look to the heavens.

IT WAS ALSO a great day for Kennedy. Seeing the secretary of state of the Vatican talking to the president of the United States, warming themselves by the fire, was a dream he never thought he would see. Then, too, the gregarious Spellman and charming Kennedy were the life of the party. Honoring the Kennedys after lunch, Pacelli, Galeazzi, and Spellman returned to New York City via Joe and Rose's Bronxville home for tea. Rose recalled how Pacelli sat on their living room sofa and Teddy, then four years old, climbed up uninvited onto the cardinal's lap to examine his cross. Incredibly, she also claimed that there was *no camera in the house* to take their pictures with Pacelli.[21] More believably, Pacelli asked that no photographs be taken. There were none taken of Roosevelt with His Eminence at Hyde Park—only of Kennedy, Pacelli, and his entourage outside the Roosevelt home.

In Bronxville, Joe reiterated to his visitors he would make sure Roosevelt appointed an ambassador to the Holy See. He could not have avoided his innate tendency to self-aggrandize, either, bragging about the family's presidential ambitions for his son Joe Jr. But had something they said made Kennedy interpret their remark as a green light for *him* to reach for the presidency in 1940? Just in case, Kennedy invited the overworked Bishop Spellman, who was also a friend of Roosevelt's, to Palm Beach that November for much-needed rest and relaxation. The more irons he had in the fire, the better.

5

PROJECT KENNEDY

Every man is said to have his peculiar ambition . . .
—ABRAHAM LINCOLN,
FIRST POLITICAL SPEECH, MARCH 9, 1832

Kennedy received a special invitation to attend Roosevelt's Second Inauguration on January 19, 1937, and was asked to bring as many of the children as possible in recognition of all he had done. Yet only Rosemary, aged eighteen; Kick, sixteen; Eunice, fifteen; Patricia, twelve; Bobby, eleven; Jean, eight; and Teddy, four, attended, chaperoned by Eddie Moore, his wife, Mary, and the children's governess, Miss Dunn.

After checking into the Brighton Hotel, they dined at the Mayflower Hotel according to Jean in her letter addressed to "Dear Daddy and Mother." At dinner, "we met monisighor Lavalle [rector of St. Patrick's Cathedral in New York], Postmaster Tauge of Boston; Mr & Mrs Joseph Maynard." Then Jean and Bobby went back to their hotel with Miss Dunn and to bed. On Inauguration Day, "we couldn't here the President's speech because it was raining so hard. Then we hired a car and rode to the white-house. . . . Then we went to lunch. There we met the Postmaster Farley, Betsey and Jimmie & The President."

There were three thousand guests at the White House luncheon, but the young Kennedys were singled out by James Roosevelt to meet the president privately. "He shook hands with us. and said well it was about time. He asked who was the oldest. We all said Hello. We went to the reception and saw the Parade and then we went home. Thank you very much for letting us go Daddy."[1]

Neither Rose nor Joe attended. Rose's sister—and last living sibling—Agnes Fitzgerald Gargan had died suddenly of an embolism in September 1936. The November visit by Pacelli and Galeazzi to the family home in Bronxville was also calculated to give solace to Rose. Blaming Rose's grief was a convenient excuse: their eldest daughter, Rosemary, had become increasingly difficult to handle "as normal." Her inability to retain what she learned at school had been rumbling on for years. To continue to believe that their eldest daughter could adapt to the Kennedys' heights of achievement was both hurtful and fanciful, and both Joe and Rose knew it. In a world that poorly understood children with special needs (Rosemary had achieved only a fourth-grade reading level), she would be doomed to a tragic life.

Rosemary adored her brothers and sisters, and often said she wished she could be more like the bubbly Kick, never realizing that she was probably the prettiest of the Kennedy girls. But as the younger siblings whizzed past Rosemary physically and intellectually, she became "disobedient." So, Rose sent her away to a convent boarding school in Maine. It was the worst decision she could have made developmentally for the girl. The headmistress wrote that Rosemary was taking "advantage of her weakness and has used it as a weapon to have her way too much. . . . she makes herself unpleasant when she finds herself in a situation in which she has to think."[2]

For a man who rarely understood failings in others, Joe thoroughly appreciated his daughter and her limitations, and defended Rosemary. It is a particularly endearing character trait—even a paradox—for a man who pushed the ideals of relentless competition and winning in his children to near breaking point. However, he did not remove her to a better environment. By 1937, Joe saw how the bright younger children could make Rosemary feel a failure. Even so, he wasn't about to hold back his personal ambitions or those he held for his other offspring. Rosemary was slow, and he would protect her as much as possible. But he had a burning ambition—sometimes bordering on rage—to raise his family above their Irish roots by his acquired wealth and visibility in politics.

STOPPING SHORT OF the pinnacle of his ambition, possibly the presidency or vice-presidency, would be folly. Kennedy thought he deserved a top post in Roosevelt's cabinet so he could reach his goal. To do that, he needed a significant cabinet position. Given the times he lived in, he was absolutely right. So, Joe let James Roosevelt know that he still wanted to be secretary of the treasury. As a self-appointed "foster father" to FDR's eldest son, Kennedy knew that Jimmy would shortly take up his duties as his father's most trusted ally and secretary.[3] Joe could not fathom why Morgenthau was trusted and he was not. For starters, Morgenthau had done a great job with a limited money supply in creating new jobs through the New Deal. Then, too, "Joe would want to run the Treasury in his own way," Roosevelt told Postmaster General Jim Farley, "contrary to my plans and views."[4]

Notwithstanding this, the president knew he could not ignore Joe for a few years again. Kennedy had published *I'm for Roosevelt* at his own expense and would never make the money back. He had brought the Catholic vote into the fold and was a key figure in turning the tide of public opinion in the president's favor with all his press and film contacts. So, in February 1937, FDR called Joe to Washington for a chat.

He offered Kennedy the post of chairman at the new Federal Maritime Commission. The president flattered him, saying that only he could sort out the woeful mess the American shipping industry had become. Characteristically, Joe exploded: "If it's all the same to you, let some other patriot take it on the chin for a while." Eventually, however, Joe allowed himself to be tempted into a job far below his expectations through presidential guile and charm and his own burning ambition. Besides, it was the only job on offer, and Joe had to take it or leave it. Putting a gloss on his disappointment, Rose later wrote: "The President wouldn't have removed Morgenthau even if he had been otherwise inclined to because Mrs. Morgenthau and Eleanor were such great friends, and dispensing with Henry could have resulted in friction not only in the Dutchess County neighborhood but in the Roosevelt home."[5]

From the start, Kennedy was determined to move on as quickly as he could for a post of his own choosing. He worked tirelessly to settle outstanding claims and forty-six unworkable mail contracts totaling some $400 million before June 30, as Kennedy bragged to his former Harvard fraternity housemate, writer and humorist Robert Benchley in 1937.[6]* Joe knew, too, that unless he made his own headlines, his work would go unnoticed by the press.

By early spring 1937, the isolationist Congress watched Europe, predicted war, and already planned how America's legislature might strengthen the Second Neutrality Act, which was due to expire that May.† Then out of the blue, before Kennedy was confirmed as maritime commissioner on March 31, 1937, he had resolved that as soon as the ailing Robert Worth Bingham retired, he would be the next American ambassador to the Court of St. James's in London. It was a clever move. Becoming ambassador to Great Britain was the highest profile job Kennedy could demand—and probably get.

THERE WERE ONLY seventy-three days to clear up the $400 million claims against the government for its poorly negotiated international postal contracts. Kennedy planned his exit from the Maritime Commission for July 1, 1937, meeting the deadline to resolve the postal contracts demands—effectively for ten cents on the dollar. While working on his solutions and a "grand announcement" on how he had saved American shipping, Kennedy turned to Arthur Krock to make headlines.

Krock later made disingenuous claims in his autobiography that he derived no "material considerations from this relationship" with Kennedy. That would be true if the $25,000 Joe paid him each year from April

---

* Straight out of Harvard, Benchley began his working career at Condé Nast's *Vanity Fair* as its managing editor, working alongside Dorothy Parker and FDR speechwriter Robert Sherwood. Kennedy asked Benchley as his "particular pet" to introduce him at their twenty-fifth Harvard class reunion, commenting "my past is safe in your hands."

† The Neutrality Act of 1935 was passed by Congress on August 31, 1935, and stated that Americans traveling to war zones did so at their own risk. The act was extended on February 29, 1936, to include Americans extending loans to any belligerent. When the Neutrality Act of 1937 came into effect that May, Roosevelt agreed to sign it so long as his "cash-and-carry" provision for the export of materials that were not "implements of war" was excluded, meaning oil. This was aimed at helping Great Britain and France in the event of war with the Axis powers (*Source:* Office of the Historian of the United States).

1936 did not count.[7]* The Krock columns of March 17 and 21 named Kennedy as "one of the outstanding figures in American life" and one of the president's "miracle-men." Henry R. Luce's *Time* magazine wrote on March 22 that "the President turned to his most effective and trusted extra-Cabinet friend, red-headed Joe Kennedy," to chair the new Federal Maritime Commission—a job no one else wanted.[8]

Krock was Kennedy's most loyal servant. "I am practical enough to know," Joe wrote to him on his deadline day at the Maritime Commission, "that the help you have given me . . . [is] the real reason that the Press of this country have given me all the breaks."[9] Just the same, Joe had others in his press arsenal, too. Back in 1931 before Clare Boothe Brokaw became Mrs. Henry R. Luce, Joe had known the delectable and witty journalist and playwright as "Bernie's Babe"—the mistress of Bernard Baruch. Clare, too, wanted to help Kennedy. So, he feigned surprise when he was told that Luce's *Fortune* magazine planned a feature article about him to appear the following September.

A young and ambitious journalist, Earle Looker, was assigned to the story. After meeting Kennedy and those who had done business with him both in government and in private enterprise, Looker had formed an unfavorable opinion of the restless, dynamic entrepreneur. The article, never published, laid Joe bare in print: he was a man driven by his own ambitions for himself and his family with scarce regard for the "institutions he touched" and was a "profiteer" at the expense of his business colleagues. On page 4, Looker wrote: "He had been one of the operators of the Libbey-Owens-Ford pool which Pecora had investigated as chief inquisitor of the Norbeck Senate investigation. . . . Out of Pecora's findings had come the Securities Act of 1933, the national blue-sky law, and the Securities and Exchange act of 1934."†

A livid Kennedy wrote to Russell Davenport, managing editor of

---

* Although Krock claimed that there were no financial incentives in his relationship with Kennedy in his *Memoirs* on page 331, the Joseph P. Kennedy papers at the JFK Presidential Library belie this claim as purposefully deceptive.

† Ferdinand Pecora led the investigations into the Wall Street crash of 1929 as the chief counsel to the U.S. Senate's Committee on Banking and Currency in 1933. He also served with Kennedy at the SEC and did not like him.

Fortune, that there were over fifty inaccuracies in the article, and that the article "is permeated with distrust of my character, dislike of my motives, and social prejudice against my origin. It is nonobjective and its facts are misleading and wrong."[10] Davenport consulted with Henry Luce and was told to placate Kennedy. That August, Joe wrote to Davenport thanking him for his "masterful handling of a very difficult situation with a very irritable young man named Kennedy." A glowing rewritten article with a color photograph of Kennedy was printed instead in the September issue. It even quoted Roosevelt and his thanks to Kennedy for his plan for "ships in keeping with our national pride and national needs."[11] Joe could not have been happier. The article was favorably timed for the next step in his grand project toward the presidency: his appointment as Ambassador to the Court of St. James's.

6

"THE LOADED PAUSE"

*One may dislike Hitler's system and yet admire
his patriotic achievement.*

—WINSTON CHURCHILL,
GREAT CONTEMPORARIES, 1937

By the spring of 1937, Jack Kennedy had been healthy for eleven months. His major at Harvard was politics because he "had already spent time abroad studying it," a reference to his brief sojourn in Paris and London in 1935.[1] Lackadaisical, fun-loving, charming Jack hadn't exactly sent the academics at Harvard swooning with excitement. Their assessment, echoing his parents', was that something had gone wrong when Jack's IQ test showed that he was much brighter than Joe Jr., the family star.

That summer was designated as Jack's time to add to the family knowledge of "what was going on in Europe," just as Joe Jr. had done when he "made a study of communism" during his brief visit in 1936 to the Soviet Union. But everything hinged on Jack's grades: with one B and three Cs, the jury was out on whether he should go. Jack had an original and independent mind, writing in his essay on Jean-Jacques Rousseau that the "Proper purpose of education" was not to parrot facts, but rather "the formation of judgement and character."[2]

At Harvard, Joe Jr. was clearly their tutor's preferred Kennedy son.

The "slender and handsome" young man with his shock of brown wavy hair and "a serious, slightly humorless manner" held a real interest in politics and public affairs. Even so, Joe Jr. "would invariably introduce his thoughts with . . . 'Father says.'" Comparing Jack to his older brother, economist John Kenneth Galbraith concluded that "unlike Joe, [Jack]was gregarious, given to various amusements, much devoted to social life and affectionately and diversely to women. One did not cultivate such students."[3]

Jack had wanted to spend the summer racing his sailboat at Hyannis Port, but his parents gave him the thumbs-down. He told Lem Billings that "the family do not want me to do it because they think there may be a war soon and I should see Europe." When a wealthier friend pulled out of the European expedition at the last minute, Kennedy arranged to pay Lem's way with Mrs. Billings—so long as he "paid him back half the amount from an inheritance due to him on graduation."

Jack wrote to his father: "I think that the best part of the trip would be getting into Spain either as Newspaper correspondents or as members of the Red Cross for about 3 weeks. If we can get in then it will affect our plans so hope you will be able to work it."[4]* It was not the first or the last time that Joe would use his international contacts to facilitate his sons' travels, often to the annoyance of those hosting the Kennedy boys.

JACK AND LEM boarded the *Washington* on July 1, 1937, with their luggage—and Jack's car—thinking they were going to have the time of their lives. Kick gave her brother a leather-bound diary engraved *My Trip Abroad* as a going-away present. Jack's first notes were: "Very smooth crossing. Looked pretty dull the first couple of days but investigation disclosed some girls." Their first glimpse of Europe from aboard ship was Ireland, the Kennedy ancestral home. Jack merely remarked: "Stayed up to see Ireland."[5]

---

* After close elections in February 1936 where the Communist Popular Front (the Nationalists) polled first, there were sporadic outbreaks of violence until the Civil War finally erupted on July 17, 1936. It lasted until April 1, 1939, with the defeat of the government by the forces of Generalissimo Francisco Franco, who would serve as Spain's fascist dictator until his death in 1975.

After docking at Le Havre, the boys drove across Normandy to Rouen and Beauvais, where they stayed at a little inn. Though Jack could afford to stay wherever he wanted, Lem could not. "It was no problem for Jack Kennedy to live as I did," Lem wrote. "He didn't mind it at all." When they got to Paris, however, Jack was driven by his raging libido to take in the hot spots like the Moulin Rouge and the Café des Artistes.

As a Catholic boy brought up primarily in the privileged world of wealthy Protestants at Canterbury, Choate, Princeton, and now Harvard, Jack found that his experiences in France—a Roman Catholic country—gave him an unexpected sense of belonging. Although his faith was always said to be superficial, during their European tour, both boys attended the Catholic mass in one cathedral or another each Sunday, with Lem more interested in the architecture, since that was his major at Princeton, and Jack comforted by the centuries-old traditions. In Paris on July 13, the boys got up early to hear Cardinal Pacelli preach at Notre Dame. There was a "terrific mob but by tagging on to an official," Jack wrote in his diary, "[I] managed to get a good seat right next to the altar. A very impressive ceremony which lasted for 3 hours. Billings had to wait in the body of the church."[6]

Joe had arranged for Jack and Lem to have lunch with Ambassador William C. Bullitt's secretary, Carmel Offie. A few days later, Offie told the boys that they would not be allowed to enter Spain. Despite their passports being stamped "Not Good for Travel to Spain," Jack insisted that they should try to get in. They got as far as Saint-Jean-de-Luz on the border in the French Basque country before they met some Franco refugees. "So we heard some pretty bloodcurdling tales," Lem recalled, "of what the non-Francos were doing in Spain. At the time we were very much shocked." They never made it past the border.

At the time, Jack was reading *Inside Europe* by John Gunther. Unlike his father and Joe Jr., Jack—always a believer in democracy—professed to be "governmental" after reading Gunther, even though he saw "St-Jean-de-Luz is a rebel stronghold." As the summer progressed, Jack became increasingly analytical, writing on July 24, staccato fashion: "England opposes Franco as they don't want Mediterranean [to be] a Fascist lake. Question of how much influence Germany and Hitler have, Russia's position. How far countries will go in having their side win? What type of government would Franco have? England and Germany?"[7]

WHEN THEY CROSSED into Italy, Jack noted, "Fascism seems to treat them well. . . . Pictures of Mussolini everywhere. How long can he last without money and is he liable to fight when he goes broke?" As they wended their way down to Rome and the Vatican, cosseted by the Kennedy friendships with Cardinal Pacelli and Count Galeazzi, Jack asked, "What are the evils of Fascism as opposed to Communism?"

An audience with the ailing Pope Pius XI was arranged at the pope's summer palace, and dinner at the Count's home. Jack and Lem could not fail to remark that Count Galeazzi—by now Joe Kennedy's good friend—was an ardent supporter of Mussolini and Fascism. Jack asked himself, "Would Fascism be possible in a country with the economic distribution of wealth as the US? Could there be any permanence in an alliance of Germany and Italy—or are their interests too much in conflict? Above all what was the true nature of fascism?"[8]

At Munich, the boys headed for the Hofbräuhaus, the site of Hitler's failed 1923 putsch. Jack's initial impression was: "There is no doubt about it that these dictators are more popular in the country than outside due to their effective propaganda."[9] Jack's observations and incessant questioning of the external forces at play, from those involved in the conflict in Spain to everyday people on the streets in France, Italy, or Germany to German hitchhikers and soldiers they picked up along their travels, showed a reflective nature well beyond his twenty years.

While in Munich, Jack visited the museum of science and technology, and found the German eye for innovation in aeronautics fascinating. It is a pity that on their whistle-stop tour of Germany, they did not go to the Munich Hofgarten to see the exhibition of "degenerate" art (*Entartete Kunst*). If they had, it might have given Jack an understanding of how Hitler had been raising millions for the war effort through the sale of fine art confiscated from his own museums.[10] This was the first exhibition of modern art, termed degenerate by Hitler. It had opened less than a month before Jack's visit to the city. An unprecedented number of visitors attended, thanks to the Nazi propaganda and the show's free entry. Without speaking fluent German or seeing it, Jack could not have known the significance of the Four-Year Plan for the sale of degenerate art and how it would help fund the coming war.

JACK SHARED HIS impressions of Europe with his father before returning to college in September. The state of Europe concerned the young man deeply, and his visit to Rome confirmed that the pope, Pacelli, and Galeazzi were particularly worried about Catholics in Spain and Germany. Jack understood that the Spanish Civil War was a proxy staging ground for the ideological conflict between Fascism and Communism. Both Hitler and Mussolini provided money, men, airplanes, and armaments to Franco's rebels by 1937. Much had been written about the struggle for Spanish Catholicism against the leftist Spanish Republic since the war broke out a year earlier. Indeed, one of the reasons for Pacelli's visit to the United States in October 1936 was to enlist Roosevelt in an anti-government campaign in Spain.[11] Joe Kennedy and James Farley, postmaster general and chairman of the Democratic National Committee, did the Vatican's bidding within the administration, ably assisted by Bishop Spellman and Count Galeazzi. Even so, Roosevelt remained aloof.

Jack also showed his father the travel diary. Joe did not blush at either of his elder sons' overactive sexuality. It was a trait they shared with their old man. Besides, it wasn't Jack's sexual encounters that interested him, but rather his astute son's take on Europe, its dictator countries, and their leaders. The time had come to implement the next critical step for "Project Kennedy": obtaining his international credentials as Ambassador to the Court of St. James's in London.

ON SEPTEMBER 8, 1937, Joe wrote a cryptic letter to Jimmy Roosevelt about his appointment that "this thing is getting terribly serious" and left it to Jimmy's conscience to "give it a little pressure" or not.[12] Kennedy had been keeping in touch with Ambassador Robert Worth Bingham—writing, rather insultingly, just before the 1936 election, "I shall be delighted to keep you posted if anything interesting comes up."[13] Back in 1935, Kennedy had shared his own health worries over his gastrointestinal problems, and Bingham reciprocated, saying that he had a serious illness no one could properly diagnose. Joe easily commiserated, as he was going through similar problems with Jack.

But the question was: Would Kennedy make a good ambassador? Unlike Jack, he could not envisage or reflect on the world situation other than in economic terms. He valued his own opinion too much to analyze the personalities he would need to assess accurately for the good of the United States and Great Britain. Jack saw that Hitler had shredded the democratic processes in Germany from the outset of his dictatorship, and unlike his father and brother, he did not like the dictators. Most significant, there was not a diplomatic bone in Joe Kennedy's body, making his heart's desire sheer folly.

Back in December 1936, Kennedy had made no comment about the British "abdication crisis." The new King, Edward VIII, demanded that his twice-divorced American mistress, Mrs. Wallis Simpson, become his queen. The British press had been gagged, but that could not stop tongues wagging, like society journalist Johnnie McMullin at British *Vogue*: "True, the Simpson situation is drawing-room gossip over here."[14] When the King refused to see reason, Prime Minister Stanley Baldwin withdrew the press ban on the affair in late November. By December 11, Edward VIII had abdicated and Prince Albert Frederick Arthur George "Bertie" Windsor became King George VI.[15] Shortly after the coronation in May 1937, Stanley Baldwin retired, and Neville Chamberlain became prime minister.

Then, too, Kennedy never mentioned the violence in the Far East or the Second Sino-Japanese War. This affected both the far-flung dominions of the British Empire and the United States. That October, Roosevelt delivered what became known as his Quarantine Speech in Chicago against "the epidemic of world lawlessness" that engulfed civilization.[16] With such widespread turmoil, a tremendous understanding of world affairs was an absolute requirement for any new ambassador, much less one without any diplomatic experience.

Nevertheless, Joe Kennedy would not be denied. Before Jack returned home, he wrote to Galeazzi on August 25, thanking him for his kindness to his second son. Then Joe wrote: "Congress adjourned two days ago and the President is taking a holiday for about a month. . . . I have informed Jimmy Roosevelt that I thought that steps like *we* contemplate would be very helpful in the not too distant future. Just as soon as there are any developments here, I will advise you."[17]

What "steps" had Galeazzi and Kennedy discussed together which were too secret to write about? Was it the hoped-for declaration of an ambassadorship to the Holy See? Maybe, but Pacelli had made his sentiments known in 1936. Roosevelt told them that the time was not ripe for an ambassadorship to the Vatican. He had also anticipated that any diplomatic representative from the United States to the Vatican could be only a "presidential special envoy" and not an ambassador and had said so to Pacelli at Hyde Park. Kennedy reluctantly understood—taking Galeazzi's view—that it was most important that neither Mussolini nor Hitler should think the Holy See was meddling in politics.[18*] So, what does the bemusing remark about informing Jimmy Roosevelt mean?

Another possibility, given Kennedy's closeness to the highest-ranking layman at the Vatican, is that Galeazzi already *knew* that Kennedy wanted to be America's ambassador to Great Britain. Taking the cryptic message from this alternative reading, Kennedy was advising Galeazzi that there had been no news as yet. Joe undoubtedly viewed such an appointment as the beginning of his greater service to the Holy See, culminating, hopefully, in running for the presidency in 1940.

To succeed, however, Joe would need to surmount ingrained prejudices against Catholics. A reasonable shortcut for a man who never held an elected office was as America's ambassador to Great Britain. Kennedy's acceptance in a Protestant country, especially in light of Britain's troubled past and present with Ireland, would elevate him to the status of "peacemaker." His visibility at the heart of international affairs, given the vast British Empire, would be enormous. Although Galeazzi and Pacelli may have privately lamented the reluctance of the American public to trust a Roman Catholic's dual allegiance to the Holy See *and* the United States, they would have celebrated the tremendous benefit Kennedy as the American ambassador to the Court of St. James's could bring. Having a strong Catholic voice so close to the president's

---

* The concordats Pacelli signed with the dictators precluded the Vatican's involvement in politics, and an ambassador's role has a political dimension.

ear would be a blessing in that year of "the loaded pause," as Winston
Churchill termed 1937.

THAT YEAR WAS truly a "loaded pause." Even the Vatican decided to
push back against Hitler. On Sunday, March 14, Pope Pius XI's encyclical
on the plight of the church in Germany, *Mit brennender Sorge*—translated
as *With Deep Anxiety*—was secretly delivered across Germany. Intended
as a condemnation of the Reich's treatment of Catholics, it failed, however, to censure either the NSDAP or Hitler by name. The encyclical
was smuggled into Germany during the Passion weekend mostly by
altar boys on foot or bicycle, avoiding public roads. The papal message
was simple: the Third Reich had "sown the tares of suspicion, discord,
hatred, calumny, of secret and open fundamental hostility to Christ and
His Church, fed from a thousand different sources and making use of
every available means ... [including] laws which suppress or render difficult the profession and practice of this faith."[19] Ensuring the success of
the Vatican in seeking peaceful worship for all Catholics was a primary
goal for Kennedy, too. France, Spain, Italy, and most of Central and South
America were predominantly Catholic.

The encroachment of communism was seen by Kennedy and the
Church as an enemy of Catholicism. Joe hadn't grasped that fascism, too,
cut across freedom of religion. He was among many powerful Americans
who believed the "red scare" was the greatest threat facing humankind.
France had a Popular Front coalition in power, with Léon Blum as its
prime minister.* Joachim von Ribbentrop, the German ambassador to
London, had been complaining officially to the British foreign minister,
Anthony Eden, of Soviet intervention in Spanish affairs on behalf of
the Popular Front Republic. What's more, Ribbentrop kept Nazi propaganda alive by feeding the press with generous portions of the "red scare"
spreading throughout Europe long after the Soviets had agreed not to
intervene in Spain.[20] Kennedy fell for the German disinformation and

---

* Blum was the first socialist and Jew to rise to such dizzying heights, and despite reforms
which attempted to mirror the New Deal, Blum was unsuccessful in tackling France's financial woes.

inadvertently disseminated it widely. Active Soviet involvement was an easy lie to believe.

SO, HOW LONG had Kennedy been plotting for his ambassadorship? Actions rather than words were often the *only* guide to Joe's intentions. There were darker corners obscuring his soul from all "outsiders," defined as anyone who was not one of the eleven immediate family members. "He wouldn't be Mr. Kennedy if you really know what his real purpose was in anything he ever did," Lem Billings confided to Jack's biographer, Nigel Hamilton.[21]

Months before Joe was confirmed as chairman of the Maritime Commission, he had sent out feelers to his European friends in the news business. Pathé's European representative in Paris, William O'Brien, wrote to Joe on January 22, 1937, about Georges Bonnet's appointment as French ambassador to Washington, and included the lowdown on the parlous state of France.[22] That June, Frank Kent of *The Baltimore Sun* wrote to Bernard Baruch about Joe's ambitions. "Poor old felt-minded Joe," Kent lamented. "What a sucker he is going to look if he does not get this appointment."[23] Kennedy had been metaphorically packing his bags all year.

Overseas was the place to be. Joe's voice had sung the praises of the New Deal too loudly as the country faced a new downturn. Distancing himself from the "Roosevelt Recession" was crucial to saving his reputation as a miracle worker. Cabinet members like Harold Ickes were blaming the "Sixty Families" of America for the renewed slump. In this climate, Joe believed any candidate who was actively super-rich with fingers in businesses from the stock market to liquor sales and a lingering influence in Hollywood was unattractive to voters. Roosevelt's inherited wealth, along with his determination to save the "forgotten man," did not have the same electoral stigma as Kennedy's rough entrepreneurship.[24] Becoming the "president's man" in Great Britain seemed a perfect solution.

In the fall of 1937, sales of liquor had trailed off considerably. If he was in London, Kennedy could glean inside information on the global economy by meeting regularly with the dapper, goateed Governor of the Bank of England, Montagu Norman. There would be plenty of opportunities to play the foreign markets through nominee accounts and make more money legally.[25] * Then, too, hobnobbing with royalty and aristocrats would more than burnish the Kennedy social credentials, pleasing Rose beyond measure.

Joe also believed he could placate Germany, and planned to meet with economics minister Hjalmar Schacht, who had saved the German economy from collapse. Recently, Schacht had devised a system of importing goods clandestinely for armaments production, then blocking payments to the exporter. He then negotiated enforced barter arrangements of German assets as payment—former privately held funds, investments, and artworks taken from "involuntary emigrants"—through a multiplicity of Swiss banking trusts.[26] Joe understood that Germany's finances were in tremendous disarray for Schacht's blocked-funds lark to remain a central feature of fiscal policy, but he was keen to understand how it all worked.

Seemingly, Kennedy did not comprehend the human misery behind the term "involuntary emigrants," or that many of these refugees had been made penniless by Hitler's edicts, automatically making them undesirables as immigrants elsewhere, too.[27] † Kennedy would regret Schacht's resignation as economics minister that November, but only because he could no longer meet the man in the normal course of European diplomatic proceedings.

---

* Nominee account holders are usually stockbrokers or lawyers who manage investments in securities and other financial instruments on behalf of a beneficiary whose name remains secret.

† "Involuntary emigrant" was the official term used for Jews, political dissidents, or priests who opposed Hitler's dehumanizing methods of ethnic cleansing.

7

THE MOVIE MOGUL
AND THE TRADE DEAL

―――――――――――

*. . . in the church there is a feeling the bars are liable to come
down on the decency problem again . . .*

—JOSEPH P. KENNEDY TO JOSEPH M. SCHENCK,
CO-FOUNDER OF TWENTIETH CENTURY FOX FILM CORPORATION,
OCTOBER 1937

To fulfill Kennedy's ambitions, the resignation of Ambassador Robert Worth Bingham was a prerequisite.* By the summer of 1937, Bingham had seen most of Europe's medical specialists to determine the cause of his malady, without success. That September, Bingham's resignation on health grounds had still not been announced, yet Rose claimed they had consulted "close friends in the Administration" about Joe's becoming the ambassador in London. But Kennedy had no close friends in Roosevelt's administration: he had alienated most of them with his blunt remarks about how they should do their jobs. Only James Roosevelt, as FDR's private secretary, remained close. Only James Roosevelt could have told Kennedy that Bingham had written to the president officially on October 19, 1937, suggesting his own replacement as ambassador: Thomas J.

―――――――――――

* Kennedy would never know that for future Kentuckians and Southerners, the Bingham dynasty would be compared to the Kennedys for their enormous wealth and shared history of tragic family deaths (*Source: New York Times,* January 19, 1986).

Watson, the chairman of IBM and head of the International Chamber of Commerce, Roosevelt's friend and unofficial ambassador in New York City.[1]

Naturally, Jimmy's off-the-record revelation worried Kennedy. So, off the record, too, Joe advised Jimmy that Watson was a poor choice: IBM was sharing advanced technology secrets with its German subsidiary and they were making that technology available to the Nazis. How did Joe know? Jack had been to the technology museum and seen it with his own eyes. Neither Jimmy nor Joe could know that eventually, the company's Hollerith punch card system made it possible "to identify, classify, manage, transport, and eventually exterminate millions of Jews."[2]

So, Joe forcefully put his own case to Jimmy. The United States was in the midst of serious renegotiations of its trade agreements around the world and was particularly interested in making inroads into the British imperial preference system. Hollywood had become a serious business in export markets, and Hollywood films were limited by the stringent tariff system in Britain, which favored the Empire and Commonwealth. Who better than he, a Hollywood insider, to negotiate that lucrative agreement and help this huge American industry that also exported American values and culture?

Kennedy was persuasive. Did Jimmy know that half of all production costs needed to be paid back within the first thirteen weeks of a film's release? In production terms, that meant that studios had to market fifty new films annually to the moviegoing public. Distribution maximized screen-time conferred to each film in a given territory. Exhibition "made screen-time available to a film only while the paying audience was sufficiently large." Together these functions created the life-and-death cycle of any film.[3] In this way, a hit movie would grab more exhibition time than a flop.

According to the 1935 statistics (the latest available), Britain's population was then 47 million, with 893 million admissions to movie theaters annually—or nineteen visits per person, paying on average ten pence per showing. In the United States, there were 2.233 billion annual admissions from a population of 127 million. Americans made eighteen trips to the "pictures," paying twenty-five cents each time.[4] This made the British market second in the world to the United States for moviegoing audiences.* Yet the British Cinematograph Films Act of 1927 imposed quotas on distributors and exhibitors by as much as 20 percent to help the British film industry develop. American distributors grudgingly took on "quota quickies" to assuage the bruised British ego, but that agreement would fall away on March 31, 1938. Who better than Kennedy to negotiate a future bonanza for Hollywood?

Jimmy knew that Joe's ongoing good relationships with the men who ran RKO, Paramount, Pathé, MGM, 20th Century Fox, and Warner Bros. were a compelling argument for him to get the job. But selling Kennedy would be a struggle. Secretary of State Cordell Hull, a tall Southern gentleman and former congressman and senator who could out-swear Joe when angered, had emphasized the importance of a broader "Anglo-American trade agreement . . . in mobilizing some forty nations behind a definite policy of economic appeasement, which in turn would facilitate political appeasement."[5]

On October 27, Ambassador Bingham wrote a long memo about the path both Canada (with British Dominion status) and the United States discussed regarding trade between themselves. Those talks, too, were stalled for up to a month "until after the information provided by the Canadians in Washington had been digested." Then, too, it had been tabled that Great Britain should send a representative to the U.S. capital for "an Ottawa Conference in Washington," to move forward trade talks with the British.[6] The British Board of Trade told Bingham bluntly that they were "desperately afraid lest wires be crossed and time fly by without concrete results eventuating" that certainly the motion picture portion of the trade deal—if not all other portions—would take on a "mystical quality" and expire.[7]

PRECISELY WHEN JIMMY told his father that Joe Kennedy wanted to be ambassador to the Court of St. James's is a matter of some conjecture. Nonetheless, some time shortly after Bingham's October 1937 letters to

---

* Since the admission price was approximately the same in each country, this made the British market worth $37.2 million as compared to the American market's being worth $571.5 million. On a strictly inflationary basis, sales in 2018 values for the British film market were approximately £2.489 billion or $3.11 billion, using an exchange rate of $1.25 to £1. Note: there were 240 pence to the pound at the time (Source: Bank of England).

Roosevelt and Hull, the matter must have been discussed in some detail. Bingham was heading to Johns Hopkins Hospital in Baltimore for exploratory surgery. The well-trodden path on the matter relates how James Roosevelt called on Kennedy at his rented mansion, Marwood, on the Potomac, and how "taken aback" he was at Joe's suggestion. "I really liked Joe," Jimmy recalled, "but he was a crusty old cuss and I couldn't picture him as an Ambassador—especially to England." Kennedy's "foster son" claimed that he tried to talk Joe out of it, but Kennedy insisted. "I've been thinking about it and I'm intrigued by the thought of being the first Irishman to be Ambassador from the United States to the Court of St. James's," Joe replied.[8]

When Jimmy passed the message on to FDR, "Sure enough . . . he laughed so hard he almost toppled from his wheelchair." The president's immediate reaction was to turn Joe down. Then he thought better of it. The motion picture industry was worth a great deal to the United States—it spread American ideals and culture around the world. Kennedy was a good businessman and organizer. Perhaps, too, he could unlock the stalled trade deals altogether?

Joe Kennedy was no pauper or professor, like Ambassador William E. Dodd in Berlin. He could afford to entertain expansively, delving deeply into his own pocket. There would be no flimflam in his reports home either. To top it all, the thought of Joe Kennedy at the London embassy appealed to Roosevelt's mischievous sense of humor, picturing an Irish Catholic in the bastion of Anglicanism. The thought that Kennedy could become another Walter Hines Page was ludicrous! * When the president took a straw poll of staff members at the White House, he saw that the concept amused others, too, but amusement soon gave way to shock and horror when he discussed it with his cabinet.

So, Jimmy was dispatched to Joe's home to try to persuade him to take a cabinet position as secretary of commerce. Kennedy was dining with Arthur Krock and excused himself from the dinner table. According to Krock, after three hours of heated debate, Kennedy's "foster son" left

---

* Walter Hines Page was the American ambassador to the Court of St. James's during the Great War and was accused of being more British than the British, convincing President Wilson to enter the war.

with more than an army of fleas in his ear. When Kennedy returned, he was "clearly very indignant, very angry and said, 'He tried to get me to take the secretaryship of Commerce and I knew it was only an attempt to shut me off from London, but London is where I want to go and it is the only place I intend to go and I told Jimmy so, and that's that.'"[9]

Krock helped Kennedy to undermine Roosevelt by making his appointment public. Without reference to the president's press team to verify if the story was true, Krock sent an overelaborate explanation of his actions to Kennedy dated "midnight December 8, 1937." The offending article was duly published the following morning, announcing the impending appointment of Joseph P. Kennedy as U.S. Ambassador to the Court of St. James's.[10]

Roosevelt's hands were duly tied, but the president never forgave Krock. FDR would always claim that the leaked story was responsible for hastening Ambassador Bingham's untimely death. The president insisted that Krock was "settling an old score" from the days when Bingham passed him over for the editorship of his Louisville paper. No wonder Krock later published the rumor that Roosevelt was shipping Kennedy overseas to "ease his plans to establish a dictatorship in Washington."[11]

The Krock article was reported in *The Times* of London on December 10, as proof "that the dispatch of Mr. Kennedy to London must mean that the President is 'grooming' him as his successor in 1940, and the fact that John Quincy Adams, who was President from 1825 to 1829, had been a Minister to Great Britain after the War of 1812–1814 is cited in support."[12] Kennedy was proud of this first public pairing of his family name with that of Adams.

8

THE LAST FAMILY CHRISTMAS

*The press of the country has presented you to the people as
something of a super-man.*

—EWING YOUNG MITCHELL*
TO JOE KENNEDY, JUNE 9, 1937

J oe could not know that Christmas 1937 would be the last time
all eleven family members would celebrate the seasonal holiday together. Ever. Nor did he know that Roosevelt had confided in Henry
Morgenthau that he was "a very dangerous man." The president also told
Morgenthau that he intended Kennedy's appointment as Ambassador to
the Court of St. James's to be a six-month sabbatical from Washington
and that he considered the ambassadorship canceled any obligation he
owed Kennedy.[1] Privately, FDR was livid that Joe had been two-faced
throughout their long association, incessantly criticizing the administration publicly. The December 9 article by Krock was positive proof of
the danger Kennedy represented.

It must be said, however, that when it came to double-dealing, the
president was an expert, too. He knew by telling Morgenthau that Kennedy was dangerous, he had struck a raw nerve. After all, Joe had lusted
after the job of secretary of the treasury for years. A recent article in the
St. Louis Star-Times even suggested that he and Kennedy were about to

---

*   Mitchell was the former assistant secretary of commerce at the time of writing, and
author of *Kicked In and Kicked Out of the President's Little Cabinet.*

swap jobs.[2] Just the same, Morgenthau opposed Kennedy's appointment because "England is a most important post and there have been so many people over there talking against the New Deal. Don't you think," Morgenthau asked Roosevelt, "you are taking considerable risks by sending Kennedy, who has talked so freely and so critically against your administration?" Roosevelt's reply was ominous: "I have made arrangements to have Joe Kennedy watched hourly and the first time he opens his mouth and criticizes me, I will fire him."

Then the president repeated the statement several times more: "Kennedy is too dangerous to have around here." As Morgenthau concluded in his diary entry for December 8, "I will certainly be glad to have him out of Washington and I take it that is the way the President feels."[3] Harold Ickes echoed their sentiments. All the same, Kennedy was oblivious to the rancor his outspokenness caused in the administration. Instead, he reveled in the special series articles on his career by his press acolytes— including Drew Pearson and Robert Allen in their syndicated column "Washington Merry-Go-Round"—and all the Hearst newspapers across the country. Many speculated on the possibility of Kennedy's achieving a higher office—that of secretary of state or perhaps president in 1940.

There was only one national dissenting voice—radio personality, syndicated columnist, and Kennedy friend Boake Carter. An Englishman by birth* and a naturalized American, Carter knew the pitfalls of the posting to London better than most. His December 14 column put it to Americans that "Kennedy is one of the most lovable souls in the world. Next to the President, I do not think that there is a man in Washington who radiates more personality. . . . He is a man who deals with things on a vast scale. Details irritate him. Delays and red tape annoy him." What's more, Carter, continued, "he is anything but a diplomat. What Irishman is?" As much as Carter liked Kennedy, he concluded that while Joe was a talented entrepreneur, he could not head a negotiating team on the trade deal because "he has not the type of personality that America needs to guide her destinies in these negotiations."[4]

---

* Harold "Boake" Carter was born to English parents in Baku, then part of the Russian Empire, now capital of Azerbaijan. He died in 1944 in Hollywood of a heart attack; some claim he might have been murdered.

Privately, Carter warned Kennedy that he was making a "terrible mistake." He was more plain-spoken than even Joe dared to be on the subject of Roosevelt. "My dear lad, agreements, mean nothing in his [Roosevelt's] life. They never have and they never will. . . . If he thinks certain things should be done as far as Great Britain is concerned, which you may think are cockeyed, you'll either have to carry them out, a la order boy, or explode and resign." Not only was Kennedy's personality wrong for the job, but he lacked the skill sets required. An ambassador needed "years of training. And that, Joe, you simply don't possess. . . . Joe, in so complicated a job, there is no place for amateurs."[5]

These tough words were the truest Kennedy would ever receive. But Joe was determined that such doom-laden language would not ruin his forthcoming appointment to the Court of St. James's. Much of the pre-Christmas period was spent responding to his hundreds of newspaper, business, and government associates either denying the *New York Times* story or, with false modesty, saying he still hadn't been confirmed, so congratulations were a bit premature.

As JOE GAZED at his family that Christmas with justifiable paternal pride, he was happy, too, that Rose was ecstatic with their elevated social position. Her neat handwritten letter to the president was understandably effusive. "I do want to thank you for the wonderful appointment you have given Joe. The children and I feel deeply honored, delighted and thrilled, and we want you to know that we do appreciate the fact that you have made possible this great rejoicing."[6] Joe never told Rose that he confided to Harvey Klemmer, who would be in London as his publicist and speechwriter, "Don't go buying a lot of luggage. We're only going to get the family in the *Social Register.*"

Rose, Joe Jr., and Jack all knew that Kennedy's plan was to use London as a stepping-stone. It was decided that Bobby, aged thirteen, and Teddy, aged six, would live with their parents at the embassy residence and attend day school in London. Eunice, Pat, and Jean would attend a Sacred Heart boarding school near the capital, with no disruption to their education.[7] Rosemary, given her special needs, was enrolled at a Montessori school in London, where Joe could monitor her progress. Kick had graduated and had been taking interior design classes at Parsons

School of Design in New York. It was decided *for* Kick that she would "drop out for a while" and help her mother with her duties as a hostess.[8] In this way, Rose's incessant travels would never be disrupted.

In January 1938, Joe Jr. began his last semester at Harvard and would finish his studies that June. It was decided with his father that his senior-year thesis should be on the Spanish Civil War and the Neutrality Acts.[9] After graduation, Joe Jr. was to become his father's secretary for a salary of one dollar and travel on the Continent as his father's *official* observer. Jack would stay on at Harvard until June 1938 with his brother, then would take a year off to be his father's other trusted eyes and ears in Europe.[10]

There is little doubt that Joe Jr., Jack, and Kick were excited about the move to London. Whenever the family convened around the dinner table, discussions were always centered around current affairs and politics. That Christmas, international politics supplanted all other topics, despite Kennedy never reading a book on modern European history. Joe had no inkling that the roots of the various issues concerning the Holy See and the political, cultural, and social causes leading to the Great War went back as far as the unifications of Germany and Italy in the nineteenth century. There was a certain naiveté, too, in how Joe assessed his new position. He hadn't appreciated that being an ambassador could make him a target in dangerous times. Only the previous August, the British ambassador to China, Sir Hughe Knatchbull-Hugessen, was seriously wounded in a bombing attack by two Japanese airplanes in Shanghai.[11] Then, too, Kennedy's last-minute education by his children required tact and diplomacy. Both Joe Jr. and Jack knew that any disagreement with their father needed to be couched as a question. It had been drilled into all the children that contradiction was disloyal and had no place in a healthy debate. And loyalty was a big thing with all the Kennedys.[12*] "Mr. Kennedy always said that the family should stick together," Lem Billings recalled. "He said the family would be happier as one unit than if they broke up into separate individual families." Rose wholeheartedly agreed.

The truth was that Joe was the sun to their planets. His magnetic

---

* They all relied on Joe Kennedy's wealth far into adulthood. In 1944, Kennedy would amend the children's and grandchildren's trust funds so that the boys would receive their money at age thirty-one, and the girls at age forty-one.

personality, quick intelligence, laughter, and candor gave his children a commanding, yet safe space in which to grow, and seemingly, to become their own people.[13] He let them know when he was thrilled with their progress, but often said how they could do better, too. If they failed at something, Joe wouldn't hide his disappointment, but then offered solutions with an unusual kindness for such a blunt individual. Even so, Joe always guided them in *his* ways, *his* goals, and *his* worldview. Above all else, he taught his children that it was winning that counted. Joe Jr. remained especially subservient to his father's will, conforming at every opportunity; where Jack, Kick, and later Bobby learned with varying degrees of pain how to cut the apron strings. Breaking free of the Kennedy clannism—and Rose's asphyxiating Catholicism—without losing their father's love became the cross which all the children had to bear.

IN EARLY JANUARY the children went back to school and Rose flew home to Bronxville. Joe began recasting the truth of how he got his plum job, writing for posterity in his *Diplomatic Memoir* that it came as an utter surprise.[14] Proof of Kennedy's disingenuity comes from separate, reliable sources. On January 4, Herschel Johnson wrote to King George VI to officially request if His Majesty had any objections to Joseph Patrick Kennedy as the American ambassador to the Court of St. James's.[15] Three days earlier, on January 1, 1938, Sir Eric Miéville at the Foreign Office wrote to His Majesty: "You probably know that about a fortnight ago I had some correspondence with Hardinge [the King's private secretary] about the rumours that were then current that Mr. Joseph Kennedy was to be appointed American Ambassador here in succession to Mr. Bingham, whose death had not then taken place."

Sir Eric confirmed that "the United States Government have now formally applied for the agrément of Mr. Kennedy and the Secretary of State is making the necessary submission to The King today." Sir Ronald Lindsay described Kennedy "as a quick, intelligent man of unusual ability. . . . He is wealthy, a devout Roman Catholic, has a pleasant wife and apparently fifteen children. He also, according to Lindsay 'dislikes society', as distinguished from company. . . ."[16] Word reached Washington soon after that Mr. Kennedy was amenable to King George VI, and the Senate of the United States duly confirmed him as United States Ambassador

Extraordinary and Plenipotentiary at the Court of St. James's on January 13, 1938.[17]

William C. Bullitt, the American ambassador to France, wrote to Roosevelt on January 10 to say how delighted he was with Kennedy's appointment, but that he should talk to Joe before he took up his post. "There is a lot of information about the Embassy plumbing that he ought to have," Bullitt confided, "and you and I are the only people I know who are sufficiently low-minded to discuss drains with him." The British, according to Bullitt, had every London embassy code, bugged both the embassy and the residence, and strategically placed British secret service employees on the inside.[18]

There is no doubt that Kennedy was ill suited for the job. Kennedy called himself "a rotten student" in a letter to John Cudahy, the newly appointed ambassador to the Irish Free State.[19] Reviewing the previous year's missives between the State Department and the Foreign Office did not appeal to Kennedy as much as a quick face-to-face meeting. For these reasons, any briefing he received from the State Department could be only of a general nature and thin on any meaningful background.[20]

That January, too, Kennedy demonstrated his unsuitability when he stated that despite the very real possibility of a global conflagration in Europe and the Far East, the Roosevelt administration had made "no clear statement of our foreign policy." If he was right, then why did Prime Minister Chamberlain write to Roosevelt on January 14 that he was "greatly encouraged to know that world affairs were engaging his attention so directly that he is willing to take so courageous an initiative" as to propose combining military forces in the Far East? Privately, however, Chamberlain referred to Roosevelt's offer as "an American bomb" hurled across the Atlantic.[21] He disliked Roosevelt's meddling in Britain's appeasement policies.

WHILE JOE WAS patting himself on the back and exhibiting his salesman's smile in most of America's newspapers and *Time* magazine, January 1938 began rather badly for the United States in its trade negotiations with Great Britain. Toward the end of November 1937, the British embassy in Washington was informed that the American motion picture industry was protesting about two amendments to the trade agreement under consideration by the British Parliament.[22] Cordell Hull wrote to the American chargé d'affaires in London, Herschel V. Johnson, that Will Hays heard that the committee reports for discussion in the House of Commons were detrimental to the American movie industry.[23] On December 10, Hull wrote again to Johnson that after Hays's trip to Washington he was "much impressed by the seriousness of the present threat to the [American] motion picture industry in Great Britain."

Hull then called on the British ambassador, Sir Ronald Lindsay, stressing that neither "government should take irrevocable action involving items of trade which are certain to come under discussion during the negotiations." In London, Herschel Johnson sought to allay some of Hull's fears by reiterating that nothing had been done to harm the U.S. motion picture industry yet, but that the bill was in its second reading in committee.[24]* By mid-December 1937, it became apparent that the British had no intention of including the motion picture deal as part of the forthcoming trade talks with the United States because the current ten-year agreement regarding American films would expire on March 31, 1938.[25] If Kennedy were to be of real use to the American movie industry, he had to hightail it to London.

Instead, that January, Kennedy headed west. Why? According to Joe, he was on the West Coast because he had not expected his appointment. In truth, there were outstanding issues to clear up at the Federal Maritime Commission before Joe's successor, Vice-Admiral Emery Scott "Jerry" Land, would take over. Roosevelt was unprepared to let Kennedy go to London unless he first handled the most burning issue facing the Maritime Commission: the potential bankruptcy of the Dollar Line and a new vision for the prosperity of Pacific coast shipping and shipbuilding.†

Kennedy's trip west was of dubious merit. Following the one-day

---

* A bill may begin in either the House of Lords or the House of Commons and is "passed" after its third reading in both houses and consideration for further amendments. It becomes law only after receiving Royal Assent.

† Joseph Raymond Sheehan, a childhood friend of Kennedy's, would become the president of the Dollar Line once the new ambassador left for London. Sheehan would administer the six-month extended government subsidy that Kennedy had approved.

conference with Dollar Line executives and other shipping leaders in San Francisco on January 7, Kennedy wended his way north to Seattle, where tensions between the International Longshoremen's Association and the local Waterfront Employers Association were tense.[26] Kennedy's poor record at labor relations continued to dog his every move. He would leave his job unfinished at the commission, with policies in disarray, chronic underfunding, ongoing labor disputes, and nothing but the postal contracts agreed upon.[27]

RETURNING EASTWARD BY train, Kennedy telegraphed Roosevelt from Shelby, Montana, that he "JUST GOT NEWS OF MY CONFIRMATION. WILL THANK YOU PERSONALLY WHEN I GET HOME. I WANT TO SAY NOW THAT I DON'T KNOW WHAT KIND OF A DIPLOMAT I SHALL BE, PROBABLY ROTTEN, BUT I PROMISE TO GET DONE FOR YOU THOSE THINGS THAT YOU WANT DONE. ROSE AND I ARE DEEPLY GRATEFUL."[28]

In the meantime, Herschel Johnson was handling the final negotiations on the motion picture agreement with his British counterparts at the Board of Trade in London.[29] On January 31, Hull wrote to Johnson that the proposed agreement was unacceptable to American filmmakers, and the Board of Trade should wait for Ambassador Kennedy's arrival. He admitted, however, that it was a pity Kennedy had been "unavoidably" delayed.

By the end of January, the negotiations had become acrimonious. So, Kennedy made a phone call around February 4 to Sir Ronald Lindsay in Washington, in which he "suggested that the passage of new British film legislation be delayed until he had a chance to discuss with Mr. Oliver Stanley and other British authorities the possibilities of working out a more satisfactory solution."* Joe was going over old ground. Jay Pierrepont Moffat, chief of the European Affairs Division at the State Department, then met with Lindsay, and reported: "It seems that Parliamentary procedure is so rigid that it is not possible to change the plans agreed upon. The schedule of legislation has been laid out, the time has been allocated et cetera." The possibility of maintaining the status quo

---

* Sir Oliver Stanley was the President of the Board of Trade in London and led the British negotiations.

for a short while was not feasible. "Sir Ronald replied that everyone had known for ten years that the legislation would expire at the end of March and must be replaced by new legislation and that thus far no new factor had been introduced."[30]

Moffat seethed, believing that it had always been the U.S. under-standing that motion pictures would be part of the mercantile dis-cussions in the overall trade agreement. Lindsay argued that motion pictures were a cultural and not a mercantile product. He would not budge, other than to say that "some of the points brought up by Mr. Kennedy would be met by the introduction of amendments at the 'report' stage." It was the equivalent of a diplomatic fistfight. Lindsay, a good friend of Roosevelt's, knew he was on strong ground. "Think of that," Lindsay concluded with great sarcasm, "think of Great Britain asking to reserve for itself 30% of the output in a great cultural prod-uct" to fulfill the public's desire to promote a British film industry.[31] What was unreasonable in that?

Both diplomats left the meeting soured by the experience. The bit-terness continued unabated through early March, with the United States and Great Britain each digging in their heels. "The British Govern-ment will understand that an alteration to the disadvantage of the United States on the very eve of trade agreement negotiations in the status of so important a product as motion pictures," Secretary of State Hull wrote to Johnson, "could hardly fail to affect the attitude of my Government toward concessions to be offered certain important British exports to the United States."[32]

Since Kennedy's own business interests were heavily linked to the ex-port of Scotch to the United States, it seems absurd that his accreditation to the Court of St. James's was delayed. The excuse used was, of course, Rose's emergency appendectomy. But this did not occur until *after* a decision to delay had been made—at the very end of January—and, moreover, seems an unlikely reason. Childbirth was potentially more dangerous back then, and Rose had delivered all her children without Joe's being present—often while he was in a different part of the coun-try. Why, then, was there a delay of a full month before Kennedy was sworn in?

Surely the Maritime Commission's issues were not more pressing—for

a man of little maritime experience and poor union negotiating skills—
than replacing the U.S. Ambassador to the Court of St. James's during
a serious trade crisis and talk of another European war? Then why did
Roosevelt delay Kennedy's swearing-in until February 18? Was the president astutely setting up Kennedy to fail? And if so, at what cost?

PART II

SUNSHINE AT THE COURT OF ST. JAMES'S

The Home and Haunt of Kings

—Edmund Spenser, 1552–1599

9

THE CELEBRITY AMBASSADOR

An unemployed man with a hungry family is the same
fellow, whether the swastika or some other flag
floats above his head.

—JOE KENNEDY TO ARTHUR KROCK,
MARCH 21, 1938

On February 18, 1938—the same day that Admiral Jerry Land became chairman of the Maritime Commission—Justice Stanley Reed administered Kennedy's oath of office, with the president and a select group of photographers looking on.

Joe claimed afterward he received no briefing in Washington on how to be a good ambassador. However, Jay Pierrepont Moffat gave Joe a personal crash course in international diplomacy, citing William C. Bullitt's Paris embassy as the model legation. Indeed, Moffat told him that Bullitt "is on such terms with Chautemps, Blum, Daladier, etc., that they not only tell him everything but actually show him telegrams received from their Ambassadors abroad."[1] Kennedy was taken through the reasons why London, Moscow, and Rome were vastly inferior embassies to Paris. Moffat held up Ambassador Dodd, who had been replaced by career diplomat Hugh R. Wilson only days earlier in Berlin, as a prime specimen of an able academic but a poor diplomat.*

---

* Dodd was American ambassador to Berlin from August 30, 1933, until December 29, 1937. He had been privately instructed by Roosevelt to protest the Nazi treatment of the

Moffat told Kennedy to maintain close contact within his comfort zone of bankers, journalists, financiers, and economists, while also courting professors, intellectuals, and aristocrats. Crucially, Kennedy was to listen to what his own *experienced* London staff thought. Above all, the new ambassador should aim to analyze and interpret the news, not only from London, but also from the vast British Empire. Then, too, if Kennedy had any questions, Moffat would be happy to be helpful. In a final word of advice, Moffat reminded Kennedy that it was a huge and weighty task he was undertaking and wished him every success.[2] Even though the suave and debonair Moffat had been in the job for only seven months, he was *the* European expert and career diplomat. Kennedy should have been glad of Moffat's personal advice.

Four days later, on the crisp, sunny Tuesday of February 22, Joe joined the president at Hyde Park for a farewell chat. The only detailed account of that discussion is Kennedy's *Diplomatic Memoir*. If one studies the document closely, some of Roosevelt's words of warning on that day are vintage Kennedy rather than FDR, like: "The United States, of course, cannot participate in any political settlements, but it can, and I believe will be able to, lead the world out of the economic morass in which it is floundering. In my opinion, the economic distress of the world these last nine years has been the root cause of most of the other troubles."[3] The *Diplomatic Memoir* always attributed words to others in direct quotes, despite having been through several drafts and refashioned by James M. Landis between 1949 and 1955. Landis himself was ill at ease with this practice, since Kennedy's contemporaneous notes could not justify the exact quotations he used. Even so, the memoir says Roosevelt also counseled Kennedy that "no matter how much we might favor or dislike the objective of any nations, we must not show our likes or dislikes." Such advice was given so Joe would keep his opinions to himself. But had FDR actually said, "We shall have to mark time until we see whether or not Chamberlain accomplishes anything"?[4] In all likelihood, yes, although the president's exact words may have been couched more as words of warning.

Jews initially, while the State Department briefed him to maintain a cordial relationship with Nazi Germany. Much of the criticism against him was unfair and came from career diplomats in the State Department.

★ ★ ★

ROOSEVELT KNEW THE curt rebuff from Chamberlain about joining forces in the Far East was an outdated anti-Wilsonian snub. Chamberlain viewed *any* American peace initiative as interfering with British foreign policy. Churchill, then out of government for nearly ten years, believed that the Conservative Party in power was filled with "blind and obstinate men," meaning Chamberlain and his cohorts, but he was powerless to do anything about it.[5] On the day before Roosevelt's talk with Kennedy, the British Foreign Secretary, Anthony Eden, and his loyal undersecretary Lord Cranborne resigned, stating to the Commons that "there are occasions when strong political convictions must override all other considerations."[6] Eden was immediately replaced with the capable, like-minded, highly religious six-foot-five-inch, willowy Edward Frederick Lindley Wood, 1st Earl of Halifax.*

The primary reason for their resignations was Chamberlain's outright refusal of Roosevelt's initiative of January 12, proposing an international conference in Washington to explore peaceful solutions to the European problems. The president asked for a reply by January 17 from the prime minister, so that Germany, Italy, and France could be invited before any guns started blazing. The dates are significant and suggest why Kennedy was not immediately sent to London when the Senate confirmed his appointment on January 13. Foreign policy was Roosevelt's special domain. His proposal was intended to stop Chamberlain from immediately giving into demands from Mussolini. The last thing Roosevelt wanted was to have a plain-spoken novice ambassador telling everyone else what to do.

Sir Ronald Lindsay in Washington had urged quick acceptance of the president's initiative. Eden had been away on holiday in the South of France but raced home to urge Chamberlain to agree to Roosevelt's offer. Chamberlain steadfastly refused. Instead, the prime minister encouraged his half brother Austen's widow, Lady Ivy Chamberlain, to continue in her unofficial role as peacemaker with Mussolini in Rome—a role she had been undertaking throughout 1937 at Chamberlain's behest with both Il Duce and his foreign minister and son-in-law, Count

---

* During Halifax's father's long life, he was known as Viscount Irwin, only inheriting to the title Viscount Halifax on his father's death in January 1934.

Galeazzo Ciano. When Lady Chamberlain passed on advice from the American ambassador in Rome, William Phillips, "to start conversations at any cost," the prime minister ignored him, too.[7]

Roosevelt knew that relations between Eden and Chamberlain had been awkward since the Nyon Conference in September 1937, when the foreign secretary secured protection of Mediterranean shipping routes against Italian piracy. Chamberlain was aghast, believing that Eden's success had been secured at the cost of Anglo-Italian relations. On February 1, 1938, Ciano wrote in his diary that he accompanied Lady Chamberlain to see Il Duce with an important letter from the prime minister. "Great Britain is ready to formally recognize the [Italian] Empire; the talks may begin at the end of the month. Mussolini approved and agreed." Then Mussolini "dictated the terms" he would accept to Lady Chamberlain.[8]

TAKEN AGAINST THESE facts, no wonder Roosevelt was deeply troubled by Eden's sudden resignation. Roosevelt was incredulous that Chamberlain would recognize the "Italian Empire"—with its latest conquest being Abyssinia. In the *Diplomatic Memoir,* Kennedy does not mention that Mussolini had signed the Anticomintern Pact with Germany and Japan in November 1937, effectively creating the Axis powers. A month later, Italy left the League of Nations allegedly due to the sanctions imposed against her for the Abyssinian invasion—but only after Mussolini received Hitler's blessing to do so.[9]

Joe's diary entry for his Hyde Park meeting blandly states that Roosevelt "discussed the foreign situation in general and the break between Eden and Chamberlain in particular." In a blatant untruth, he says that Roosevelt "did not seem to resent the position Chamberlain has taken of trying to make deals with Germany and Italy in order to fend off a crisis, but he seemed to regret Eden's passing from the picture."[10] There are two possibilities as to why Kennedy wrote this. Either he made this entry *after* becoming great friends with Chamberlain and sought to mask Roosevelt's wariness of the British prime minister in January 1938; or he was genuinely unable to discern the president's true thoughts. Either interpretation did not bode well for the future.

★ ★ ★

WHAT *DID* CONCERN Kennedy was all the press he was getting—at home and in Britain—about whether he would wear ceremonial knee breeches or not to his accreditation to the Court of St. James's. Apparently, the president's mother was worried that he would.[11] The subject was one of Roosevelt's crueler jokes. It seems that in late 1937 while Joe was in the Oval Office lobbying for the post of ambassador, the president asked Kennedy, "Would you mind taking your pants down?" Joe reluctantly obeyed. Then FDR roared with laughter. "You are just about the most bow-legged man I have ever seen." Roosevelt explained that during the ceremony the ambassador *has* to wear knee breeches and silk stockings. "When photos of our new ambassador appear all over the world, we'll be a laughingstock."[12]

At a stroke, Roosevelt's Oval Office striptease humiliated Kennedy, yet made him feel a White House insider with whom the president could let his hair down. It also kept Joe guessing if his bowlegs might be an impediment to his ambassadorship. What he did not realize was that many an ambassador had been accredited in native regalia, and other European royal courts had accredited women wearing dresses.* The brouhaha was a media tempest in a teacup.

ON FEBRUARY 23, Kennedy boarded the SS *Manhattan*. "Newspaper men, casual well-wishers, old friends and strangers by the thousand, it seemed to me, pressed into my cabin until we all nearly suffocated," Joe said.[13] In order to have a private chat with Jimmy Roosevelt, they had to weave through the mob into the cabin bedroom. Neither recorded what was said. After all the guests had been sent ashore, Joe went out to wave goodbye to the eight children (except Jack) who had come to see their father off.† They were "standing in the rain, waving and throwing kisses."[14]

Winter crossings on the Atlantic are notoriously rocky. Kennedy described the voyage as rolling across the ocean, intimating that he had fared worse; but claimed tiredness would keep him in his cabin for the

---

* When Joachim von Ribbentrop was accredited at the Court of St. James's, he gave Edward VIII a highly formal Nazi salute and ostentatiously clicked his heels. The press had a field day, calling him Herr von "Brickendrop."

† Rose was still recovering from her appendectomy.

duration of the voyage. Given that he had taken along as his personal press "handler" (at Arthur Krock's suggestion) a young journalist called Harold Hinton, as well as Harvey Klemmer, a speechwriter who had worked with Joe at the Maritime Commission, secluding himself alone in his cabin was hardly an option. Arthur Houghton, borrowed from Will Hays's office in Hollywood, completed the foursome.* Klemmer, Hinton, and Houghton had a lot of studying to do on the eastbound journey.

Kennedy was not a man to admit that he was overwhelmed by his exciting, momentous burden. He does not give many details of this crossing, unlike earlier and later ones. It is possible, too, that he remained in his cabin for fear of retribution by the National Maritime Union members who staffed the *Manhattan*. After all, he was a union-buster and widely viewed as their archenemy. But when a crew spokesman said that "Our members will give Mr. Kennedy every courtesy, no matter what they think of his attempts to wreck their union," Joe apparently relaxed. Before the journey was over, Kennedy visited the crew's quarters and agreed that their living conditions were not fit for human habitation. That said, he did not make any recommendations to Admiral Land.[15]

As they approached England, the British newspapers the *News Chronicle* and the *Daily Mirror* interviewed Joe via the ship-to-shore telephone. "Their questions were not very promising," Kennedy lamented to his diary, "and I wondered if my interviews on landing would be so inconsequential."[16] Fortunately, the wet and chilly English weather had forsaken the British Isles since mid-February. When the *Manhattan* docked at Plymouth on March 1, the day had been partly sunny with a high of fifty degrees.† For once, there were no high winds buffeting the harbor, no swell of the icy waves onto Plymouth Hoe. Unusually, most of that month would remain unseasonably warm, with no rain to speak of for the first twenty-three days across the entire south of England. A spring drought would follow.[17] Kennedy could be forgiven if he thought the sun shone purely for his benefit.

---

* Joe hadn't known that Hinton had a severe drinking problem, and he would be compelled to send Hinton home the following September.

† Ten degrees Celsius.

10

HITTING THE GROUND RUNNING

My impression is that Hitler and Mussolini,
having done so very well for themselves by bluffing . . .
are not going to stop bluffing.

—JOSEPH P. KENNEDY TO PRESIDENT ROOSEVELT,
MARCH 11, 1938

As anticipated, the press was out in force. Kennedy, a master manipulator of the American newshounds, set to work on the British. At
the dockside, Joe flashed the Kennedy smile, kept his comments brief
and folksy, and applied the Kennedy charm with a trowel. His main
statement, printed in *The New York Times* the following morning, was
that there would be "regular transatlantic air transportation between the
United States and Great Britain by 1940" and that he would like to be
one of its first passengers.[1] His boast charmed the British.

Kennedy and his personal staff lost no time boarding the night train,
reaching Paddington Station at seven the next morning. Joe had been
told before sailing that the U.S. government did not provide its ambassador with a car and was disgruntled at having to take a taxi to the residence at 14 Prince's Gate. He would soon correct that omission when
his brand-new Chrysler LeBaron arrived from New York.[2]

Although Joe was impressed with the fifty-two-room new home, he seemed more concerned with rolling up his sleeves for duty than with describing his ambassadorial townhouse. That said, Kennedy noticed that 14 Prince's Gate was within easy walking distance from Rotten Row, where all the "topside people"—as Kennedy would call the social elite—rode their horses.

In fact, the ambassador's new home was a building of national significance, constructed in 1849. The six-story beaux arts style residence had been the gift of J. P. Morgan Jr. to the American government in 1920.* It had a carved Portland stone facade with heads of Native Americans cut into the keystones over the arches of the ground-floor windows. The octagonal front hall with its black-and-white marble floor and the grand staircase with its marble columns were impressive. There was a fancy open-cage lift, or elevator, which gave access to all six floors. Joe, however, thought that despite the residence's size, it was unsuitable for a family of eleven, claiming it would take a fortune to renovate to his liking, not to mention heating it and paying for its upkeep. His salary as ambassador was a meager $75 a week.

FIRST OFF, JOE met the residence staff, then breakfasted with his personal team, Bill O'Brien and London Jack (whose salaries were paid from his own bank account), for an update on the latest British and European news.[3] Soon enough, they would be joined by another Kennedy cohort from Joe's Hollywood days, Jim Seymour. "Please feel you have in me a flying ambassador who keeps his mouth shut and whose loyalty never waivers one iota," Seymour wrote to Joe in May 1937.[4]

Straight off, Kennedy told O'Brien that he was unhappy with how the Plymouth newsreel was shot, and ordered another, more flattering one to be made, in the embassy gardens.[5] That same afternoon, while the light lasted, Pathé News would be on hand as demanded. Joe acted as his own director, shouting, "Cut!" whenever he stumbled over his words spoken to the camera.

---

* The building at 14 Prince's Gate was extensively remodeled internally once J. P. Morgan Sr. acquired number 13 Prince's Gate and incorporated the two terrace dwellings into one home. Externally it looked like two homes, but internally, numbers 13 and 14 were one residence. During the Great War, the house was loaned to the Professional Classes War Relief Council, who used it as a maternity home.

Then, without pausing to rest, Kennedy strode out for the embassy, which was situated at one of London's premier addresses, 1 Grosvenor Square. Joe was tremendously disappointed when he saw it. While it was within easy access of the ambassadorial residence, to his mind, the embassy was not fit for its purpose. The stylish neo-Georgian building on the eastern side of the square had been part of a redevelopment scheme led by Hugh Grosvenor, Duke of Westminster, and the U.S. Embassy was its first occupant in 1938.*

Joe asked Jimmy Roosevelt in his March 3 letter to pass on "that I have a beautiful blue silk room and all I need to make it perfect is a Mother Hubbard dress and a wreath to make me Queen of the May." Insultingly, even for those days, Joe wrote, "If a fairy didn't design this room, I never saw one in my life." Then Joe added, "Not only was the designer a fairy, but. . . . If there was ever a badly laid out building for which the United States Government has to pay regular money, this tops it all."[6]

WHILE IN LONDON, Kennedy was determined to maintain his American lifestyle. It is always difficult moving to a foreign country to work, but with a family of eleven—and a grown child with special needs—the challenges were multiplied many times over. Neither Rose nor Joe were taking any chances that they would need to give up their creature comforts. For Joe, that meant importing American products at regular intervals like Maxwell House coffee; over seventy pounds of candy at a time—including thirty pounds of "Mr. Kennedy's mixture" from Windmill Sweets in South Chatham, Cape Cod—at a 25 percent discount; dozens of cans of New England clam chowder; Nivea Creme; Jergens lotion; Cheracol cough syrup and more—essentially anything that the family regularly used which was not easily available in England. Kennedy provided for his own needs in spirits through the British Distillers Company. Fine wines, wholesale fresh fruit and vegetables, and even flowers and cigars were ordered through William Bullitt's chargé at the U.S. Embassy

---

* The U.S. Embassy occupied the building until 1960, when the Americans moved across the square to its purpose-built monstrosity in 1961. The Canadian High Commission took over the old building. The Canadian High Commission moved out in 2014 when the building was sold to a developer and is currently being marketed by Knight Frank real estate agents as forty-four luxury flats (*Source*: Knight Frank Estate Agents).

in Paris. Nonetheless, the most significant import Joe made was the chest freezer he had shipped from New York.[7] No Kennedy child would go without ice cream.

Before joining her husband, Rose had written to the State Department to discover if she should bring or send over items. She was rather shocked to discover that bed linen, dining room linen, and bath mats were lacking, and there was no sewing machine, despite there being a sewing room. "A careful comparison of the attached lists with the inventory cards indicates that the Embassy residence is quite completely furnished with high grade furniture." Then the writer, who signed with the initials *BK,* continued: "Of course I have no way of ascertaining the present condition of the various pieces. . . . Curtains and drapes appear to be adequate for the whole building, as well as rugs and lamps." There were only eight bedrooms—two single and six double. That said, there were thirteen bedrooms for the servants and nineteen beds for them. So, Rose poached some bedrooms from the servants' quarters to have individual bedrooms for each of the children and guests, "as necessary." The good news was that in 1931, the State Department had paid $506.52 for sixty-eight blankets. However, the walls of the residence had been stripped bare since Andrew Mellon had donated his entire art collection to the National Gallery in Washington in 1933,* so Joe arranged a loan of some of William Randolph Hearst's overpriced art from St. Donat's Castle in Wales to fill the empty wall space.[8]

IT WAS LATE afternoon when Kennedy made his first official call on the British Foreign Secretary, Edward Wood Lord Halifax, at the Foreign Office. As the former Viceroy and Governor-General of India, Halifax was deemed an excellent replacement for Anthony Eden. Prior to being introduced to him, Joe must have been warned about Halifax's extraordinary height and appearance. Kennedy was prepared to look up to the six-foot-five-inch reed-thin and sad-eyed foreign secretary. He should have been told, too, that Halifax was born without a left hand and that a

---

* Andrew W. Mellon was U.S. Ambassador to the Court of St. James's from February 5, 1932, until March 17, 1933.

prosthetic one had been fitted—in the form of a clenched fist with the thumb poised to move by a spring.[9]

Death overshadowed much of Halifax's youth until he was ten years old. He was born the sixth child and fourth son in his family. Sadly, his three elder brothers died in rapid succession, leaving Edward heir to his father's enormous fortune and seat in the House of Lords. His childhood and his High Anglican upbringing made him very religious, leading Churchill to call him "The Holy Fox." The only drawback to Halifax as Foreign Secretary was that he could not speak or sit in the House of Commons, which Chamberlain called "the centre of gravity" of British politics.[10] Instead, Halifax's forum for airing the government's views was in the upper House of Lords. Given Halifax's years of diplomacy and cool reactions, Chamberlain saw his new foreign secretary as the perfect foil for Churchill's alleged recklessness.

KENNEDY MADE NO mention of Halifax's extraordinary appearance, his aristocratic stoop, receding hairline, magnetism, slight lisp, or sad, kindly eyes. Instead, Joe tells how he "talked pretty frankly . . . about the isolationist tendencies at home and found him [Halifax] prepared for that point of view."[11] The "isolationist tendencies at home" were graphically presented by the staunch isolationist Kennedy, who as the father of four sons was quite naturally adverse to talk of war. Halifax wrote to the British ambassador in Washington that Kennedy was "in good form and made even more generous use than usual of the American vernacular to emphasize his point."[12] In other words, Joe swore like a trooper.

While serving as Viceroy and Governor-General of India in the troubled years of 1926 to 1931, Halifax came to believe in forbearance and face-to-face negotiation. Although Kennedy didn't know how to restrain himself, he, too, believed in the personal touch. Halifax did not understand economics like Kennedy did, and was always "inclined to trust the responsible professional" in these matters.[13] What Joe hadn't understood was that Halifax, like many Europeans, had a scant regard for American diplomacy stemming back to the errors of the Wilson era.

Kennedy was perhaps unaware that Halifax was the coauthor of Chamberlain's appeasement policy based on his experiences in India, but was thankful for Halifax's determination not to "slight the German amour-propre." The foreign secretary believed that both Indians and Germans were a great people and that "the main difference between the two nations is that a mild Hindu is probably less alarming than a vigorous Prussian."[14] That said, neither Halifax nor Kennedy grasped that Hitler was no Prussian, with all its connotations of military prowess, noble heritage, and honor.

TWO DAYS LATER Kennedy was summoned to 10 Downing Street, the official home of British prime ministers. "I found him a strong decisive man," Joe wrote about Prime Minister Neville Chamberlain afterward, "evidently in full charge of the situation here. Perhaps those at home who regretted the departure of Anthony Eden are backing the wrong horse."[15] Chamberlain was a seasoned politician who was first elected to the House of Commons at the mature age of forty-nine for the constituency of Birmingham Ladywood. He hailed from one of the toughest political fighting families of the late nineteenth and early twentieth centuries.

Both his father, the former Colonial Secretary Joseph, and his elder half brother, the former Foreign Minister Austen Chamberlain, had been touted as future prime ministers in their heyday, but neither succeeded in their ultimate goal. Given this heritage, it came as no surprise that Neville Chamberlain ran his appeasement policy with a merciless attention to detail within the Conservative Party, using the Whips at every turn.* He also masterfully controlled the British press. Yet, Neville felt he lived in their respective shadows. According to Churchill, Neville's father was a colossus who made the political weather in his day. No such accolades touched his son.

Chamberlain served in both Ramsay MacDonald's and Stanley Baldwin's governments throughout the 1930s in various cabinet positions, before finally becoming prime minister on May 28, 1937.† The *Daily Telegraph* said: "Despite his stiff and somewhat forbidding exterior . . . he was in fact 'very human' . . . 'and as devoted to his briar pipe as Mr

---

* The Whips are the parties' "enforcers," maintaining party discipline and ensuring that MPs vote in accordance with party lines rather than with any individual ideology. When the Whip is withdrawn, that MP loses any association with the party.

† This was two weeks after the Coronation of George VI.

Baldwin to his cherry.'" Chamberlain was also said to be a "good judge of claret." He was a formal man of definite ideas, aloof and difficult to read. He was rabidly against Britain's socialist Labour Party and hid his thoughts and personality behind a veneer of Victorian public duty and propriety.[16] Chamberlain's appearance was rather lugubrious: tall but stooped, he rarely smiled and had a hawklike nose and dark sullen eyes peering steadfastly from beneath bushy eyebrows. In combination with his usual dress of old-fashioned dark suits, his Victorian wing-collared shirts, and his ever-present umbrella, he resembled an undertaker. Together with Halifax, they were known (behind their backs) as "the undertaker" and "the priest" respectively.

Like Halifax, Chamberlain had been prepared for Kennedy's tough talk about America's not intervening in any European conflict. Unknown to Joe, it was music to his tired ears. The British prime minister said he was making his own plans for "pacification or fighting, as things might develop."[17] The burning issue regarding motion pictures seemingly was not discussed, despite Cordell Hull's telegram to Herschel Johnson that same day asking to be kept "currently informed" of the trade negotiations going on in London.[18]

On his return from Downing Street, Kennedy called in the press to give them "the lowdown." With his shirtsleeves rolled up to his elbows, his hands clasped behind his head, Kennedy leaned back, "cocking his feet on his desk," as the journalists rolled in, somewhat shocked at his demeanor. His day had started well enough, Kennedy told them. He rode that morning in Hyde Park's Rotten Row on a rented horse before seeing Chamberlain. As they fired more salient questions at him, Kennedy couldn't—or wouldn't—answer, grinning and saying, "You can't expect me to develop into a statesman overnight." The British newsmen stood goggle-eyed when Kennedy volunteered what precisely had been said about no American intervention. He added gleefully that the average American was far more concerned about "how he's going to eat and whether his insurance is good, than in foreign politics. Some, maybe, even are more interested in how Casey Stengel's Boston Bees are going to do next season."[19] The American press laughed. The British feigned laughter, too.

British traditionalists, however, took a dim view of Kennedy's antics from the start. Montagu Norman, the long-serving Governor of the Bank of England and a man Joe undoubtedly admired, "disliked Kennedy as a person, partly because he was an Irish-American, a Roman Catholic and therefore 'of bad stock,' partly because he displayed in private some of the unpleasant traits of a man permanently on the make."[20]

Some had axes to grind, like the American-born MP and diarist Sir Henry "Chips" Channon, who feared America's cultural and economic juggernaut. Within days, complaints about Kennedy reached as far as Rome, where Ambassador Phillips received a nasty surprise. While extolling Joe's virtues, Phillips was shocked by the stony silence from the wife of a British MP. Later she explained that when dining in Parliament she had seen how *all* the MPs "had expressed themselves thoroughly disappointed in Kennedy; that he was not at all the type of man to represent the United States at this time." Josiah Wedgwood, a powerful Liberal MP, wrote to Harold Ickes that he was frankly disappointed the United States had not sent its best man at such a critical moment. Joe's gaucheness and myriad faux pas, like rushing to be the first to dance with the Queen at a ball, served only to anger the British establishment.[21] Nonetheless, despite these loud stage whispers, Kennedy's official British press remained favorable.

EVEN SO, KENNEDY wasn't in London to please the British. To fulfill his dream of becoming president of the United States, he would also have to appeal to voters other than Catholics. Joe's embassy briefings made it clear that there was a growing concern over the fate of Jews in Europe. Taking his solipsistic viewpoint, he came to regard the plight of the German Jews and their increasing desire to immigrate to Palestine as a godsend to his presidential ambitions. If he could help these Jews, surely that would translate into winning the Jewish vote in the United States without too much trouble?

Early in March, Dr. Stephen Wise, a prominent American rabbi and faithful supporter of the Catholic presidential candidate Al Smith in 1928, happened to be in London conferring with the Zionist Executive and Jewish Agency leaders Chaim Weizmann, David Ben-Gurion, and Blanche "Baffy" Dugdale. Tall, with wide-set eyes and many infectious enthusiasms, Baffy was the niece of Foreign Secretary Arthur Balfour, who in 1917 made the Balfour Declaration for the founding of a Jewish homeland in Palestine British government policy. Baffy, an Anglican, was an ardent friend of Zionism, making it her life's work.

On March 9, the day after Kennedy was presented to George VI for his accreditation to the Court of St. James's, the Foreign Office launched a fresh attack on the government's Palestine policy to greatly reduce Jewish immigration. This "about-face" was believed to be kowtowing to Mussolini, who was using Palestine as a pawn in his talks with Chamberlain. The prime minister was compliant because he was desperate to reach an agreement with the Italian dictator. Dr. Wise had come to London to discuss this policy reversal and made it his business to call on Kennedy to warn him about the present situation and Chamberlain's horse trading.[22]

Wise was delighted with Kennedy's response. "I know you will be glad to hear ... that J.K. has already made a very good impression," Wise wrote to FDR. "These Britishers will hear, of course in private, language from him to which their dainty ears are not accustomed. ... J.K. is going to be very helpful, as he is keenly understanding and there is just enough Irish in him to make him sympathetic to those of us who resent the British promise that is in danger of being broken."[23] Although Wise had seen all sorts of machinations in his long and active life working for a Jewish homeland in Palestine, he did not see that Kennedy's sympathies were aimed to impress him personally and gain a toehold with the American Jewish vote.

They say that talk is cheap, and Kennedy did a lot of that. He did not meet with Weizmann or Ben-Gurion or Baffy that March; nor did he speak to them while they were in London. It would not be until after Kristallnacht that he would seriously turn his attention to "the Jewish Question." Even then, he would act only out of self-interest.

II

"SPRING MANOEUVRES"

———————

If you take my word, these quick bulletins
will be newsy but still unimportant as far as the United
States of America's policy goes.

—JOE KENNEDY TO PRESIDENT ROOSEVELT,
MARCH 11, 1938

The highlight of Kennedy's one-week-old diplomatic career was a hole in one at the new Stoke Poges golf course in Buckinghamshire. Apparently, Joe had motored through his first "London fog" to get there. When he came up to the second tee and struck a "fine tee shot," the ball "trickled into the cup." Both Joe Jr. and Jack sent their dad telegrams asking where Arthur Houghton had been standing, since their father had never hit a hole in one in his life.[1] Whether the fog had lifted and Joe could see 128 feet down the fairway, much less its 128 yards, or if Houghton had tampered with the ball didn't matter. It was a good tale and made for dozens of lighthearted articles.

On Tuesday, March 8, Kennedy's big day was finally at hand. He wrote that "the coaches, with their scarlet-coated drivers and footmen, came for us at the Embassy a little after eleven." The horses, too, wore their official regalia for the occasion. Joe was accompanied by Herschel V. Johnson, counselor and chargé d'affaires; the first and second secretaries of the embassy; and the financial, commercial, agricultural, and military attachés. Sir Sidney Clive, the King's Principal Diplomatic Marshal, responsible for all court presentations, rode with Kennedy in his gilded coach. For some reason, Joe chose that moment—in what was the culmination of his political career so far—to discuss scrapping presentations of American debutantes at Court that spring. Kennedy found it remarkable when Sir Sidney became "jittery," and that "any refusal on my part [to include American debs] might mean the United States is snubbing the new King."[2]

MOST AMERICANS DIDN'T understand that the British were still sensitive about His Majesty. Aged forty-two, "Bertie" became George VI in December 1936 after the grueling ordeal of his brother's abdication to marry the twice-divorced American, Wallis Simpson. It was a job Bertie had never been trained for and hadn't wanted. His speech impediment, so beautifully portrayed in the film *The King's Speech,* remained problematic. And yet Bertie *did* become King, gaining everyone's respect and admiration.

In fact, Robert Worth Bingham wrote to Roosevelt on January 5, 1937, just three weeks after the abdication, encapsulating what George VI meant to those who had dealt with both monarchs: "The British have passed through their dynastic crisis successfully. I have no doubt they are much better off for the present and for the future than would have been possible under the previous regime." In that same letter, Bingham said also that "the Duke of Windsor [formerly Edward VIII] was surrounded by a pro-German cabal and many people here suspect that Mrs. Simpson was actually in German pay."[3] Kennedy had no such insight, writing: "The show at Buckingham Palace was set up to expectations, and I chatted informally with the King for five minutes. I found him charming in every way. Lord Halifax was there. The King said he liked to play golf, but could not for the moment because of an infected hand. He mentioned that he plays tennis left-handed."[4] And that was all he had to say.

In contrast, Kennedy waxed lyrical about his luncheon at the Savoy with the Association of American Correspondents afterward. He told his friendly press boys "quite frankly" what he thought about his new job. "I was by no means sure that an American ambassador could accomplish anything here just now; that I would be home very shortly if I found that to be the case." Kennedy also told them that "I would deal with them exactly as I had done with their colleagues in Washington, as soon as I discovered what custom and ethics were prescribed for such relations." That tidbit begs the question: Why was he talking to them about procedures before he was certain what they were? Buried deep within his series of off-the-cuff remarks was the familiar refrain that he "had no political aspirations whatever and any reports they had seen to the contrary were unfounded."[5]

TWO DAYS LATER, Kennedy was invited to luncheon by the Right Honourable (Rt. Hon.) Oliver Stanley.* Also present were Sir Thomas Inskip, Coordinator of Defense; Sir Alexander Cadogan, Permanent Undersecretary of the Foreign Office; Sir Alexander Hardinge, Principal Private Secretary to the King; the anti-appeasers Alfred Duff Cooper, First Lord of the Admiralty; Ronald Tree, MP; the aging banker Lord Charles Montagu; the obese and balding Anglo-Irish nobleman Valentine Browne Lord Castlerosse; and playwright and librettist Frederick Lonsdale. "I find these men no more worried than I am," wrote Kennedy, "that war is breathing on their necks."[6]

Kennedy was talking to men who recognized that they had not changed the inevitable. As early as November 1936, Anthony Eden had initiated what became known as the "Guessing Position" in his speech at Leamington in Warwickshire. It was a simple strategy: so long as Germany was uncertain if the British would intervene in Central Europe, and the French were never sure if they would, a conflict could be avoided. It had been formulated as a response to Hitler's occupation of the Rhineland on March 7, 1936.

But Hitler was better at the game than the British. In his February 20, 1938 speech to the Reichstag, he said the British and French "statesmen, politicians and journalists" were a "rare mixture of arrogance and pitiful ignorance which more than once presumed to sit in judgement"

---

* The title Right Honourable refers to a member—past or present—of the monarch's Privy Council. Kennedy erroneously refers to Sir Oliver as "Lord Stanley" in his diary. Sir Oliver was the President of the Board of Trade, leading the trade treaty negotiations in London. His elder brother, Edward, heir to the title, joined the cabinet in May 1938, when he became Secretary of State for Dominion Affairs. They were the sons of the 17th Earl of Derby, also called Edward and styled as Lord Stanley.

on Germany.[7] In the weeks following Austrian Chancellor Kurt von Schuschnigg's February 12 summons to Berchtesgaden, there had been rumors of German troop movements on the Austrian border. These had been discounted by the new German foreign minister Joachim von Ribbentrop as the usual "Spring Manoeuvres." In an attempt to salvage his position, Schuschnigg designated March 13 as the date for a plebiscite to vote on the question of unification of Austria with Germany—better known as the Anschluss.

Since 1933 a disbelieving Europe had been inching along its own Via Dolorosa toward another war with Germany—one where a dishonest, immoral, gangster dictator with tremendous popular magnetism vowed "to make Germany great" again. Hitler held no fear of bloodletting and gave his simple message—at times bombastically and hysterically—to the German people about their superiority of body and spirit while reawakening dreams of pan-Germanism from the Great War. The Nazis had successfully harnessed German pride, frustration, and pent-up aggression, hitching it to one of the most successful propaganda machines ever invented.

ON THURSDAY, MARCH 10, the British government hosted an official luncheon at Downing Street in honor of Foreign Minister Joachim von Ribbentrop, the former German ambassador to London.[8] Three days later, Chamberlain wrote to his sister Hilda, still upset with "those wretched Germans." Indeed, after he had "spent 20 minutes after lunch talking earnestly to Ribbentrop about a better understanding and mutual contributions to peace by Germany and ourselves," official news of German troop movements and successive ultimatums to Schuschnigg were delivered into Chamberlain's hands. "I had to immediately call Ribbentrop into my room downstairs, sending his wife home alone, and there Halifax and I talked to him most gravely and seriously begging him before it was too late" to ask Hitler to halt his "swallowing Austria."

Despite these "grave" discussions, Chamberlain admitted that he found Ribbentrop "so stupid, so shallow, so self-centred, so self-satisfied, so totally devoid of intellectual capacity that he never seems to take in what is said to him." In fact, Ribbentrop was at a loss to see what the objection to Germany's methods had been.[9] Chamberlain had an intense dislike of anyone who was "muddle-headed" and ineffectual. This extended to the Labour Party in the House of Commons, too, where Chamberlain had consistently given the impression for years that he regarded them as socialist filth.[10] The distrust and dislike for the prime minister was shared by the opposition in equal measure.

BY MARCH 11, Kennedy was concerned about his Pilgrims Society speech he had dispatched to Roosevelt and the State Department for approval. The speech was Hinton's primary test as speechwriter for Kennedy on foreign affairs, too. Regarding Austria, Joe blithely wrote to the president, "in the words of the French Ambassador this morning, nothing is likely to happen except to have Schuschnigg eventually give in unless there is some indication that France and England are prepared to back him up."[11]

Prior to leaving Washington, Kennedy was briefed about George S. Messersmith's February 18 memo.* The State Department knew that the razor-sharp Messersmith felt "a certain group in England, which has been fostering such [appeasement] agreements" must recognize that Hitler was not a man of honor, adding, "I have myself never been able to understand why these illusions should persist." Messersmith recognized when Hitler summoned the Austrian chancellor, Kurt Schuschnigg, to Berchtesgaden in February that "in no uncertain terms he [Hitler] made demands which, if carried through, would leave Austria without any shred of real independence."[12]

Within hours of Kennedy writing to Roosevelt, Arthur Seyss-Inquart, the former Austrian minister of the interior and local Nazi leader, replaced Schuschnigg as head of state. Yet when it came to the importance of the Anschluss, Kennedy missed the point entirely. "My own impression is that Hitler and Mussolini, having done so very well for themselves by bluffing," Joe wrote, "they are not going to stop bluffing until somebody very sharply calls their bluff." But there was no "bluff" filling Hitler's sails over Austria. Kennedy reported that everyone felt "the United States would be very foolish to mix in" and that this "feeling is almost unanimous among the top-side people."[13]

* At the time, Messersmith was the U.S. assistant secretary of state and former ambassador to Austria.

Chamberlain shared Kennedy's viewpoint. "What a fool Roosevelt would have looked if he had launched his precious [January] proposal," he wrote to Hilda. "What would he have thought of us if we had encouraged him to publish it as Anthony [Eden] was so eager to do? And how we too would have made ourselves the laughing stock of the world."[14]

Halifax, however, saw the situation with considerable clarity. "But the experience of all history went to show that the pressure of facts was sometimes more powerful than the wills of men," he wrote to his ambassador in Germany, Sir Nevile Henderson, at 11:30 P.M. on March 10, "and if once war should start in Central Europe, it was impossible to say where it might not end or who might not become involved." Naturally, Ribbentrop toed the Nazi Party line to both Halifax and Chamberlain, accusing Schuschnigg of phrasing the plebiscite's question on an independent Austria badly and saying that he represented a gerrymandering minority.[15] But, of course, Ribbentrop already knew that the Schuschnigg plebiscite vote to guarantee Austria's independence would never take place.

APPARENTLY OBLIVIOUS TO Halifax's views, Kennedy thought he was settling in rather nicely, taking on board what was then a British swearword "bloody" to add to his vibrant lexicon of American expletives. He dutifully paid social calls on more senior ambassadors.* Visits to the French, Spanish, Argentine, and Russian embassies were first on his list. At each meeting, Joe gave the same message: he harbored grave concerns about the economic outlook. Each ambassador asked what he thought about a European war. "In my mind," Kennedy wrote in his March 9 diary entry, "no general war is visible in the immediate future."[16]

PERHAPS MOFFAT'S WORDS about taking a wider view rang in Joe's ears. A better perspective might be gained by inviting Winston Churchill and his son, Randolph, to luncheon. Kennedy was unaware that "word was passed around before his arrival to be nice," according to Randolph. "Consequently the Establishment went to work. They [the Kennedys]

---

* Protocol dictates that the most recently accredited ambassador pays calls on the other ambassadors the first time.

were invited to house parties, dinners, golf and shooting by dukes and earls."[17] Joe never suspected that he was being managed.

Kennedy had read the younger Churchill's piece in the *Evening Standard* about his accreditation to the Court of St. James's. Randolph bitingly commented that only Kennedy and the less important waiters present wore long trousers.[18] As expected, when Joe could get a sentence past Winston, he burbled on about how America would not become involved in another European war. Kennedy's "plain-speaking" and inability to "listen plainly" closed down any meaningful communication.

That said, Winston, too, would be heard. According to Kennedy, Churchill "harped" on his differences with the government and said how much he regretted Eden's resignation. Churchill maintained that Mussolini had been rescued by Chamberlain's desire for an Anglo-Italian treaty. Chamberlain's actions had cost Britain its credibility and prestige with the smaller European countries it had always protected. Further, the prime minister's methods gave sustenance to the dictatorships and ruined any chances of a more important Anglo-German accord. Damning the government further, Churchill repeated Ribbentrop's words that "England must close its eyes to the procedure in the East."[19]

That afternoon, Kennedy sent a letter to Roosevelt, saying if Chamberlain could work out "some kind of a deal" with either Germany or Italy, "he will be a hero." Reiterating his mantra that the United States should not mix in, Kennedy added a twist: that the British—across the board—thought American intervention was a bad idea. This more accurately reflected Chamberlain's viewpoint than Churchill's. Furthermore, "I am more convinced than ever that the economic situation in Europe is becoming more and more acute and if our American business does not pick up so that trade is generated for these countries, we will have a situation that will far overshadow any political maneuverings."[20] While Joe liberally quoted from his meeting with the French ambassador, Charles Corbin, he had perhaps not known that Corbin's London friends were the Francophile anti-appeasers Sir Robert Vansittart—known to everyone as Van—Churchill, and First Lord of the Admiralty Duff Cooper.*

---

* Joe forgot to mention that the third government of Prime Minister Camille Chautemps had collapsed the day before writing and that no successor was in the offing. The French

Curiously, Kennedy does not relay his discussions with the Spanish ambassador. The two-year-old war Civil War in Spain was discussed, however, with Cardinal Arthur Hinsley, archbishop of Westminster and primate of the Catholic Church in England. Through Hinsley, Kennedy passed on the "inside information" from the Italian-born cardinal currently serving in Spain that there remained some 20,000 Italian troops on the ground fighting with General Franco's army. The feeling was that the war would be over shortly.[21] A more accurate estimate to the number of Italians fighting in Spain then was between 80,000 and 100,000 men. Hinsley knew that the Spanish Civil War was divisive in Britain, particularly among the intelligentsia. Young intellectuals were far more concerned about the death of Spanish democracy, and together with the working classes, formed the International Brigades of volunteers to help defend the faltering Spanish Republic. Kennedy was well schooled by Count Galeazzi that the leftist government forces represented the downtrodden poor, mainly peasant, and working-class majority; in contrast, the rebels were fighting to maintain the status quo of the elite and the Catholic Church.

ON THE EVENING of March 11, as German troops amassed on the Austrian border, Kennedy attended a reception at the German embassy in London. He met the new German ambassador, Herbert von Dirksen, a dour-faced, bespectacled, balding diplomat. An unmitigated snob born into a parvenu noble Prussian family, Dirksen sported a Heidelberg dueling scar on his cheek and had been trained since childhood to hold himself like a superior Prussian *Junker*. The German had previously served in Poland as chargé in the 1920s and was known as "the enemy of Poland" before he took charge of all of the Eastern Bloc German diplomatic services. Given his background, Dirksen felt that Kennedy was beneath disdain, but feigned friendship from the first handshake.

Third Republic was extremely unstable in the 1930s, with the public distrust of politicians running at a fever pitch after the fraud of the Stavisky Affair was exposed in February 1934. There were six different governments between 1934 and 1939, with Chautemps serving three times as prime minister.

Then, too, Kennedy was pictured at the reception with Ribbentrop—also a parvenu nobleman who had bought his "von" from an impoverished adopted aunt. Since Joe's diary entry for that day has been excised and he remained silent about meeting the German foreign minister, it is possible Kennedy overstepped the bounds of diplomacy by assuring Ribbentrop that America would remain neutral. The British press had made much of Kennedy having been "specially appointed by President Roosevelt," so Ribbentrop, possessed of a low cunning, would have taken such assurances as coming direct from the U.S. president.

Other diplomats were there that evening, too. It was the first time Kennedy met the dapper Chicago-born Sir Henry "Chips" Channon. When Chips got home, he wrote that he had "talked to Mr Kennedy the new American Ambassador, whose chief merit seems to be that he has nine children."[22] Kennedy was photographed with John Whelan Dulanty, the Irish High Commissioner, who was also tasked with trade negotiations. Kennedy made it his business to "help" Dulanty in some unspecified way in the future. Halifax was in attendance, too, watching attentively alongside the Chief Diplomatic Adviser to the Foreign Office, Sir Robert Vansittart.[23]*

AT FIVE A.M. on Saturday, March 12, mere hours after Kennedy's presence at the German reception in London, three divisions of German infantry and one division of trucks crossed into Austria. The skies over Vienna were darkened by two hundred transport aircraft landing at a rate of fifty planes per hour, carrying two thousand German troops to Aspern Airport.† The Viennese were deafened by hundreds of German bombers purposely flying low over the city. By daybreak, three divisions of German infantry had crossed the border. By eleven A.M., German storm troopers marched down Vienna's streets to a rapturous welcome. Huge swastika flags were unfurled from upper-floor apartment windows, almost touching the pavement below. Gestapo agents armed with Hitler's Black Book containing the names and desired possessions of enemies of the new Ostmark, as Austria would become known, raced into action. Austrian culture was subsumed, then

---

*   Under Eden, Van had been the Parliamentary Permanent Secretary before Cadogan.

†   Aspern Airport was replaced by Vienna International Airport in 1954.

obliterated. Overnight, Austria's 200,000 Jews were dehumanized under the laws of the Third Reich. Vienna's most famous Jew, Sigmund Freud, hurriedly scrawled across a whole page of his diary: *Finis Austriae*—Austria is finished.[24] The Anschluss, or annexation of Austria, was completed by midday. It was a precise, macabre ballet—well planned and minutely rehearsed. Two days later, Hitler would receive a messianic welcome.

Joe Kennedy did not comment directly on the Anschluss other than to write in his diary on March 12 that "the extraordinary cabinet meeting called today to consider the Austrian developments robbed me of the company of Lord Halifax on the motor trip I was to take to Oxford."[25] The purpose of his sojourn—some sixty miles from central London— was to act as one of the electors for the Harmsworth Professorship of American History.

Kennedy was smart enough to know that he was at sea regarding the politics of the moment. Even so, he opted rather unusually to consult with the Vatican rather than with Moffat. On March 15, Cardinal Pacelli replied in a lengthy telegram: "As to your investigation towards the new rulers in Austria and the possibility in this regard between the Holy See and the Nazi Government, I am happy that you brought up this matter as to allow me to give you my personal views which of course . . . are just delivered to your confidential use."[26] Most of the communiqué related to the message from the archbishop of Vienna, Cardinal Theodor Innitzer, "praising" the Anschluss, and ignoring the concordat signed with Hitler.

An indignant Pacelli had recalled Innitzer to Rome immediately, where a clarification was issued on April 6. The original declaration was amended to "the solemn statement of the Austrian bishops on 18th March this year did not intend evidently to express an approval of what was not and is not reconcilable with the Laws of God, with the freedom and the rights of the Catholic Church. Furthermore that statement cannot be interpreted by the State and the Party as a duty of conscience of the faithful nor must it be used for propaganda purposes."[27] The message was duly passed on to the State Department for its consumption, but as far as Kennedy was concerned, Pacelli's telegram said it all.

12

THE PILGRIMS

*It was the most isolationist utterance that has come from any
American Ambassador in many years.*

—Dr. Abraham Flexner, director of the Institute for
Advanced Study at Princeton, to Thomas Jones,
former deputy cabinet secretary to four prime ministers,
march 21, 1938

Rose Kennedy had boarded the SS *Washington* with Kick, Pat, Bobby, Jean, and Teddy a few days earlier on March 9. At Harvard, Joe Jr. was putting the finishing touches to his senior thesis, "Intervention in Spain," supporting American isolationism and the Neutrality Acts and chronicling the activities of the "Hands Off Spain" Committee. Joe Jr.'s loyalty was to his father, the Catholic Church, and Franco. He planned to go with Jack, Rosemary, and Eunice to join the family in London at the end of term.

In the meantime, the ambassador concentrated on his forthcoming Pilgrims Society speech. The "State Department cabled that the Pilgrim's speech is in good shape" and suggested only minor changes, Joe wrote; but he had underestimated the strength of Washington's objection. After Hull read it, making significant deletions, he asked Moffat to edit the speech a second time. The internationalists at the State Department feared that Kennedy was promoting the isolationist message. Given that the Anschluss had just occurred twenty-four hours earlier, it was both impolitic and undiplomatic to reiterate that Americans were not inter-ested in European affairs—as Kennedy's speech did—particularly when he did not represent the president's feelings.

As a novice diplomat, Kennedy seemed unaware that any public state-ment made on the international situation would appear to have been sanctioned by the U.S. administration. Moffat's cable informed the am-bassador that his Pilgrims speech was open to misinterpretation. Hull weighed in advising Kennedy that given the seriousness of the Austrian situation, it was up to *him* as secretary of state to clarify the government's position. Hull would set that out for the press on March 17, the day before Kennedy's speech.

Using a visit on Tuesday, March 15, from Viscount Waldorf Astor (owner of *The Observer*) as a pretext for a transatlantic telephone call, Joe said Astor claimed that "immediate war is a greater danger than they like to let the public know." Kennedy backed this up with his fears that Churchill and his anti-appeasers might carry the parliamentary debate about Germany, angering Hitler.[1] Hull replied that it was not Kennedy's place to speak out. Rather than accept Hull's intervention, Kennedy ex-ploded.[2] He told Hull to "keep quiet," and that the secretary's speech would not help one iota. Moffat, grabbing the telephone from a hoarse Hull, thanked Kennedy for his frank viewpoint. But Joe would not be placated. He asked to be put through to the president, so Moffat lied, saying he had just received a note that Roosevelt was with his dentist and was unable to talk just then. After consulting with other senior de-partment officials, including undersecretary Sumner Welles, Moffat noted in his diary that "a few of them were quite brutal in their comment that Kennedy wanted the Secretary's speech canceled" so that his isolationist Pilgrims Society speech could "receive a better play."[3]

After a mere two weeks on the job, Kennedy had assumed that *his* opinions and *his* role put him in a better position to speak for the U.S. administration than Secretary Hull. It was the beginning of a private war declared by Kennedy against the State Department, rendering his posi-tion untenable unless he backed down.

ROSE AND THE children landed at Plymouth on March 16 and were whisked up to London by a beaming husband and father. Although she was happy enough with the residence, Rose feared there would be "no place" large enough to accommodate "all the rest" when they came "with their friends from Harvard and Princeton." On the morning of the Pilgrims Society speech, Joe presented Rose to Queen Elizabeth at Buckingham Palace, where, "precisely to the minute of our appointed time," they were ushered into the "beautiful and very comfortable sitting room. The Queen walked toward them in greeting." Rose was awed and terrified. The Queen asked her to sit with her on the small sofa by the fire. Joe sat opposite in a comfortable armchair. The Queen, so used to making people at their ease, asked Rose all about the young Kennedys, "their ages and school plans" and whether they were happy to be in England. She volunteered that her daughters, Princess Elizabeth (now Queen) and Princess Margaret Rose, were about the same ages as Bobby and Jean.[4]

That evening, Lord Halifax introduced Kennedy to the assembled great and good at the Pilgrims Society dinner held at Claridge's Hotel. The new ambassador rose to applause and flashed his famous smile. He made a few ad-lib remarks about how surprised he was to see such unremitting sunshine since his arrival and thanked Halifax for commenting on his horsemanship in Rotten Row. Kennedy read a short paragraph to thank the Pilgrims, and acknowledged Lord Derby, Edward Stanley, who presided.* Joe began by reading, "It must be realized that the great majority of Americans oppose any entangling alliances." He did not notice the quick intake of breath from some in the audience. "Some believe that our country would not fight under any circumstances short of actual invasion," he continued. "Not accurate. Others imagine that the U.S. could never remain neutral in [the] event of a general war. That is just as dangerously conceived a misapprehension as the other."

Kennedy continued: "The resulting destruction of manpower and painfully accumulated capital wealth would bankrupt the world to a point where a new civilization and new form of society would have to

---

* Edward Stanley, 17th Earl of Derby, had been Secretary of State for War in the Lloyd George government in 1916 and from 1918 to 1920 was ambassador to France. He was also one of the most important Thoroughbred horse owners and breeders of the early twentieth century (*Source*: ODNB, 17th Earl of Derby).

be slowly and haltingly evolved." Then he backed away from a definition of what he meant, saying, "To the President and Secretary Hull there appears to be a remedy for the present impasse in world affairs. They call it economic peace. This is an aspect of international relations in which America is prepared to take an active interest. We regard the establishment of more friendly commercial relations as imperative. Economic appeasement . . . means a higher standard of living for the workers of the world."[5] Contrary to Kennedy's message, neither Roosevelt nor Hull believed any longer that "economic peace" would resolve Hitler's bloodlust. The speech concluded with: "You cannot run down a customer with a bayonet. If the nations of the world would trade liberally and naturally among themselves a new kind of security would be born—a security based on intelligent self-interest and not on force."[6]

When Kennedy sat down to polite applause, he knew his speech had fallen flat. To break the silence, the Duke of Kent rose and toasted the Earl of Derby as one of Britain's "great institutions."* Afterward, the duke said for the record that "Mr. Kennedy and Lord Halifax would need support to straighten out their problems, not political support only, but support from those who wished to make the world a better place to live in." Halifax said that the "Government was trying to steer a straight course in the light of principles which were equally valued by Mr. Kennedy's Government and not withstanding differences of outlook they could give great help to one another in the cause they both favoured."[7]

Kennedy mistook the Duke of Kent's and Lord Halifax's post-speech comments as a seal of approval for his stance. In fact, their remarks were calculated, given Kennedy's outspokenness, to say very little that might harm the foundering trade negotiations. Halifax was treading on an appeasement tightrope, already shaky in his belief that Hitler would stop at swallowing Austria.

Kennedy's speech directly contradicted Hull's March 17 statement that failure to accept international responsibilities would lead to America's

---

* Prince George Edward Alexander Edmund Windsor (1902–1942) was the fourth son and younger brother of Edward VIII and George VI. While he was a noted rake prior to his marriage and was closest to Edward VIII, he became a tremendous supporter of George VI once he became King.

increased insecurity. One of the polite applauders listening to Kennedy was Thomas "T.J." Jones, the former deputy cabinet secretary to four prime ministers and reputedly "the keeper of a thousand secrets." Shortly after Kennedy's speech, Jones received a letter from Dr. Abraham Flexner, first director of the Institute for Advanced Study at Princeton. It included a few local press cuttings showing that the Pilgrims speech "had been either written or carefully examined in Washington" and that the aside from the "cautious reference to Anglo-American relations," the rest of it was "the most isolationist utterance that has come from any American Ambassador in many years. In my opinion," Flexner maintained, "all these things are explicable only in one way, that is, that America is disgusted with Chamberlain, absolutely ignorant of Halifax, and thoroughly distrustful of Mussolini, Hitler and the pro-German influence in Great Britain." Flexner hoped that if he sent the press clippings—or "rubbish" as he called them—to Jones, his friend might "do something to open the eyes of those who make popular opinion in England to the effect that they are guessing wrong on America."[8]

KENNEDY MAY HAVE been briefed by advisers like Bill O'Brien that Halifax, as Master of the Hounds in Yorkshire, had traveled to Germany in November 1937 under the pretext of "shooting foxes in Pomerania" with Reichsmarschall Hermann Göring. Halifax's invitation came through an advertisement in the magazine *The Field*. The British ambassador to the Third Reich, Sir Nevile Henderson, encouraged Halifax to go, believing appeasement must be the first solution to Europe's woes, saying: "I hope you will speak as you yourself suggested to me about Nazism in general, quite apart from the political side."[9] Then, at an official dinner for the Yugoslav foreign minister shortly after, both Eden and Chamberlain in a "joint exhortation" urged Halifax to go to Germany.[10] Halifax went and not only "shot foxes in Pomerania" but also met with Hitler and understood that the dictator's "Nationalism and Racialism" was "a powerful force." This November 1937 trip became the basis for Halifax's appeasement policy.

By March 1938, Halifax could only pray he'd been right. He had his doubts, though he still held firmly to appeasement. Henderson advised Hitler's Anschluss was the "desired . . . consolidation of National-Socialism and the Reich" at a time when Austria was already "Nazi to the core."[11]

KENNEDY, HOWEVER, NEVER saw the political when the economic could be argued. He firmly believed that Hull was wrong to preempt his own speech. Britain could not count on the United States in the event of a general war. Nor did he see that his tough talk ran counter to Hull's earlier March 12 speech entitled, "Do American Principles Require American Interventionism?" Kennedy failed to appreciate, in Halifax's words, that "this country [Great Britain] was set very close to parts of the world where the atmosphere was charged with highly combustible material and whether we wished it or not it was impossible to dissociate ourselves from the anxiety of this environment."[12]

"The march of events in Austria made my first few days here more exciting than they might otherwise have been," Kennedy wrote to Krock on March 21. "After three weeks in London, I still find myself able to evaluate European events against the background of our public opinion at home, as I understand it, and not against the semi-hysterical attitude which the professional diplomats here adopt whenever another unforeseen step occurs." There was certainly debate, but no hysteria, among the same men whom Joe had described only days earlier as "no more worried" than he.

"All this means, as I size it up," Kennedy continued, "that there will be no war if Chamberlain stays in power with strong public backing." The British were about to sign an agreement with Mussolini "which will include a trade agreement and arrangements for restricting naval force in the Mediterranean. Germany will get whatever it wants in Czechoslovakia without sending a single soldier across the border."[13]

WHILE KENNEDY MADE predictions that were far from his official remit, he was ignored by 20th Century Fox in London in its efforts to save their lawyer in Vienna, Dr. Paul Koretz, an Austrian Jew. An appeal was made by the company direct to the Foreign Office to send a telegram to the British legation in Vienna, requesting Koretz's presence at an important company consultation, stipulating "that he should now live outside [Vienna] and continue in their employ."[14] Fortunately, Captain Thomas J. Kendrick of the British SIS* was stationed in Vienna in the passport division and reacted promptly to the Foreign Office request "in view of Koretz's value to British commercial interests."

Kendrick and his team were swamped by the distressing sight of terrified Jews clamoring for visas from the legation and were processing over two hundred people daily. In one of his thousands of "rule-bending" moments, Kendrick issued Koretz a visitor's visa, assuring him that once he was in England, he would never be forced to return to Austria.[15] *If* Kennedy had known about Dr. Koretz from 20th Century Fox, he was not involved in his rescue.

ON MARCH 24 Chamberlain initiated the debate about European affairs in the House of Commons. Joe and Rose Kennedy listened from the Peers' Gallery. Given the ongoing war in Spain, the Anschluss, and the potential threat to Czechoslovakia due to the millions of Germans living in the Sudetenland portion of the country, Chamberlain stated, "I do not deny that my original belief in the League [of Nations] as an effective instrument for preserving peace has been profoundly shaken." Yet, "the value of any guarantee which we may give or of any treaty obligation into which we may enter must in the last resort depend upon our ability to implement the obligations or the guarantees upon which we have entered."

Chamberlain thought that restoring confidence in peace was the greatest challenge facing His Majesty's Government. It was "how to maintain the rule of law in international affairs, how to seek peaceful solutions to questions that continue to cause anxiety." The Czechoslovak situation and its Sudeten German minority was "necessarily most present to many minds," and engaging in a peaceful solution was paramount to Chamberlain. "In the meantime," the prime minister concluded, "there is no need to assume the use of force, or, indeed, to talk about it. Such

---

* The British SIS, or Secret Intelligence Service, was established by British Prime Minister Herbert H. Asquith in July 1909. For more information, see https://www.sis.gov.uk/our -history.html.

talk is to be strongly deprecated. . . . It must interfere with the progress of diplomacy, and it must increase feelings of insecurity and uncertainty."[16]

The New York Times's opinion was that Chamberlain had merely kept "the rest of the world guessing" if Britain would go to war over Czecho-slovakia. Even so, Kennedy was elated with Chamberlain's statesman-ship. He praised the prime minister's speech as "a masterpiece" to Arthur Krock, finishing off his letter predicting that "Great Britain ought to be in for something of a mild boom soon, I should think. Chamberlain has given the rearmament program full priority over the ordinary commerce of the country, practically as in war-time. This means that money will be spent in large amounts."[17]

13

THE ENGLISH SWANS

Rose, this is a helluva long way from East Boston.

—JOE KENNEDY TO ROSE KENNEDY,
WINDSOR CASTLE, APRIL 9, 1938

The Anschluss and fears over Czechoslovakia delayed Kennedy's shaking things up "American-style." At seven P.M. on March 18, just before the Pilgrims Society dinner, Kennedy sent a "confidential for the President and the Secretary" dispatch to Washington. He had raised the issue of presenting American ladies at Court during the London Season "on several occasions," because "there is no doubt in my mind that they are seriously concerned at the possible effect of our adopting a rule of no presentations."[1] Such a rule would reflect badly on the King personally, and the greater Court circle, and would also lose the "means of friendly propaganda in the United States." Nonetheless, as with Hull over the Pilgrims Society speech, Kennedy persevered. A compromise was suggested that "the presentations might be strictly confined to young ladies of debutante age, whether residents of the United States or daughters of Americans in England representing American business enterprise."

Joe was attempting to combine his desires for his family with his political aims as a presidential hopeful, and this led him to the idea of approaching the debutante issue through the guise of social democracy. Given the ages of Rosemary and Kick, Joe had always wanted to limit the Court presentations to American debutantes *resident* in Great Britain,

rather than have a blanket ban. Using the pretext of the British sensitivities that no American debs would adversely affect the King, Kennedy
sought Hull's and Roosevelt's guidance about changing "all our minds"
and proposed the residency requirement.[2] Roosevelt told Hull on March
21 that he agreed with Kennedy's revised position. American debutantes
without any ties to England who flocked to Court to be introduced
to foreign royalty stuck in Roosevelt's throat. It implied that American
culture—and its *Social Register*—were inferior to British polite society.
For Americans, it was certainly undemocratic, anachronistic, costly, and a
waste of a busy ambassador's time. But nothing was finalized until after
Easter.

TRADITIONALLY, THE LONDON Season had been the backdrop for aristocratic girls from their country seats to be introduced to London society
by their mothers and to be "brought out" as debutantes each spring in
a round of grand balls, crowned by their presentations at Court. "The
Season" was the culmination of their mothers' years of work in raising these girls to perfection. For British parents, the Season's object was
matrimony. With the advent of the American nineteenth-century "dollar heiresses"—whose money kept those same country seats afloat and
British aristocrats in ready cash—the tradition had mushroomed out of
all proportion. Although Joe could never put a stop to British girls participating in the Season, he fully intended to stop Americans without any
reason for attending the Court presentations—especially those who, by
lineage, might outclass his daughters. After all, Kick and Rosemary were
the granddaughters of a Boston Irish saloonkeeper on their father's side.[3]

Kick Kennedy was eighteen, and both parents had every intention
that she should glow brightest during *her* Season. Not that they were
husband-hunting for a young aristocrat to become her spouse. That
would have meant marrying a Protestant—an anathema to both parents.
Instead, they had their eye on an American Catholic with oodles of
money: J. Peter Grace. As the heir to the W. R. Grace chemicals fortune,
the twenty-five-year-old Grace was a fine catch, and he adored Kick.

Getting themselves into the *Social Register* and having Kick presented
at Court was a meaningful goal for both Rose and her daughter—and
for Joe, a sock in the Brahmins' eyes in Boston. So, the talk about no debs

was mere window dressing for the benefit of Hull and Roosevelt. Having *fewer* debs presented would make the effervescent Kick—and the pretty Rosemary—shine in a select group of young American women. But first Kick would have to understand "how the English lived."*

KICK'S EDUCATION BEGAN with Eights Week in Oxford on April 2. Eights Week was a long-held tradition of boat racing between Oxford and Cambridge universities. Cambridge had won it for fourteen years until 1937, when Oxford finally triumphed. On that blustery April day in 1938, the Oxford side hoped to repeat its victory. Since Joe was the guest of honor that evening at the Queen's College in Oxford, it was natural he brought Kick along as his "plus one" for the whole day.[4]

Though petite in stature, Kick loved competitive sports and winning. Her experiences sailing on Cape Cod helped her appreciate that the boys who were racing were well drilled. There was a strong westerly blowing across the Isis (as the Thames is called through Oxford), with a hint of a northerly, which would affect the competition. When the starting gun sounded, Kick cheered unrestrainedly for Oxford and its second victory in two years. Nevertheless, there was an unspoken concern among all the boys that pervaded the day. In his 1938 book *The Boat Race,* rower G. C. Drinkwater ominously wrote: "And so we leave the race which it may be hoped will never again be interrupted as it was in 1914–1918."[5][†]

Kick's naturalness and ebullience made her a favorite among the undergraduates. At the Queen's College that evening, she listened intently to her father's speech, winning her even greater praise from the boys. Girls, in their experiences, were not interested in politics, but Kick was. What she hadn't known was that the dewy-eyed Magdalen College man,

---

* Neither Joe nor Rose felt that Rosemary should be passed over for the presentation at Court. Even so, they recognized that including her in the presentation ceremony was purely to try to make Rosemary feel special about doing the same thing Kick did.

† There would be no boat race in 1939. George Drinkwater, an Oxford Blue rower, died in an air raid in 1941.

Tony Loughborough, aged twenty-one, and the heir to the 5th Earl of Rosslyn, was smitten with her.

THE FOLLOWING DAY, Joe attended a dinner at Lord Waldorf and Lady Nancy Astor's London home. The Kennedys had known them since Rose visited England in 1928, when she promised Lady Astor, on behalf of Joe, a copy of the Pathé newsreel of their arrival in America.[6] Joe told Nancy all about his marvelous daughter and asked Lady Astor to introduce Kick to some fine young people her own age.

Born Nancy Witcher Langhorne of Danville, Virginia, Nancy became British on her marriage to Waldorf Astor in May 1906,[*] and frequently went out of her way to help her fellow native-born Americans meet the British aristocracy. She had already planned Easter weekend festivities at her magnificent country home, Cliveden, for her grown children and their friends; so within days, Kick duly received her first invitation of the London Season to join them.

Kick had been in England just over a month when she first saw Cliveden, the Astors' impressive mansion and estate in Berkshire near Taplow, which stands proudly overlooking the Thames. Originally built in 1666 as a hunting lodge by George Villiers, 2nd Duke of Buckingham—a notorious roué and boon companion of King Charles II—Cliveden was twice destroyed by fire. With each incarnation, it rose from the ashes more resplendent than before. It had been the scene of many a political and social moment throughout its near three-hundred-year history, and a favorite haunt of kings and queens since the 2nd Duke of Buckingham's times. When Queen Victoria, a frequent guest in her day, heard that William

---

[*] Waldorf Astor became 2nd Viscount Astor on the death of his father, William Waldorf, in October 1919. Waldorf was obliged to vacate his seat for Plymouth Sutton in the House of Commons and took his father's seat in the House of Lords. Nancy stood for her husband's constituency and won the election, becoming the first woman to sit in the House of Commons. Waldorf was also the chairman of Chatham House, the Royal Institute of International Affairs—a highly respected think tank for political discussion and action.

Waldorf Astor had bought Cliveden in 1893, she was not amused to see the estate pass into foreign hands.[7]*

Kick would discover at Cliveden how very different she was from British girls her age. "She didn't hang back shyly or demurely," Andrew Cavendish, Duke of Devonshire, told Kick's biographer Barbara Leaming. Like any self-respecting Kennedy, she hurled herself into the melee, laughing and joking with the boys' rough-and-tumble discourse, just as she was accustomed to do with Joe Jr. and Jack. Although she was an innocent and her brothers protected her, she had been to nightclubs with them, and was adopted by Jack's friends as their mascot. Her Catholic education contrasted sharply with all she had learned from her brothers, Hollywood movies, and Broadway shows. As a result, she seemed far more worldly than her female contemporaries. Though nineteen-year-old Jean Ogilvy had been asked by Lady Astor to look after Kick that weekend, Jean immediately realized that it was hardly necessary to protect the "Little American Girl."[8]

The boys who had been invited to Cliveden included Andrew Cavendish, younger brother of Billy Hartington (heir to the Duke of Devonshire); Andrew's cousin, David Ormsby-Gore—whom Jean had a crush on; the politically minded Hugh Fraser; the eldest Astor son, Michael; and the jokester in the group, Jakey Astor. Hugh Fraser ignited the conversation about the "shameful" Cambridge and Oxford debates of 1932 and 1933 respectively, where the vote returned stated under "no circumstances" would the students fight for King and Country. Fraser and his friend Julian Amery were leading the battle to reverse the "ever shameful" King and Country resolution at Oxford.† While Hugh and the other boys spoke of these weighty matters, the girls, aside from Kick, peeled away.[9] Naturally, in the politically charged Kennedy household, the results of the debates were known at the time. Jack had taken

---

* Cliveden is most famous for the Profumo affair. In 1961, when the War Minister John Profumo met "model" Christine Keeler at Cliveden's swimming pool during the height of the Cold War, he began an affair with her. Profumo was discredited when the story broke in 1963, and it was revealed that Keeler and her friend Mandy Rice-Davies were also sleeping with the Soviet military attaché.

† Julian was the younger son of Leo Amery, a Member of Parliament and close friend of Winston Churchill's.

a particular interest from his sickbed and concluded that the British had become decadent, abandoning their creed of duty and honor. Talking about politics was second nature among all the Kennedy children.

Kick became fast friends with Jean Ogilvy that weekend and could not have been happier. In her thank-you note to Nancy, Kick said that Cliveden was "the best thing that ever happened to me."[10] She had been a smashing success with the younger British aristocracy.

JOE AND ROSE, too, were embarking on the experience of a lifetime. From April 9 through 11, 1938, they would spend the weekend with the King and Queen at Windsor Castle. The other invited guests were the prime minister and his wife, Annie; Lord and Lady Halifax; Lord and Lady Elphinstone (the Queen's brother-in-law and elder sister Mary); and Major the Honorable Sir Richard Molyneux, equerry to Queen Mary the Queen Mother.

Rose made sure she was freshly coiffed at Chez Antoine that Saturday morning. They arrived by an embassy car through Windsor Great Park at seven P.M. promptly. Understandably, Rose was awed at the sight of the castle, built from 1070 by William the Conqueror. She loved history, and certainly felt its resonance as they wended their way to meet the master of the household, Brigadier-General Sir Smith Hill Child. He then conducted the Kennedys to their apartments in one of the towers with a splendid view of the park. The red damask upholstered furniture caught Rose's eye, as did the accessories picked out in gold and white. Liveried servants wearing perukes were "especially appointed" to attend to their every need and led the way whenever the ambassador and his wife left their suite of rooms. After a small sherry was served, they were left alone to relax. Joe reeled around to face his wife and said, smiling, "Rose, this is a helluva long way from East Boston."[11]

At the appointed hour of 8:20 exactly, the footman came to escort the Kennedys to the Green Reception Room, where the Chamberlains, Halifaxes, Elphinstones, and Major Molyneux joined them. Ten minutes later, as the clocks chimed, the King and Queen entered, greeting their guests by shaking hands. Still, the ladies curtsied and the men bowed low. When dinner was called, the King and Queen led their party into the dining hall. The royal couple sat opposite each other at the center of the table. Rose sat at the King's right and Mrs. Chamberlain to his left; Joe was to the right of the Queen, with Mr. Chamberlain on her left. The table decorations were sumptuous, but the tall flower arrangements made it tricky for the King and Queen to see and speak to each other. Liveried musicians played softly in the background throughout the meal.

It is a wonder Rose managed to converse at all with the King; but practiced as he was in putting guests at ease, he turned the conversation to the subject of her nine children. Not wishing to seem like a bumpkin, Rose commented on the picture of Queen Victoria hanging on the wall behind the Queen's chair. She asked about the "blue ribbon" Victoria wore, and the King explained that it was the Order of the Garter, and what it meant. Apparently, Victoria had complained to the artist that the Order was not painted the correct hue of blue and sent one of the garter ribbons to him so he could match it in the painting.[12]*

After dinner, the ladies and gentlemen adjourned into two separate drawing rooms.† Lady Dorothy Halifax was appointed to bring the other ladies, one at a time, to come speak to the Queen, who stood in front of the fireplace. Rose chatted first with Queen Elizabeth for around fifteen minutes. When she asked Rose how she managed to sleep in noisy London, Rose replied that she "put wax in her ears." Rose admitted, too, that she had great difficulty saying "ma'am"—to rhyme with "ham"—and the Queen told her not to bother. Rose could not help but be impressed with the Queen's great dignity and charm, her simple manner, pleasing voice, and "English rose" complexion.[13]

When the gentlemen joined the ladies, they were shown some of Windsor's treasures on a private tour. Rose was most impressed by the jewelry worn by Mary Queen of Scots and the original blue garter from which the Order of the Garter took its name. At precisely eleven P.M., the King and Queen said good night, shaking hands again, and the Kennedys were escorted to their apartment. As Rose lay in bed, pinching herself

---

* The artist thought that he had been decorated by Victoria and began a correspondence with her thanking her for the honor. Naturally, Victoria disputed granting him any such thing. So, the artist never retouched the color blue, and neither did anyone else afterward.

† The British term "drawing room" derives from the original "withdrawing room," where people *withdrew* after a meal.

that she was the guest of the King and Queen of Great Britain, her admiration for them knew no bounds. They had not wanted to take on the awesome task shunned by Edward VIII, but they bore the duty as if they had been born to their roles.

THE NEXT DAY, "at luncheon, the Queen wore a bluish-green dress, no hat, and an aquamarine bracelet," Rose recorded in her diary. "The princesses were in rose dresses with checked blouses, red shoes with silver colored buckles, white socks, and necklaces of coral and pearl. Princess Margaret had a ribbon in her hair." Rose sat next to Neville Chamberlain and told him that he reminded her a great deal of Joe, with their business backgrounds, their fondness for classical music, and their love of walking. Later, when she told her husband, he scolded her for speaking out of turn.[14]

Yet Joe himself had not understood that he ignored the etiquette of refraining from business discussions at the dinner table. Lady Dorothy Halifax, as a Lady-in-Waiting to the Queen, tried to veer him away from mentioning the political turmoil. But Joe would not be deterred. Instead, he related the plight of thirty-four Sacred Heart nuns trapped in Spain, as told to him by the mother superior at the Convent of the Sacred Heart in Roehampton, where Eunice, Pat, and Jean were at school. What could Lady Halifax do beside wish him every success in evacuating them?

A Scottish piper signaled that luncheon was at an end by walking through the room playing; and as before, they went to their separate drawing rooms for port and informal conversation. For the gentlemen, this was the time when weightier matters might be discussed, and Joe again brought up the Sacred Heart nuns. He also claimed that he talked to the King about going to America. The British were getting bad press, Joe prattled on, and he suggested that the King "should have the right people contact the American press so that both sides of all questions should get proper hearing." Kennedy could hardly know that a personal invitation by President Roosevelt had been extended at George VI's Coronation in May 1937.

Nonetheless, Kennedy should have realized it was entirely inappropriate to sidestep the Foreign Office and the political machinery surrounding the royal family for a public relations matter. Joe was unaware of his breach of protocol and perplexed why the King should grimace as if he had "trouble concentrating" while the ambassador talked. So, that afternoon Kennedy compounded his gaucheness when he "talked with one of King's secretaries, who handles press" telling him he "thought the King and Queen might stop off in America, at Washington, New York and Boston after they had visited Canada in a couple years."[15]

AFTER DINNER ON Saturday, when the gentlemen and ladies were re-united, Kennedy brought up the Sacred Heart nuns trapped in Spain again—this time to Mr. Chamberlain. First, he boasted about his good re-lations with the Vatican, and that he "had written to Rome about Austria and would advise him [Chamberlain] if he heard anything." "It would be a great stroke," Joe repeatedly said, if the nuns could be rescued. Naturally, the prime minister "hoped it would happen, but they had such bad luck trying to get people out that he was not holding his breath."[16]

In light of Kennedy's approach to the Vatican, which the British viewed as friendly to Hitler, Chamberlain was hardly going to share the successes British intelligence had had in Vienna and elsewhere. The prime minister had been informed by the British ambassador to Rome, Eric Drummond 7th Earl of Perth, that he no longer believed in a com-pliant Vatican working against the dictators ever since Pacelli's concordats with Mussolini and Hitler. Other British diplomats echoed his opinion. Perth personally found Mussolini "hateful" and "the boasting, the postur-ing, the rampant nationalism, the gross misrepresentations of the British attitude, the absurd egotism and conceit . . ." was "enough to turn the least Anglo-Saxon stomachs." Even so, Perth was a seasoned diplomat and recognized that peace with Italy was better than war and had developed a closer relationship with Count Ciano and Mussolini.[17]

THE NEXT DAY was Palm Sunday. It had been arranged for the Kennedys to go to the Catholic mass in Windsor after a private breakfast in their sit-ting room. On their return, they saw the Changing of the Guard, which left Rose speechless. Then they walked in the park surrounding the castle and spied Princess Elizabeth, aged thirteen, hiding in the bushes—hatless and wearing a pink coat. She smiled coyly at them, and the Kennedys understood they were interrupting a game of hide-and-seek.

At leisure before luncheon, both Joe and Rose could not resist writing the children and friends on letterhead from Windsor Castle. "We both felt the whole thing wasn't real," Joe wrote in his diary. "It was like playing soldier and turning back the pages of history," he added. For their last meal that Sunday, Joe sat next to Princess Elizabeth and asked if she liked the movies. She replied that she did, and that *Snow White and the Seven Dwarfs* was her favorite, especially the bit when Snow White talked to the animals. Annie Chamberlain joined in their conversation and asked her which subject she liked best. The Princess replied that she was especially fond of geography and had just finished studying the Atlantic coast of the United States.

Before leaving, Joe said "the King joined Chamberlain and me and said he was thinking over what I said . . . about the American Press getting all sides. We all three agreed it was important."[18] Joe noted in his diary, too, that Chamberlain said any agreement with Germany was "not too promising," since every time "he tried to get the Germans to say what they wanted they became indefinite." The once-burning issue of the return of Germany's colonies had been kicked into the long grass for discussions in "six or ten years from today."[19]

The last point Kennedy raised with Their Majesties—again in a breach of protocol—was his idea of restricting the American debutantes. The Queen, according to Kennedy, agreed it was "snobbery and was glad" the ambassador wanted to curtail the ceremonies.[20] And so, on Monday April 11, Kennedy's final decision about the debutantes was covered extensively in the British newspapers. The *Daily Mirror,* owned by the diminutive Canadian-born Max Aitken Lord Beaverbrook, headlined: AMBASSADOR STOPS U.S. DEBS PESTERING. The *News Chronicle* led with MR. KENNEDY CUTS THE 'DEBS'; BLOW TO U.S. SOCIAL CLIMBERS.

Although Arthur Krock did not break the news, his column of April 12 in *The New York Times* gave the most comprehensive reportage. Krock wrote that a good deal of Kennedy's "training" to be an ambassador revolved around his social duties, which "irked him deeply. The most distasteful of these social obligations was the Court presentations of American debutantes, their aunts and their mamas." Worse still, Kennedy was told that senators, congressmen, governors, and "social climbers, social leaders, and woman-harried rich paterfamiliases would shower him with requests and endorsements, from among which he must choose a very few.

"Mr. Kennedy decided that here was a pressure group which has no place under the American flag. . . . He considered this both unfair and undemocratic." And so, before leaving the United States, Mr. Kennedy approached Senator Henry Cabot Lodge Jr. of Massachusetts with whom "a mutual respect was held" and who also felt that the custom had gone too far. It was agreed that Kennedy should write to the senator, declining his application on behalf of an unnamed Back Bay debutante. Naturally, the State Department needed to voice its disapproval, too, since it was keen that the Court and the Foreign Office understood there was no offense intended against the British monarchy. But the stage management involving Lodge's response went awry.

The British press were sent Kennedy's letter to the senator, without notifying Lodge. The State Department, too, handed out the "tiara-shaking" one-pager in America without telling Lodge or giving him a final copy. The senator was caught off guard. One reporter, according to Krock, wrote: "The nation's capital is guffawing at the blunt but neat manner in which Joe Kennedy had 'hoist Senator Lodge on his own petard' and noted that Mr. Lodge 'climbed aboard the bandwagon before the letter could be made public.'"[21] Lodge went from being a co-conspirator to an undone Boston Brahmin. Privately, he was incensed. The Krock article was written at the behest of Kennedy, to assuage the wounded pride of the injured senator. Thankfully for Kennedy, the Queen was not quoted publicly. It would have been a huge, potentially long-term damaging gaffe from which Kennedy would have found it difficult to recover.

AFTER EASTER, THE mad rush was on for Rose, Rosemary, and Kick to have their dresses made for the debutantes' presentation at Court. Not any off-the-rack gown would do, so Kick and Rose headed for the home of haute couture, Paris. Mothers had to present their daughters, so Rose needed to be just as glamorously attired. Granted there had been London appointments at the fashion designers Molyneux and Schiaparelli in March, and both Kick and Rose had fittings with Molyneux before the visits to Cliveden and Windsor Castle.[22] By the time Eunice and Rosemary landed at Plymouth late in April chaperoned by Eddie and Mary

Moore, all was ready for their presentation at Court on May 2—the first of the four Court sessions.

Rose's dress was designed by the foremost British couturier Molyneux, who knew the precise needs for a presentation at Court, including the length of the matron's train. Her gown was white lace embroidered with silver and gold beading. Rosemary's gown was white net trimmed in silver, also by Molyneux. But Kick had opted for a gown designed by the French couturier Lelong, also of white net with silver croquettes. Each wore the obligatory three ostrich plumes of the Prince of Wales at the correct angle in her hair, but Rose, as the matron, also wore a diamond tiara, lent to her for the occasion by Lady Bessborough. Suffering through long rehearsals on what to do and how to stand and how to calculate the distance between themselves for the ceremony to avoid tripping over one another's trains, Rose likened the presentation to a ballet.

Admired by Joe, Bobby, and Teddy for their Cinderella-like appearances, the three ladies and Joe, in his white tie and tails, went to the palace. Rose recalled the Grand Stairway, and passing from anteroom to anteroom, attended by footmen in their royal livery, until at last they arrived at the Grand Ballroom.[23] Kick managed the delicate timing perfectly despite an attack of nerves: "My train not fastened on—only put on at last minute. Walked by very quickly," she confided in her diary. Sadly, Rosemary stumbled on her train and nearly fell over.[24] Their presentations were over in a matter of seconds. Rose, however, would only ever mention *her* role; she said she would retain the fondest of memories of all the preparations and that evening forever.

14

TRADING INSULTS

The tragedy of the American diplomatic service for years
has been its unabashed obeisance before the
throne of British foreign policy.

—Drew Pearson, "Washington Merry-Go-Round,"
April 22, 1938

After one month in London, Kennedy had a sense that he was invisible and ineffective. Dining at the Savoy or Claridge's and visiting stately mansions was fine, but it made no difference in keeping the United States out of another European conflict. Kennedy's economic outlook had hardened, too. "If we keep lagging behind" in the United States, then Britain would be unable to "make the grade alone," he wrote to Krock.[1]

As talk of war spread that spring, too, America's ambassador made it his duty to support Chamberlain's appeasement policy back home. In Washington, Kennedy's political standing suffered with every step he took as the prime minister's champion. His lengthy April 15 memo to Roosevelt applauded the Anglo-Italian agreement: "Should the president share these views I need hardly say how grateful the prime minister and myself would be should he feel able to give some public indication of his approval of the agreement itself and the principles which have inspired it."[2] Kennedy added, "Ninety percent of the people in Great Britain will hail it [the Italian accord] with great acclaim and there is no question about its being the beginning of a step in the right direction."[3]* Chamberlain had pushed through the Anglo-Italian agreement with a reaction from the Foreign Office that "would have frozen a Polar Bear!" he wrote to his sister Ida, emphasizing that "anything that pleases Musso must be bad for us!"[4]

Kennedy was out of step with U.S. policy regarding Italian aggression. Roosevelt had made it abundantly clear that the United States heartily disapproved of the Italian Abyssinian campaign of 1935. "And when you come down to it," Roosevelt said a few weeks earlier in Gainesville, Georgia, "there is little difference between the feudal system [Communism] and the Fascist system. . . . I am as opposed to Fascism as I am to Communism."[5] He understood that Great Britain wanted to relieve dangers from the Mediterranean, but the deal with the Italians was by no means laudable. The principle of nonrecognition of an aggressor was paramount, and the president was not prepared to give the U.S. seal of approval to any attacker.

Roosevelt's reply to Kennedy began with these frosty lines: "As this government has on frequent occasions made it clear, the United States, in advocating the maintenance of international law and order, believes in the promotion of world peace through the friendly solution of peaceful negotiation. . . . It does not attempt to pass upon the political features such as that recently passed between Great Britain and Italy." Nonetheless, Kennedy extracted a comment from a recalcitrant State Department that the agreement between Great Britain and Italy, initialed on April 16, was "proof of the value of peaceful negotiations."[6] † Shortly after, Hull commented that the American policy of nonrecognition of conquests by aggressors remained "absolutely unchanged."[7] Churchill would describe the Italian pact as "a complete triumph for Mussolini, who gains our

---

* It was Halifax who had asked Kennedy to get the president to publicly approve the agreement.

† While the agreement was initialed in April, as of October 1938, it still had not been ratified and carried out due to the continuing Italian fighting forces and military support for Franco in Spain.

cordial acceptance for his fortification of the Mediterranean against us, for his conquest of Abyssinia, and for his violence in Spain."[8]

JUST THE SAME, Kennedy truly believed that Chamberlain could avoid war, but the prime minister did not have the ambassador's clout with the American press. So Joe intervened. Without consulting the State Department or the White House, Kennedy wrote "Private and Confidential" letters to American journalists who were sympathetic to him and would carry his message in their papers. Roosevelt and Hull were livid. Kennedy was muddying foreign policy by communicating with the press without instruction or approval. Worse still, the president could not recall Joe after a piffling six weeks without raising serious questions about his own judgment. Instead, it was agreed to teach Kennedy a lesson.

Bob Allen, who co-wrote the "Washington Merry-Go-Round" nationally syndicated column with Drew Pearson, was one of many journalists tapped on the shoulder by the State Department that April. In reply to the offending letter from Joe, he warned: "Just as a friend, Joe, I'd keep my fingers crossed on Chamberlain and his Tory Party. You are going to see important changes in the British government in the not too distant future. . . . From the inside information we get, the Chamberlain government is about as competent as Hoover's was and is rapidly becoming as unpopular."[9] Although Allen's intelligence was premature by two full years, it was nonetheless sound advice. Already Joe seemed to be another Walter Hines Page—the eponymous ambassador accused of bringing Wilson's administration into the Great War in 1917. Just the same, Kennedy remained unrepentant. Keeping the American press informed of his opinions, he felt rather perversely, was an integral part of his job. Besides, how else could his tour of duty in London achieve his goals? Kennedy was determined to feed important stories that showed him in a good light to the press hounds and the isolationists on Capitol Hill.

Two weeks earlier, a scoop appeared in the "Washington Merry-Go-Round," revealing that 19.8 million cubic feet of helium was to be sent to Germany by the U.S. government. Reichsmarschall Hermann Göring was an official of the German zeppelin company (Luftschiffbau Zeppelin) and was "clamoring for the helium" from America—and a further 40 million tons over the next two years. A zeppelin required 6 million cubic feet of helium, but the order would be enough to use in bombs over Madrid, Prague, Paris, or even London. "Since Congress passed the [helium] act, however, Europe has been seething," Pearson and Allen wrote, "and Hitler has given every indication that he will provoke war if anyone thwarts him."[10] Harold Ickes gladly halted the transaction.*

Then came the "Washington Merry-Go-Round" article about a so-called secret Anglo-American agreement to help Generalissimo Francisco Franco win the Spanish Civil War. The Neutrality Acts—which the Helium Act should have been appended to—prevented the sale of arms and instruments of war to either side in Spain. A growing number of senators argued that the U.S. and British embargoes favored the fascists, since they were receiving substantial aid from Germany and Italy, and several senators repeatedly urged the Roosevelt administration to consider revising the arms embargo. Yet, Pearson and Allen wrote, "any American move to lift the Spanish arms embargo would be a terrific slap at Prime Minister Chamberlain, would largely nullify the British government boast already being made in diplomatic circles throughout Europe that Britain has American foreign policy in its hip-pocket."[11] Their source was not revealed, but the gist, timing, and language smacked as coming from Kennedy.

Next, Joe wrote to the powerful isolationist Republican Senator William E. Borah of Idaho, who sat on the Foreign Relations Committee, that "the more I see things here the more convinced I am that we must exert all of our intelligence and effort toward keeping clear of any involvement. As long as I hold my present job," Kennedy affirmed sincerely, "I shall never lose sight of this guiding principle."[12]

THAT SAID, KENNEDY could not control his columnist friends. The dynamic "Washington Merry-Go-Round" duo—who *did* get some crucial components of their reporting wrong—headlined an April 22 piece LADY ASTOR'S PRO-FASCIST CLIVEDEN GROUP IS WOOING JOE KENNEDY. Referred to as "genial Joe," Kennedy is portrayed as some housebroken British

---

* The United States had held a virtual monopoly on helium since the *Hindenburg* zeppelin disaster in 1937. During Ickes's honeymoon to London in May with his bride, Jane (niece of Ambassador Cuhady), Chamberlain, Halifax, and a host of others Ickes had met congratulated him on stopping the shipments.

poodle. Indeed, "American career diplomats hold the British Foreign Office in reverence almost as if it were a Deity," Pearson and Allen wrote.[13] They viewed Nancy Astor's politics in black and white from the Democratic streets of Washington, D.C., and dubbed the alleged "Cliveden Set" as a group of aristocrats and plutocrats wishing to retain its privileges at the expense of Europe. In fact, the "Cliveden Set" was the invention of the rather disreputable Stalinist editor of *The Week,* Claud Cockburn.[14]

Joe was insulted and mad, writing to Pearson that "I know you and Bob don't want to hurt me unless you have definite reasons. Your story on the Cliveden Set is complete bunk. . . . It is unfortunate when I am working as hard as I can to keep this situation straight that this kind of story should be published. The repercussions over here have been extremely bad."[15] Actually, they were bad on both sides of the Atlantic. Pearson's reply, confirming that the State Department was his source, should have made Kennedy see that his relationship with the press had badly upset his superiors.

Even so, Kennedy saw nothing wrong with fascism. For him, it was the best bulwark and the lesser of the evil doctrines against the rule of law and world order. Even Winston Churchill told Mussolini in 1927 that he, too, would have supported Il Duce—the Italian expression for "the leader"—in his "triumphal struggle against the bestial appetites and passions of Leninism."[16] The British widely believed that Mussolini's fascism had saved Italy in 1922 from the communists. As the world polarized throughout the 1920s and 1930s into isms of the left and right, many believed fascism was the best political ideology to stop the spread of communism.

European plutocrats wanted to believe Hitler had worked the same miracle as Mussolini in Germany. The British aristocracy was naturally pro–German, too, because of the centuries-old ties between the royal family, the aristocracy, and German principalities. Many royal and aristocratic brides and grooms had been taken from Protestant German royal households over several generations. However, after the Nuremberg Laws of 1935 and the flood tide of recently impoverished émigrés fleeing Germany, those who still held to the myth that Hitler was "peaceful" and "good" had chosen to close their eyes and see no evil. While Kennedy was an economic wizard, he had not computed the meaning of numerous diplomatic dispatches that described Nazi atrocities in Germany and Austria. Nor had he comprehended that Hitler possessed a limitless fount of resentment against the world. Joe blithely accepted that Europe, in the words of the British ambassador in Berlin Sir Nevile Henderson, would "have to dance as Hitler pipes."[17]

Kennedy's blindness to the misery caused by Hitler and Mussolini was so their end game would not become America's fight. He steadfastly believed that all political turmoil was caused by economic hardship, too. If governments could eliminate fiscal problems, everything else would fall into place. Using British rearmament as an example of how this worked, he wrote to Moffat that the "British military and diplomatic engine has now been put from second into high—jerking somewhat and with some cylinders definitely missing fire, but the speedometer [meaning the economy] begins to register an increase." He predicted, too, that "there will be no war for any predictable time in the future."[18]

REMARKABLY, KENNEDY ACTED as he wished, unaware that the State Department intended to keep him on a tight leash. From Washington's perspective, Joe had proved he was like the proverbial loose cannon on the deck in a stormy sea. Roosevelt and Hull were in agreement that they must keep Kennedy focused. He was appointed to negotiate the trade deal and resolve the issue of sovereignty of the strategic Canton and Enderbury Islands in the Phoenix archipelago for military use in the Central Pacific. Period. The quandary about the Pacific islands was tackled first. Roosevelt's suggested resolution, as communicated through Kennedy, was to share administration of the islands between the United States and the United Kingdom indefinitely. Chamberlain, urged by Kennedy, agreed.[19]

The trade agreement proved more problematic. The British position regarding motion pictures as a cultural product remained unchanged, just as Hull continued to insist that movies were a trade commodity. The State Department's dogged determination to reopen negotiations on the newly passed Films Act while Hitler had just raped Austria was highly inappropriate and caused Kennedy considerable agitation. As the mad rounds of entertainments fizzed throughout the London Season that April, Kennedy tried time and again to make Hull see he had done what he could for the American motion picture industry. He reiterated this to Sam Goldwyn and Douglas Fairbanks Sr. when they dined with him at the residence on April 6.[20] Kennedy, while a novice diplomat, knew that his timing to hustle the British into resurrecting the issue of motion pictures *and* negotiate a meaningful trade agreement could not have been worse.

"I have already taken up the films question with Halifax, Stanley, and Cadogan," Kennedy wrote to Cordell Hull as early as March 16, "and there is nothing to be gained by further protests on our part." The Films Act had been passed into law on March 30, with some important tweaks here and there, granted as an appreciative nod to Kennedy's astute wrangling.[21] Hull fumed that the British should dare to develop their own motion picture industry at the cost of imported American movies. Kennedy, however, appreciated that the British wanted to portray their own values, problems, and way of life. On April 26, he cabled: "It will be unwise as well as useless to attempt [asking] the British to alter existing legislation" in respect to films, since the new act had built into it "considerable discretionary powers" that could be decided by the Board of Trade on its own. Without prior reference to Hull, Kennedy had "already discussed" these matters and how best to horse-trade with the British.[22]

Hull's May 3 reply was icy. The British trade delegation in Washington was ill informed about the new film act and the motion picture industry generally. In fact, the British delegation was specifically barred from discussing motion pictures other than to pass American inquiries to the appropriate ministers in London. Although Kennedy had acted out of turn and Hull would have preferred to reprimand him, the British had forced the secretary of state to "negotiate" any further deals through Kennedy rather than the trade delegation encamped in Washington. For a man who loathed compromise and disliked people who did not listen to him the first time he gave an order, privately Hull—an inveterate gentleman swearer—was at his vituperative best.

"You are requested to initiate conversations with the appropriate British authorities at the earliest convenient date," Hull wrote, undoubtedly gnashing his teeth, "looking to the conclusion of an understanding between the two countries regarding the treatment to be afforded to American motion picture films and the American motion picture industry in the United Kingdom." Ignoring all of Kennedy's previous correspondence, Hull added: "We regard a satisfactory arrangement respecting motion pictures as an important part of the trade agreement negotiations."[23]

Three days later, Kennedy informed Hull that Oliver Stanley was ill and not expected to return to work for at least ten days. "It is not politically possible to have the Films Act changed so soon after enactment," Kennedy cabled Hull. "Under that Act, the Board of Trade is bound to consult the Films Council before making certain decisions." A month later, nothing had changed the British viewpoint, and Kennedy again cabled: "I recommend therefore that conversations on this topic be dropped." Fortunately for Kennedy, Hull had been masking his serious illness—a tubercular-style disease called sarcoidosis that no one knew about—and the secretary of state was "on vacation" at the time. These "vacations" would multiply as Hull's health failed.[24] And so it was Sumner Welles as acting secretary of state who finally agreed with Kennedy, thereby ending the correspondence. As Hull had frequently bemoaned, "when I do go away, mistakes are made around here which cannot be undone.[25]

YET, THE BRITISH trade delegation in Washington bore the brunt of the early discussions, not Kennedy. Historically, textiles—cotton and woolen—had been the most significant export items of the empire, and the British felt that the U.S. stance on import duties was detrimental to the British pound and inward foreign investment. The British reported in an open memorandum that "the task of His Majesty's Government will not be made easier by the lack of balance in the visible trade between the two countries, which has become even more marked in the first quarter of this year."

When Kennedy spoke at the UK Chamber of Shipping in April, he tried to bring the conversation around to the idea of cooperation between English-speaking nations. "We want to see the channels of trade unclogged," Kennedy told his audience. "Therein lies our hope of prosperity, not only for shipping, but for other industries as well."[26] That spring, there was much work to do, since it was broadly agreed that the only point on which the parties concurred was "that only harm would result from an agreement which could not justly be represented to public opinion in the countries concerned as fair and equitable."[27]

Kennedy understood films and finance, but when it came to worldwide trade and trade-offs in a looming war economy or Britain's needs for a healthy foreign exchange and foreign investment, he may have felt out of his depth. During March, he met with Montagu Norman of the Bank of England to sound him out on the European economic situation and Great Britain's ability to financially withstand a war. Their ongoing monthly conversations led Kennedy to report that the British could not possibly fight a long conflict. The country simply did not have the funds. According to Norman's wife, her husband took a dislike to Kennedy early in their relationship as a man on the make. Norman's good friend, Sir John Reith, the first director-general of the British Broadcasting Company (BBC), found Kennedy's level of ignorance about the British rather surprising. "For an hour and a half afterwards," Reith wrote of their first lunch together, "all sorts of questions about procedure and people. . . . He said that he would like advice on any matter but especially he hoped to hear when he made mistakes."[28]

15

THE EMERALD ISLE AND "CASE GREEN"

*. . . get it into the very thick heads of the Germans
that if they insist on stepping on the string
the gun was very likely to go off.*

—HALIFAX TO HENDERSON, MAY 1938

Neville Chamberlain was often the first to pat himself on the back. He thought he was doing a splendid job overriding his cabinet, acting as his own foreign secretary, and masterfully controlling the press. That April, Chamberlain summarized his latest achievement in Ireland as having "got the Irish agreement in the bag all right. It doesn't look good on paper but I believe most people will be pleased that we have settled that old quarrel and they will be encouraged by the thought that the new policy is delivering the goods." In fact, according to "the American ambassador," Chamberlain added gullibly, "De Valera had said to him that I was the only British minister he had met who made him feel that he could believe what I said."[1]

The Anglo-Irish Trade Agreement of 1938 put an end to the trade war of the previous five years and was intended to end the political differences of the past. While the Irish still wished to discuss Britain relinquishing Northern Ireland to the Irish Free State, only matters of defense, finance, and trade were agreed.* Crucially, the deal gave the naval bases at Berehaven, Cobh (Queenstown), and Lough Swilly back to the Irish Free State, making Britain dependent on Ireland alone to protect its "rear door." Churchill was incredulous, as the naval ports—negotiated between him and Michael Collins back in 1922—were, in Collins's own words, "necessary for your life."† Queenstown and Berehaven were fueling bases for destroyer flotillas in the Atlantic and narrow seas. Lough Swilly was vital to protecting the approaches to the Clyde and Mersey.[2]

Kennedy had been badgering the Dominions Secretary Malcolm MacDonald, intent on giving his advice on the Irish agreement and claiming he had the ear of "Dev"—the nickname for the Irish Free State's prime minister Éamon de Valera. Sir Ronald Lindsay wrote to Halifax to explain Kennedy's interest: "The O's and the Macs are still numerous in Congress and throughout American political life. . . . Politicians generally find it worthwhile to testify from time to time their affections for Ireland and their sympathy for Irish aspirations."[3]

Just the same, Kennedy spent more time with the U.S. ambassador John Cudahy in Dublin negotiating his honorary degree from Trinity College than he did in helping the British and Irish to reach an accommodation. From the Foreign Office and Dominions documents available, Kennedy's influence was nonexistent. Roosevelt told intimates that Joe really wanted an honorary degree from Trinity College "for the sake of his children and he took the occasion of the negotiation of the settlement between Ireland and England to press his claim indirectly through John Cudahy."[4]

Kennedy's actions did not sit well in British government circles. Privately, he had been dubbed as the worst sort of self-promoter by the British. MacDonald waited until after the deadline for the evening papers

---

* Protestants were the overwhelming majority of the population in Northern Ireland, meaning that the Northern Irish population was not in favor of joining with the Catholic Irish Free State. In the 2011 census, 48 percent of Northern Ireland's population was Protestant, 45 percent Catholic, and 7 percent other religions. In the last election, Sinn Féin, the left-wing Irish Republican political party, became the majority political party in Northern Ireland.

† At the time, Churchill was Colonial and Dominions Secretary dealing with the Irish Settlement.

to announce that the agreement with Ireland had been signed on April 25, in the main to avoid a preemptory statement by Kennedy.

To CHURCHILL, THE Irish ports were essential in the event of war, and he had seen war looming since Hitler's seizure of power in 1933. In the intervening years, the führer had been meticulous in his deception among the German-speaking peoples that he abided by law and order. The fact that he changed the laws at will and was creating his own order was immaterial. The Anschluss was proof. As soon as Vienna was occupied on March 13, Hitler announced his own Austrian plebiscite, excluding Jews naturally. The question permitted only a yes-or-no response: "Do you adhere to our leader Adolf Hitler and thus to the reunion of Austria with the German Reich which was carried through on March 13, 1938?" The result was a foregone conclusion.

Almost immediately, reports of widespread looting, a new Nazi police force, and "details of 'Nazi clean ups'" were common knowledge at all the embassies. At the British legation, the spymaster Thomas Kendrick and his team worked tirelessly to save as many lives as their particular brand of bending of the rules would allow. Kendrick would soon pay for his trouble with his own arrest and three days of Gestapo interrogation before he was deported back to England.[5] Kennedy, however, failed to report in his dispatches to the State Department or the president about the rush of Jews and political opponents of the Nazis to England, or to relay the horror stories they told.

The American legation in Vienna, however, reported that "This is [a] period of efficient terrorism. . . . Money and private property being seized wholesale. Jewish department stores plundered. Suicides continue. Last night Major Fey killed wife and child and self."* Incredulous at what was going on, the chargé d'affaires warned the State Department that the preponderance of "non-Aryans" in Vienna "implies situation of great and

---

* Emil Fey was a proponent of Austrofascism and had been the vice-chancellor of Austria from 1933 to 1934 under Engelbert Dollfuss. He was known as Hitler's most vociferous opponent. On March 15, 1938, he was interrogated by the Gestapo agents. On his return home, disconsolate, he wrote a letter for help, but shot his son Herbert, his wife, and himself the following day before he received a reply. He was not Jewish.

tragic consequences. Austrian Jews unable to leave. Many with contacts in America calling at Legation."[6]

CZECHOSLOVAKIA WOULD BE next, but neither the British nor the Americans knew Hitler had ordered the military to begin preparations for its invasion—"Case Green"—on April 21.* As the Czechoslovak crisis heated up in May, Kennedy advised the State Department that neither the French nor the British believed that "even Hitler himself knows what the course of events will be." He wired that the Foreign Office viewpoint was "the Sudeten-Deutsch . . . have now become more Nazi than Hitler himself and are running ahead of Henlein." Asserting his own beliefs as fact, Kennedy concluded that the British and French governments "would not go to the extent of telling [the Czech prime minister Edvard] Beneš that he would have to compromise the ultimate sovereignty of his state."[7] And yet Chamberlain had already voiced his opinion that there was not a great deal that could be done to placate Herr Hitler, other than getting "the Czechs to face up to realities and settle their minority problem."[8]

In fact, Chamberlain feared that the "small countries" like Czechoslovakia would only attempt to defraud British interests and embroil the country in unnecessary conflict. Unlike Halifax, he did not yet think the threat of a strong Germany was a problem.[9] Chamberlain—and Kennedy—believed that a German economic powerhouse was not "necessarily a bad thing" and perhaps such dominance could assuage Hitler's bloodlust.[10] As a result, neither Chamberlain nor Kennedy considered Halifax's efforts to curtail German economic influence beneficial.

Around this time, a mild note of alarm began to creep into Kennedy's cables. After a lunch with Sir Warren Fisher, the Permanent Secretary to the British Treasury and head of the Civil Service, Kennedy wired that the British Secret Intelligence Service (SIS) *knew* that Germany was rearming rapidly (a fact known for several years), and that if war should be declared on Great Britain, "the issue would be decided within 30 days

---

* Konrad Henlein was the leading Sudeten German political leader prior to the invasion of Czechoslovakia by the Nazis. On March 28, 1938, Henlein secretly met with Hitler, where it was agreed that he would begin to demand autonomy for the Sudetenland.

and that Germany is designing an air force designed to demolish London in one fell swoop." Yet he reassured the State Department that all British ministries were advised by him that they must "make their war plans without looking for any support or help from America."[11] Kennedy's conclusion was aimed at his American readers. The possibility that America would become involved had not yet entered the British mindset.

ON MAY 3, Hitler traveled with his entourage of five hundred party officials, diplomats, and journalists to Rome. He pressed Mussolini for a military alliance, which Il Duce asked for time to consider. To make the Italian leader more relaxed with his ultimate decision, Hitler announced at the state banquet on May 8 that Germany regarded the Italian frontier as "forever unchangeable." On Hitler's return to Berlin, he ordered fortification lines to be made to the west to ensure that France and Britain would find protecting Czechoslovakia impossible.[12] The German *Westwall*, or Siegfried Line, faced France's Maginot Line and stretched from Kleve on the German border with the Netherlands to Switzerland— some 390 miles. It housed 1,800 bunkers, secret tunnels, and tank traps. Soon after, Mussolini confirmed that he was indifferent to Hitler's designs on Czechoslovakia and the Sudetenland.

In mid-May, the stern-looking, bespectacled Sudeten leader Konrad Henlein came to London. The trip had been carefully planned after a successful wooing campaign of the British by the Sudeten Germans to put pressure on Prague for their "mistreatment." Using the most modern propaganda methods—and German money—they were incredibly well organized. MPs were entertained on "lavish junkets to Bohemia," where they were taken to beauty spots first, and then on trout fishing expeditions, before being shown the most stricken parts hit by high unemployment in the Sudeten-Czech heartland.[13] For those who hadn't known precisely where Czechoslovakia was on a map and who continued to call it "Czechoslavia" or "Czechoslovenia," such educational outings proved unfailingly to win over the hearts of most who saw the country's natural beauty juxtaposed against the beastly conditions of the Sudeten Germans.

Henlein's arrival was well timed, too, for Chamberlain, who hoped that "we may get through without a fresh demonstration of force."[14] For him, like many, Czechoslovakia was "a faraway country" that incorporated a place called Bohemia, which was last written about in English at the beginning of the seventeenth century by William Shakespeare in *The Winter's Tale*. Erroneously called "a desert country, near the sea," the play comprised most people's knowledge of the place. The Czech ambassador, the amiable Jan Masaryk, was often heard to remark that he had to explain to the gentlemen he dealt with that "Czechoslovakia was a country and not a contagious disease."[15]

Kennedy's "great friend" Waldorf Astor, as chairman of the Royal Institute of International Affairs (RIIA), invited Henlein to speak to the political elite during his sojourn. Kennedy apparently did not attend Henlein's talk at the RIIA headquarters at Chatham House in St. James's Square, but may have heard one of the Sudeten leader's speeches while in London. Quite astutely, Henlein preyed on the British establishment's fears of communism, telling his packed audiences that the 1935 pact with Moscow had transformed his country into "Russia's aircraft carrier," infecting Czechoslovakia with "the bacillus of communism."[16]

Winston Churchill had luncheon with a "few friends"—namely Sir Archibald Sinclair and Professor Frederick Lindemann—and Henlein on May 13,* and thought that the Sudeten German leader's visit to London was "a hopeful sign."[17] Churchill wrote to Halifax afterward that they were heartened by their private talk. Winston had spoken to Jan Masaryk, too, who shared his viewpoint except on the issue of rescinding the treaty with the Soviets—nonetheless, a huge "except."[18]

ON MAY 10, Sir Horace Wilson, one of Chamberlain's two éminences grises, "a clever, cunning and somewhat cynical fellow, well-versed in the politics of trade, a dab-hand at formulating compromises, and an ardent defender of the interests of British industrialists and traders," approached the diminutive, intelligent, highly observant, Jewish, and unappreciated Soviet ambassador, Ivan Maisky. The canny Maisky wrote in his diary that

---

* Sir Archibald Sinclair, a man of movie-star good looks, was the leader of the Liberal Party and MP for Caithness and Sutherland. Professor Frederick Lindemann, originally from Baden-Baden in Germany, was a naturalized British subject, and Churchill's prime scientific adviser regarding German rearmament. He was noted for his arrogance and intellectual prowess.

he never saw Wilson exhibit "an understanding of international politics, still less a desire to be engaged in those complex and sensitive matters."

Wilson had asked for a tête-à-tête with Maisky about any potential Russian military involvement if Hitler invaded Czechoslovakia. The Russian listened patiently to Wilson expounding on the well-trodden path of Hitler's next objective being to set up a "Mitteleuropa" to the east, swallowing up various smaller countries and directly threatening the USSR. "All these mitigating factors shall certainly come into play," Maisky replied. "Germany's empty stomach will be filled." Maisky understood immediately that Wilson was letting the Russian in on Chamberlain's latest thinking: if the Russians would not play ball with the British, Russia would perish under the Nazi boot.[19] Maisky took it as an empty threat rather than a friendly warning. Had he passed the message undiluted on to Stalin, it might have escalated the Soviet schemes to make a pact with Hitler, so Maisky said nothing.

KENNEDY GAVE HIS personal slant to the Sudeten crisis, writing later in May to the State Department that the British were fearful the Sudeten Germans could start a war that would embroil America. In fact, the British had been urging the Czechs to resolve the matter of their 3.5 million Sudeten citizens' rights for some considerable time. The Anschluss, however, had brought the issue into sharp focus. Sir Nevile Henderson in Berlin incessantly reminded the Foreign Office that the Sudetens had a "moral right to self-administration and eventually to self-determination." Then Henderson went further: it was "morally unjust to compel this solid Teuton majority to remain subjected to a Slav Central Government in Prague."[20] Where America stood in the matter was immaterial to the British.

A calmer Kennedy reported to Roosevelt that Konrad Henlein had come to London to explain his position—and that the Czech minister, Jan Masaryk, and Kennedy found his "requests" quite reasonable.[21] Then after Henlein left, a more excitable Joe wrote to Moffat that "the British are more concerned than they allow to appear over him [Henlein] and his Sudeten Germans. It is feared here that these people may provoke by their extreme conduct some incident which will end up in fighting."[22] Evidently Kennedy had been talking to Chamberlain. The British establishment, however, understood that Henlein's trip was part of the latest Nazi propaganda campaign to win over their hearts and minds, and was largely successful.

WHEN TWO SUDETEN farmers were shot on May 21, everyone feared that Hitler had been behind the deed. The Czechs mobilized that same day, believing this was the beginning of the invasion. Halifax hastily telegraphed Ribbentrop, promising that His Majesty's Government would "exert all possible influence at Prague for avoidance of further incidents and will continue to do so." He also hoped that Ribbentrop would do the same in Berlin, since its leaders should not "count upon this country being able to stand aside if from any precipitate action there should start European conflagration."[23] Only Hitler and his generals knew that the military was not ready to invade Czechoslovakia under Case Green until the fall.

SOCIALLY, MAY WAS a busy month. The saving grace for no progress on the trade agreement was the unabated wining and dining of the Kennedys from country mansion to city palace. On May 5, at a gathering at the Astors' London home, Joe and Rose met the pioneering aviator Charles Lindbergh and his wife, Anne Morrow Lindbergh, the bestselling author and daughter of the former U.S. ambassador to Mexico. Also present were George Bernard Shaw, William C. Bullitt (American ambassador to France), and Geoffrey Dawson, editor of *The Times.*

The Lindberghs had moved to Kent in England after the 1932 kidnapping and murder of their little boy and lived for a while with Harold Nicolson MP and his wife, the writer Vita Sackville-West. Lindbergh complimented Joe on his recent pronouncements and felt an immediate connection. "It was one of the most interesting lunches I ever attended," Lindbergh wrote in his journal. "Kennedy interested me greatly. He is not the usual type of politician or diplomat. His views on the European situation seem intelligent and interesting. I hope to see more of him."[24] Lindbergh's views about America's neutrality were echoed in Kennedy's speeches, and Lindbergh believed that German military superiority— particularly in the air—made them invincible.

Old friends from New York came that May, too. Henry Luce, the publisher of *Time, Life,* and *Fortune,* was on a fact-finding mission, and brought along his beautiful wife, Clare. She had begun negotiations with London producers to stage her play *The Women* in the West End, but there were fears that its risqué script would run afoul of the British censors. Clare, who rarely failed in anything she set her mind to, was aghast that the Lord Chamberlain's Office found her hospital scene in act 2 objectionable.*

The Luces and Lindberghs were guests at an embassy dinner held in honor of Lord Halifax and his wife. Never one to miss an opportunity to show off his Hollywood connections, Kennedy screened the film *Test Pilot,* starring Clark Gable and Myrna Loy.[25] He was happy that Lindbergh thought the aerial dogfights looked realistic. Soon after, Joe arranged for another embassy dinner in the Luces' honor. Afterward, Clare sent the outrageously expensive gift of stud earrings to Rose in thanks.

Clare—a die-hard Republican and active hater of Roosevelt—would not have hesitated to tell Joe that his popularity and visibility was flagging in the United States. Of course she had heard the rumors about "Kennedy for President" and may well have played up to him about these. Undoubtedly, at that stage, Clare was hoping Joe would return to the United States to put his marker down for the 1940 presidential election. Within days, Kennedy announced that he would be returning home in June to attend Joe Jr.'s graduation from Harvard. He telegraphed Hull that "the Ambassador in London should be ordered home at least twice a year and that he wanted to discuss 'very definite impressions with him about the situation here' and to meet with Roosevelt."[26]

---

* The offending scene had one of the lead actresses drop her cigarette ash on her newborn child while nursing.

16

TO BE OR NOT TO
BE — PRESIDENT

BRITISH PRESS SETS TASKS FOR KENNEDY—
"INSIDE" REPORTS SAY ENVOY—ON HIS 9-DAY VISIT IN THE
U.S., WILL REVISE OUR FOREIGN POLICY—
MUCH MORE IS EXPECTED
—*NEW YORK TIMES* HEADLINE,
JUNE 15, 1938

Kennedy again preempted the State Department by telling the press that he had to have a face-to-face with the president to discuss the European situation. He also asked Arthur Krock to step in. "I think it would be a very helpful thing if agitation could be started to have me address the Senate and House Foreign Relations Committee in Executive Session," Joe wrote to Krock on May 24. "I feel that I certainly have the most interesting story that has come out of here for many years and I think it is bound to affect their judgment when they hear it." Certainly the European crisis, as seen from the United States, was bewildering. Americans could hardly rely on their newspapers—unless they could read between the internationalist or isolationist lines. "By the time you arrive," the Pulitzer Prize–winning Krock replied on June 1, "I think you will find everything ready unless the members have all got out of town by then. Congress is set to adjourn not later than June 15."[1]

Joe had made his arrangements to sail to New York on the *Queen Mary* with Henry and Clare Luce. By then Joe and Clare had become lovers, and she "made no secret of reveling in 'Joe's' company." Her biographer, Sylvia Jukes Morris, diplomatically wrote that "Harry enjoyed it less." The photograph of the Luces disembarking show two extremely unhappy newlyweds.[2]

Krock arranged for Kennedy to be treated with the respect and attention reserved for a presidential candidate or a movie star. The June 15 *New York Times* article expected that during his nine-day stay in the USA the ambassador would:

> First, reshape the foreign policy of the United States;
>
> Second, end the negotiations for the Anglo-American trade treaty and bring off the treaty itself;
>
> Third, indulge in mysterious currency manipulations to do with the devaluation of the dollar; having far-reaching effects on the world monetary situation;
>
> Fourth, arrange a deal whereby the United States will build planes for Britain while Britain builds ships for the United States Merchant Marine;
>
> Lastly, settle the war debts [from the Great War].[3]

Roosevelt, Hull, Welles, Sir Ronald Lindsay, Chamberlain, and the heads of departments in the British government all read the June 15 headlines with dismay.

WHEN THE *QUEEN MARY* docked, Joe was surrounded by a mob of reporters in the dockside quarantine area. His official reception committee was there, too, comprising, among others, Admiral Jerry Land and Jimmy Roosevelt.* Joe was pleased to answer all their questions and flash that famous Kennedy smile. He declared "emphatically that he would not

---

* Land, Kennedy's replacement at the Federal Maritime Commission, was also Lindbergh's cousin.

consider being boomed for president in 1940," as it would be a "breach of faith with the president." Asked if he'd consider heading up the New York Stock Exchange, Joe answered, "not even if it were offered to him."[4]

The following morning, he was whisked from the Waldorf Astoria to meet with the president in his private office at Hyde Park. Kennedy, however, had misread the situation. The only written record of what happened comes from the diary of Harold Ickes. Apparently, Kennedy let loose a torrent of abuse at the president for his many speeches criticizing fascism. He ranted on about foreign policy, maintaining that Roosevelt was getting it all wrong. Then Joe instructed Roosevelt. It was okay, Joe said, to attack Nazism but not the fascists. When the president asked why he felt that way, Kennedy expounded on his theory that "very frankly" the United States "would have to come to some form of Fascism here." Ickes wrote that the "President thinks that Joe Kennedy, if he were in power, would give us a Fascist form of government. He would organize a small powerful committee under himself as chairman and this committee would run the country without much reference to Congress."[5] Roosevelt did not share with Ickes his wrath at Joe's blatant presidential ambitions.

Kennedy had persuaded himself that democracies could not put the economy back on the rails—possibly through conversations with Galeazzi and in consideration of the accommodation the Vatican had reached with Mussolini. Though he far preferred the freewheeling world of the rugged individualist and free market economy, Joe had come to believe that the capitalist system was broken and that only a select group of individuals could take control of the engine of government.

Of course, the idea of fascism in America was abhorrent to Roosevelt, but it was closely linked to the possibility in the minds of some Democrats and Republicans as to whether FDR would run again in 1940. No one had run for a third term since George Washington refused a third term for himself. The tradition had become an unwritten law. But Roosevelt had not ruled out breaking with tradition himself, despite the fact that his wife, Eleanor, urged him to prepare for his successor. "Franklin always smiled and said he thought people had to prepare themselves," Eleanor later recalled, "that all he could do was to give them opportunities and see how they worked out."[6] While there were other presidential hopefuls—like the Catholic James Farley, postmaster general and chairman of the Democratic National Committee—Roosevelt was certain that whoever ran on the Democratic ticket in 1940 would have to finish the work he himself had begun on the economy and would have to face a terrible world conflagration.

Until that fateful meeting in June, Joe's mistakes—his uninhibited manipulation of the press, his speaking out against the president, and his passing his own opinions for State Department policy—had ruled him out for Roosevelt's support. The "secret circulars" Kennedy had submitted to Arthur Krock; Boake Carter; Russell Davenport of Henry Luce's *Fortune*; Frank Kent of *The Baltimore Sun*; and Drew Pearson and Bob Allen were supplemented by personal weekly briefings by letter to newspaper publishers like William Randolph Hearst; Roy Howard; Colonel McCormick of the *Chicago Tribune*; and Arthur Sulzberger of *The New York Times*. His actions had plainly angered Roosevelt, Morgenthau, Hull, and Ickes. And now he had insulted the president by his overbearing and wrongheaded demands. No wonder the president would dismiss Kennedy's "publicity tactics" as "part of the presidential fever that commonly bit all ideological shapes and sizes of men."[7]

UNKNOWN TO ROOSEVELT and Hull, Kennedy had made far more serious blunders. He decided to keep the White House and the State Department in ignorance about two vital pieces of information. The first—and potentially less serious—one was that Halifax had broken ranks with Chamberlain to stop the influence of Germany on foreign economies. This was no secret in the British Cabinet. Kennedy, thanks to Chamberlain, was aware of this, too. Halifax battled against the prime minister to stabilize the Chinese currency and deny the Germans its vast mineral resources by buying all of China's tungsten*—required for electronic circuitry in weapons.

Buying Rumanian oil before Germany could was proposed, too. Halifax also met with executives of Imperial Tobacco to explore the possibility that if he bought all of Greece's tobacco crop to reduce German economic influence in southeastern Europe, could it be successfully blended with Imperial's Virginia tobacco?[8] On June 1, Halifax warned

---

* Tungsten is often called wolfram in other languages, as it was first discovered in wolframite.

the Foreign Policy Committee: "We are now confronted with the prob-ability that German influence would penetrate throughout the whole of Central and South-Eastern Europe in the economic sphere, leading to the likelihood of Germany dominating this great area in the political sphere."[9] Had Kennedy thought this was unimportant? Or was he at-tempting to mitigate more bad press in the United States for Germany?

The second—and more significant—occurrence took place on June 10, when Kennedy and Ribbentrop exchanged "frank" views in Lon-don. No one in the White House or the State Department knew that Kennedy had come to New York fresh from meeting the German for-eign minister and the new German ambassador in London, Herbert von Dirksen. Immediately afterward, Ribbentrop reported to Berlin that they discussed "the subject of the agitation against us in the American press. The American Ambassador replied that he intended to do everything in his power to stem this press agitation.... His main objective was to keep America out of any conflict in Europe, and he would do everything in his power to accomplish this."[10] It was tantamount to Joe's showing his poker hand before the bets were on the table.

Two days before leaving for New York, Kennedy met again with von Dirksen. The ambassador's report to Berlin said that the purpose of Ken-nedy's forthcoming trip was "to give President Roosevelt detailed in-formation about European conditions.... The President desired friendly relations with Germany. However there was no one who had come from Europe and had spoken a friendly word to him regarding present-day Germany and her Government." Dirksen agreed with Kennedy's assess-ment, too, about Germany's poor press in America. "Kennedy added that he *knew* he was right. Most of them were afraid of the Jews and did not dare to say anything good about Germany; others did not know any better, because they were not informed about Germany." Dirksen was clear, too, that Kennedy had brought up the Jewish Question. The Jews were of "great importance" to good relations between Germany and the United States, Joe said. Then Kennedy launched into a regrettable, clearly anti-Semitic statement: "In this connection, it was not so much the fact that we wanted to get rid of the Jews that was so harmful to us, but rather the loud clamor with which we accompanied this purpose," Dirksen imparted to Ribbentrop. "He himself understood our Jewish policy completely; he was from Boston and there, in one golf club, and in other clubs, no Jews had been admitted for the past fifty years. His father had not been elected mayor because he was a Catholic; in the United States, therefore, such pronounced attitudes were quite common, but people avoided making so much outward fuss about it."[11]

Effectively, Kennedy was making a leading American foreign policy statement to the German hierarchy without the knowledge of the State Department or the president. He was exchanging "views" with the Germans when the British had just survived the May Crisis in Czechoslovakia and were reassessing their appeasement position on economic grounds. On a political and economic level, his statement gave a terrible mixed message against both American and British foreign policies and interests. On a human level, it was unpardonable. Kennedy knew about the concentration camps.* He knew that Jews had been systematically dehumanized; were denied an education and employment; and had all their worldly possessions stolen from them. He knew that thousands had been killed and thousands more had been made homeless. He knew that the Jews had been made stateless throughout the Reich, and that hundreds of thousands were trying to flee to safety.

Kennedy also knew that no nation wanted a destitute Jew—irrespective of that person's qualifications as a doctor, lawyer, accountant, politician, journalist, baker, teacher, or goldsmith. He knew that Jews and their children had been spat upon in the streets; had had the clothing ripped from their backs; and were made to do menial tasks while the general population laughed at them. He knew Jews were even made to act against other Jews to save the lives of their families. It was a shameful statement by Kennedy

---

* The concentration camps located in Germany, Austria, and Czechoslovakia in 1938 were not as yet designated as death camps. Although many died in these prior to the decision to exterminate the Jews with the Final Solution in 1941, they were primarily used for the torture of political opponents and Jews. The camps were a means of "persuasion" for Jews to sign over their worldly goods, and many who walked out alive also tried to leave the country. Kennedy knew about the violence in Austria after the Anschluss in tremendous detail from the American embassy there and had ample access to all of the information available to George Rublee's Intergovernmental Committee on Refugees, the offices of which were at the American embassy in London. For America's role in the silencing of knowledge of the coming Holocaust, read David S. Wyman's groundbreaking book *Paper Walls: America and the Refugee Crisis 1938–1941* (University of Massachusetts Press, 1968).

to compare the unmistakable early signs of the Jewish Holocaust to not being admitted to a country club.

The Dirksen and Ribbentrop conversations were never reported by Kennedy to the State Department or to the White House. The British and Americans discovered his treachery only when the Allies captured the bulk of the German Foreign Office archives in 1946. It would be nearly another two decades before these were published in English. Kennedy's disingenuous defense was that Dirksen had misunderstood him.

AND SO, WHEN Roosevelt met with Kennedy that day at Hyde Park, he was in total ignorance of Joe's remarks to the Nazi hierarchy. Just the same, FDR was outraged at how his ambassador ordered him around and told him what to do. So, he smiled at Joe, then without explanation summoned Eleanor, asking her to "feed him lunch at her cottage and then to see him onto the train" to New York.[12] Eleanor was aghast at her husband's sudden rudeness. Kennedy, however, seemed unaware that a private war had been declared. When Krock wrote to him suggesting that there had been a cooling in the relationship, naming the White House press secretary, Steve Early, as his source, Joe assured him it would all blow over.

On June 23, the day after Kennedy and Roosevelt met, Early spoke to Walter Trohan of the *Chicago Tribune* and William Murphy Jr. from *The Philadelphia Inquirer*. Each published almost identical stories about the friction between Roosevelt and Kennedy. The *Chicago Tribune* ran a front-page leader: KENNEDY'S 1940 AMBITIONS OPEN ROOSEVELT RIFT—PRESIDENT TURNS ICY TO ONCE FAST FRIEND. The articles quote an "unimpeachable source" that "copies of a secret circular" to Washington correspondents had been relayed to the president. "The circular, according to reports, contains information on the progress of British debt and trade negotiations which have not been reported to the state department."

The article continued: "It has also been reported that Kennedy has besought a prominent Washington correspondent to direct his presidential boom from London. . . . Joe Kennedy never did anything without thinking of Joe Kennedy, a high administration official said. And that's the worst thing I can say about a father of nine kids." A dozen more stories were printed about how all early contenders for the Oval Office seemed to be frozen out by Roosevelt. To boot, Kennedy was lambasted in another article for "stirring up a hornets' nest" by canceling the July 4 celebrations at the London embassy by Americans Abroad and the Daughters of the American Revolution.[13]

Murphy's *Philadelphia Inquirer* article clarified Roosevelt's attitude to presidential hopefuls by pointing to the disfavor which former Indiana governor Paul V. McNutt endured after he let it be known that he wanted to run for the presidency in 1940: McNutt was made ambassador to the Philippines. A "high official of the present Administration is reliably quoted to have inquired, 'Is that far enough away?' when McNutt's appointment was suggested." The same could be said of Vice President John Nance Garner when he thought of throwing his hat in the ring.[14] Roosevelt disliked dark horses, as Joe had proved to be, but he rarely let his dislikes get the better of him. The president was, of course, behind the articles.

BY THE TIME these were published, Joe had left New York to attend the pre-commencement celebrations known as Class Day at Harvard. Joe Jr.—who would graduate *cum laude* the following day—was chairman of its organizing committee. Contrary to previous remarks, Joe told a reporter from *The Boston Globe* that he would "probably not attend" the commencement exercises the next day because he wanted to watch Jack sail for Harvard at Wianno on the southern coast of Cape Cod, and he doubted he could get back to Cambridge in time.

Even if Joe had wanted to avoid press vultures scenting blood, his reasons for not attending were more personal. Harvard had refused to grant him an honorary degree. Instead, the university favored Walt Disney and thirteen other candidates. Kennedy believed it was due to his refusal to sign a petition to honor Justice Louis Brandeis (a Jew) some months earlier. When Kennedy's slap to Brandeis was made public, Joe told the press that it was "outrageous for Harvard to have to be petitioned to honor so famous an alumnus as Brandeis."[15] After this, Kennedy refused to give another cent to the illustrious university, even after they honored Jack.

AT A WHITE House meeting a few days later, Roosevelt showed no signs of his displeasure. Instead, he played up to Joe's enormous ego, begging him to do one more favor before returning to London. At the urging of the White House, U.S. Steel had agreed to cut its prices to help stimulate the U.S. economy. Afterward, however, the company revealed it also intended to cut wages. Such cuts could lead only to a decline in consumption and increased unemployment.

The following morning, accompanied by Arthur Krock as his note-taker, Kennedy met Thomas Lamont, the representative of J. P. Morgan who served on the U.S. Steel board. Kennedy urged Lamont to accept a reasonable alternative: prove that your revenue losses materialize within ninety days before cutting wages. He was persuasive enough to make Lamont understand that it was in no one's best interests to fail to cooperate with the president. Although Lamont never "signed off" on any deal, he listened to Kennedy and did not cut wages because steel revenue did not plummet as feared by the board. It was a simple solution for anyone who understood both government and business.

THEN KENNEDY WAS hit with another broadside. The day before he was set to sail back to Europe in the company of Joe Jr., Jack, and Krock, *The Saturday Evening Post* came out with an article about Jimmy Roosevelt's insurance business. It claimed that Jimmy's business had been dramatically boosted by Kennedy, suggesting, too, that there was something sinister in Joe's relationship with the younger man. This was the first time any publication had broken ranks on the subject, and Kennedy was deeply perturbed. So, he checked into the Mayo Clinic to avoid comment.

That same evening, while he was safely hidden away, several process servers in the lawsuit of Mr. J. Edwards Jones, an oilman who was claiming a million dollars in damages against Kennedy for ruining his business while he was chairman of the SEC, tried to serve a summons on Kennedy at the Waldorf Astoria.* Once aboard the *Normandie,* Kennedy told everyone the amusing story about how these men hunted him down in room after room at the hotel in a comedy worthy of the Keystone Kops.[16] While they came up empty-handed, Joe prepared his statement about the *Saturday Evening Post* exposé, too: "This magazine article tries to make me out a phony, but if all of it is as true as the part I have read about myself, it is a complete, unadulterated lie."[17]

---

* Jones's lawsuit was unsuccessful.

17

RETURN TO ALBION

I will not cease from Mental Fight, . . .
In Englands green & pleasant Land.
—WILLIAM BLAKE,
"JERUSALEM," 1804

Kennedy brooded over his unsuccessful trip to America. He regretted writing to Bernard Baruch to delay sailing, too.[1] If he had known that Baruch was traveling on a fact-finding trip for Roosevelt, and anything he said to Baruch would find its way back to the president, he would have exploded. As it was, before leaving, Joe spat fire and brimstone at Trohan of the *Chicago Tribune* and Murphy at *The Philadelphia Inquirer*, and resolved to fight back.

So, Kennedy briefed Pearson and Allen in Washington, and they lost no time throwing dust in the administration's eyes. Once he had sailed, they reported "those sensational dope stories giving the real lowdown for Ambassador Joe Kennedy's hurried visit were just about as accurate as the idea that Alf Landon will run again in 1940." Now *they* would reveal the truth. The British were not interested in either the war debt or the trade agreement because "they are too preoccupied with rearming and the TNT-loaded European situation to give it much thought." Pearson and Allen informed their readers that "the real purpose of Kennedy's trip was to confer with Roosevelt about the tragic German and Austrian refugee problem."[2] That was pure Kennedy puffery.

Pearson and Allen were told Joe advised the president that the lives of German and Austrian Jews were in grave danger, and unless a solution could be reached at Évian, their lives could be forfeit. "On top of all the other refugee complications," the columnists wrote, "Kennedy reported that the secret policy of the Nazis is to demand ransoms for the release of those people whom they claim they are anxious to get rid of."[3] Kennedy thought his remarks to Pearson and Allen would make Roosevelt and Hull see that he possessed some magical knowledge. Instead, relations cooled even further.

As a result, when Myron C. Taylor, the former head of U.S. Steel, was named as chairman of the Intergovernmental Committee on Refugees due to meet at Évian-les-Bains on July 6, Joe seethed with rage. Roosevelt had not even considered him for the job. Kennedy swore blind that the chairman of this committee was *the* plum job that would land him in the White House, and it had been snatched away without cause by Roosevelt.* He was sure to tell a British representative, Colonel Walter Horace Samuel, 2nd Viscount Bearsted MC, with unmistakable disdain, precisely what he thought of Taylor.†

THE KENNEDYS ARRIVED in London just in time for the July 4 celebrations. As Joe Jr. and Jack dressed to attend the dinner and ball of the American Society in London at the Dorchester Hotel, Joe put the finishing touches to his speech. Anthony Eden and Joe Kennedy were each scheduled to speak about Anglo-American relations from their nation's perspective. Kennedy's speech implied that he made foreign policy, stressing the need for Britain to resolve its differences with Germany without delay, adding that America wanted Hitler and Mussolini to make territorial concessions before there could be real peace. Eden, on the other hand, made it clear that the United States should not be "asked or

---

* Initially, the impetus came from the president himself. On March 23, 1938, two weeks after the Anschluss, President Roosevelt invited twenty-nine governments to a conference at Évian-les-Bains in France. The result was the Évian Conference and the formation of the Intergovernmental Committee to find a solution regarding the Jewish refugees (*Source:* Royal Institute of International Affairs, London).

† Bearsted, a Jew, was an anti-Zionist. Nonetheless, he was very influential in promoting Jewish affairs, but wanted only peace in Palestine, not a Jewish state.

expected to pull British chestnuts out of the fire, though there are beginning to be quite a few chestnuts that concern us both."[4]

On July 5, Kennedy called on the prime minister. He asked about the Czech situation, and Chamberlain replied he "had no reason to expect an immediate explosion." When the ambassador briefed the prime minister about his talks with Hull and Roosevelt, he got a bit carried away. "Kennedy has come back with the most roseate accounts of the change in American opinion," Chamberlain wrote to his sister, "and of the President's desire to do something to help. And if it be true that American papers are expressing that sort of view one may be sure that the Germans are aware of it."[5]

Then two days later, *The Times* of London reported that Kennedy had flown to Dublin to receive his honorary degree, dining afterward with the first minister Éamon de Valera at Dublin Castle.[6] No wonder Roosevelt told Ickes on July 3 that Joe was "having the time of his life although he cries 'wolf.'" He also said that Kennedy was unnecessarily pessimistic about the British, leading Ickes to conclude, "I do not think Joe is fooling him [Roosevelt] very much. He said, for instance, that he did not expect Joe to last more than a couple of years in London because he was the kind of a man who liked to go from one job to another and drop it just when the going became heavy."[7]

After lingering in Ireland to visit the ancestral home of his forebears, Kennedy made arrangements to have dinner with Sir Oliver Stanley, President of the Board of Trade on July 14. Kennedy wrote immediately afterward to Hull that according to Stanley the "trade agreement was pretty well settled with the exception of five or six points. I said I had not been so advised." In an attempt to become involved, Kennedy said, "Everybody is planning to get out of town by the 29th July. Is there anything I can do on this?"[8] Kennedy's main concern was he could not honestly claim credit for his involvement in the trade deal, other than tinkering around its edges in motion pictures and sending messages from and to negotiators as a messenger boy.

Hull let Kennedy sweat for four whole days before answering. Mr. Stanley's notion "of progress differs materially from our own," but only insofar as timber being the stumbling block. In a veiled remark about his own summer vacation plans, Hull pointedly finished his telegram: "I plan to remain in Washington constantly in order that I may be in direct touch at all times with these negotiations."[9] Hull knew that Kennedy had rented a villa on the French Riviera for the summer and was talking about himself leaving town on "the 29th July."

Then on July 21, Kennedy asked if he could advise the prime minister "that this was the final position of the United States on the trade agreement?" Hull's immediate response was that Kennedy was advised to speak to the prime minister *only* about the deadlock. Hull was testy, claiming that the British alone were responsible for the "unduly protracted delay" in coming to terms. The Americans were critical about "uncertainty in business circles. Should there be a suspension of negotiations for six weeks to enable the British ministers to take their holidays, this criticism would, of course, become intensified."[10]

Neville Chamberlain's letters are silent about any further discussions with Kennedy that July. Kennedy did, however, have lunch with the prime minister at 10 Downing Street on July 26, and might have delivered Hull's message then. Kennedy was rapidly becoming disparaging of the secretary of state, calling him "the old man" who knew nothing of business or Britain's prior international trade obligations. Kennedy did have a point, particularly as Britain had a prior agreement with the Scandinavian countries about their "most-favored-nation" status with regard to timber.[11]

A four-page coded report was sent from Stanley to the British ambassador in Washington on July 27—two days before the alleged British disappearance on holiday. The first point Stanley made was that he was surprised to learn that "the Ambassador had told Washington that ministers would shortly be leaving London and that consequently it would be difficult to conclude the Agreement during the first half of the recess."* Apparently, America's ambassador had said, too, that the secretary of state regarded the negotiations as "hopeless"—which Stanley said was "unjustified." What's more, Kennedy had asked Stanley "whether there was now any chance of an Agreement." The President of the Board of Trade was compelled to take Kennedy back to "where they had got to in their negotiations" and "how the United States Administration had

---

* Meaning the first six weeks after Parliament adjourned for business.

appeared to change their mind from time to time." Stanley emphasized to Kennedy that "later, after detailed negotiations in Washington
it appeared that all the Americans wanted was a small Agreement but
recently they had returned to the idea of a big Agreement."

Stanley finished off the coded report in a fit of pique: "In reply to the
Ambassador's query whether the approach he was instructed to make to
the Prime Minister would be likely to assist a settlement, the President
[of the Board of Trade] said it depended upon the manner in which
it was put." Self-evidently, it would not help the situation if the prime
minister was told that "the American Administration were demanding
quite impossible concessions as a price of an Agreement."[12] Stanley was
perplexed about the American position. Much of that confusion was
caused by Kennedy, and what the British had begun to call "Kennedyiana," a freewheeling diplomacy initiated by the American ambassador
that needed to be deciphered without any hope of possessing the codes.
One thing, however, had become abundantly obvious to the British negotiators: both the State Department and the White House wished to
keep their ambassador out of the loop.

ON SENSITIVE ISSUES, the British joined in the game, too. Kennedy was
not advised about the secret visit of Hitler's personal adjutant, Captain
Fritz Wiedemann, on July 18. The tall and handsome envoy had been
Hitler's commanding officer in the Great War, and his coming to London
was viewed with optimism by the prime minister. It was decided that
Lord Halifax and Sir Alexander Cadogan should meet with Wiedemann
in a discreet location—the Halifax home in Eaton Square.

Wiedemann had come "with the full knowledge of the Führer to en-
quire about the possibility of Göring coming to London to continue the
talks begun by Halifax the previous November" in Germany. Halifax was
"delighted in principle" but suggested that it would be best if the Czech
situation had been settled first. Hitler's envoy "cooed softly as any dove"
and gave the Foreign Secretary "binding assurance" that the führer was
planning "no forcible action" in that country, so long as there were no
incidents or massacres of the Sudeten Germans.[13]

Halifax seemed convinced of Wiedemann's sincerity, and according
to the envoy's report to Hitler, he had asked to be remembered to the

führer. Wiedemann goes so far as to quote Halifax as saying that it would be the culmination of his work to see "the Führer entering London, at the side of the English King, amid the acclamations of the English people."[14] If Halifax had actually said such a thing, it was meant that Hitler would be invited to the palace as the friend of George VI. The Foreign Secretary could hardly have known that Hitler and Ribbentrop were conniving to install the Duke of Windsor on the throne again after the planned British surrender.[15]

ON JULY 20, Kennedy received word that the stranded Spanish Sacred Heart nuns whom he had been championing for over three months were at long last aboard a British warship bound for England. Kennedy, in need of good press, "decided to let the newspapers know of the rescue. . . . I wanted to emphasize that the Jews from Germany and Austria are not the only refugees in the world."[16]

The New York Times reported: "Their arrival will be another reminder to the British public—perhaps the most striking since the arrival of 4,000 Basque children last year that not all political or religious refugees nowadays come from Central Europe." Chamberlain and the Home Office received thanks, too, for the roles they played in the rescue.[17] Since the report was a distortion of the facts, it is probable that the British ambassador was instructed to ask the *New York Times* publisher, Arthur Sulzberger, to explain why this rescue was compared as "perhaps the most striking" in comparison to the plight of four thousand innocent Basque children. The newspaper's July 30 article, headlined EUROPE—BRITAIN'S FRONTIER IS NOW AT THE DANUBE, redressed the situation, reporting that there "is fresh evidence that the key to the European situation is not Spain but Czechoslovakia."[18]

Seemingly, Kennedy could not put a foot right. He continued his confidential discussions with the German ambassador in London. When he wrote to Roosevelt that the European situation was not as critical as the president thought, Kennedy's opinion was based on Chamberlain's wishful thinking and Dirksen's lies. He had been reassured quite plainly by Dirksen that matters were progressing as planned in Czechoslovakia, and he should not listen to all those overblown reports about more refugees. In reply, Kennedy explained that American public opinion was turning against Germany because of the "insecurity" all those refugees were creating throughout Europe, and even the world. "The average American," Dirksen reported back to Berlin, "blamed Germany for the general insecurity which prevailed in the world and which prevented economic recovery. Germany was accused of wanting to provoke war."[19]

But Kennedy had alarmed Dirksen, too, with his gloomy picture of the American economy. As proof, Joe repeated an alleged conversation with J. P. Morgan about how Morgan wanted to "give up his business." Kennedy's loyalty to Chamberlain—rather than to Roosevelt—shined through as well. He lied when saying that the president backed, and would continue to back, the Chamberlain government. Nonetheless, Dirksen drew his own conclusion, believing that it was "obvious" that "the United States regards itself as the protector and helper of England, which in turn, however, has to pay for this help with subservience and obedience." When the German ambassador to Washington read Kennedy's remarks, he wrote "erroneous" in the margin of his copy of the document.

Less damaging, Kennedy repeated to Dirksen the current scuttlebutt at the House of Commons that Anthony Eden would be replacing Sir Ronald Lindsay on his retirement, as the next British ambassador to Washington.[20] Kennedy was reduced to passing on rumor as truth, when he had personally admonished embassy officials for repeating any unverified gossip as fact only four months earlier. A burgeoning lexicon of Kennedyiana was the natural result of his growing isolation.

Dirksen also advised the German secretary of state, Ernst von Weizsäcker, that their discussions then ranged "back to Kennedy's plan to visit Germany in order to establish contact there with the persons in authority." In order not to arouse any comment, Kennedy suggested that as the president of the International Wheat Advisory Committee, which had met in London a few weeks earlier, he could attend their meeting in Berlin, scheduled for September 1938. Kennedy had, according to Dirksen, an elaborate plan to improve German/American relations through his personal diplomacy. To that end, a Kennedy meeting with Hitler was of the utmost importance to world peace.[21] Essentially, Kennedy had taken on the role of making American foreign policy without reference to the White House or State Department. His purpose was to keep Congress in isolationist mode.

Kennedy informed Hull only after he had taken these unwelcomed initiatives with Dirksen. He mistakenly thought that the State Department and the president would be pleased with this "new method" of "investigation and mediation." Both ignored him. Then he learned that the highly respected Liberal politician Lord Walter Runciman had been selected to go on a mission to Czechoslovakia in an attempt to break the deadlock between the Czech government and the Sudeten Germans. Joe was venomous in his criticisms, describing Runciman as "wily as a serpent" and President Edvard Beneš of Czechoslovakia as "slippery as a snake."[22]

What Kennedy hadn't realized was that Runciman was very much Chamberlain's personal choice. The prime minister announced in Parliament on July 26—without consulting his cabinet—that he had decided to send Runciman as his personal envoy in early September. He thereby single-handedly put Britain right in the middle of the crisis. In a "long talk" with Walter Runciman that very day, Baffy Dugdale and he agreed that: "(1) it brings England back on to the map of Europe for good or evil, with a vengeance and decisively, (2) whether Runciman succeeds or fails, things cannot be the same again, (3) Neville is probably too stupid to perceive the implications of what he has done, (4) He has completely regained the initiative over Anthony [Eden]."[23] Indeed, it hadn't occurred to Chamberlain that hurried special initiatives could possibly make matters worse.

These events make Kennedy's July 29 telegram to the State Department misleading: "The Foreign Office had considered the matter of an international commission but for a number of reasons this was not adopted. The Foreign Office had gradually come to the conclusion that it would be necessary for an Englishman to undertake the task of mediation and Lord Runciman who in every respect was most qualified agreed to undertake it."[24] Having flown off the handle earlier, Kennedy learned that Runciman was an old friend of Halifax's and a personal choice of Chamberlain's, "as a Downing Street memo makes plain, because he 'could be relied upon to put the results across.' His background, political career and Establishment credentials left him naturally capable" without having to constantly refer back to London.[25]

WHILE JOE STRUGGLED to understand his own continued role in London, his family were having the time of their lives. Just after he had left for the United States, a stunning photograph of Rosemary appeared in *The Sketch* and Rose had had an interview with *British Vogue*. But the Kennedy who had shone above all others was Kick. She was an accepted member of "the cousinhood"—sons and daughters of the aristocratic elite. Jean Ogilvy had become Kick's great friend; and Kick was the latest American curiosity to be invited to all the best country house weekends. Whether it was at the Astors, at the Airlies, or even at that bastion of Anglicanism, Hatfield House, the home of the Cecil family, Kick proved that she was a deserving member of the exclusive club.[26]

On June 24, when Joe was in Massachusetts fuming over Harvard's snubbing him, Kick and Jean watched the tennis at Wimbledon. That evening, Jean's parents, Lord and Lady Airlie, gave a small dinner party. Momentously, David Ormsby-Gore—flashing his new set of false teeth that he wore with pride after crashing his car into the back of a truck at ninety-eight miles per hour—introduced Kick to his cousin, William Cavendish, known as Billy. His title was the Marquess of Hartington, and as the eldest son, he was the heir to his father's title of the Duke of Devonshire. Billy and Robert Cecil (who would become the 6th Marquess of Salisbury) were deemed the two most eligible bachelors in London.[27]

Billy was an undergraduate student at Trinity College Cambridge studying history. At six foot four, he was unusually tall, and appeared even taller next to the diminutive Kick. Where Billy's younger brother, Andrew, was extremely exuberant, the fair-haired Billy, with his charming half-smile and gentle manner, seemed to radiate an air of calm. Like Kick, Billy loved "a good talk," and Jean noticed from the first moment he met her that they didn't stop chatting between themselves as if there was no one else in the room.[28] When the time came for Kick to leave the others, as they were going on to a dance at the Palace of Westminster, both Billy and Kick became visibly distressed. Her "publicity-mad" father had arranged yet another photo shoot and she was "forced" to return to

14 Prince's Gate. David Ormsby-Gore said he'd rescue her and pick her up to go on to the dance. When David rang the bell, Billy Hartington was with him.[29]

The couple met again at the birthday party of another Cavendish cousin, Charlie Lansdowne, at Bowood House in Wiltshire on July 1. Three days later, Joe Jr. and Jack exploded onto the scene. Joe Jr., who everyone had been told would one day be U.S. president, was touted as the handsomer, brighter, oldest brother. But it was Jack, with his self-deprecating charm that so resembled Kick's, who became the heartthrob. Their father may never have realized that Joe Jr. "soon developed a reputation among the girls of the set for what Fiona Gore and Jean Ogilvy described many years later as roughness and aggressiveness."[30] Like his father, if Joe Jr. saw a woman he wanted, he went after her.

18

A FRENCH INTERLUDE

A Frenchman's Home is where another man's wife is.
—MARK TWAIN

The summer of 1938 at Cap d'Antibes was not momentous, but it would be unforgettable. The English expatriate community was out in force. The Kennedys were happily ensconced at their villa and were members of the beach club of one of the most magnificent hotels in the world—Hôtel du Cap. Not yet known as a "sunny place for shady people," the Côte d'Azur was home to deposed foreign aristocracy, like Czar Nicholas II's uncle, Grand Duke Michael Mikhailovich; as well as the man who gave up his British throne for "the woman he loved"—the Duke of Windsor. Maharajahs, kings, queens, princesses, and their councilors all made the Côte d'Azur their summer home. The Kennedys were the least famous among the sparkling glitterati.

Winston Churchill vacationed at the home of American Maxine Elliott, the former actress and theater owner. Somerset Maugham wined and dined the Windsors that August, who had already decided to buy their rented villa, Château de la Croë. Maugham also had the Churchill supporter, Harold Nicolson, to stay at his home, La Mauresque. In his letter to his wife, Vita Sackville-West, Nicolson described how of a "soft warm evening" he sat out among "the red and white oleander in the pink dusk and watched the sun set over Cap d'Antibes until the lighthouses began to wink across the purple water."[1] This was the magical kingdom where the beautiful people—le beau monde—breathed in the sun-kissed Mediterranean breezes with a sigh and unalloyed pleasure.

The year 1938 was the first summer when Joe installed his family on these sugar-sand beaches. Kennedy had, of course, ventured to Cap d'Antibes before with Gloria Swanson. Then, too, Joe knew the Americans Frank and Florence Gould, who owned a chain of hotels and casinos along the coast, but he also knew the sex-mad Florence intimately.[2] * Even so, Joe probably did not know that Frank and Florence were being investigated by the French Sûreté for money-laundering that summer. At the time, Florence was also sleeping with (among others) the American ambassador to France, William C. Bullitt.

THAT SUMMER, THE bestselling German author Erich Maria Remarque began work on his novel *Arch of Triumph* in his darkened room at Hôtel du Cap, while his mistress, Marlene Dietrich, took to sunbathing. Marlene, never one to do things by halves, even had her long-suffering daughter, Maria Elisabeth Sieber, concoct her personal sun lotion—"a mixture of the finest oil and iodine, with just a hint of red wine vinegar."[3]

"While our 'famous author' labored in his shadowed room high above the sea, his lady, sexy in a fitted white bathing suit," the attentive Maria wrote, "befriended the sexy Irish politician on the cliffs below." To Maria, Ambassador Kennedy was "kind of rakish." For "a man with such a patient little wife, who had borne him so many children," Maria wittily added, "I thought he flirted a bit too much, but outside of that, Mr. Kennedy was a very nice man." As for the nine children, they were simply "wonderful!" They "all had smiles that never ended, with such perfect teeth each of them could have advertised toothpaste."[4]

Aged thirteen, Maria was more Patricia Kennedy's age than Rosemary's, yet she often spent time with Rosemary, who was seen as "the damaged child" wedged between these "effervescent and quick-witted children." Maria cast herself as a fellow misfit with Rosemary, "comfortable in

---

* Frank J. Gould was the youngest son of the railroad robber baron Jay Gould. They owned the Hôtel Provençal at Juan-les-Pins less than two miles away from Hôtel du Cap and several properties in Nice.

each other's company. We would sit in the shade, watching the calm sea, holding hands."[5]

Marlene's daughter described Joe Jr. as "the heir, broad and chunky, a handsome football player with an Irish grin and kind eyes." Kathleen took Rosemary's place as the "official" eldest sister and somehow "seemed to have matured too soon" as a result. Eunice was "opinionated" and "not to be crossed," clinging jealously to her identity as "an intellectual achiever." Jack was "the glamour boy, the charmer of the wicked grin and the 'come hither' look—every maiden's dream, my secret hero." Pat, although Maria's age, was neither "gawky" nor "fat" and hadn't "a pimple in sight." She called Bobby "the fixer." He was the one who knew everything and was happy to share his information with all and sundry. Jean was the kind, gentle girl who "picked up forgotten tennis rackets and wet towels—a concerned mother in the making." Little Teddy, "with his chubby little legs," was always running, striving to keep up with his older and longer-legged siblings. As for Rose, she was always kind, and often invited Maria to their villa, which was adjacent to the hotel. In the Kennedy family, no one "starred," for they all had starlike qualities.[6] Soon Maria observed that Joe was spending far too much time in Marlene's cabana, and stopped going there herself. For a girl who had been kept at her mother's side rather than attend school (except for a frequently interrupted stint at Brillantmont International School in Lausanne, Switzerland), Maria was quite perceptive.

By August 1, Germany called up three quarters of a million troops for "military maneuvers," while Joe spent as many daylight hours as possible with Marlene inside her beach cabana at Cap d'Antibes. Twelve-year-old Bobby Kennedy danced with Canadian-born British comic actress and singer Beatrice Lillie, and it was rumored (as in the 1939 Cole Porter song "Well, Did You Evah!") that Mars would collide with Earth. Then one evening Jack Kennedy crossed the crowded dance floor to ask Maria, frozen in a stiffened white net formal gown, to dance the Lambeth Walk with him.[7]

On August 2, the French ambassador to Germany, André François-Poncet, reported to Sumner Welles that the German army was in a "state of preparation such as to make immediate mobilization possible." Apparently,

"Hitler was full of venom on account of the loss of prestige which he and his government had suffered on May 21 [the Czech Crisis], and he was determined that the 'miserable little country' [Czechoslovakia] . . . should not be able to put Germany in such a position."[8]

This, of course, meant that the Runciman mission was doomed before it had begun. The French foreign minister, Georges-Étienne Bonnet, met with Ambassador Bullitt on August 12, confirming that the French government believed Runciman's mission could only keep the Germans from invading Czechoslovakia for about two weeks. Mussolini was behaving as if he had lost "his mental balance" and wanted immediate war. "If France should have to continue to arm at the present rate," Bonnet warned Bullitt, "it would be necessary to regiment the entire country on soldiers wages and soldiers rations. In no other way could the present level of the franc be maintained and the essential military expenditures made."[9]

On August 6, a distraught Jan Masaryk met with Soviet ambassador Maisky in London and had much to say to his country's ally. Sir Nevile Henderson received strict instructions by Halifax to tell Ribbentrop that the heavy concentration of German troops on the Czech borders "might have grave consequences for the world; that Czechoslovakia would respond to any German aggression with armed resistance, which would entail military interference by France and the USSR . . . let Hitler consider whether it would be in his interests to see the British Empire among Germany's enemies, and in light of this prospect, assess his subsequent moves." Ribbentrop apparently rounded on Henderson, screaming, "Your British empire is an *empty shell*. It is rotten and decaying. . . . Britain is governed by Jews, ha-ha-ha! Isn't it so?"[10] Six days later, Ambassador Maisky (a Jew) warned Herschel V. Johnson, as the American chargé, that the Soviet Union believed Czechoslovakia was a mere pawn in Hitler's struggle for continental domination.[11]

NONETHELESS, NEITHER CHAMBERLAIN nor Halifax believed that their communications were reaching Hitler. They had "at least half a dozen" Secret Intelligence Service reports that pinpointed a German attack on Czechoslovakia after Hitler's Nuremberg Rally on September 12. Leave for all serving members of the German armed forces had been canceled from August 1, bolstering their belief that Hitler was preparing for an invasion.[12]

On August 3, Chamberlain wrote to Dirksen (who was already on holiday) that he hoped the ambassador understood Lord Runciman's mission had not been decided yet. Halifax was certain that "in von Ribbentrop's present temper there was a real danger that he might suppress his letter of July 28, and not show it to Hitler at all."[13] So Chamberlain sent a copy of that letter to Dirksen, hoping he could get past Ribbentrop. Then on August 10, despite the preparations, Field Marshal Walther von Brauchitsch gave Hitler a memorandum from General Ludwig Beck that the German army was still not in a state of readiness for an armed conflict.[14*]

IN MID-AUGUST, KICK and Jack decided to take a short holiday in the former Austria, to see what was going on. Joe Jr., at his father's behest, headed to Paris, to see history being made. Kennedy, however, remained at Cap d'Antibes. Ewald von Kleist-Schmenzin, the emissary of Colonel-General Ludwig Beck and Admiral Wilhelm Canaris, undertook a secret mission to Churchill and Vansittart in England. While visiting Chartwell, von Kleist-Schmenzin discussed the coup d'état planned by the generals to bring "a new system of government within 48 hours. Such a government, probably of a monarchist character, could guarantee stability and end the fear of war for ever," Churchill reported to Halifax.[15] Chamberlain immediately discounted the von Kleist-Schmenzin report as a pipe dream and saw Churchill's enthusiasm for such a plan as another example of Churchillian folly. A leader as well loved and well protected as Hitler could never be overthrown, Chamberlain asserted.

Just the same, the German chargé d'affaires in London, Theodor Kordt, begged Chamberlain to listen to the secret envoys and encourage any anti-Hitler resistance in Germany. Kordt believed that if Chamberlain immediately stopped all negotiations with the dictator it would give rise to a groundswell of support within the country to topple the führer. He even told the prime minister that Germany was preparing for war. Then,

---

* Beck resigned on August 27, in protest of Hitler's continued aggression against Czechoslovakia. The resignation was not made public.

too, despite warnings from the military, Hitler firmly believed that he would not have to fight the British to overrun Czechoslovakia. To Hitler, "the senility of the British was a self-evident truth, that could be shaken by no considerations."[16]

THE CZECHS, MEANWHILE, were not taking any bets that the French, Soviets, or British would come to their aid. Their government trusted no one, and with good reason. The British felt the French would not uphold their treaty obligations, and then there was the fact that Chamberlain refused to deal with Stalin. On August 22, Sir Nevile Henderson was recalled from Berlin. Herschel Johnson advised Kennedy that Chamberlain had called an emergency cabinet meeting on August 26 and expected the full cabinet to be back in London. The next day, Ribbentrop received a note from the Italian ambassador in Berlin. Mussolini wanted to know "that Germany would communicate in time the probable date of action against Czechoslovakia to be able to take in due time the necessary measures on the French frontier."[17]

PART III

SUNSET AND "THE GATHERING STORM"

You may come to the moment when you
will have to fight with all the odds against you
and only a precarious chance of survival.

—WINSTON CHURCHILL,
THE SECOND WORLD WAR: THE GATHERING STORM

19

THE "FARAWAY COUNTRY"

THERE WILL BE NO WAR

—LORD BEAVERBROOK, *DAILY EXPRESS*, SEPTEMBER 1, 1938

Kennedy was still in Cap d'Antibes when, on August 24, the American chargé Herschel Johnson introduced to Lord Halifax the Washington lawyer George Rublee. As the new director of the Intergovernmental Committee on Refugees, Rublee* was on his way to Paris to meet with Hugh Wilson, the American ambassador in Berlin. Rublee wanted "to discuss with him [Wilson] whether and in what form it might be possible for an approach to be made to the German government" on the Jewish refugee crisis. There was no mention of Kennedy in the communiqué. Yet, on August 28, Joe was in Paris to join the meeting with Ambassador Bullitt, Myron C. Taylor, and Rublee.[1]

On August 26, the first emergency cabinet meeting took place with the British ambassador Henderson from Berlin and the full cabinet present. Chamberlain described it as having "the crisis atmosphere."[2] Halifax, too, was frankly alarmed. The best news, he told the prime minister, was that Pacelli at the Vatican intimated Mussolini "had his hands full enough not to want any new adventures." Viscount Chilston† in Moscow cabled

---

* Rublee served as the director of the Intergovernmental Committee on Refugees on Roosevelt's personal recommendation as agreed at the Évian Conference.

† Aretas Akers-Douglas was 2nd Viscount Chilston. He was the British ambassador to the Soviet Union between 1933 and 1938.

that "the Soviet Union would do its best to help Czechoslovakia." Lord Runciman advised that the Sudeten area should have the equivalent of "Swiss cantonal autonomy" as a preliminary position in talks with the Germans. A British official in Bucharest, known only as Mr. Farquhar, wired that the German minister there believed it was up to France to honor its guarantee to the Czechs. From Prague, the British ambassador Basil Newton's report noted that London's *Daily Telegraph* remarked: "A successful issue to the Sudeten negotiations is impossible so long as freedom of the Sudeten Party is limited by outside influences." Newton urged that Hitler's malevolent influence needed to be brought out into the open. Halifax had directed Newton to speak his mind, and his report pointedly concluded that it would require an "official government approach" to resolve the crisis.

The cabinet had a few days to ruminate these weighty matters before its second meeting on August 28. Halifax wondered aloud if either he or Chamberlain should propose a visit to Hitler.[3] It was then Chamberlain asked his cabinet if the government should issue a formal ultimatum to Hitler stating that the British would defend the territorial integrity of Czechoslovakia by force. After several uncomfortable hours in discussions, it was eventually agreed that Henderson should be sent back to Berlin to speak sternly to Hitler.

ON AUGUST 29, Kennedy returned to London full of solutions regarding what should be done for the Jews and met with Chamberlain at 10 Downing Street. It is probable that Kennedy had upset Rublee in Paris, since on August 30, Kennedy was ordered by Hull to "render full support" to the Intergovernmental Committee on Refugees.[4] Joe was out of touch with the realities of the moment in London, too. He had returned to a Britain focused solely on Czechoslovakia, not on the insurmountable issue of refugees.

Kennedy had misconstrued the facts discussed in the two emergency cabinet meetings, too. He hadn't realized that Chamberlain proposed military intervention and Halifax had pulled the prime minister back from the brink. Chamberlain freely admitted to his sister Ida on September 3 that he was "depressed"; that he kept racking his brain "to try to devise some means of averting a catastrophe if it should be seen to be upon us."[5] Surely, in his conversation with Kennedy, Chamberlain bemoaned that British lives would be lost to protect some "faraway country" about which he knew little. And now Chamberlain had to make his annual visit to see the King and Queen at Balmoral Castle. What could he tell them?

"He does not look well," Kennedy cabled Hull. "The gist of the conversation was that he is very much disturbed about the Czechoslovakia situation. . . . Hitler has made up his mind to take Czechoslovakia peacefully if possible but with arms if necessary." Then he mistakenly reiterated that only Chamberlain stood between war and peace. "He is worried but not jittery."[6]

There is, however, an alternative slant to Joe's discussions with the prime minister and, later, Halifax. Kennedy's relationship with the press and his "plain-spokenness" were well known. Then, too, Joe saw eye to eye with the prime minister about averting another European war. So, why on August 30 had Halifax asked Kennedy about the American position should Britain refrain from the fight—if there was one—in Czechoslovakia? Halifax knew he should have contacted Ambassador Lindsay in Washington for an appropriate American response. Nonetheless, Joe said he would cable the State Department for its position. Then, foolishly, he called in a number of international journalists *before* the State Department replied. Kennedy told them about the Foreign Secretary's request, adding that military aid from the United States had been suggested, too, when it had not. Had Kennedy and Chamberlain combined forces in a clever piece of disinformation? Or was Joe being duped?

Of course, the Neutrality Acts made any American intervention impossible. On August 31, the New York *Daily News*, along with hundreds of other American newspapers, reported that Kennedy had been "sounded out" by Chamberlain on the American position in the event of war. Whether the British were conniving with Kennedy's knowledge or not, the announcements were aimed at Hitler. It was one thing to fight Czechoslovakia, the USSR, France, and Great Britain, but surely even Hitler wasn't mad enough to take on the United States, too.

On September 1, Soviet ambassador Maisky motored down to Churchill's home in the rolling Kent countryside. They discussed that the USSR intended to come to the aid of the Czechs if Germany attacked. Churchill thought that before battle commenced, Britain, the USSR, and

France should deliver a joint communiqué vehemently protesting Hitler's saber rattling. In that instance, Churchill believed Roosevelt would give his moral support. Maisky sagely noted in his diary:"I simply cannot believe that Chamberlain would agree to join with the USSR in standing up to Germany."[7]

The September 3 edition of the *Chicago Tribune* carried its version of Kennedy's talks under the headline: BRITISH CRITICIZE U.S. ENVOY; SAY HE TALKS TOO MUCH—PIQUED BECAUSE HE BARRED BID FOR WAR AID. Although the paper claimed Kennedy's popularity was undiminished, "the British are dismayed at his outspokenness about diplomatic secrets." Kennedy's revelations "to a mixed audience of newspaper men on Wednesday" to discuss "a subject considered a dark secret is best known to himself."[8]

As a result,"a little worried" French chargé in Washington requested to meet urgently with Moffat. The press emanating from London "that Great Britain was pressing us" was causing consternation, Moffat wrote, "for a definition of what we would do and what our attitude would be in the event that Britain went to war." He could tell the French chargé only that the press reports were "scarcely accurate." Before the Frenchman's visit, on September 1, Moffat had written, "Joe Kennedy's star is not shining brightly these days."[9]

WHEN THE ARTICLES appeared, Kennedy and Jack were in Scotland laying a cornerstone of a memorial chapel to Samuel Seabury at St. Andrew's Episcopal Cathedral in Aberdeen. Duly reprimanded for his earlier precipitous actions, Joe sent through his next speech to the State Department for review, marking the paragraphs which might "broadly speaking" be of concern. Unwisely, Kennedy had continued to present his personal views as American policy, which were clearly at odds with the administration and which might also be unnecessarily provocative toward the Reich. After all, Kennedy was simply laying a cornerstone of the Samuel Seabury Memorial Chapel, and the only statement to make was about Seabury's life,* the memorial, links between Scotland and America, and how he was honored to lay the cornerstone. It is tantalizing

---

* Samuel Seabury (1729–1796) was the first American Episcopal bishop.

to speculate if Jack—newly returned from Hitler's Austria with a distaste for what he saw and already far wiser in foreign affairs than his father— had anything to do with Joe's apparent about-face. On receipt of the speech, Moffat noted, "All of us thought that the Secretary should have Presidential authority to reject the paragraphs."[10]

Roosevelt was incandescent when he read the speech and told Morgenthau, "The young man needs his wrists slapped rather hard."[11] Not only had Kennedy violated diplomatic protocol several times, but the president had just heard from Morgenthau that Kennedy was sounding off about Hull as "the old man," and how Kennedy had obfuscated over the motion pictures deal with the secretary of state to benefit the British.* To boot, the president could hardly credit that the British had taken Joe, an Irish Catholic, to their hearts.

However, Roosevelt also saw the bigger picture and chose not to act, other than to have the offending paragraphs be stricken from Kennedy's speech. Knowing the British to be Machiavellian statesmen who had been in the game of international politics for over a thousand years, Roosevelt felt that Kennedy was at best being played; at worst, treacherous. He knew, too, before confirming Joe to the post of ambassador that Joe was unfit for the role. Nonetheless, he had removed Kennedy from Washington for his own purposes. One reason was that isolationism was keeping the president from acting fairly in international affairs, and like Churchill, he saw war clouds gathering. Roosevelt hoped that by keeping Kennedy in London, shooting off his plain-spoken mouth, he would ultimately demean or abandon isolationism in an ever-darkening world.

So, understandably, the president decided he would not recall his errant ambassador. Kennedy could side with Chamberlain as much as he pleased and create as many isolationist headlines contrary to United States foreign policy as he wanted. All Roosevelt had to do was to deny Kennedy's interpretation of foreign policy matters that were well beyond his scope as ambassador. From London, Joe could be denied the oxygen of power in American politics, while still maintaining his substantial weight among

---

* Morgenthau, too, was vacationing at Cap d'Antibes and duly noted down all of Kennedy's negative remarks to be repeated on his return to Washington to the president and the cabinet.

America's 25 million Catholics. He could cry from the rooftops through Hearst's newspapers, *The New York Times,* and his key syndicated columnist friends any isolationist fake news he chose to holler. Roosevelt, like Churchill, knew that Hitler would not stop at Czechoslovakia. Then, too, with Kennedy in London, the president could still get his ambassador's endorsement for a third term in 1940—should he decide to run.

BY THE END of the first week in September, Chamberlain was fed up with the Foreign Office chant "We must keep Hitler guessing." He admitted, too, that he was "obsessed" with the Czech situation in a letter to his sister Hilda.[12] After Chamberlain returned from Balmoral, matters seemed even more hopeless. On September 10, the *Daily Mail*'s Paris edition splashed the "most gratuitously mischievous" headline that "at midnight" the British government had sent an ultimatum to Hitler stating that if the German chancellor used force in Czechoslovakia, the British would at once declare war. A furious Chamberlain immediately dispatched telegrams to Paris, Prague, and Berlin denying the report.[13] But the *Daily Mail* was right: an ultimatum had been sent to Henderson—but to be delivered to Ribbentrop, not Hitler.

That same day Kennedy met with Halifax. Subsequently, he cabled Hull that the British had stated Hitler had only three options: (1) to stir up trouble in the Sudeten area, thereby bringing in the German troops "to put down the bloodshed"; (2) to call a plebiscite to get public opinion on his side; or (3) "to march" in and "bomb Praha" [Prague]. "Their secret advices are that Hitler has already made his decision."[14] Halifax said that while there "cannot be any good in war," the destruction of "this impossible Nazism" is the only way the democracies can survive. When Kennedy asked Halifax what Chamberlain thought, the prime minister had apparently replied that "this is really not as much fun as shooting grouse." The British, according to Joe, were "quite calm but I feel they sense great danger in the air."[15]

On September 12, Halifax fed Kennedy information that the British were considering "the idea of starting a little movement of the destroyer fleet" and that they would let Kennedy know later that evening. Halifax then wrote to Lindsay in Washington: "The Ambassador felt that it was essential to take every possible step to avoid misunderstanding in

Herr Hitler's mind and that only overwhelming argument would suffice to prevent us sending the final warning that we had in mind. . . . The Ambassador said," Halifax continued, "that American opinion was much more excited against Hitler than he had ever known it; in his own words 'twenty times as excited as in 1914'. If war should come . . . and . . . London was bombed, he thought there would be a strong revulsion of feeling."[16]

Next, Kennedy went to see Chamberlain at 7:30 P.M. that evening.[17] His purpose was for some German agency to report back to Ribbentrop that he had been called in at short notice, encouraging German speculation "that our countries were apparently keeping in close touch." Kennedy did not notify the State Department, or indeed tell Roosevelt or Hull later, that his ruse was intended to frighten the Germans into believing the United States was working on some sort of "joint declaration or action." By then Kennedy already knew neither Roosevelt nor the State Department was going to make any statement to back Britain—no matter which way it chose to jump.[18] Unlike later deceptions practiced by the OSS (Office of Strategic Services) or the British Secret Intelligence Service, it was a clumsy attempt at disseminating disinformation.

Not realizing the dangers of how his actions would be interpreted back home, Kennedy went a stage further: he leaked his ruse to the German counselor of legation as fact. The next day, Theodor Kordt sent a cable to Ribbentrop marked *Geheim* (secret), stating he had irrefutable evidence that "President Roosevelt has made it known through the Ambassador that Great Britain could count on the support of the United States if she should become involved in a war." A second dispatch quoted Kennedy saying that "he himself had two sons" of military service age and he would continue to work to keep America out of any European conflict. Even so, Kennedy affirmed to Kordt that the United States would ultimately join Britain.[19]

Theodor Kordt's cable also stated that Kennedy reiterated if Hitler refrained from bloodshed, world public opinion toward Germany would become positive. The United States would be the first to congratulate Hitler on exercising restraint. Indeed, the führer would be looked upon as a "benefactor." Hitler's "ideas in the social and economic field which were responsible for such extraordinary achievements in Germany [that they] would be a determining influence on the economic development of the United States and economic cooperation between all nations."[20] These were Kennedy's personal views, and wholly at odds with the Roosevelt administration, which he served. Kennedy intimated that he *made* foreign policy rather than *followed* foreign policy enacted by others. In speaking out so recklessly about some spurious "joint declaration" or "joint action" without either Roosevelt's or the State Department's approval, Kennedy had gone rogue.

HITLER'S LONG-AWAITED SEPTEMBER 12 speech at Nuremberg before thousands of supporters thundering *Sieg Heil!* did not declare war on Czechoslovakia. He did, however, call the Czechs "dishonest" and their behavior "revolting," as they were acting under the "gruesome defiance" of their peoples. He defended Mussolini's actions in Abyssinia; berated the Jews for their "unimaginable cruelty" to Germany and Western democracies for protecting them; and finally said that Czechoslovakia's only raison d'être was as "a base in the event of war for launching aerial attacks and dropping bombs upon German cities and industrial plants." The Sudeten Germans had a right to their own way of life, just as any other people do, he screamed.[21] Despite the baseless accusations, the repetition, and the ranting, both France and Britain were momentarily relieved.

Afterward, according to the prearranged plan, Konrad Henlein's Nazi followers began their attacks: rioting against Czech police and soldiers followed by looting Jewish shops. The Czech government declared a state of martial law. When it looked as though Henlein's Sudeten Party would be overpowered, because most locals had not joined in, the Sudeten leader fled to Germany.

Then, in the evening of September 13 to 14, the French prime minister, Édouard Daladier, contacted Chamberlain, suggesting that they should make a joint approach direct to Hitler. "Things should be tried when they look blackest," the prime minister wrote after, "and that they should come as a complete surprise."[22] So, without advising Halifax or his cabinet, Chamberlain cabled Hitler, proposing to come to see the führer for a tête-à-tête. His decision not to tell anyone—except Hitler—was breathtaking. Even Daladier was kept in the dark. Although the prime minister informed his cabinet the next day, they had no opportunity to digest this tidbit before Hitler answered, inviting Chamberlain to Berchtesgaden.

The British prime minister departed at once, accompanied by his éminence grise, Sir Horace Wilson. The Czechs were "astonished that at the very moment when for the first time they had the internal situation in the Sudeten areas in hand the British Prime Minister should himself pay a direct visit to Hitler."[23] The Beneš government had already proposed administrative measures that far surpassed Henlein's official requests and Chamberlain's wishes. The result was that the prime minister's precipitate action gave the führer the initiative in the negotiations.[24] So, as Chamberlain descended from his aircraft to the roaring chant of *Sieg Heil!*, Ribbentrop and Dirksen gave the prime minister the latest news. Henlein just announced over German radio that he was demanding annexation of the Sudetenland to the Reich.

IN WASHINGTON, MOFFAT received the French ambassador, this time asking about America's position regarding Chamberlain's German trip. All Moffat could say was the secretary of state would undoubtedly be questioned about it at his press conference later, and he would say something positive about any move that aimed to preserve peace. Indeed, Hull's statement issued to the press was clear: "The historic conference today between the Prime Minister of Great Britain and the Chancellor of Germany is naturally being observed with the greatest interest by all nations which are deeply concerned with the preservation of peace."[25]

Nonetheless, Joe was taking no chances and told Rose to return to London from Cap d'Antibes. She had been led to believe that her husband's constant presence had "given great moral support" to Chamberlain, when in fact Kennedy, too, was desperate for firsthand information. After Chamberlain's return to London on September 16, Kennedy was none the wiser. With the persistence of an attack dog, he called several times without an appointment at Downing Street and buttonholed anyone who would speak to him. The American papers, of course, followed his every move, and scurrilously reported that Joe was acting on behalf of the U.S. government. But it was all fluff. Kennedy knew nothing, and neither did Hull. Finally, Cadogan agreed to meet with America's ambassador on September 17. Kennedy cabled Hull afterward that

Chamberlain "found Hitler in a very bad mood. Those around him had just reported another incident in which three hundred Sudetens were killed. Chamberlain said he knew nothing of that and urged Hitler not to take it for granted unless it was confirmed."[26]

During Chamberlain's three-hour man-to-man talk with only Hitler's interpreter, Dr. Paul Schmidt, present, the prime minister found that "for the most part H. spoke quietly and in low tones. I did not see any trace of insanity but occasionally he became very excited and poured out his indignation against the Czechs in a torrent of words." Chamberlain told Hitler that he "didn't care two hoots whether the Sudeten were in the Reich or out of it according to their own wishes." Then Chamberlain suggested that they break off their talk for now, hold consultations, then meet again. Hitler agreed "that is a possible procedure," but was solicitous that a man of the prime minister's age need make a second journey. It was agreed, nevertheless, that the men would meet near Cologne and Hitler would not make a move until he heard back from Chamberlain.

Despite Hitler's record since taking power in 1933, Chamberlain wrote to his sister Ida on September 19 that "he had established a certain confidence which was my aim[;] and on my side in spite of the hardness and ruthlessness I thought I saw in his face I got the impression that here was a man who would be relied upon when giving his word."[27]

WHEN CHAMBERLAIN FINALLY briefed Kennedy in person, he implied that the British military strength lagged far behind Germany's. If the British joined the French to defend Czechoslovakia, both men feared London would have air raids within days. It is difficult to imagine that Kennedy, the ultimate quick-thinking problem solver, had not gone through options with the prime minister and seen that he was hinting for American military aid. Chamberlain confided he had sent a personal message to Beneš that Hitler would accept nothing but annexation of the Sudeten area. Kennedy told Hull in a triple priority dispatch that the prime minister most feared Hitler calling a plebiscite.[28]* Chamberlain's greater fear, however, was the possibility that Hitler would then raise

---

* Chamberlain's fears of a "democratic" plebiscite were based on Hitler's winning the hearts and minds of those living in the Sudetenland portion of Czechoslovakia. Chamberlain

the subject of German minorities in Hungary, or worse still, in Poland. Where would it all end?

On September 18, the French premier and foreign minister came to London to discuss a united Anglo-French position and agree on a schedule for Chamberlain's next trip to Germany. A downtrodden Cadogan told Kennedy that things were not looking good. There was a split in the cabinet. Edward Turnour, 6th Earl Winterton (speaking to the House on behalf of Viscount Swinton), Walter Elliot (Secretary of Health), Oliver Stanley (President of the Board of Trade) and Alfred Duff Cooper (First Lord of the Admiralty) "were not at all enthusiastic concerning the whole proposal and that [the] Minister of War [Leslie Hore-Belisha] would possibly incline to their side."[29] Cadogan did not say that Halifax was also teetering on the edge.

NEVER ONE TO let the cards fall how they may, Kennedy decided to act unilaterally once again. On September 19, he cabled Charles Lindbergh in France asking the aviator and his wife to come to London. Although he also wrote to Hull that day, no mention was made of Lindbergh or why he was asked to come so urgently. Then, on September 21, Kennedy was advised that Beneš was having great difficulty getting his cabinet to accept the British and French plan for annexation and that the Czech prime minister Milan Hodža had resigned. Kennedy intended to ask Lindbergh, who was the most knowledgeable American aviator on the German Luftwaffe, for help because Chamberlain had freely admitted to him "that he did not believe it possible for England under peace time operations to ever catch up with Germany's preparations for war."[30]

Two days later, on a cool, misty day with the smell of coal smoke hanging heavily in the air, Charles and Anne Lindbergh had lunch with Joe and Rose Kennedy at Prince's Gate. After the meal, the men discussed the crisis, aviation in general, and the military situation in Europe. Kennedy avowed that "everyone in [the] embassy is extremely worried. Hitler told Chamberlain that he would risk a world war if necessary." Kennedy said that public opinion was pushing Chamberlain toward war.

---

still did not realize that European domination and Aryan ascendance were Hitler's immediate goals.

Lindbergh replied the English were in "no shape for war" and that their fleet, which had always protected them from the enemy in the past, could no longer be counted on with the advent of aviation. "I am afraid," Lindbergh confided to his journal, "this is the beginning of the end of England as a great power."[31] Kennedy asked Lindbergh to write a report on the military aviation situation in Europe to share with others, and the aviator agreed.

After lunch, Lindbergh went to see Herschel Johnson at the embassy to get another take on events. They were interrupted when Kennedy barged in, announcing that Chamberlain was going to meet Hitler again, this time at Bad Godesberg. Joe feared if Hitler made more demands, England would declare war.[32] Kennedy had failed again to see matters from a British perspective. Many viewed Hitler's posturing as "Danegeld"— the blackmail paid to the invading Danes to keep Anglo-Saxon lands from being ravaged. By now the British cabinet knew—even if the prime minister chose to ignore the reality—that any deal with Hitler would be short-lived.

Next, Lindbergh met with the highly respected Colonel Raymond E. Lee, the American "London Observer" (military attaché), for supper at Lee's home. While they were dining, the report came in that discussions between Chamberlain and Hitler had suddenly broken off, meaning Lindbergh would compile his report for Kennedy amid preparations for war. At the same time Sir Oswald Mosley, leader of the British Union of Fascists, pontificated from his soapbox in Piccadilly Circus; Communists paraded with red banners; and the Air Raid Precautions (ARP) gas mask station busily fitted the queuing crowds to their new masks. Sandbags were hauled into place, police and ARP wardens were on maneuvers, and emergency information in the event of air raids was broadcast on the radio and at nearly every street corner.[33]

By September 22, Lindbergh's report, written at great speed, was delivered to Kennedy. Its sole intention was to inform. Its effect terrified all who read it. Kennedy quoted liberally from the text in a cable to Hull that same day in "Special Gray Code":

I feel certain that German air strength is greater than that of all other European countries combined, and that she is constantly increasing her margin of leadership. I believe that German factories are now capable of producing in the vicinity of 20,000 aircraft each year.... The Quality of German design is excellent and the extensive research facilities ... [imply that] Germany now has the means of destroying London, Paris and Prague if she wishes to do so. England and France together have not enough modern war planes for effective defense or counter-attack. France is in a pitiful condition in the air. England is better off but her air fleet is not comparable to Germany's. France is probably now building in the vicinity of 50 planes per month; England probably in the vicinity of 200 first-line aircraft.... It is not possible to estimate Russian air strength.* The Russians have copied American factories and purchased American machinery of the most modern type.... Judging by the general conditions in Russia, I would not place great confidence in the Russian air fleet. However Russia probably has a sufficient number of planes to make her weight felt in any war she enters.... For the first time in history a nation has the power either to save or to ruin the great cities of Europe. Germany has such a preponderance of war planes that she can bomb any city in Europe with comparatively little resistance.[34]

AT 11:45 A.M. on September 23, Chamberlain cabled the latest from Bad Godesberg. In Hitler's "Godesberg Memorandum," the goalposts moved again: "The boundary he [Hitler] proposes is based on a language map and he has so drawn it to give the most favourable results to Germany ... failing acceptance of his proposals ... he intimates that he will be obliged to seek a military solution and in that event he will draw, not a 'national frontier' but a 'military and strategic frontier.'" At four P.M. Halifax cabled the British ambassador in Prague that the "French and British Governments could not continue to take the responsibility of advising them not to mobilize."[35]

Dejected, exhausted, facing an increasingly fractious cabinet—and most of all, a resolve from Halifax that Hitler would never be satiated—Chamberlain decided to address the nation and the empire. Kennedy militated several times for the broadcast to be aired in America, too. Sumner Welles, who managed Kennedy better than others, was deputized

---

*   Lindbergh had recently returned from the USSR.

to tell the ambassador that while the American government could not interfere in radio broadcasts or dictate to companies what they could or could not air, neither Roosevelt, Hull, nor he felt it was appropriate. Just the same, on September 26, Roosevelt made a direct appeal to Hitler: "On behalf of the 130 millions of people in the United States of America and for the sake of humanity everywhere I most earnestly appeal to you not to break off negotiations looking to a peaceful, fair and constructive settlement of the questions at issue."[36]

The following evening, Chamberlain's fateful words were taken into homes, restaurants, and offices around the globe. The wireless at Prince's Gate was tuned in, with Joe listening anxiously, Joe Jr. at his side. Jack had returned to Harvard. The younger Kennedys and Rosemary had been sent to relative safety in Ireland, in the event of a sudden attack. Kick Kennedy listened, too, from a Scottish friend's home; while Rose was on holiday at the Gleneagles Hotel.

The prime minister's voice crackled over the airwaves: "How horrible, fantastic, incredible, it is that we should be digging trenches and trying on gas masks here, because of a quarrel in a faraway country between people of whom we know nothing. . . . Armed conflict between nations is a nightmare to me; but if I were convinced that any nation had made up its mind to dominate the world by fear of its force, I should feel it must be resisted." The prime minister tried to give a balanced broadcast, also saying that Herr Hitler had promised him "that after the Sudeten German question was settled, that is the end of Germany's territorial claims in Europe."[37]

Shortly after his historic radio appeal, Chamberlain received a reply from Hitler that he would "join in a guarantee of the new frontiers of Czechoslovakia," but that this offer, known as the Godesberg Memorandum, would expire at two P.M. on Wednesday, September 28. Chamberlain drafted a personal message to Hitler: "After reading your letter I feel certain that you can get all essentials without war, and without delay. I am ready to come to Berlin myself at once to discuss arrangements for transfer with you."[38]

On September 28, Joe Kennedy sat between Count Dino Grandi, the Italian ambassador, and Jan Masaryk, the Czech minister, in the diplomatic gallery of the House of Commons to hear the prime minister tell his fellow members about his travails. In front of the assembled Parliament, the haggard prime minister became visibly relieved when a note from Mussolini and Hitler was delivered to him. He theatrically held up Hitler's invitation to Munich alongside Italy and France to decide on the carving up of Czechoslovakia.* The whole house rose in cheers on both sides of the aisle, and the noise was "terrific," according to Kennedy. "Now I can spend Christmas in Palm Beach as I planned," a grinning—and ever injudicious—Kennedy said to Masaryk. Shortly afterward, at the request of the Foreign Office, Joe arranged with the Hays film office for the censorship of the Paramount newsreel in which "British editors criticized the appeasement policy" of the government. A. J. Cummings of the *News Chronicle* was particularly outspoken, and his words "our statesmen have been guilty of what I think is a piece of yellow diplomacy" were stricken.[39]

A VICTORIOUS CHAMBERLAIN returned from Munich on September 30. War had been averted. Czechoslovakia had been betrayed by its allies (save the Soviets), foremost among them the British. However, the prime minister had returned with Hitler's signature on a separate "piece of paper" assuring the British that: "We are resolved that the method of consultation shall be the method adopted to deal with any other questions that may concern our two countries, and we are determined to continue our efforts to remove possible sources of difference, and thus to contribute to assure the peace of Europe."

When the prime minister landed at Heston airfield, he waved the joint declaration and read it aloud to the assembled crowd. As Chamberlain's car drove through the adoring, cheering masses into central London, Halifax became gloomy. "All this will be over in three months," he warned. Yet nothing could dampen Chamberlain's elation. From the

---

* The Czechs were not invited and did not know of the meeting in advance. Only after immense pressure from the British did they accede to Hitler's demands. Kennedy claimed to be sitting next to the Italian ambassador, Dino Grandi, but omitted Masaryk's name. Kennedy was between Grandi and Masaryk, according to Edward R. Murrow's notes.

window of 10 Downing Street, the prime minister waved his miserable piece of paper again and said, "This is the second time in our history that there has come back from Germany to Downing Street peace with honour. I believe it is peace for our time."[40] Neither Chamberlain nor Kennedy understood that after Munich, appeasement was a bankrupt policy.

20

TRAFALGAR DAY

My character and my good name are in my own keeping.
Life with disgrace is dreadful.

—Horatio Nelson,
March 10, 1795

The European wolves smelled blood. Poland and Hungary wanted their own slices of Czechoslovakia. Poland demanded and received the Teschen area from Hitler after October 1, and promptly occupied it with Polish troops. Hungary would have to wait until November 2 to carve out its slice of southern Slovakia and Carpathian Ruthenia. Nonetheless, the important thing for Kennedy and Chamberlain was that peace had been maintained. Neither man doubted his rightness.

The führer fooled them both into believing that he admired the prime minister. "Hitler could see in the marvelous reception accorded Chamberlain by the German people," Joe wrote in his diary, "their wish to keep out of war and their great respect for Chamberlain who not for one minute allowing diplomacy to bog down entirely and who really made the only warlike or prepared gesture he could in the mobilization of the British fleet."[1] Kennedy also alleged that he had had "several American cruisers sent to England simply for the effect on Germany. He went to see Chamberlain one day on business, and then went back a second time for no reason at all," an awed Lindbergh wrote in his wartime journal, "except to have it known that the American Ambassador went twice on the same day to see the Prime Minister about the crisis."[2] Kennedy said that the prime minister thanked him for "the help I had given him during the last month . . . he depended more on me than on anybody for judgment and support."[3] The first statement was undoubtedly true. The second smacked of what the British now firmly called Kennedyiana.

ROOSEVELT, HOWEVER, BELIEVED that England and France had committed an international outrage. They will need to "wash the blood from their Judas Iscariot hands," he said to Harold Ickes in the middle of September. Roosevelt, Churchill, their close colleagues, and their advisers had not recognized that Germany was unprepared to fight a European—much less world—war in 1938. If France, Britain, and the Soviet Union had joined forces, as General Alfred Jodl* testified at his trial at Nuremberg in 1946, a 1938 war "was out of the question, with five fighting divisions and seven reserve divisions in the western fortifications, which were nothing but a large construction site, to hold out against 100 French divisions. That was militarily impossible. Even Hitler was thankful his 'generals had urged restraint.'"[4] Once Germany had taken over the Czech fortress line, the führer confided that "what we saw [of the Czech military strength] greatly disturbed us; we had run a serious danger."[5]

TEN DAYS AFTER Munich and "peace for our time," Hitler made a speech at Saarbrücken, capital of the reclaimed Saarland on the border with France. He told the thousands listening that sadly any document signed with a democracy was only of a transitory value. Democracies were fickle: "At any time they may lose their position to make way for others who are not anxious for peace. . . . It only needs that in England instead of Chamberlain Mr. Duff Cooper or Mr. Eden or Mr. Churchill should come to power, and then we know quite well that it would be the aim of these men immediately to begin a new World War."[6]

In early October, Kennedy wrote to Hull "the feeling of relief which began to sweep through . . . Great Britain on [last] Wednesday afternoon has now been largely supplanted by a mood of analysis. . . . The debate

---

* Generaloberst Jodl (a four-star general) was the chief of the Operations Staff of the German High Command.

now taking place in the House of Commons is of course stimulating reaction."[7] Chamberlain was incensed Alfred Duff Cooper had resigned as First Lord of the Admiralty, and that twenty of his Conservative members had abstained from the vote to support the government on Munich. Hundreds of letters poured in supporting the offenders, who were mockingly referred to as "The Glamour Boys."[8] Clement Attlee MP, Leader of the Opposition Labour Party, had abandoned his earlier pacific stand, and was like-minded to Churchill, feeling that Munich was "nothing but an armistice in a state of war. . . . We have felt that we are in the midst of a tragedy. We have felt humiliation."[9]

President Roosevelt's October 5 cable to Kennedy requested he "call upon" the prime minister on his behalf to relay his message "as time may be of the essence." Roosevelt hoped that in the aftermath of Munich, the best opportunity had arisen for "the establishment of a new order based on justice and on law." The president considered that "the present German policy of racial persecution, which has perhaps done more harm than any other to the estimate of Germany held by public opinion in America, regardless of class, race or creed," needed to be addressed urgently. "While it may be too much to expect an early change in the basic racial policy of the German Government," Roosevelt continued, ". . . it would seem reasonable to anticipate that the German Government will assist the other Governments upon which this problem has been forced by relaxing pressure upon these people sufficiently to permit the arrangement of an orderly emigration and by permitting them to take with them a reasonable percentage of their property."[10]

Roosevelt's message was particularly ill timed from a British perspective. Kennedy had been silent on the burning shame and rearmament issues consuming the dazed British cabinet. Of course, the State Department and the White House had access to British newspapers, but other than *The Times* of London, they were not deemed to be "reliably" close to the prime minister. By October 5, Munich was called the "breathing space" in which Britain could rearm. However, neither Kennedy nor Chamberlain saw that Germany continued arming, too, albeit at an exponentially terrifying clip. On October 9, Hitler announced from Saarbrücken: "I have therefore decided . . . to continue the construction of our fortifications in the West with increased energy." All those who had rejoiced days earlier shuddered when they heard Hitler add: "It would be a good thing if in Great Britain people would gradually drop certain airs which they have inherited from the Versailles epoch. We cannot tolerate any longer *the tutelage of governesses.*"[11]

WITH THE ACQUISITION of the Sudetenland, Germany had also gained 3.5 million further foot soldiers and reaped the rewards of war without firing a shot. The Czech military machine was well oiled, with 1.5 million rifles, 750 modern aircraft, 600 tanks, 2,000 modern field guns, rich mineral resources, Czech stockpiles, and timber.[12] Worse still, the Škoda ironworks came under German control. While the company is noted today for its cars, in 1938, it was one of the largest manufacturers of armaments in Europe. By the end of the year, Reichswerke Hermann Göring had acquired a controlling stake in all three manufacturers of armaments in Czechoslovakia, significantly increasing Germany's military might. The production of armaments at Škoda alone between October 1938 and the outbreak of war in September 1939 was nearly equal to all British arsenal factories in the same period.[13]

By mid-October, the Committee of Imperial Defence asked the Chamberlain cabinet if it should recall all the distributed gas masks. Evidently, they were unaware that the Škoda factory was the primary manufacturer and it would be impossible to order replacements. Simultaneously, all the other armed services departments were busily ordering all manner of arms, referring to the "alarming shortages" that the Czech Crisis had exposed. Even so, Chamberlain scaled these demands back in compromise, hoping not to "disturb the trade of the country or irritating the Germans and Italians by large-scale measures."[14]

Both Kennedy and Chamberlain failed to see the worst blunder of the Czech Crisis was the missed opportunity to join forces with the Soviet Union against the Nazis. Of course, there were ample reasons for not trusting Stalin, who had decimated his senior military officials in the purges of 1937. Chamberlain had enough trouble dealing with the socialist Labour Party (which he never did), much less dyed-in-the-wool Bolsheviks. The loss of the "Grand Alliance" of the Soviet Union in the East and Britain and France in the West as advocated by Churchill was, in fact, enormous—and one the Western allies would come to regret.* It would have meant that from September 30, 1938, instead of June 22, 1941, Hitler would have been obliged to fight a war against armies on two fronts. Then, too, he would have had to do this without Czech armaments. By ignoring the Soviet offers of men and matériel, the British and French opened the way for Stalin to think the unthinkable: an alliance with the Nazis.[15] Roosevelt, too, believed unfailingly that with England, France, and the Soviet Union all pounding away at Hitler's enlarged Reich, "Germany would find it difficult to protect itself even with its present preponderance in the air."[16]

For many, the disgraceful wholesale abandonment of the Czechs was an abomination. The brilliant and arrogant German-born British physicist and Professor of Experimental Philosophy at Oxford University, Frederick Lindemann, had been advising Churchill since the early 1930s about rearmament. A daring pilot, Lindemann became Churchill's "chief adviser on the scientific aspects of modern war and particularly air defence, and also on questions involving statistics of all kinds."[17] Although Churchill agreed with Lindbergh that Britain was ill prepared for war, he disagreed that Germany would destroy London from the air. So did Kennedy's military attaché to London, Colonel Raymond E. Lee.

Kennedy, never an historian, could not see that the principle of collective security, upon which Europe's peaceful existence had been reliant since the end of the Great War, was betrayed along with the Czechs. He disliked Churchill's disloyal declaration in the House of Commons that "we have sustained a total and unmitigated defeat." He heard only the widespread admiration for Chamberlain's Herculean efforts.[18] He never understood that Churchill could not reconcile being English with the fact that Munich meant peace without justice. Nor could Kennedy see why President Beneš of Czechoslovakia protested on resigning, "before the world against a decision in which they had no part."[19]

THE KEY PERSON in the aftermath of Munich was not Chamberlain or Kennedy, but Halifax. He wrote to the prime minister on October 11 that "as we were saying the other day, while hoping for the best, it is also

---

* On September 24, six days before Munich, the Soviets had mobilized 330,000 men to come to the aid of Czechoslovakia.

necessary to prepare for the worst."[20] That meant not only rearming, but also a government of national unity. So, Halifax proposed a change in policy: to bring the opposition parties, and even Anthony Eden, into the government. Before the end of the month, Halifax wrote to the British Ambassador to France Sir Eric Phipps that he hoped "very shortly to reach conclusions that would greatly speed up our rearmament." Four days later, he told Phipps, "It would be fatal for us to be caught again with insufficient armed strength."[21]

Chamberlain ignored Halifax's urging to create a new cabinet, which, to his mind, would spend much of its time challenging him. The prime minister never knew that his boast about "peace with honour" made Lord Halifax "shiver" when he heard it.[22]* Indeed, for Halifax, it was a very dangerous fiction unless the time gained could be used to good effect. But instead, a weary Chamberlain retreated north to the River Tweed for a rest and a spot of fishing.

Even before Munich, Halifax was tackled by phone, mail, and personal pleading from old friends whose opinions he respected, like Leo Amery MP,† Oliver Stanley, and William George Stewart Adams, the Warden of All Souls College Oxford. All of them urged Halifax to halt any further coercion of the Czechs. Notwithstanding this, Chamberlain's grotesque vanity and ability to delude himself, as he put it to the September 22 cabinet meeting, prevailed. "Herr Hitler had certain standards . . ." Chamberlain said, "he would not deliberately deceive a man who he respected and with whom he had been in negotiation."[23] Halifax's conversion away from appeasement—the very policy which he had helped to formulate—can be traced to September 24. Alec Cadogan talked to Halifax that day, and the foreign secretary had his first sleepless night. The next morning, he thanked Cadogan for his lack of sleep, recognizing that continued support of appeasement would be an empty gesture to his own pride.

---

*   Other supporters wanted Chamberlain to call a general election in support of Munich. Churchill applauded the prime minister's urge to resist it.

†   Leopold Charles Maurice Stennett Amery MP was a contemporary of Churchill's at Harrow School and met Halifax while he was studying at Balliol College, University of Oxford. He was a former First Lord of the Admiralty and Colonial Secretary under Baldwin. He was also a faithful Churchill supporter.

While Chamberlain hailed Munich as a "triumph of restraint and dignity" in the Commons, Halifax was not entirely loyal. In the House of Lords, he was at pains to show "eleven ways in which Munich had been an improvement on the Godesberg demands," but called the outcome "an abomination." The Foreign Secretary felt compelled to write to his school and Christ Church Oxford contemporary, Lord Francis Scott, on October 18, "No one I imagine can think that the arrangements made at Munich were anything but the choice of the lesser of two horrible evils."[24]

THE MOOD OF the rebel British political elite was shared by Roosevelt and rejected by Kennedy. In future, Halifax would work for rearmament. Even Chamberlain had told Parliament of Britain's need to rearm during the Munich debate. However, just how and when rearmament would occur remained an incoherent strategy in the weeks that followed. Ever loyal to Chamberlain, Kennedy decided he would lead from the front.

On October 19, the American ambassador was the keynote speaker at the Trafalgar Day dinner of the Navy League commemorating the victory of Admiral Horatio Nelson against the combined French and Spanish fleets. It was a Pyrrhic victory that had cost Nelson his life and was always treated with great reverence. Joe Kennedy was the first American ambassador in history to be given this honor. Harvey Klemmer and Kennedy had spent ten days drafting his speech, but sent it to Hull only two days beforehand at six P.M. London time.* "He spent ten days on it and expected us to vet it in one," an exasperated Moffat wrote. "A large part of it is an endorsement of Chamberlain philosophy of government, but being expressly advanced as the Ambassador's personal views there was nothing to do but pass it" verbatim.[25]

LORD LLOYD OPENED the dinner's speeches by telling the distinguished audience that the recent mobilization of the navy as "the only effective argument [which] contributed to the conversations that took place on the other side of the Channel."[26] After the toast to Nelson, Kennedy rose,

---

* Harold Hinton had been sent home for repeated drunkenness.

toasted the Royal Navy and the Merchant Navy, then began jokingly
with what his wife—and mother of his nine children—would and would
not allow him to say. The "recent events would undoubtedly stimulate
the already frenzied race for arms," *The Times* reported. When Kennedy
gave a short, sharp blast against the "vicious circle of misdirected energy" of world rearmament, a discomfited hush descended on his naval
audience.

The nations of the world would have to get together, if they wanted
to maintain their standard of living, to reduce the arms burden on each
and every nation, Kennedy said. He advanced his own theory that "instead of hammering away at what are regarded as irreconcilables, they
[the democracies and the dictatorships] could advantageously bend their
energies toward solving their common problems by an attempt to re-
establish good relations on a world basis. . . . But there is simply no sense,"
Kennedy rambled on, "common or otherwise, in letting these differences
grow into unrelenting antagonisms. After all, we have to live together in
the same world, whether we like it or not."[27] The pro-Chamberlain and
semiofficial organ of government, *The Times,* made no comment other
than to present Kennedy's speech in full.

American newspaper reactions, however, varied. Some discounted taking "the utterances of our representatives too seriously," as in the *New
York Herald Tribune*; there was unalloyed outrage in the *New York Post*.[28]
Walter Lippmann's October 22 syndicated column headlined AMBAS-
SADOR KENNEDY ADVISED TO REFRAIN FROM SPEECHES was more scathing. "The professional career men, the men who spend their lives in
the foreign service, preserve the rule of silence except when specifically
instructed," Lippmann wrote. "The amateur and temporary diplomats
take their speeches very seriously. Ambassadors of this type soon tend to
become a little State Department with a little foreign policy of his own.
The Secretary of State back in Washington, can only groan and wring his
hands in the privacy of his office."[29]

Frank Kent's column in *The Wall Street Journal* was equally sardonic. He
credited his fellow columnist and sometime contributor to the Algon-
quin Round Table, Heywood Hale Broun, with the idea of "dropping
Mr. Kennedy in Boston harbor on his return, so that his Americanism

might be restored by resting awhile amid the alien tea." However, Kent finished his article with the insightful statement that the administration found Kennedy's publicity-seeking nature distasteful and that he had used his Trafalgar Day speech as an overt attempt to boost his presidential aspirations. Certainly, Kent concluded, it would be understandable if the White House was enjoying some ambassadorial floundering in the un-relenting hot water of press comment. Even Arthur Krock had to admit that "the speech has caused confusion in the minds of the public as to what our policy is."

And that was the point of the uproar. Kennedy, with his phony London state department of little foreign policy, forced Roosevelt to step in. "Peace by fear has no higher or more enduring quality than peace by the sword. . . . There can be no peace if national policy adopts as a delib-erate instrument the threat of war," Roosevelt declared. Political changes needed to be made by due process and with "due regard for the sanctity of treaties," the president added, taking a swipe at Chamberlain. "It means self-restraint to refuse strident ambitions which are sure to breed insecu-rity and intolerance."[30]

THE FUROR CONTINUED unabated for weeks. When it became pub-lic knowledge that Kennedy had been involved in the censorship of the Paramount newsreel, newspapers like the *Chicago Tribune* referred to America's ambassador as the "office boy of empire." Kennedy's blatant partisanship for Chamberlain underlined the impropriety of that rela-tionship. "The columnists are still writing about the Kennedy speech," Moffat wrote in his diary. "Dorothy Thompson calls names, Walter Lipp-mann says that however satisfactory career Ambassadors may be in certain lines, they are perhaps less of an evil than political Ambassadors who try to play individual roles instead of merely as members of the team."[31]

Despite the negative publicity, Kennedy had not given up on a pres-idential or vice-presidential future. To his mind, all he had set out in his Trafalgar Day speech merely reiterated his belief that war was bad for business. Free trade was the answer to the world's ills, even in fascist coun-tries. What Kennedy had failed to grasp was that Nazism traded in lives. Jews and political opponents were reduced to an unwanted commercial commodity, once they had escaped the Reich as paupers. There was no economic discussion to be had, nor was there any safe haven for Hitler's Jews. They had been robbed of their dignity, their families, and their possessions. Even so, for Joe Kennedy, the Jews still represented his best chance of becoming a presidential hopeful in 1940.

21

THE AMBASSADOR
AND THE JEWS

75% of the attacks made on me by mail were by Jews.

—JOSEPH P. KENNEDY TO TOM WHITE,
NOVEMBER 12, 1938

I n Washington, Moffat was made the scapegoat for failing to censor Kennedy's speech, but he noted in his diary, "In the long run, however, no one is going to be hurt unless it be Mr. Kennedy himself."[1]

On October 1—the day Germany took over the Sudeten territories—Jan Masaryk joined an after-dinner discussion with Chaim Weizmann, Baffy Dugdale, David Ben-Gurion, and a select group of others involved in the Zionist cause. Masaryk recounted the "black shame" of Munich and how Halifax had told him only four days before to mobilize and "For God's sake, do it quick!" While in Munich, according to Masaryk, Chamberlain was shown a "bogus record of telephone conversations between Jan and Beneš—plotting to bring down the present [British] Government!" Worse, the prime minister believed it. Those present concluded that "there can be no doubt that telephones are tapped, and people's movements watched, here in London." Masaryk blamed John Simon, then Chancellor of the Exchequer, as the man responsible for Britain's lack of preparedness. Simon was a "guilty man," who, for Masaryk, was even unworthy to "let my dog lift his leg in his left eye."[2]

Naturally, the discussion veered onto the issue of Palestine. Most worrying for Baffy, Weizmann, and Ben-Gurion was their renewed fear that the British government would give in to Arab pressure to sell "the Yishuv"—Jewish-owned lands in Palestine—to the Arabs. "The lesson of the Czechs reinforces the lesson to trust only ourselves," Baffy confided to her diary that evening.[3] If the British could abandon a strategic ally like Czechoslovakia, why not the Jews already in Palestine and those who wished to emigrate there? That same week, Malcolm MacDonald, the Dominions Secretary,* told Weizmann that he was "trying to stand firm under renewed pressure of Cabinet and Arab Kings. I [Baffy] said to Chaim we must listen to him, work with him, but never trust him, or one of them, ever again."[4]

It was against this background that Joe Kennedy launched himself into the tangled web of failed diplomacy, successful German propaganda, unrelenting hopes, and unmitigated political deceit surrounding the complex "Jewish Question" without fully appreciating its tortuous history or murderous future. Of course, he knew that the British Mandate in Palestine came about as a result of the defeat of the Ottoman Empire in the Great War. But Joe was not a man for detail.

THE BALFOUR DECLARATION, named after Britain's Foreign Secretary, Arthur Balfour, was made public on November 2, 1917, in the form of a letter to Lord Rothschild. It stated that the British government favored "the establishment in Palestine of a national home for the Jewish people" on the clear understanding that there was no disadvantage to "the civil and religious rights of existing non-Jewish communities in Palestine, or the rights and political status enjoyed by Jews in any other country." That principle became the eternal sticking point in all Jewish and Arab negotiations. Less than a month after the Balfour Declaration, Jerusalem was liberated by British troops, ending 673 years of Turkish rule.[5]

Although the declaration has since been considered a unilateral act,

---

* Malcolm John MacDonald was the second-born son of Prime Minister James Ramsay MacDonald and the first minister to advocate the Commonwealth as a desirable successor to the Empire. It was MacDonald, not Kennedy, who settled the British/Irish trade war and the annuity of the "treaty" ports in 1938.

the French government had also advocated "the renaissance of the Jewish nationality in that land from which the people of Israel were exiled so many centuries ago." President Woodrow Wilson and his administration also supported the Balfour Declaration. On July 24, 1922, the British pledge for a "Jewish National Home" was specifically included in the text of the League of Nations mandate, which called for the implementation of its terms and was agreed by all fifty-one member states.[6] When David Ben-Gurion testified to the Peel Commission* on January 7, 1937, he said that the Bible was the real Jewish Mandate and that the Balfour Declaration "is only the recognition of this right."[7]

Inventing his own statistics, Hitler distorted the scope of the Jewish Question to suit his racial policies. When he seized power on March 31, 1933, there were officially 503,000 Jews in Germany, making up 0.76 percent of the total population of over 68 million. A third lived in Berlin, and more than half of them had married outside the Jewish religion. Since 1871 (when Jewish integration into German society had begun in earnest by the formation of Reform Judaism), the Jewish population decreased from 1.05 percent to 0.76 percent by virtue of conversion to other religions. German Jews were overwhelmingly *not* Zionists and had no wish to "return" to Palestine.[8]

JOE KENNEDY WAS certainly aware that from the outset of Hitler's Third Reich, Jews faced racial persecution by the Aryan population.† By November 1938, the raft of anti-Semitic laws prohibiting Jews from owning or managing most businesses; working in the sciences or education; and participating in leisure activities—including sunbathing on any beach or pool or going to the movies or theater—accelerated the Aryanization of the economy. Not only were Jews deprived of their livelihood, but their bank accounts and other assets were used by the central bank of the German Reich. By 1939, Berlin's Jewish population fell by 50 percent

---

* The Peel Commission, formally called the Palestine Royal Commission, was convened in November 1936 to investigate the rising unrest and violence in Mandatory Palestine in the aftermath of the six-month Arab general strike from April to October that year. The conclusion was that the League of Nations mandate was unworkable, and it recommended partition.

† The term "Aryan" meaning the Nazis' mythic proto-Nordic race.

to 80,000 people. Berlin's total population in 1939 was an estimated 4.34 million people.[9]

Kennedy may not have known that the Nazi Party began to work with the small Zionist movement in Germany and Jews in Israel to "assist" Jewish emigration. Initially, a citrus-planting cooperative in Palestine called Hanotea applied to the Reich Ministry for the Economy for permission to transfer capital from Germany. When an emigrant from Germany arrived in Palestine, he "received an equivalent value in real estate," less whatever percentage the German government raked off the top. This became the model for the later Haavara negotiations and agreement.[10*]

But Haavara was imperfect, as it depended on the Reich's goodwill. Initially it cost 50 percent of the value of the emigrants' own capital employed as an exorbitant "flight tax." Soon enough the Reich's share grew to 100 percent, stopping the flow of legal German Jewish refugees.[11] Hitler shrugged his shoulders. If the Zionists would not pay for their Jews to immigrate, then who would?

Kennedy became aware that other methods of taking assets owned by Jews had been devised from downright thievery to the semblance of law by decree. We are "only paying these people back what they deserve," Hitler said. "When the German nation was, thanks to the inflation instigated and carried through by Jews, deprived of the entire savings which it had accumulated in years of honest work, when the rest of the world took away the German nation's foreign investments . . . the western democracies did nothing."[12] Hitler believed the Jews caused the Great War and the terrible hyperinflation of the early 1920s.

WHEN ROOSEVELT CALLED for the Évian Conference in March 1938, he had high hopes for success. Kennedy was not involved or consulted in the early phases of planning, despite his best efforts. That June, Joe sent a telegram full of thinly veiled disgruntlement claiming that the British would like to be informed precisely when and in "which building" the conference would take place in Geneva. Hull's terse reply said that the

* These agreements have led several notable and ill-informed anti-Semites to claim that "Hitler was a Zionist."

French were handling everything, and that if the British wanted to know more, they should contact them.[13]

Simply put, Jewish refugees were never in Kennedy's remit. And why should they be when he was noted for referring to Jews as "kikes" and "sheenies" and other ethnic slurs? This, combined with his self-aggrandizing publicity, certainly made Roosevelt wary of including him in any solution. Kennedy's only knowledge of Évian was conveyed in a general telegram sent to all American ambassadors stationed in participating countries. It set out the American definition for "all refugees from Germany": whether or not they had already left the country and irrespective of their religion. It established a system of documentation; set up a continuing body in a European capital to be designated; and prepared a resolution to carry out further work.[14] At the end of the day, the European capital selected for Évian's ongoing work was London.

Kennedy was right when he predicted that without the cooperation of the Third Reich, Évian was a conference without meaning. On the day after the conference opened, the German secretary of state, Ernst von Weizsäcker, sent a circular message to all ambassadors abroad advising them that "No country was prepared to receive the emigrating German Jews, particularly if they were without means. The question therefore arose whether the Reich Government was prepared to cooperate in the transfer of capital in Jewish hands." As far as the Reich was concerned, all Jewish money was "payback" for the evil Jews had inflicted on Germany. The British ambassador to the conference, Lord Winterton, was told that the Jewish Question "was an internal German problem that was not subject to discussion . . . a transfer of the capital accumulated by the Jews—especially after the [Great] war—could not be expected of Germany."[15]

Through a combination of objections from Latin American countries, based on threats of commercial reprisals against them by Germany, Évian, like the League of Nations, proved yet another watered-down and failed measure at collective diplomacy. The closing declaration drafted by Myron C. Taylor quoted the League of Nations resolution of May 14, 1938, on German (and Austrian) refugees, further defining who the refugees were: those forced to emigrate for political beliefs, racial origin, or religion.* The next meeting of the new Intergovernmental Committee would take place in London on August 3, 1938.[16] Kennedy was still at Cap d'Antibes when it convened.

In response to the publication of Mussolini's *Manifesto della razza* (Racial Manifesto) on July 14, Pope Pius XI nominally entered the fray, denouncing racism on July 30.† Mussolini's son-in-law and the foreign minister, Count Galeazzo Ciano, was asked to deal with the Vatican. "I summoned the Papal Nuncio and I warned him," Ciano wrote in his diary, "if they continue down this path, a clash is inevitable because the Duce considers the racial question to be fundamental" specifically with regard to the Amhara uprising in Abyssinia. "Tomorrow he [the Papal Nuncio] will confer with the Holy Father. I believe that it is better to act so as to avoid a crisis, but if the Church wants it, we shall not be the losers."[17]

ON HIS RETURN to London on August 29, Kennedy had hoped to become involved in the Jewish Question directly, only to find events in Czechoslovakia had overtaken him. Yet, ten years after his Trafalgar Day speech, Kennedy continued to blame the Jews for all his negative press in the fall of 1938. "There were a few, however, who willingly contemplated a course leading to war, and even hoped that it might occur. Among these were a number of Jewish publishers and writers....The tactic of this group may some day be analyzed."[18] Wishing to deflect attention from his own actions, Kennedy asserted that Jewish publishers and writers in America wanted war to help their fellow European Jews. Of the many journalists criticizing him, only Walter Lippmann was Jewish. Arthur Krock, his stalwart supporter and loyal servant, was also

---

* Taylor also wrote an outline of their economic and social adaptability, explaining how their acceptance would fit into the laws and future legislation of countries prepared to take them.

† There were only 44,000 Jews in Italy in a population of 44 million, many of whom had intermarried with Catholics. The Italian anti-Semitic laws mirrored the Nuremberg Race Laws of September 15, 1935. Jews were prohibited from being Italian citizens and it was illegal to educate a Jew. That said, the Italians did not believe the propaganda, and being Italian, many privately ignored the laws. For a fascinating portrait, read Primo Levi's autobiography, *The Periodic Table.*

Jewish. Diplomatically, Jack Kennedy, writing from Harvard, highlighted that the Trafalgar Day speech "seemed to be unpopular with the Jews etc. [it] was considered to be very good by everyone who wasn't bitterly anti-Fascist."[19]

That September, telegrams from George Rublee became increasingly frustrated. Chile had pulled out of any arrangement to take German Jews. Hull mistakenly persisted in believing that something could still be negotiated with the Third Reich. Myron Taylor searched for a way to capitalize on the "friendly" relationship between Chamberlain and Hitler, culminating in the president's personal message to Kennedy for Chamberlain on October 5.[20]

Chamberlain's reply to Roosevelt came two days later. "I hope as you do that it will prove possible to persuade the German Government to make a practical contribution [i.e., letting Jews leave with *some* assets] to the solution of the problem and I warmly welcome your suggestion that the first suitable opportunity should be taken of urging them to do so." While agreeing entirely with the president's message, Chamberlain hinted that it was up to Rublee's Intergovernmental Committee to pursue that avenue, not him.[21]

Rublee telephoned Welles and told him that only Kennedy held sway with the prime minister to make him take the matter seriously. Yet "my impression is that Ambassador Kennedy is not disposed to take a strong line," Rublee continued. "He feels that our undertaking is hopeless. He does not want to go out on it because he has other matters he considers more important. I don't think it's hopeless, but it is very difficult."[22]

Independently, Kennedy had been meeting representatives from the American Zionist community. Ben V. Cohen, an American Zionist leader, a New Deal lawyer, and one of the "Gold Dust Twins,"* visited in early October as an unofficial emissary of Justice Brandeis and Felix Frankfurter. Kennedy arranged for Cohen to meet with Dominions Secretary Malcolm MacDonald. Rose Gell Jacobs, an executive of the American Jewish Agency for Palestine, was another emissary. Kennedy started his

---

* Benjamin V. Cohen was an early New Dealer and was often paired with the other "Gold Dust Twin," Tommy Corcoran. Together with James M. Landis, they wrote the Securities Act of 1933, often referred to as the "truth in securities" law.

conversation with her saying that he had met with Chaim Weizmann on November 2.* This gave him the necessary credentials to expand on his personal viewpoint about the Jews. The only way through the impasse was to "negotiate a deal with Hitler" directly, he told Jacobs. He reiterated he was "ready to listen to any scheme that will work, as he has not yet come across any." Where Weizmann believed that Kennedy was an ally, Jacobs reported back he "was not fully in tune with Zionist aspirations." Kennedy revealed to Jacobs, too, that he had had prior knowledge that the British were not going to allow increased immigration to Palestine.[23]

In both instances, Kennedy was trying to cold-towel his anger at the American press and treat the Jewish refugee problem as a "deal-doing exercise." Despite his obvious shortcomings, Kennedy instinctively saw the specific sticking points. As distasteful as it was, without Hitler's agreement to allow Jews to exit with some assets *and* the British agreeing to increase Jewish immigration to Palestine, nothing would be resolved.

THEN THE UNEXPECTED happened. On November 7, an enraged young Polish Jew, Herschel Grynszpan, was pushed to the brink of reason when he discovered his parents were among the tens of thousands stuck in no-man's-land between Poland and Germany. His rage boiled over and he killed a junior German diplomat in Paris. In retaliation, Hitler unleashed his hounds of hell for Kristallnacht—the Night of Broken Glass—in the evening of November 9–10. Hitler's SA (*Sturmabteilung*, or paramilitary wing of the Nazi Party) and ordinary German citizens in the enlarged German Reich took part. It was a savage pogrom of all the physical edifices that housed Judaism.

Over a thousand synagogues were burned down, the Judaica within destroyed, pillaged, or turned into "state property." Shops and their contents were smashed and ransacked, and thousands of Jews were beaten.

---

* Oddly, this meeting is not recorded in the original of Kennedy's diary, but it is listed in his appointments for that date, implying that either the meeting was not important to him or that Kennedy wished to keep secret what was said. Also, Kennedy did not report the brief Jacobs meeting to the State Department. On November 7, he told Hull that Weizmann was meeting with MacDonald, and that the British "had been influenced months ago by pressure from the United States" not to curtail Jewish immigration to Palestine (*Source:* FRUS, 867N.01/1258 Telegram: Kennedy to Hull, November 7, 1938).

Although "only ninety-five people" were killed according to the German press, more than 30,000 Jews were arrested and herded into concentration camps. Over 7,500 stores had their shop fronts smashed. Lynching Jews on sight by the frenzied mobs was widely reported.[24]

Two days later, dozens of Nazi edicts required all Jewish businesses to be liquidated and their stocks, bonds, and precious metals to be "sold" to the Reich. These would be valued (for the equivalent of ten cents on the dollar) and go collectively to pay a $400,000 "atonement fine" to the government for the damage they had caused to the Reich. Fearful that the general population who had benefited from the looting would flood the market with their ill-gotten booty, a new ordinance to protect the value of Jewish property called the Order Concerning the Utilization of Jewish Assets was issued. The *Times* headline read A BLACK DAY FOR GERMANY, whereas the *Daily Telegraph* featured on its front page GERMAN MOBS' VENGEANCE ON JEWS.[25] No newspaper mentioned that it was the fifteenth anniversary of Hitler's failed beer hall putsch in Munich, and a national holiday on the Nazi calendar.

Kennedy was appalled. With each passing day, the German ambassador von Dirksen sent more and more ominous cables to Berlin. The world reaction was unanimous in its revulsion against Germany. The German ambassador to Washington, Hans-Heinrich Dieckhoff, sent a wire to Berlin: "Even the respectable patriotic circles which were thoroughly . . . anti-Semitic in their outlook also begin to turn away from us."[26] New York mayor Fiorello La Guardia posted an all-Jewish police detail to guard the German consulate against anti-Nazi rallies and bomb scares. Moffat in the State Department believed that "the wholesale confiscations, the atrocities, and the increasing attacks not only on Jews but on Catholics have aroused opinion here to a point where if something is not done there will be combustion. . . . The final decision was to order Hugh Wilson home [from Berlin] for 'report and consultation.'"[27] Wilson and the post of American ambassador was permanently withdrawn until 1945. Sir Nevile Henderson had withdrawn from Berlin the previous month for emergency surgery for throat cancer. He would return to his post in February 1939.[28]

CHAMBERLAIN WAS SLOW to recognize that this venal outburst of barbarism put appeasement and belief in anything Hitler said into the detritus of history. *The New York Times* printed an article on November 10 (before the full extent of the atrocities were known) that Chamberlain wanted "this government to be a go-getter for peace"—borrowing the Americanism from Kennedy, who was trying to put some backbone into the prime minister's infrequent public statements.

On Sunday, November 13, Joe, Rose, and Joe Jr. were invited to luncheon at Malcolm MacDonald's home in Essex. Kennedy "dominated the discussion by *putting forward his solution* to the Jewish Question. If Great Britain would take the lead in opening territory for Jewish resettlement, other nations would fall into line and the onus would be taken off the Chamberlain government for not opening up Palestine to Jewish refugees." Rose phrased Joe's comments differently: "Interesting discussions, especially one about the ultimate solution of the Jewish question about which there is constant agitation now. Joe feels that some countries, like Australia, for instance, might find a haven for them."[29] This was, of course, not an original thought, since Australia had already offered to take some five thousand Jews at the behest of George Rublee—back when they were still called "involuntary emigrants."

"Some concrete thing should be attempted instead of everyone deploring the conditions but nothing definite volunteered," Rose continued. Joe rammed his point home that Sunday by postulating that "if England put it up to each nation what they would do, then the responsibility would be theirs and not entirely hers [England's] in the disturbance in Palestine." He erroneously said, too, that "conditions had improved since Jews went to Palestine due to increase of money and capital brought there by them."[30]

Kennedy had forgotten his own advice that some deal needed to be done with Hitler. To MacDonald, he appeared shockingly ill informed about the financial realities, ignorant of the wider facts, and mischiefmaking. Since June 1938, the Reich had prohibited any emigrant's acquisition of *sperrmarks*—meaning Reichsmarks left behind by emigrants with the central bank of Germany. Even conversion of gold to *sperrmarks* resulted in the loss of 92 percent of the value to the emigrant. The Haavara system for emigration to Palestine had been better; but since February 1938, this, too, had become unviable. In any event, Haavara and all the other financial systems devised were intended to benefit the parlous foreign exchange status of Germany, not to help the Jews. Kennedy should have understood this. Besides, a telegram highlighting all these issues had been sent by Myron Taylor from the American embassy in London on August 15, 1938, while Joe Kennedy was on vacation.[31]

WHAT KENNEDY SAW in the Jewish refugee problem was simple: it presented *the* opportunity to resolve what he saw as essentially a financial matter; to burnish his credentials for the 1940 elections by keeping America out of any future war; and most important of all, to keep his sons safe.

The Kennedys' unfailing moral compass guides—the Catholic Church, Galeazzi, and Pacelli—remained silent about the growing humanitarian disaster. "Had Catholics protested, specifically, Kristallnacht and the rise of anti-Semitism," John Cornwell wrote in *Hitler's Pope* about Pacelli's lack of action in 1938, "the fate of the Jews in Nazi Germany and indeed throughout Europe might have been different."[32] With an additional population of 10 million ethnic Germans since March 1938, the greater Reich's Jewish population had also grown to nearly a million people. Myron Taylor's estimate that August that there were now 300,000 Jews at risk was woefully shy of the mark.[33]

So, without reference to the British or American administrations, Kennedy advised his friends in the American press that he had a plan. On November 15, Joe was portrayed as the modern-day savior of the Jews: headlines in dozens of papers across the United States and Canada ran hotly from BRITAIN COLD SHOULDERS and U.S. PLAN TO SAVE THE JEWS to EMPIRE AND AMERICAN NATIONS WILL BE ASKED TO JOIN "KENNEDY PLAN."[34] Taking its less sensational lead from the American press, *The Times* limply commented that it had understood that there were "conversations between the American Ambassador, Mr. Joseph Kennedy, and the British government on the subject of future action to afford relief to the Jews."[35]

Roosevelt sidestepped the furor, commenting he would say nothing about those conversations, but "that the refugee commission in London was still at work." Moffat noted "he [Kennedy] has never so much as reported a word to the President, the Secretary, or Mr. Rublee." This made the sub-headline from *The New York Times*, KENNEDY SHARES IN TALKS, look like a puff from Krock.[36]

On November 18, Clare Boothe Luce cabled Kennedy: YOU ARE A REMARKABLE FELLA BLESS YOU. LOVE CLARE.[37] It is no surprise, given Joe's relationship with her, that *Life*** embroidered Kennedy's efforts as *his* plan to resettle the Jews and that the plan was "already widely known as the 'Kennedy Plan.'" The article even went on to predict that if the "Kennedy Plan" was successful, "it will add new lustre to the reputation which may well carry Joseph Patrick Kennedy into the White House."[38]

The facts speak more softly, but truer, than the Kennedy hyperbole. After the Sunday lunch at Malcolm MacDonald's home, Kennedy went to see Halifax and MacDonald officially on Tuesday, November 15. Joe was at his fiery best, proclaiming that "the effect in the United States of the German Jewish policy was a violent reaction against 'appeasement,' and opinion in America was definitely less sympathetic to Great Britain." Halifax's Private Secretary, Oliver Harvey, wrote in his diary the same day that Halifax sharply chided Kennedy for presenting his own pet theories as U.S. policy, and wrote an official rebuke to Ambassador Lindsay in Washington that he was "at a loss to understand why American opinion should blame His Majesty's Government because the German Government persecuted the Jews, especially as the United States did not show much desire to do anything substantial."[39] After all, America, too, had vast open spaces.

"I told the Ambassador [Lindsay] that if Mr. Kennedy had any plan he had not reported it to us," Welles stated for the record. "This Government had not sent any instructions to Mr. Kennedy in the matter, nor had it instructed him to present any plan."[40] When Welles addressed the issue by telephone, Kennedy was unrepentant. Roosevelt and the State Department had seen the secret SIS documents which categorically judged the so-called Kennedy Plan as impractical.† The Nazis had no intentions

---

* Clare originally had the idea for the pictorial newsmagazine *Life* while working as an editor at *Vanity Fair*. She approached publisher Condé Nast about it, but he was in no financial position to launch another magazine. Her husband, Henry Luce, later took on the idea in 1936. It was an immediate financial success.

† The FBI was poorly equipped to handle its overseas role of collecting reliable intelligence in 1938. It did not even know that there were over seven hundred Nazi-backed organizations within the United States. The Office of Strategic Services (OSS), the precursor to the CIA,

whatsoever of letting the Jews emigrate when they were used as slave labor *and* their capital was employed for the Third Reich.

Despite Kennedy's unwanted and unnecessary intervention, it had been decided in the Monday, November 14, cabinet meeting—the day before the Kennedy articles appeared in the press—that "owing to the Jewish persecutions it was no good trying to attempt further progress with the Munich settlement and any question of making an offer of colonies must be set aside." Halifax along with MacDonald pushed through the motion "to try and produce a large-scale and impressive plan for settlement" of the Jews. "British Guiana is now suggested as possibly able to take 10,000, and the rest of the Colonies and Dominions are being approached."[41]

Halifax shared the SIS reports in committee. These showed that the "Nazi hotheads" were in the ascendant and that "Hitler himself attaches less importance to an agreement with Great Britain. . . . Indeed, Hitler was angry with Great Britain because P.M. was getting the credit and not himself [for Munich agreement]." At that same cabinet meeting, it was decided that Halifax and Chamberlain should go to Italy to try to improve relations with Mussolini, and thereby weaken the Axis, during the second week of January 1939. Halifax strongly urged a National Register to initiate a draft, but Chamberlain remained dead set against it.

The formulation of the revised British plan had taken place at the behest of a reenergized Halifax, and certainly not by Kennedy's influence on Chamberlain. Nor was there ever a real "Kennedy Plan." Whatever plans existed, these had been devised by others—in some cases, over a period of many years—and they were appropriated by Kennedy and publicized through his relationship with the press. Taken together with Kennedy's role in the censorship of the Paramount newsreel, there were a growing number of people in London, including Halifax, who began to share Roosevelt's view that Joseph P. Kennedy was indeed "a dangerous man."

---

did not exist as yet. Roosevelt only tapped Major General "Wild Bill" Donovan on the shoulder in the summer of 1941 to begin "officially" gathering American intelligence.

22

A WELTER OF RUFFLED FEATHERS

Men rise from one ambition to another: first they seek to
secure themselves from attack, then they attack others.

—NICCOLÒ MACHIAVELLI

That November, during the tortuous discussions about the Jews, another long-standing debate was suddenly settled: the Anglo-American trade agreement. "After careful consideration, I have decided, with the President's approval, to accept the pending British offers (slightly modified in several respects) and to proceed forthwith to the signature of the trade agreement," Hull informed Kennedy out of the blue on November 3.[1]

Instead of being happy to have this administrative burden lifted from his shoulders, Kennedy objected through the press. He had been expressly cut out of the final round of negotiations. "Joe has always been lukewarm toward the treaty," Drew Pearson wrote in the "Washington Merry-Go-Round" column of October 31. "Joe frequently wired the State Department . . . for details. But the State Department never obliged."[2]

Apparently, Kennedy phoned Welles in a flap, too, but there is no record of their conversation.[3] The Reciprocal Trade Agreement was signed in Washington on November 17. Given Kennedy's other gaffes, it was a much-needed boost to Anglo-American relations. On a personal level, however, the fact remained that Kennedy had not negotiated the trade deal—the raison d'être for his becoming ambassador. Then, too, he had arrived too late to make a significant impact to the British Film Act. Since the outset, he had rubbed the State Department the wrong way. Kennedy, of course, realized he had been sidelined. So why didn't he quit for "personal reasons," as he had done twice in the past?

Joe Jr. encapsulated his father's reasons beautifully. "After ten months of carrying out his ambassadorial duties, Dad is rather tired of his work," Joe Jr. noted with more than a hint of understatement on December 10. "He claims that he would give it up in a minute if it wasn't for the benefits that Jack and I are getting out of it and the things Eunice will get when she comes out next Spring. He doesn't like the idea of taking orders and working for hours trying to keep things out of his speeches. . . . He also doesn't like the idea of sitting back and letting the Jewish columnists in America kick his head off." The loyal eldest son, now aged twenty-three, backed his father to the hilt: "The papers have made up a pile of lies about him, and he can't do anything about it but he claims that he is going to let a few blasts when he gets back there in a couple of days."[4]

ON NOVEMBER 29, Sumner Welles announced that Kennedy was returning to the United States on leave for the Christmas holidays. The "Washington Merry-Go-Round" headline of December 8, however, told a different story: JOE KENNEDY RETURNING TO MEND POLITICAL FENCES, BUTTER UP THE PRESS; NOT ASKED TO COME; CRITICISM HURTS HIS AIM FOR 1940 VICE-PRESIDENCY. "What he is secretly after is the 1940 nomination for Vice President," Pearson wrote in the story as a stand-in for Kennedy. "Joe has had a number of jolts lately. . . . One American correspondent quoted Joe as complaining, 'I wish Roosevelt had as much confidence in me as Neville Chamberlain.' [. . . .] The recent barrage of brickbats has greatly disturbed him. They could scuttle his vice presidential aspirations just as completely as his friend Chamberlain sunk the trusting Czechs."[5]

There is little doubt that the "Washington Merry-Go-Round" article held considerable sway with the White House, even when others clamored for Kennedy to be replaced for his censoring the Paramount newsreel and backing the "yellow" Chamberlain government.[6] But when Arthur Krock wrote his editorial in defense of Joe for *The New York*

Times, A DAY IN COURT FOR AMBASSADOR KENNEDY, Roosevelt was left in no doubt that he should keep Kennedy in London as long as possible in the run-up to the 1940 presidential election.

Krock's article was a fierce defense of his paymaster and friend, setting out that "the criticisms and attacks began some weeks ago, and they have multiplied and proliferated." Sources close to leading New Dealers were mounting an effective "campaign" against Kennedy. "They know well when they offer 'inside information' to a newspaperman that he, because of their intimacy with the White House, is under reasonable compulsion to assume that the information is correct."[7] Kennedy planned to return on the *Queen Mary* on Saturday, December 10, with Joe Jr. for a two-month leave, and the best advice Krock gave him privately was to take the bad press like others before him. A week was, and is, a long time in politics.

Nonetheless, if fence-mending had been his priority, Kennedy should have admitted his mistakes. Instead, he marched into the State Department with a report he had *his people* in London complete to prove the rightness of his position. In his cover letter to Roosevelt, Kennedy called the document "merely the viewpoint of one of the half dozen people whom I have working on this situation." The ten-page memorandum dissected the entire world situation as these people saw it by answering one question: "What would be the effect on the United States of the decline or collapse of the British Empire?"[8]

Kennedy concluded that if the British were defeated in a general war, the enemy would demand the transfer of all military assets, including bases, as well as all dominions and colonies. The transfer of control of the seas would lead to the rise of Germany, Italy, and Japan to the detriment of the United States. Loss of the British Navy would put the entire onus of defense of the Pacific on America and would close the Mediterranean to trade routes. In that event, the United States could survive only if it became "Fortress America," with its boundaries extending "1,000 miles from her shores," and stayed out of the conflict.

To avoid anarchy, there would need to be an integration of the European states "through the dominating influence of one or more of the great powers," and through this method, a "decent level of living" and peace could be perpetuated. Kennedy pointed to the Third Reich as the ascendant model: "It is, in fact, taking place in the latter form through the predominance of the Third Reich to-day. It may be fatal to France and England alone. But it would not be fatal to a democratic world united in self-defence."[9]

There was nothing original in Kennedy's premise that the European states should become more integrated. Collective security and the foundering League of Nations had attempted to do that for nearly twenty years. Holding up the Third Reich as an exemplar of this newfound integration was a gross distortion of the facts and wishes of most Europeans. What Kennedy, among many others, failed to see was that fascism was not a vaccine against communism; that appeasement was a bankrupt policy; and most important, that responding to force with force was the only way democracies could maintain the way of life they had come to cherish.

JUST BEFORE JOE left for home, he wrote a letter to Enrico Galeazzi, revealing that "I may decide to remain there."[10] Evidently, Kennedy felt Galeazzi was utterly trustworthy in sharing his half-formed thoughts on paper. It is thought-provoking that both Galeazzi and Pacelli had remained publicly silent on the Jewish Question throughout the autumn and winter of 1938/1939, too. Pacelli, as the secretary of state of the Holy See, had made no official statement about Kristallnacht; even though he controlled the Vatican press, *L'Osservatore Romano*, and held considerable influence over the notoriously anti-Semitic *Civiltà Cattolica*.[11]

And yet, "It is impossible for Christians," Pope Pius XI said with tears in his eyes in the autumn of 1938, to participate in anti-Semitism. "We recognize that everyone has the right to self-defense and may take the necessary means for protecting legitimate interests," the pontiff added, referring to Germany. "But anti-Semitism is inadmissible. Spiritually, we are all Semites."[12] From all appearances, there was a divergence of thought between Pius XI and Pacelli.

IN LONDON, ROSE was shopping for the family skiing trip at St. Moritz at Lillywhites on Piccadilly Circus. Jean and Patricia joined her in town, even though the school holidays had not begun. While Paris haute couture salons were more to Rose's taste, nothing beat London's top retailer in sporting goods for kitting out a large family for Switzerland. She was quite amazed at how ice skates had evolved into a fine art form, where you chose the shoe "in certain color, quality and then skates of a certain quality were attached."

Rose visited Rosemary the following day "at her convent where she is studying kindergarten work." No other remark about her eldest daughter was made, which speaks volumes. Before Rose could shop for Eunice, she came down with a bad cold and took to her bed "for the first time" in her life. After all, she had to be on her best mettle to be surrounded by seven of her children without Joe over the Christmas holidays. Missing church and feeling low, Rose telephoned her parents for a short three-minute ($15) conversation, where she told them about their plans and mentioned that Joe was leaving early for Florida, so that she could go to Egypt in March as she wished. She had to be circumspect in what she said, "as people listen in," and Joe was adamant no one should know when he was returning stateside.[13]

By the time Kennedy and Joe Jr. traveled to Plymouth on December 6 to speak at the annual dinner of the Plymouth Chamber of Commerce and the Plymouth and Devonport Mercantile Associations at the request of Nancy Astor, Rose had mostly recovered. Although Nancy "pretended that Dad and she were only friends for the evening," Joe Jr. wrote, "she [Nancy] ballyhooed the press, spoke indirectly about letting Jews in, and really got away with wholesale murder."[14]

Unabashed, Joe stood before the assembled audience and said, "We should doubtless solve our difficulties if we did not cry ourselves into a belief that all was lost." It seemed to Kennedy that the majority of the problems facing the world had roots in worsening economic conditions. Political means were now required to solve economic hardships of the past. "We are faced today with a grave responsibility. There is no doubt about that. It will require everything we have of courage and resourcefulness if disaster is to be diverted," Joe warned. "Even so we may not be able to avert catastrophe."[15]

AFTER KENNEDY SAILED, a British aeronautic expert, Sir Roy Fedden, Chief Engineer at the Bristol Aeroplane Company, had been invited for his sixth visit in six years to the Lilienthal-Gesellschaft 1938 conference in Germany. Fedden reported to the government adviser, Tom Jones, afterward how impressed he was with the "size and organisation of the aircraft factories" but also "with the training schemes for the young. The quality of workmanship of the boys of 14 was astounding," Jones wrote in his diary. "They were fitted to render first-aid to damaged aeroplanes." When Jones told Chamberlain, begging him to invite Fedden to Down-ing Street straightaway, the prime minister gave a wave of the hand and told Jones to "send him to Kingsley Wood," the Secretary of State for Air. Jones was outraged. "L.G. [Lloyd George] would have pressed a but-ton and had Fedden to breakfast tomorrow morning if not to tea that afternoon. . . . Neville, said L.G. once, has a retail mind in a wholesale business."[16]

Many parliamentarians were in the doldrums that December and felt the sting of Kennedy's attack on British "defeatists," as he decried at Plymouth. "All that they could do was die grandly after having lived fee-bly," Robert Bernays MP wrote to his sister, equating the feeble British leadership to the French aristocracy at the time of the French Revolu-tion. Bernays had made a speech back in 1934 demanding support for all measures on rearmament to boost national safety. Five years on, he felt everyone was to blame, but most of all Baldwin. Eden, for all his fine oratory, never admitted publicly "even to himself that a strong foreign policy must mean strong armaments."[17] Nearly three months after Munich, Chamberlain had done little to prepare the nation for what most saw as an inevitable war.

There was a great deal to be pessimistic about. "With every month that passed, from 1938 onwards, the German Army not only increased in numbers and formations and in the accumulation of reserves, but in quality and maturity," Churchill wrote. "The advance in training and general proficiency kept pace with the ever-augmenting equipment." In fact, the Germans had done most of the expansion of its air force before the war would begin, where the British were only just launching the replacement of the old Gladiator biplane fighters from the Great War with the workhorse fighters of the future, Hurricanes and later Spitfires. In December 1938, there were only five squadrons of Hurricanes. The lack of tried and tested air pilots made the "Munich Winter," as Churchill called it, bleak.[18]

IN WASHINGTON, KENNEDY'S discussions were brief. FDR agreed to meet Joe, but the meeting had no small talk, no drinks, no meal. Roosevelt was on his best behavior, swallowing hard as he listened to Kennedy sound off about how he had been poorly treated. How dare the president not defend his ambassador to the press? Kennedy fulminated. Why hadn't he been consulted on matters of primary importance to his position? he asked rhetorically. Roosevelt usually avoided these types of confrontations; however, he had been quite prepared for this one. FDR donned the persona of the charmer and oozed charisma. Joe was doing a fine job in London, he just needed to smooth egos at the State Department and all would be good. No one had dared mention anything smacking of a recall to him. Resignation? Why in the world would Kennedy want to resign? Joe was playing an historic role and he was the president's chosen man in London.

Placated, Kennedy left for New York to join Jack, who had decided to take the next semester off to serve as his father's private secretary in London.* Joe spent a night at the opera, then flew to Palm Beach with Jack for the next six weeks. Jack and Joe Jr. had friends to stay, while their father had, at various stages, David Sarnoff, Boake Carter, Walter Winchell, Arthur Houghton, and London Jack. It was a "chums" dream holiday, cossetted by Kennedy money, booze, food (just how Joe liked it) in the Kennedy compound, and playing golf at the Palm Beach Country Club.

The only bright spot for the British that December was Anthony Eden's charm offensive in the United States. Set up and encouraged by Joe Kennedy, Eden accepted the invitation from the National Association of Manufacturers to address their annual conference on December 9 to help deflect the increase in anti-British sentiment. And so, Eden sailed to New York on the *Aquitania* with a case of champagne, courtesy of Joe. With his Hollywood good looks and British charm, Eden was hailed by the hyperbolic American press as "Prince Charming. He is St. George

---

* As with Joe Jr., the role of private secretary filled by Jack was not sanctioned by the State Department. Neither son was on the U.S. government payroll.

fighting the dragons. . . . He can stand up till the last round and come back after a knockout. He is an Englishman."[19]

IN ROOSEVELT'S STATE of the Union message on January 4, 1939, he told the Senate and House of Representatives that while war had been averted in Europe, "peace had not been assured." On many occasions in the past, he had reminded Congress of the many disturbances abroad "and the need to put our own house in order in the face of storm signals from across the seas. . . . All about us rage undeclared wars—military and economic. All about us grow more deadly armaments—military and economic. All about us are threats of new aggression—military and economic. . . .

"There comes a time in the affairs of men when they must be prepared to defend, not their homes alone, but the tenets of faith and humanity on which their churches, their governments and their very civilization are founded. . . . At the very least, we should avoid any action, or lack of action, which will assist, encourage and build up an aggressor," Roosevelt warned. The American neutrality laws flew in the face of common sense, worked unevenly and unfairly, denying help to the victims of aggression.[20] Roosevelt's speech made Kennedy's continued stance for appeasement, while remaining *his* ambassador, patently incongruous. Yet Kennedy remained.

On January 10, 1939, both Kennedy and Bullitt were summoned to appear before the House and Senate military committees. Each described the European situation as "dismal" and "utterly chaotic." Each painted such a grim picture that some skeptics listening thought they should rethink their stance on American defenses. Kennedy told them, too, that in the event Great Britain should enter into a declared war with Germany, it would be defeated, and the loss of its navy would endanger America.[21] Both ambassadors testified in private, without direct newspaper access.

The "Lindbergh Report," with which both ambassadors were well acquainted, formed part of their testimonies, too. As they gave evidence, Roosevelt was working with his military advisers on a national defense message to Capitol Hill, for what many expected to be "one of the monumental defense papers in American history calling for the greatest peacetime array of armed might in the history of the country, answering the challenge thrown down to democracies by totalitarian states."[22] Roosevelt wanted a minimum defense budget of $552 million.

Somehow Kennedy's testimony was leaked to *The New York Times,* predicting that the Chamberlain government might pacify Hitler with the offer to permit Germany to build military bases in Canada. An official denial from Joe was swift in counteracting the "baseless" rumor: "I never said anything that could possibly be interpreted in such a way."[23]

IN LONDON, THE Foreign Office discovered that Chamberlain was "keeping a side line out to the dictators" by "working behind the Foreign Secretary's back." In fact, Chamberlain had been acting peculiarly toward Halifax since mid-October. The Governor of the Bank of England, Montagu Norman, was encouraged by the prime minister to go see the Reichsbank president, Hjalmar Schacht, in Berlin. When Halifax remonstrated, Norman stormed into the Foreign Office in a rage, claiming he was not going there for his pleasure, but to discuss a plan for helping "German credit and imports in connection with Jewish expatriation."[24] Less than three weeks later, Schacht was summarily fired and replaced by the economics minister, Walther Funk.* There had been other revelations, too. Chamberlain was in contact with the German press agency without telling Halifax. The prime minister's speech to the Foreign Press Association mid-December lacked backbone, and when Halifax inserted a paragraph, Chamberlain took it out for fear it "would give offence in Rome."

Undeniably, their forthcoming visit to Rome on January 10 had many worried. Halifax told the cabinet that "our main principle should be 'nothing for nothing'. We should make no concession to Signor Mussolini unless he would help us to obtain the détente which it is our policy to obtain." Chamberlain's ambitions were to persuade Mussolini to

---

* Schacht had been minister of economics and president of the Reichsbank until 1937, when he resigned at his own and Göring's request. He was fired as president of the Reichsbank on January 20, 1939. His "plan" for Jewish emigration came about as a result of his unalloyed criticism of Kristallnacht. Schacht was acquitted at Nuremberg in 1946 for crimes against humanity. Funk was found guilty at Nuremberg on three counts and became known as "The Banker of Gold Teeth," referring to the gold teeth extracted from concentration camp victims, euphemistically called "non-monetary gold."

"prevent Herr Hitler from carrying out some 'mad dog' act."[25] At the end of the day, neither wish was fulfilled. Mussolini and Ciano were adamant that they were delighted to be in the German camp. They boasted that Franco would soon be in control of Spain. The king of Italy and Pope Pius XI met Chamberlain and Halifax, too, but they offered no solutions. One of the most incongruous photo opportunities of their visit showed Mussolini and Ciano dressed as gold-braided men of war, with their heavily brocaded hats dwarfed by black-coated British ministers towering over them "like a couple of undertakers' mutes."[26]

On his return home, Chamberlain told Herschel Johnson that he would welcome Joe Kennedy's early return. Roosevelt was informed and summoned Kennedy to the White House on February 9, cutting his vacation short by two weeks. After Kennedy berated the president again for the treatment meted out to him, a certain bonhomie returned, with both men taking potshots at Bernard Baruch. Roosevelt once again good-naturedly assured Joe that he had his every confidence. Hull reconciled his feelings by believing that with Kennedy's return, at least they should know what Chamberlain was thinking.

23

A CORONATION TO REMEMBER

---

*This is the first time that the head of the British Government
has submitted to a foreign Government the outlines of one of
his speeches. It's a bad sign for them.*

—CIANO'S *DIARY*

Roosevelt sent Kennedy back to London due to disclosures made to the Foreign Policy Committee of the British Cabinet on January 26, 1939. The top secret information was forwarded to Roosevelt on February 7, revealing Germany was planning an attack in the west. Holland was considered the most likely avenue, since it would be impossible for the British to prevent the Netherlands from being overrun. Such an assault, all but Chamberlain agreed, must be regarded as a direct challenge on Britain and a casus belli. The French, too, had received similar information through their intelligence network, although it had not detected troop movements.[1]

On Kennedy's return, many insiders noted that there was a resurgence in Chamberlain's appeasement rhetoric. While Joe appeared to make a fresh start as "the president's ambassador" and energetically visited as many British government representatives and foreign ambassadors as possible, he remained, by dint of his character and outlook, incapable of change.

Nevertheless, Kennedy was shocked to see that Chamberlain was out of touch with European affairs. Barcelona had fallen to Franco late in

January, and the Spanish Popular Front government wanted to negotiate against reprisals if it surrendered. Yet at Kennedy's dinner with Chamberlain, the prime minister was unconcerned, telling Joe he did not believe the intelligence received about a strike in the west and that he placed no significance on abnormal troop movements in Italy.[2] Like Kennedy, Chamberlain was infected with an "insidious conviction" that only *he* saw the future clearly. On February 19, Chamberlain wrote: "With the thrush singing in the garden, the sun shining, and the rooks beginning to discuss among themselves the prospects of the coming nesting season . . . All information I get seems to point in the direction of peace."[3]

Sumner Welles wondered if the prime minister was deluded and felt obliged to ask Ambassador Lindsay point-blank if Chamberlain was "all right." Lindsay diplomatically responded that while the prime minister was a logical and clear thinker, he was not one to muddle his thinking with "the imponderables of the human factor." Then Lindsay confided that increasingly the Foreign Office was on tenterhooks. But he did not tell Welles that Halifax's permanent secretary, Oliver Harvey, had already begun to canvass MPs to see if they would support a Halifax leadership challenge.* Eden was "in" and Churchill "is well pleased with H but does not trust the PM," Harvey noted in his diary. Winston added that he was quite dissatisfied with the ARP (Air Raid Precautions), and that he feared "that Mussolini may precipitate a crisis and that Bonnet [French foreign minister] may run away."[4]

That February, Kennedy wrote a lengthy memo to Roosevelt on the European situation. It is a peculiar document. The first two paragraphs read more as if they were written by his historian son, Jack. It continually puts Britain into an historical perspective. It also stressed Lindbergh's line that the Empire had lost its preeminent position due to the advent of aviation, then asks: "Can the United States afford to run the risk of seeing Britain and France defeated by the totalitarian regimes?"

Command of the sea no longer counted with the advent of aviation and fighter planes, just as the Victorian cousinhood—all those royal,

---

* In the UK, the prime minister is the "first among equals," meaning that the office is held by the leader of the political party in power. A successful leadership challenge would mean the new party leader would become prime minister.

ruling foreign descendants of Queen Victoria—belonged to the past. The "Pax Britannica" of 1814–1914 was over. Kennedy's memorandum, like others beforehand and many to follow, was defeatist. His message was that the United States should become "a regimented industrial order under Government control." This American Fascist State would remain "free" and "competitive" in world markets. To defeat fascism, America "would have to adopt totalitarian methods. . . . America, alone in a jealous and hostile world, would find that the effort and cost of maintaining 'splendid isolation' would be such as to bring about the destruction of all those values which the isolation policy has been designed to preserve." Kennedy's implicit solution was to come to an accommodation with the dictators before the United States found itself without options.[5] Although Roosevelt never replied directly to Kennedy's memorandum, he was more than happy to use its terrifying estimates of German military strength. So, he confidentially disseminated these to the military chiefs to help boost the looming defense budget appropriations.

WHILE KENNEDY WAS still in Washington, Pius XI died after a long illness.* Two weeks later, Kennedy wrote to Galeazzi from London, thanking him for the medal he'd sent, commemorating the seventeenth year of Pius XI's pontificate. Although Joe professed to be in "great shock" at the pope's death, "I was concerned about the future of our friend. I talked with the president about it before I left, and it was his sincere hope that great honor would come to him."[6] Whether this was more Kennedyiana or not, such a letter from the American ambassador would wield significant influence in the right hands at the Vatican. "When the new pope is elected, and the ceremonies take place," Joe added, "I'm going to try to find some reason to be sent to Rome."[7]

Intriguingly, given Kennedy's well-publicized interest in the Jewish Question and close relationship with Galeazzi, he did not know that Pius XI had commissioned a new encyclical on anti-Semitism entitled *Humani generis unitas* (*On the Unity of the Human Race*). The document was a thorough condemnation of the state-sponsored German terror against the Jews. Though it existed only in first draft form before Pius XI

* Pius XI died on February 10, 1939.

died, at some point prior to the conclave to elect the new pontiff, Pacelli quashed it.[8]* In a recently discovered version, the draft encyclical defends the Catholic Church against charges of anti-Semitism. The document's tortuous argument defends the Church from becoming embroiled in the "purely man-made" political debate that would compromise "Christian principles and humanity." The Church's primary function was in "upholding her legacy of Truth. . . . The purely worldly problems, in which the Jewish people may see themselves involved, are of no interest to her."[9]

THE PAPAL CONCLAVE was called for Wednesday, March 1, and all sixty-two cardinals were present. Cardinal Eugenio Pacelli was nominated pope on the third ballot the next day. Joe telephoned the president the following Sunday to ask if he could go to the coronation. Roosevelt replied, "Yes, by all means." Seemingly, FDR toyed with Joe, saying he was thinking of naming Phillips, what did Joe think? That said, William Phillips, American ambassador to Italy stationed in Rome, had reminded the State Department and the president earlier that it would be undiplomatic if they sent a temporal ambassador (meaning him) to the religious Vatican ceremony.[10] Then the president deftly slipped into the conversation, "After 1940, I am going to look at the performance instead of acting in the play." Joe then lobbied Sumner Welles to become the official representative to the coronation, and the president confirmed his approval. Kennedy wired in reply: "Dear Sumner, I can't tell you how much I appreciate your kindness. If I have one real virtue, I never forget."[11]

ON MARCH 7, Kennedy received the telegram confirming his request had been granted. No president had ever sent a representative to the Vatican for a papal coronation. Naming Kennedy as the president's "personal representative" killed the proverbial two birds with one shot: not only was it a high honor for Kennedy, but it was also a reminder to Pacelli, soon to be crowned Pope Pius XII, of their fireside chat and the hand of friendship that the president had extended in 1936.

---

* Pius XI commissioned three different experts to write the encyclical on his behalf. The only known surviving copy of the "lost encyclical" was discovered (in French) around the turn of the twenty-first century.

Galeazzi would follow the new pope upward as his main "keeper of secrets." Henceforth, Kennedy would view himself, rightly or wrongly, as the primary liaison between the Vatican and the White House. Without a thought to protocol, Kennedy wired Phillips that he would be bringing the whole family—including governesses Elizabeth Dunn and Luella Hennessey, and let's not forget Arthur Houghton, Mary and Eddie Moore, and Joe's butler, Stephens. Then he sent word to Rose, who was on holiday in Egypt, to join them in Rome.[12] It never occurred to him that seats for the coronation were at a premium, or that he should have asked the Vatican if he could attend with sixteen others to avoid logistical problems. Hull knew better than to take things for granted, specifically cabling: "Transportation and per diem for yourself only authorized from London to Rome and return subject to Travel Regulations as well as per diem of $6.00 while in Rome. Travel by air if you desire is authorized."[13]

BEFORE LEAVING, KENNEDY received a note from the Irish legation to the Holy See to attend a dinner on March 12, where the Irish prime minister, Éamon de Valera, would be present. Kennedy did not accept immediately, saying he would have to advise them after his arrival. Perhaps he had hoped for a private dinner with the new pope, or at least, Galeazzi?

Joe and Jack flew from Croydon Airport on the southern outskirts of London to Paris on the morning of March 11. There they joined the remaining seven children and their entourage, traveling on to Italy by the Rome express train. In Rome, the family met up with Rose. Only Joe Jr. did not attend, as he had gone to Spain after his skiing holiday to report back on the conclusion of the war and Franco's ultimate victory. Soon after the family were reunited, they heard Joe Jr. was safe at the American embassy in Madrid.[14]

The most beautiful weather shone on Coronation Day, Sunday, March 12. The Kennedys awoke at dawn to prepare for the day ahead. Crowds had been gathering in St. Peter's Square since four A.M., and an estimated 400,000 souls were expected. The children and their chaperones traveled in three separate cars: Rose and Joe drove with Count Galeazzi, who would be their personal escort. No car was permitted to enter the square, so the Kennedys were ushered in on foot by Galeazzi, who then ensured that they were seen to their seats.

Of course, accommodations had been made for two Kennedys—Joe and Rose—but now there were eight children and five extras.* When Count Ciano and his Countess, Mussolini's daughter Edda, entered, they found that the Count's seat was occupied by a junior Kennedy. Unaware that they were being observed by the future pope Paul VI, Ciano verbally threw his toys out of his crib, waving his arms and threatening "to leave the Basilica and to desert the ceremony." Of course, the situation was immediately resolved, "but there remained in our memory the procession of the children of Ambassador Kennedy," Paul VI recalled, perhaps with a mirthful glint in his eye.[15]

Joe and Rose sat in the front row, "next to De Valera. Rose, De Valera and I talked all the time, principal subject England should permit Northern Ireland come in with Southern and, if necessary, let them all return their privileges. I never understood this but I could see he was whipping himself into his campaign for U.S." Evidently Joe had decided to ignore the friendly warning from James F. Byrnes: "DON'T OVERDO ENTIRE WORLD OBSERVING."[16]

As the mass followed its centuries-old traditions, all the Kennedys were overawed by the splendor of the occasion and the ceremony. They were accorded places of extreme privilege—directly opposite the pope's throne while mass was said. "Here we heard that Ciano was mad because England's representative [Duke of Norfolk] was ahead of him in Procession. Said 'Italy' was insulted. After watching him march through the church giving Fascist salute and bowing and smiling, I was convinced he was a swell-headed Muggo," Joe said. Cardinal O'Connell overheard Kennedy's remark and muttered, "Oh, will Joe ever learn?" After mass, the Kennedy contingent proceeded onto the balcony overlooking the devoted multitude, just "to the Pope's left as he faced the crowd and then saw him crowned." The entire ceremony took six hours, and Joe "never tired."[17]

---

* Arthur Houghton, Eddie and Mary Moore, Elizabeth Dunn, and Luella Hennessey. Presumably, the butler Stephens did not attend. Rose's French maid would have a separate audience with the new pope the next day. Franklin Gowen, second secretary at the U.S. embassy in London, was present, too.

The next day at 11:30 A.M. the entourage (including Rose's French maid) had a private audience with the new pope. Taken through the maze of rooms with the guards at attention, they arrived in the papal anteroom just as the Duke of Norfolk, Sir Bernard Marmaduke Fitzalan-Howard, came out. The children were laden down with packages and had their arms full of all manner of holy objects for Pius XII to bless. Galeazzi and Kennedy entered together first, without the family, and Joe wrote how "the Pope 'rejoiced' that President had sent me to Rome," recalling all those wonderful times back in 1936. They talked about recognition by the U.S. government of the Vatican by sending an ambassador. When Kennedy told the pope that his own Catholic "hierarchy were against it [including Cardinal O'Connell] because I thought they were afraid they would lose power" in their diocese, Pius XII disagreed.* The new pope gave Rose a larch box with a rosary in it, blessing her. "He talked to her so much and so kindly and intimately I thought she would faint."[18]

Jack Kennedy slid back into the comfortable anonymity of his large family, but couldn't resist writing to his friend, Lem Billings, that "Pacelli is now riding high, so it's good you bowed and grovelled like you did when you met him." He also divulged that his father had been offered the title of papal duke, which "will be hereditary and go to all of his family which will make me Duke John of Bronxville and perhaps if you suck around sufficiently I might knight you. However," Jack revealed with a sigh, "he's not going to accept it."[19]

Jack's jokiness was sheer bravado. The entire Kennedy family were swept away, utterly breathless with emotion as eyewitnesses to Catholic history, as Joe's press release to the Associated Press on March 13 shows: "A day overwhelming in its memory, in its significance, in its universal appeal," it began. "It seems to us no longer the figure of a man but a godlike figure with lips moving in prayer and the fragile hand blessing all men. We felt here was one to whom the world could turn for sublime spirituality, for undaunted courage and for justice to all men." That same day, the German ambassador to the Holy See cabled Ribbentrop that Pius

---

* Kennedy had been warned not to trust anyone in Rome, and both Cardinals O'Connell and Hinsley cautioned him against sending an ambassador (denoting political recognition) to the Vatican. The ambassador revealed their confidences to Pius XII.

XII's letter announcing his election "reveals the hand of the Pope as . . . expressly reserving the treatment of German questions for himself."[20]

WHILE JOE ATTENDED a reception at Castel Gandolfo, the papal summer palace, Halifax was informed that Slovakia had declared herself independent—with German support—from the Czechs. The Czech minister of foreign affairs was on his way to see Hitler, and there were reports that Germany was appointing two *Statthalters*—one for Prague, the other for Bratislava—and that German troops were on the move that very night. Oliver Stanley's visit to Berlin to discuss improved trading relations was immediately called off.[21]

That same evening, Phillips told Kennedy about the latest European developments.* Rose had already left for Paris to shop for her spring wardrobe. Joe joined the Phillipses in the receiving line. Always with an eye for the ladies, Kennedy noted that there was "quite a nice looking group of young as well as old people there." Phillips explained he had to have these young attractive Italian girls there for Ciano or else he wouldn't turn up. At dinner, Kennedy was seated next to Edda, Countess Ciano, who asked him directly if the United States would fight. Joe replied affirmatively. "I felt if we didn't there was no point in telling her so." Ciano joined their table later, "surrounded by three or four young girls," and "all the time he was talking he was looking around as if he had St. Vitus dance."[22]

AT SIX A.M. on March 15, the German army crossed into Czechoslovakia. At the same time, Teddy Kennedy dressed for his First Communion to be given by the pope at that morning's mass. Before Teddy and his father arrived at the Vatican, the Germans had occupied Prague. That afternoon, Joe boarded the express train for Paris. At least he could stay long enough to see his youngest son's ceremony and hear Pius XII say to Teddy, "I hope you will always be as good and pious as you are today."[23]

---

* Phillips neglected, however, to tell Kennedy that the Italians had been spying on him quite successfully and that he had just discovered that the Italian spy in the embassy had duplicate keys to the safe and had taken all the codes. He became aware of the Italian undercover operation only when he went to retrieve his wife's tiara for the evening's festivities and found it was missing.

24

"A WAVE OF PERVERSE OPTIMISM"

Churchill Must Come Back

—SLOGAN ON THOUSANDS OF POSTERS, SPRING 1939

The Rome express pulled into Paris at eight A.M. on March 17, two days after Hitler's invasion of Czechoslovakia. Joe found Rose, not at the Hôtel Ritz as planned, but on her knees praying at l'Église de la Madeleine "with her eyes closed."[1] Both recognized that they were running hard to keep up with events, and with Joe Jr. still in Spain, Kennedy needed to understand if their son was in real danger. So, after he dropped Rose back at the hotel, Joe headed for the American embassy. Ambassador Bullitt had been put in charge of the negotiations to recognize the Franco government.

As Joe Jr. had intimated earlier, Kennedy stayed in his post to advance his sons. At a Cliveden weekend party in late February, Kennedy read aloud Joe Jr.'s letter to the assembled guests, including Chamberlain, Philip Kerr Lord Lothian,* the Duke and Duchess of Devonshire, the Lindberghs, and Geoffrey Dawson of *The Times*. Anne Morrow Lindbergh likened Joe's pleased expression to "an Irish terrier wagging his tail (a very nice Irish terrier)" needing approval. Dawson noted in his diary,

---

* Lothian had just been named as replacement to the retiring Sir Ronald Lindsay in Washington.

"An American ambassador full of a letter from his boy in Spain."[2] Three days later, at an embassy dinner for British newspaper publishers, Dawson mockingly wrote that "Joe K. tells us (seated) 'what was in Roosevelt's mind.'"[3] More Kennedyiana was the conclusion.

Great Britain and fifteen other countries had recognized Franco's fascist government on February 28, on the proviso there would be no reprisals against the loyalists. Now, in Paris, Bullitt reassured Kennedy that the discussions were progressing nicely, and that Franco's Spanish representative had given him a "well-worded" declaration that had been accepted.* Neither Joe nor Joe Jr. had anything to worry about.[4]

Bullitt also told Kennedy he had asked Roosevelt to denounce the latest Nazi aggression and push for the repeal of the Neutrality Act. Bullitt, too, predicted that the next pinch point would be the Polish Free City of Danzig, formerly part of Germany. Finally, Bullitt told Joe he had been instructed to order Kennedy to call on Chamberlain immediately on his return and repeat everything Bullitt said about the Poles and fears that the French would abandon them. Kennedy came away from his session feeling as if he had slithered down the pole into the lower division of ambassadors.

DURING KENNEDY'S ABSENCE, Churchill put his finger on Chamberlain's lack of understanding when writing, "A wave of perverse optimism had swept across the British scene during these March days."[5] The prime minister refused to see that his rosy account of the alleged progress toward peace was dishonest. As late as March 10, Chamberlain had bullied Dawson of *The Times* to follow his directive that "the Spanish affair would soon be over" and that discord between France and Italy would be tackled next. The rest of the established British press followed suit, claiming that soon the "armaments race" would be halted and it would follow that there would be an improvement in "Anglo-German relations."[6]

That said, in London "breakaway" independent newspapers—for example, *The Whitehall News Letter* and *The Arrow*—sprang up like toadstools,

---

* There were, of course, reprisals against the Popular Front government officials. Many of them were on a "most wanted" list if they returned to Spain and were only "pardoned" and given reparations after Franco's death in 1975.

with journalists such as Charles Tower of the *Yorkshire Post,* Iverach Mc-
Donald of *The Times,* Harold Nicolson MP, and Robert "Bobbety" Cranborne MP acting as their contributors.* *The Arrow's* first issue on January
6, 1939, warned that "a nation that is prepared has a very different spirit,
a different policy, a different resolve from a nation that is unprepared."
Then, too, there were Claud Cockburn's more salacious *The Week* and
Commander King-Hall's *News-Letter*—which flourished and prospered
for their forthright search for the truth when the established daily press
presented a united front for Chamberlain.[7] It is little wonder that by mid-
March posters suddenly appeared throughout central London calling for
the return of Churchill to the government.

The Foreign Office, too, was in disarray—physically and philosophi-
cally. When Ivan Maisky visited Rab Butler there, he saw the construction of an antiaircraft and gas shelter in the basement. Maisky came to
warn Butler of an imminent attack in the west, more than likely also
knowing that his boss and mentor, Maxim Litvinov, had become isolated
since Munich. Indeed, Soviet foreign policy had passed into the hands of
Stalin and Vyacheslav Molotov.

At the annual Soviet embassy reception on March 1, Chamberlain,
thirteen members of his cabinet, and five hundred pillars of business,
banking, and the aristocracy attended for the first time ever. Halifax
had pressed Chamberlain and the others into the show of solidarity on
hearing Maisky's news and had consulted with Churchill, too. Both men
believed that an alliance between Poland, the Soviet Union, Turkey, Rumania, France, and Britain might just stop Hitler.

Maisky kept prodding the British to act, *without* informing Moscow.
He told Butler he had heard from a reliable source that Hitler's long-
term objective was to first destroy the Soviet Union, then break it up
into smaller states that would remain friendly to Germany. But before

---

* The *Yorkshire Post* was the only established newspaper not to follow Chamberlain's direction. From 1935, Joseph Ball, the partner civil servant to Sir Horace Wilson, who did Chamberlain's secret bidding, owned the old radical publication *Truth,* which had been founded by
Henry Labouchère in 1877. Sir Robert Vansittart commissioned a private inquiry into *Truth*
in 1941, which revealed the "previously unknown connection between Ball, the Conservative
Party, and the newspaper." Its records were destroyed by Ball before his death (*Source:* Richard
Crockett, *Twilight of Truth: Chamberlain, Appeasement and the Manipulation of the Press,* 10).

Hitler could embark on such a complex undertaking, he would need to secure his rear—meaning an attack in the west. At a lunch with American publisher Roy Howard (who had been granted an exclusive interview with Stalin) and Lord Dufferin,* Churchill concurred with Maisky. The attack on Czechoslovakia was merely to get his hands on the Czech arsenal, thereby reinforcing Germany with weapons, ammunition, aircraft, and their excellent armaments factories.[8] Despite Halifax's unstinting efforts, there would be no six-party pact against Hitler. With its long history of Russian invasions, Poland would not trust Stalin.

By early March, Halifax tended to exchange views with Alec Cadogan, Oliver Harvey, and Sir Robert Vansittart, unable to persuade Chamberlain that appeasement was dead. To Halifax's horror, Chamberlain and Horace Wilson briefed the press on March 10, portraying their preposterously rosy picture to the public. When Halifax heard Chamberlain had said, "I think the foreign situation is less anxious and gives me less concern for possible unpleasant development than it has done for some time," Halifax knew his "get tough" policy lay in tatters and wrote to the prime minister, barely disguising his anger. "They [the Germans] will be encouraged to think that we are feeling the strain, etc, and the good effects that the balance you have up to now maintained between rearmament and peace efforts is tilted to our disadvantage."[9] Of course, Chamberlain was covered in shame on March 15 when Hitler invaded the rump of Czechoslovakia. Halifax immediately recalled Sir Nevile Henderson from Berlin, as rumors of German ultimatums against Rumania, Turkey, the Netherlands, and Poland flooded into his office.

KENNEDY HAD JUST returned to England when Chamberlain made his March 17 speech in Birmingham to the Conservative Unionist Association. As Chamberlain spoke, the Rumanian minister, Viorel Tilea, called on Halifax in London. Rumania had received an economic ultimatum from Germany that in exchange for "a monopoly of Rumanian exports, Germany would guarantee Rumania's frontiers." The purpose of the call was to ask for His Majesty's Government to support Rumania, and to

---

* Basil Hamilton-Temple-Blackwood, 4th Marquess of Dufferin and Ava, was the Parliamentary Undersecretary of State for the Colonies 1937–1940.

see if a joint "proclamation of the Balkan Entente to guarantee each other's frontiers" would help. Halifax fired off the necessary telegrams to Paris, Warsaw, Ankara, Athens, Belgrade, and Moscow to ask for their viewpoints.[10]

Chamberlain's speech took Kennedy by surprise. Delivered the day before the prime minister's seventieth birthday, Chamberlain asked, referring to the swallowing up of what remained of Czechoslovakia: "Is this the end of an old adventure, or is it the beginning of a new? Is this the last attack upon a small State, or is it to be followed by others? Is this, in fact, a step in the direction of an attempt to dominate the world by force? Those are grave and serious questions," the prime minister continued. "I am not going to answer them tonight. But I am sure they will require grave and serious consideration not only from Germany's neighbours, but of others, perhaps beyond the confines of Europe." Chamberlain's sudden change of heart prompted Churchill to urge "the anti-aircraft defences should forthwith be placed in full preparedness."[11]

Although the Birmingham speech signaled a parting of the political way between Kennedy and the prime minister, America's ambassador thoroughly commended it to both Chamberlain and Halifax. In Kennedy's view, if Britain decided to support the Balkan Entente, then the United States would take a more favorable view against any British actions taken. Kennedy did not communicate this to the State Department and had again spoken out of turn.[12]

Bullitt's message to Washington, however, gave the correct intelligence: Hitler was on his way to "inspect" Memel—the German port ceded to Lithuania at the end of the Great War—and would "soon be making plans to visit other spots in Europe.* "Some day someone will have enough guts to pull a trigger and the affair will begin. The British seem to be awake at last and the French definitely are awake. . . . There is a quiet courage and serenity in France today," Bullitt added.[13]

Eastern Europe presented an incredibly complex picture. The Poles had gained the Teschen region in the carving up of the former

---

* The Lithuanian government agreed to voluntarily return the entire Klaipėda Region effective March 22, 1939, including Memel, which had been cut off from Germany by the Treaty of Versailles (Source: *New York Times*, March 23, 1939).

Czechoslovakia. It was, of course, a temporary gift from Hitler that served to silence Poland and keep the Poles worried about the Soviets' intentions. Neither Poland nor Rumania would accept Soviet intervention, given their mutual histories of occupation by Russia, nor would Poland work closely with Rumania. Hungary had already declared for Germany.[14] Although Chamberlain had a "profound distrust of Russia," and worked only halfheartedly toward the Grand Alliance of six nations, it was Poland that made any Soviet alliance impossible. And more is the pity. The German ambassador to the Soviet Union cabled Berlin that he had been unable to corroborate the rumors about a grand alliance. For once, the Germans were guessing about the aggressive intentions of others.[15]

As a result, Kennedy's work to develop an economic relationship between Germany and Great Britain was dead. Chamberlain abandoned the project completely. The State Department thought it was a wise move, potentially sending the wrong signals to an aggressive Reich. Welles, for one, was relieved. He never believed in the Kennedy-promoted policy.[16]

On March 31, before a packed House of Commons, a reinvigorated prime minister moved to the dispatch box. "As the House is aware, certain consultations are now proceeding with other Governments," Chamberlain began. "I now have to inform the House that during that period, in the event of any action which clearly threatened Polish independence, and which the Polish Government accordingly considered it vital to resist with their national forces, His Majesty's Government would feel themselves bound at once to lend the Polish Government all support in their power." He then added: "The French Government have authorised me to make it plain that they stand in the same position in this matter as do His Majesty's Government."[17]

As if the loud rattling of sabers from the east was not enough to worry Kennedy, Madrid fell, and there was no word from Joe Jr. Several days later, the errant firstborn returned unscathed to London. His parents were unaware that Joe Jr. had written from Irún (on the Spanish border with France), opening with "I'm in an awful mess here so I thought I would write you this note and let you know what's what in case I get interned for a couple of days." Joe Jr. had crossed into Fascist Spain and was found to have Republican currency on him. He explained that since Franco had taken Madrid, he was taking the worthless currency as a souvenir to his little brother, Bobby. Young Joe was sent back to San Sebastián, where the censor discovered communist newspapers from Madrid among other newspaper cuttings in his belongings. He was accused of being a "dirty Russian spy. . . . It takes so long to send a wire from this side that I decided to drop you this note in case they try to jail me." Luckily, he talked his way out of trouble, arriving home before his letter.[18]

BACK IN FEBRUARY, Jack had sailed with his father across the "plainly rough" North Atlantic to England. He delighted in meeting queens, kings, aristocrats, and world-famous politicians, as if he had been born to the role. "Met the king this morning at the Court Levee," Jack related to Lem Billings. "It takes place in the morning and you wear tails. The king stands up and you go up and bow." After meeting Queen Mary, he went to tea with "Princess Elizabeth with whom I made a great deal of time," he added in a rakish Kennedy boast. "Thursday night am going to Court in my new silk knee breeches, which are cut to my crotch tightly and in which I look mighty attractive."[19]

Jack also told Lem that he had gone to the Grand National at Aintree Racecourse near Liverpool with his dad that March. What made it all the sweeter was that the winning jockey was Irishman Tim Hyde riding Workman—a 100/8 shot. Jack did not say that they had been taken to Aintree on a private train with an aristocratic crowd of horse breeders and habitués of the racecourse, or that they hadn't bet on Workman. It was here that Jack first saw the giant figure of Prince Monolulu, the feted horse-racing tipster. Monolulu and Joe had been acquainted for some time, and it was Monolulu who had helped the ambassador to win his bet at Ascot the previous year.

"Everyone thinks war inevitable before the year is out. I personally don't," Jack told Billings, "though Dad does."[20] Jack was twenty-two and having far too much fun. Even more "fun" for Jack would be to see firsthand all the political hot spots he could, just as Joe Jr. had done. The overriding emotions in the Kennedy children were the rivalry and competitiveness their father had bred into them.

Yet, without recognizing the signs, Jack was becoming an internationalist. After Aintree, he went to work at the American embassy in Paris at the invitation of Ambassador Bullitt and his chargé d'affaires, Carmel Offie. Back in June 1938, both Kennedy boys stayed on and off with Offie in his rue de Rivoli apartment until shortly before the Munich crisis in September. The boys enjoyed themselves, "invited to various parties in the diplomatic corps where they could meet young ladies," Offie later recalled. "No one took them very seriously."[21] Considering the fact that Bullitt and Kennedy actively disliked each other—Joe because he was resentful of Bullitt's ongoing good relations with FDR, and Bullitt because of Joe's utter lack of diplomacy—it became a rather long, if not arduous, babysitting job.

Now, in April 1939, Jack was wined and dined again at the expense of the American taxpayer. "Was at lunch today with the Lindberghs and they are the most attractive couple I've ever seen," Jack remarked. The young Kennedy was looking at them as eye candy and not listening to what they had to say. Charles Lindbergh was convinced that Hitler was a man of peace. He was negotiating a high-profile but (unknown to Lindbergh) phony deal to sell German airplane engines and parts to France on Göring's behalf.[22]

ON APRIL 5, 1939, Hitler gave the order for all children aged ten to eighteen to be conscripted.*

Three days later, Italy invaded the Kingdom of Albania. King Zog and the royal family fled, taking much of Albania's gold reserves with them.† Other royals would follow within a year. Jack Kennedy knew he was living history and longed to be in the thick of things. After a skiing

---

* Until that time, boys aged ten to fourteen had been mandatory members of the Jungvolk, indoctrinating them into the ways of the Third Reich. Boys who were aged fourteen to eighteen automatically joined the Hitler Youth. However, from that April, the two organizations were amalgamated, with boys as young as sixteen taking charge of teaching paramilitary war games to as many as five hundred boys who had previously been in the Jungvolk.

† The Albanian royal family settled for about a year in France until Ian Fleming, a naval intelligence officer and later author of the James Bond novels, aided them to escape to England as France fell. The first monarch in exile in England was Haile Selassie, emperor of Ethiopia. Many members of the Dutch and Danish royal families also took exile in London.

trip to Val d'Isère, he set off on a somewhat chaotic route to the Balkans, the Soviet Union, and the Middle East, hoping to finish off in Greece so he could spend the summer on the Mediterranean again. Like his older brother, Jack sent his father regular reports and updates from places he visited. Just the same, Joe never read Jack's incisive letters aloud, or bragged about them. Similarly, Joe never tried to bribe newspaper editors or publishers to print Jack's letters, as he had done with Joe Jr.'s accounts of the fall of Loyalist Spain.

Yet Jack's letters were full of historical insight and current-day imperatives. From Jerusalem, he summarized the intractable problem between the Arab and Jewish populations with a striking ability. "During the [Great] war, the British Government, desiring both the assistance of the Jews and the Arabs, made separate promises to both, one in the MacMahon, the other in the Balfour declaration. . . . In considering the whole question now, it is useless to discuss which has the 'fairer' claim," Jack wrote to his father. "The important thing is to try to work out a solution that will work, not try to present a solution based on these two vague, indefinite and conflicting promises."[23]

The MacMahon-Hussein correspondence of 1915–16 to which Jack referred was a British government promise to aid the Arabs in freeing themselves from the yoke of the Ottoman Empire and establish their independence. "The limitations and restrictions placed upon this promise have always been held by the British Government to have excluded the area of Palestine. The Arab leaders, however, have insisted that Arab independence was promised there as elsewhere."[24] And therein lay another complicated skein to the tangled tale.

Jack also deduced that the exile of the Palestinian Arab spiritual leader, the Grand Mufti, condemned them to weakness and a subservient position to the Jews, who had Western money, ideas, and eloquent leaders. Jerusalem, then as now, was the battleground.[25] The British White Paper of May 23, 1939, tried to take a middle-of-the-road approach and pleased none who were intimately concerned: "The objective of His Majesty's Government is the establishment within 10 years of an independent Palestine State in such treaty relations with the United Kingdom as will provide satisfactorily for the commercial and strategic requirements of both countries in the future. The proposal for the establishment of the independent State would involve consultation with the Council of the League of Nations with a view to the termination of the Mandate."

The White Paper also stated that this new "independent State should be one in which Arabs and Jews share government in such a way as to ensure that the essential interests of each community are safeguarded."[26] The primary purpose of the single-state solution was simple: to quell the Arab revolt that had begun in 1936 and was occupying over 50,000 soldiers.* As anticipated, the White Paper limited Jewish immigration to Palestine at a time when several hundred thousand Jews were displaced in Europe. The government pledged only 25,000 Jews could immigrate "as soon as they could be absorbed."[27] Kennedy would have done well to listen to Jack, particularly as he was under renewed attack from a host of those involved with the question of Jewish immigration to Palestine.

On April 30, Moshe Sharett, the Zionist movement's and Jewish Agency's ambassador to Great Britain, was delegated to go talk to Kennedy. Sharett wondered in his diary if he wasn't wasting his time: not only was Kennedy no decision-maker, but he had "no faith in Kennedy's good will." Sharett was right. Joe cut the meeting short, simply because he had nothing to add to the British position and the president would not interfere in a "British internal matter."[28]

---

* There is ample evidence that both Italian and German propaganda resources as well as some small arms were put at the disposal of the Arabs in the revolt, which lasted until September 1939.

25

THE LAST SEASON

Time can seldom have been purchased more dearly—and
never have been more wantonly wasted afterwards.

—RONALD CARTLAND MP, IN *THE ISTHMUS YEARS, 1919–1939*

A ggression is like water," Ivan Maisky told Halifax on April 11, "if
you block it in one direction, it finds another."[1] Three days later,
President Roosevelt cabled Hitler and Mussolini requesting them to
guarantee the independence of thirty European and Middle Eastern
countries from attack or invasion, since "you have repeatedly asserted
that you and the German people have no desire for war.* If this is true
there need be no war." If Germany gave these assurances, the president
would seek identical undertakings from those nations and call for an
international conference to limit armaments and increase world trade.
Hitler and Mussolini were dismissive of Roosevelt's "infamous" propaganda campaign against the peace-loving Germans.[2]

A week earlier, in a "Personal and Confidential" letter, circumventing
State Department's official channels, Kennedy offered his services sotto
voce to Welles to act as the unofficial liaison to the new pope. "I had a
couple of talks with the Holy Father—one at rather great length, both

---

* The countries and their territories FDR wanted assurances for were Finland, Estonia, Lat-
via, Lithuania, Sweden, Norway, Denmark, the Netherlands, Belgium, Great Britain and Ireland,
France, Portugal, Spain, Switzerland, Liechtenstein, Luxembourg, Poland, Hungary, Rumania,
Yugoslavia, Russia, Bulgaria, Greece, Turkey, Iraq, the Arabias, Syria, Palestine, Egypt, and Iran.

as to conditions in the United States and the conditions in Europe," Kennedy advised Welles. "His influence in Italy is probably stronger than that of any Pope for the last 100 years." Though Kennedy admitted that Pius XII could never prevent "Mussolini from fighting," papal influence "could be utilized for the cause of peace in ways under the surface rather than in a big gesture."[3] Welles did not fall for Kennedy's sales pitch.

Two weeks later, Joe went to Edinburgh to address Scotland's capital city. He also collected an honorary Doctor of Law degree from the University of Edinburgh. Kennedy asked permission to speak out, focusing on Roosevelt's cable to Hitler and Mussolini. The State Department cabled back that he was to do no such thing. Joe's sarcastic answer confirmed his pique: "All international affairs omitted, talking about flowers, birds and trees. The only thing I am afraid of is that instead of giving me the freedom of the city they will make me queen of the May."[4] In Kennedy's opinion, the president was laying the groundwork for replacing aggression with better trade and the prospect of peace—in other words, *his* plan. Joe could not comprehend that this was a matter for the president of the United States, not for an ambassador.

THERE WERE SOME important American businessmen who agreed with Kennedy regarding substituting trade for aggression, like James Mooney, president of General Motors Overseas, who had been awarded the Order of the German Eagle in 1938 (as had Charles Lindbergh). Mooney had his own contacts with the Vatican, also through Francis Spellman, and would be described in 1940 by George Messersmith as "dangerous and destructive" and "eager to see the fall of Britain." Messersmith even went so far as to say of Mooney—a man he considered to be his friend—that he was "part of an Irish Catholic Group of influential Americans 'so blind in their hatred of England that they are prepared to sell out their own country in order to bring England down.'"[5]

On April 25, Mooney paid a courtesy call on Kennedy in London, at the behest of the German Reich. He told Joe about his meeting with Dr. Emil Puhl,* vice-president of the Reichsbank and a director of the Bank

---

* Puhl was most notorious after the war for the secret maneuvering of Nazi gold. He was not only in charge of the gold stolen from the countries conquered by Hitler but also of the

for International Settlements in Basel, Switzerland. Helmuth Wohlthat, one of Göring's main economic advisers on the Four-Year Plan, was also present. They had proposed to Mooney that in exchange for a gold loan to the Third Reich, the Germans would reverse the discriminatory Nuremberg Laws, which had led to the cessation of trade with Great Britain and the United States. "We'd give it all up," Puhl and Wohlthat told Mooney, "if we thought there was the slightest chance of our ne-gotiating a gold loan and come back into normal trading arrangements." Kennedy immediately proposed a secret meeting with the Germans in Paris to discuss the matter. Puhl, Wohlthat, and Mooney knew their man when they approached Kennedy. But they hadn't expected the ambas-sador to send a "Strictly Confidential" cable to Sumner Welles about the deal. Welles discussed the matter urgently with Hull. After a careful preamble to spare Kennedy's feelings, Welles said: "I hope very much . . . that you will not undertake this trip at this moment" on the grounds that such a meeting in Paris would create too much publicity and comment.[6]

Mooney insisted that it would be a slap in the face to the Germans if Kennedy canceled the Paris meeting. But Joe, unable to reach Roo-sevelt, had not taken Welles's "no" lightly. Just the same, since the State Department had asked him only not to go to Paris, Kennedy suggested that Wohlthat come to London instead. His actions were the mark of a desperate man, anxious to be at the heart of political power brokering. Wohlthat was responsible for the scandalous "repatriation" of Czech gold on deposit through the Bank for International Settlements (BIS) at the Bank of England a month earlier.* Mooney would reappear again in var-ious guises during the war, once as an unofficial emissary of Roosevelt

---

"non-monetary" gold from the concentration camp victims. He was convicted in the last of the Nuremberg Trials and sentenced to five years' imprisonment for war crimes.

* In one of the murkier episodes of March 1939, John Simon as Chancellor of the Exchequer lied to Parliament about the status of the Czech gold on deposit with the Bank of England because Montagu Norman, Kennedy's idol, lied to Simon. While it was within the power of Norman to stop the Nazi demand for the "return" of the Czech gold—and it would have been absolutely legal to do so—Norman, as a director of the BIS and the governor of the Bank of England, failed to act even though he had been amply warned by the National Bank of Czechoslovakia that its directors had requested the return of the gold "under duress," as they had been threatened with torture and the murder of their fami-lies (*Source:* David Blaazer, "Finance and the End of Appeasement: The Bank of England,

to Germany, but his most notable involvement was with the Nazis to reinstate Edward VIII on the British throne once Germany defeated the United Kingdom.[7] At the time, no one at the State Department learned that Kennedy had met with Wohlthat alone in the German's room at the Berkeley Hotel in Mayfair.

Wohlthat returned to London in July to stir up more trouble. Sir Horace Wilson and Robert Hudson, a junior minister in the Department of Overseas Trade, offered that if Germany disarmed under international supervision, His Majesty's Government would give a loan of a billion pounds sterling to buy raw materials and return Germany to a peace economy. It seems that Kennedy had initiated this maneuver, which Wilson carried out on behalf of the prime minister. When the story broke in the *Daily Telegraph* and the *News Chronicle*, Wilson denied that any such plan was discussed. "The story is calculated to do infinite harm to the Soviet negotiations and to U.S. opinion," Oliver Harvey confided to his diary, "where our *bona fides* are not so above suspicion as not to be easily called in doubt. . . . I hope Halifax will tackle the P.M. about it, but he has not yet."[8] Kennedy's personal initiative had backfired badly.

YET ALL WAS not doom-laden for Joe Kennedy and his "hostages to fortune" that last spring and summer of peace. Though the "London Season" normally began in earnest after Easter, 1939's season started early due to the Royal Tour of Canada and the United States. The King's Levée, attended by Joe and Jack Kennedy on March 7, was the last before the outbreak of war.[9]

Two days later, Rose Kennedy presented her daughter Eunice at Court. Thereafter, Eunice was invited to virtually all the Season's parties. On the first day of spring, Tuesday, March 21, the president of France, Albert François Lebrun, and his wife, Marguerite, came to London. They were met by the King and Queen at Victoria Station and taken straight to Buckingham Palace for the State banquet that evening in the Throne Room. The royal gold dinner service, along with large gold centerpieces, gold platters, and gold chargers upon which white plates trimmed with

---

gold and a golden crown in the middle were placed, more than rivaled the bejeweled dignitaries. The menu, printed on gold-edged cards crowned with the king's GRE monogram, told the guests that they were to have eight courses. From the Consommé Quenelles aux Trois Couleurs and the Filet de Truite Saumonée George VI to the Mignonettes d'Agneau Royale, Salade Élysées, the Corbeille Lorraine, and the Bombe de l'Entente Cordiale, the menu reflected the royal and Anglo-French friendship. The accompanying wines were, de rigueur, *bien sûr* French and the finest from the royal cellar. These were served in the impressive Windsor service of Garter crystal, each piece engraved with the Rose of England and the badge and motto of the ancient Order of the Garter.

The King and Queen sat at the head of the horseshoe-shaped table on gold and red damask armchairs. The Queen glittered brightly, dressed in gold and silver and wearing some of the crown jewels. Marguerite Lebrun, in silver lamé and also adorned with splendid jewels, hid her homeliness admirably. But the outstanding ensemble of the evening belonged to Rose Kennedy, with her copious hooped skirt of aquamarine satin generously studded with real diamonds and rubies. Joe was thrilled at the sensation her ballgown created. Rose had standards to maintain, too, as one of the world's best-dressed women.[10]

A YEAR HAD passed since Kick Kennedy's introduction to the young British aristocracy at Cliveden. Like many, Kick breathed more easily when Chamberlain waved his flimsy paper proclaiming "peace for our time." She would not be sent back to America, and Billy Hartington would not be sent to war. Since then, however, Kick heard Billy and his friends had lost patience with the illusion of peace and Chamberlain's policy of wishful thinking. Billy worried, too, that British foreign policy had not been moral. Just as Joe tried to reshape appeasement in his own preferred economic image, Billy was adamant that the prime minister's despicable foreign policy had undermined the very traditions of honor and duty that made Britain great. For Billy, Czechoslovakia was not alone in Chamberlain's betrayal at Munich: the finest of British values had been sacrificed, too.

It came as no surprise to Kick that Hugh Fraser and Julian Amery, who had failed once to reverse the dishonorable Oxford Union's King and

TOP: A portrait of the Kennedy family in their living room, Bronxville, New York, 1938. From left: Joseph P. Kennedy Sr., Patricia Kennedy, John F. Kennedy, Jean Kennedy, Eunice Kennedy, Robert Kennedy, Kathleen Kennedy, Edward Kennedy, Rosemary Kennedy, Joseph P. Kennedy Jr., and Rose Kennedy. (Courtesy of Getty Images. Photo by Bachrach/Getty Images)

BOTTOM LEFT: Joseph P. Kennedy, circa 1925. He was already a multimillionaire "Wall Streeter" and bound for Hollywood to make his second fortune. (Courtesy of Getty Images. Photo by New York Times Co./Getty Images)

BOTTOM RIGHT: James Roosevelt (left), the oldest son of President Franklin D. Roosevelt, chatting with Joseph P. Kennedy on the links of the Palm Beach Country Club, just prior to Kennedy's taking up his post in February 1938. (Courtesy of Bettmann/Getty Images)

TOP: President Roosevelt looks on as Joseph P. Kennedy takes the oath from Supreme Court Associate Justice Stanley Reed as the new U.S. envoy to Great Britain, Washington, D.C., February 18, 1938. (Courtesy of Getty Images. Photo by Underwood Archives/ Getty Images)

BOTTOM: Joseph P. Kennedy leaves the U.S. Embassy to present his credentials to the King at Buckingham Palace, London, March 8, 1938, accompanied by Col. Raymond E. Lee (far left) and Sir Sidney Clive, Marshal of the Diplomatic Corps (third from right). (Courtesy of Getty Images. Photo by Becker/Fox Photos/Hulton Archive/Getty Images)

TOP: Left to right: Kick Kennedy, Rose Kennedy, and Rosemary Kennedy dressed for their Court presentations, May 1938. (Courtesy of Getty Images. Photo by Derek Berwin/Getty Images)

BOTTOM LEFT: March 16, 1938: Ambassador Joseph Patrick Kennedy, with his wife and five of their nine children, at the Princes Gate home in London. Left to right: Kathleen, Joseph Kennedy, Edward ("Teddy"), Rose Kennedy, Patricia, Jean, and Robert ("Bobby"). (Courtesy of Getty Images. Photo by H. F. Davis/Topical Press Agency/Getty Images)

BOTTOM RIGHT: The Duke of Kent, brother of King George VI, is shown (center) with Rose Kennedy and Ambassador Joseph P. Kennedy arriving at the Dorchester Hotel in London for the Fourth of July banquet. (Courtesy of Bettmann/Getty Images)

TOP: Ambassador Kennedy with Rose Kennedy escorted by Count Enrico Galleazzi. Kennedy was the official U.S. representative at the Papal Coronation of His Holiness, Pope Pius XII. The fascist Galleazzi was a close personal friend of the new Pope and Kennedy. (Courtesy of Bettmann/Getty Images)

BOTTOM LEFT: Papal Coronation, March 1939: Ambassador Joseph P. Kennedy (wearing glasses in back row), Rose Kennedy (center), and eight of their children standing between two guards outside the Papal residence at their special audience with the Pope, at the Vatican. (Courtesy of Getty Images. Photo by Hulton Archive/Getty Images)

BOTTOM RIGHT: March 11, 1940: Sumner Welles calls at 10 Downing Street in London for talks with the British Prime Minister, Neville Chamberlain. Left to right: Lord Halifax, the Foreign Secretary, Sumner Welles, Neville Chamberlain, and Joseph P. Kennedy Sr. (Courtesy of Getty Images. Photo by Fox Photos/Hulton Archive/Getty Images)

TOP LEFT: American Ambassador to Great Britain Joseph Kennedy with the English statesman Winston Churchill outside 10 Downing Street, London, circa 1939. (Courtesy of Getty Images. Photo by Keystone/Getty Images)

TOP RIGHT: Left to right: U.S. Undersecretary of State and President Roosevelt's Special envoy to Europe Sumner Welles, U.S. Ambassador to Great Britain Joseph P. Kennedy, and First Lord of the Admiralty Winston Churchill in March 1940. (Courtesy of Bettmann/ Getty Images)

BOTTOM: Left to right: Joseph P. Kennedy Jr., Ambassador Joseph P. Kennedy, and Jack Kennedy (the future 35th President of the United States). (Courtesy of Getty Images. Photo by AFP via Getty Images)

TOP: Ambassador and Mrs. Joseph P. Kennedy are shown at a party given at the American Embassy in London, May 11, 1939, for Britain's King George VI. Left to right: Mrs. Kennedy, King George VI, Queen Mother Elizabeth, and Ambassador Kennedy. (Courtesy of Bettmann/Getty Images)

BOTTOM LEFT: Rose Kennedy with Jack Kennedy's good friend Lem Billings, circa 1938. (Courtesy of John F. Kennedy Library)

BOTTOM RIGHT: Left to right: Joseph P. Kennedy Jr., Kick Kennedy, and future president John F. "Jack" Kennedy entering the Houses of Parliament on September 3, 1939. (Courtesy of Getty Images. Photo by Fox Photos/Getty Images)

TOP: Ambassador Joseph P. Kennedy walking behind a bank of sandbags as he leaves the Treasury Building in London on September 28, 1939. (Courtesy of Getty Images. Photo by New York Times Co./Getty Images)

BOTTOM LEFT: Marlene Dietrich with her daughter, Maria Riva. (Courtesy of Vogue Images. Photo by Horst P. Horst)

BOTTOM RIGHT: Portrait of Gloria Swanson behind lace, 1928. (Courtesy of Vogue Images. Photo by Edward Steichen)

TOP LEFT: Clare Boothe Luce, circa 1936. (Courtesy of Vogue Images. Photo by Cecil Beaton)

TOP RIGHT: Mary and Eddie Moore, who accompanied Rose and seven of the Kennedy children to St. Moritz, Christmas 1938. (Courtesy of John F. Kennedy Library)

BOTTOM: William Cavendish, Marquess of Hartington, with his bride, Kathleen "Kick" Kennedy, smiling happily at their wedding in London in May 1944. Behind them, left to right: Lady Nancy Astor, Joseph P. Kennedy Jr., and Edward, the Duke of Devonshire, the groom's father. (Courtesy of Bettmann/Getty Images)

Country Resolution of 1933, would try again. In that spring of 1939, Fraser and Amery made the case for conscription in the wake of the shameful abandonment of the Czechs and in light of the German invasion of what remained of Czechoslovakia only days earlier. It was a hot topic, filling the Union hall with over a thousand people crammed into every inch of available space, including window recesses. Fraser asked Amery to propose the motion: "In view of this country's commitments and the gravity of the general situation in Europe, this house welcomes conscription." Not only were the pair arguing for a rapid change in official government foreign policy, but their motives stretched to changing the perceived image of decay that the 1933 resolution helped create. The debate lasted well into the night. The result was that the King and Country Resolution of six years earlier was overturned.

Kick understood and privately applauded their moral position, even though she dreaded anything happening to Billy and their friends. At a dinner party she gave at the ambassadorial Prince's Gate residence, Joe Kennedy showed a movie about the Great War. "As the images of slaughter in the trenches began to play, Ambassador Kennedy suddenly leapt in front of the screen. Pointing to the pictures of soldiers being mown down by gunfire, he warned Billy and the other young men, 'That's what you'll be looking like in a month or two!'" Kick was appalled at her father's behavior and whispered to Billy, "You mustn't pay any attention to him. He just doesn't understand the English as I do."[11] That May, the Military Training Act was passed by Parliament. It required all young men between the ages of twenty and twenty-two to undertake six months' military training. Over 240,000 young men registered.[12] And so, while the great homes of London broke out the packing crates, miles of tape for their grand windows, and white sheets so redolent of a nation preparing for war, the most resplendent London season also got under way.

ON MAY 4, 1939, Ambassador and Mrs. Kennedy hosted a banquet in honor of Their Majesties. Joe had made much of the royal couple's tour of Canada and the United States, and "his role" in making it happen. Both he and Rose fretted over the evening, since it was specifically intended as their grand send-off. Kennedy was convinced he had made it all possible. And yet his name is not mentioned anywhere whatsoever in the preparations so carefully kept in the Royal Archives at Windsor, other than to note "Dine with the Kennedys" on May 4.[13] In fact, the tour was first mooted by Canadian prime minister Mackenzie King at George VI's and Queen Elizabeth's coronation on May 12, 1937, long before Kennedy was appointed ambassador. President Roosevelt's letter of August 25, 1938, to King George does not mention Kennedy, either. Then, too, the president wrote to James Gerard, a former U.S. ambassador to Germany and presidential representative at the Royal Coronation in May 1937 that he thought Gerard would like to know *his* approach to Their Majesties at their coronation had been successful.[14]

Indeed, on September 17, 1938, Roosevelt sent a sealed letter to the American embassy and asked Kennedy to transmit it unopened to the King. "I am asking Mr. Kennedy to give you this," he wrote, "but I think that we can keep any talk of your visit out of diplomatic channels for the time being. Your Ambassador, Ronald Lindsay is a very old and close personal friend of mine."[15] Thereafter, all communication was channeled through Lindsay. The King and Queen sailed for Canada on May 6 aboard the *Empress of Australia* for their seven-week tour of North America, five days of which were spent in the United States.[16]

Shortly after the royal departure, the London Season erupted in earnest. The dark, amusing, and absolutely the "most chic" Mrs. Reginald (Daisy) Fellowes was back in town from Paris.* California-born Maud "Emerald" Cunard, who loved the mix of ancient aristocracy with "the lions of the literary world," entertained that May, too. For the Kennedys, the debutante season was again upon them, and this time it was Eunice's turn to crave the world's attention. Joe, Kick, and Eunice Kennedy attended Nancy Astor's London ball given for her niece, Dinah Brand, that June. The Duke and Duchess of Gloucester, the Duke and Duchess of Kent, the Duchess of Marlborough, and the Duke and Duchess of Devonshire attended, too. In an era of lavish floral decoration, the Astor ball outdid all others: brilliant gold tassels of laburnum swayed overhead, a rich abundance of mauve, pink, and purple flowers adorned the ballroom,

* Daisy was the niece of the American Winnaretta Singer, Princesse de Polignac, and raised by Winnaretta after her mother's death when Daisy was only six years old.

while white gardenias and arum lilies perfumed the sitting-out room with their dreamy, exotic scents.[17]

As May rolled on into June, the pace of the partygoing picked up, supplemented of course by the rowing regatta at Henley-on-Thames, horse racing at Royal Ascot, tennis at Wimbledon, and cricket at Lord's. Ronald Cartland, the young and independent-minded MP for Birmingham,* wrote: "And so we go on: playing cricket, waiting for the racing specials, planning summer holidays. . . . But are we awake? Worse, have the gods sent us mad before destruction falls?"[18]

On May 24, Rose Kennedy sailed to New York on the French ocean liner *Normandie*. The vessel's return journey brought Clare Boothe Luce to London and Joe Kennedy's welcoming arms. She cabled him a few days before leaving New York: "Save me lunch and or dinner chat alone love Clare." Always the ardent lover, Joe met her at Southampton and drove her back to London. During her stay, "Joe" appears as the most frequent entry in Clare's diary. A weekend at Lord Beaverbrook's country home together, then back to the embassy for a movie, was only the beginning. "As well as entertaining à deux, 'Joe' squired her to the Ascot races and an evening performance of her play *The Women*." She had snuck back to London the previous October on the same ship, leaving only a tantalizing cable to Joe—GOLLY THAT WAS NICE—as the sole proof that she was ever there.[19]

WHILE JOE ENTERTAINED and enjoyed this most spectacular of Seasons, Kick and Billy had fallen more deeply in love than either imagined possible, given her Catholicism. Kick was known personally to the pope. Billy and his family were pillars of Anglicanism. Billy turned twenty-one in December 1938 and had a celebration to commemorate the actual date, which Kick attended as his companion, but his "coming-of-age" party was reserved for that August. Kick suspected that Billy might ask her to marry him beforehand, so Joe and Rose ensured that she would be at Cap d'Antibes with the family instead.

But Lady Sarah Churchill's most resplendent ball of the Season at Blenheim Palace opened Kick's eyes to how difficult obtaining approval for

---

* Cartland was the younger brother of romance novelist Barbara Cartland.

marriage to Billy would be.* Virtually all of the aristocracy and ruling elite were guests, waited upon by bewigged and liveried footmen dressed in eighteenth-century costumes. "I had never seen anything like it," diarist Chips Channon wrote. "The palace was floodlit, and its grand baroque beauty could be seen for miles. The lakes were floodlit too and, better still, the famous terraces.... It was gay, young, brilliant, in short, perfection.... Shall we ever see the like again?"[20] Eunice Kennedy was elated at taking part in the most amazing weekend of the Season, and wrote a short piece entitled "A Weekend at Blenheim Palace" for the family.

But Eunice's impressions were lost on Kick. That sultry July evening, the Catholic Veronica Fraser (sister of Hugh) appeared on the arm of Julian Amery, and not with the man she loved, Robert Cecil. Robert's father, Lord Salisbury, had ordered them to see less of each other. That evening, too, Billy told his father, Edward Duke of Devonshire, that he wanted to marry Kick. The duke forbade it, reminding his son and heir that he could not pick and choose his duty to King and country. Kick's hopes of remaining in England in the event of war were dashed.[21]

How Rose and Joe became aware of the "danger" lurking in Kick's love affair with Billy has gone unnoted. More than likely, it slowly dawned on them from Billy's birthday in December 1938 and the "threat" of his coming-of-age party in August 1939. Joe wrote to Boake Carter that he "had hoped to get back after the end of July and possibly spend some part of the vacation at Cape Cod," and this was undoubtedly true. But the threat of war meant he would have to stay in Europe, while physically distancing Kick from Billy. Joe could not send his daughter home on her own as war loomed. To send his entire family home before war had been declared would tar him with the brush of "coward." And so it was decided to rent a house at Cap d'Antibes again, and indirectly forbid Kick from going to Billy's coming-of-age party.

THROUGHOUT JUNE, JOE was boasting about his superior understanding of the European situation, and how England didn't stand a chance of

---

* Blenheim Palace is the ancestral home of the Dukes of Marlborough, given to John Marlborough by Queen Anne for defeating Louis XIV. It is also the birthplace of Winston Churchill.

winning any war. When Walter Lippmann visited London, Kennedy told him that Hitler "has every reason to go to war and is able to win. The British fleet is valueless. . . . Franco is surrounded. . . . All Englishmen . . . in their hearts *know* this to be true."[22]

In July, Kennedy's dependable ally Arthur Krock wrote for *The New York Times*: "The Senate Committee on Foreign Relations had voted by a majority of one to hold over until the next session the administration's proposals to revise the so-called Neutrality Laws." Nonetheless, Krock continued, Roosevelt viewed the European situation as being at "a critical pass" and that "none abroad shall rumor any executive division over foreign policy" and that Joseph P. Kennedy, "the president's foremost informant on European affairs, has foregone an earnest wish to be relieved of his duties immediately."[23]

That summer at Cap d'Antibes, Joe's great accomplishment, aside from playing golf, was to advise Marlene Dietrich to take the role of Frenchy in *Destry Rides Again*. Worried about imminent war, she asked "Papa Joe"—her new nickname for Kennedy now that there were other "Joes" in her life—if she had to take her family with her to America. "You are the Ambassador to England," Marlene said. "You must know that the gaga Chamberlain with his pretty boy Eden, they are not going to be able to stop Hitler. So what will happen? I can't be away making a stupid film if anything happens!" Kennedy assured her that "if and when he felt the danger of war was imminent, he would evacuate his family back to England and safety and that her family would be given the same protection as his."[24] Marlene had tired of Joe as a lover, transferring her affections instead to a woman named Jo in that last summer of peace. Kennedy was not heartbroken, contenting himself with a pretty French girl who acted as his golf caddy, and who was "good in every respect."[25]

26

"THIS COUNTRY IS AT WAR WITH GERMANY"

May He defend the right.

—NEVILLE CHAMBERLAIN, SEPTEMBER 3, 1939

S ince the beginning of May, the inevitable march to war was a cer-
tainty. Jack Kennedy reported that Danzig was completely "Nazi-
fied."[1] On May 3, Chamberlain directed Dawson of *The Times* to come
up with the headline DANZIG IS NOT WORTH A WAR and a letter to the
editor (probably written by Sir Horace Wilson under the signature of
Lord Rushcliffe), leading the Halifax faction to believe that "No. 10 is at
it again behind our backs." Oliver Harvey wrote: "Appeasement is raising
its ugly head again."[2]

On May 12, the Anglo-Turkish agreement was signed to guarantee
joint action against aggression in the Mediterranean. The Pact of Steel
was signed between Adolf Hitler and Benito Mussolini ten days later.
On May 23, Hitler announced his intentions to move into Poland. That
same day, the British government concluded it would make a *single* state
in Palestine—not a homeland for the Jews—to become independent by
1949. And in May, too, negotiations with the Soviet Union reached a
stalemate. Joe Kennedy had a hand in only the last of these events.

Any possible alliance with the USSR was an anathema to Kennedy.
When the American ambassador to the Soviet Union, Joseph E. Davies,

came to London that spring, Kennedy violently disagreed with him about the Russians' sincerity. Davies warned Kennedy that if he could not help to persuade Chamberlain and Daladier of France that the Russians truly wanted this alliance, they would "drive Stalin into Hitler's arms." Davies further warned that the obvious snubs by the Western allies made the paranoid Russian leader distrustful of any alliance with them.[3]

"The attitudes of the broad masses of the [British] population are sharply anti-German everywhere, except for a part of Scotland," the Soviet ambassador Maisky wrote on May 2 in his journal. "Reconstruction of the Government. This is considered absolutely inevitable now, and even the Beaverbrook press has started a campaign to this effect. But Chamberlain is stubbornly postponing the entry of such figures as Eden, Churchill and others into the Cabinet until the very last moment."[4] Maisky's protector and foreign minister Maxim Litvinov would be fired the following day and replaced with Vyacheslav Molotov. For Maisky personally, as well as for Russia, the British failure to accept the Soviet proposals delivered "the smashing blow to the policy of effective collective security."[5]

Chamberlain's mealymouthed approach to the Soviets was encouraged by Kennedy during his weekend of May 13–14 at Chequers. Also invited were the Oliver Stanleys, David Margesson (the Government Chief Whip), and Lord and Lady Lee of Fareham.* Kennedy's constant pessimism about the Russian deal was reflected in his assurances to Hull that Chamberlain was "not at all sure that he will not call the whole thing off." Like Chamberlain, the ambassador was exasperated with what was seen as Russian prevarication. Just the same, it was Kennedy who helped drive the prime minister's own hesitation by asking unnecessarily loaded questions.[6]

Chamberlain and Kennedy failed to recognize that much of the problem from the Soviet side was caused by the change from Litvinov to Molotov at the Soviet foreign ministry. In June, the Soviets wanted an amendment that Britain should come to the aid of the Baltic states in

---

* Arthur Hamilton Lee was a former cabinet minister under Lloyd George. It was Lee who gave Chequers to the nation in 1917 as the residence and retreat of successive British prime ministers.

the event of "indirect aggression." This was interpreted by Chamberlain as possibly including a coup d'état in favor of the spread of communism. When the Russians tried to make it clear the proposed clause related only to German aggression, Chamberlain refused to believe them.[7] "I had a very tiresome week over the Russians whose methods of conducting negotiations include the publication in the press of all their despatches and continuous close communication with the [British] opposition [parties] and Winston," Chamberlain wrote to his sister Ida.[8]

The Soviets were losing patience, too. The objections to any sort of agreement with the Finns, Estonians, and Latvians, combined with the Polish and Rumanian desire for an agreement with a guarantee for their safety by anyone but the Russians, made any meeting of minds impossible. The Soviet's new hard man, the stony-faced Molotov, was incandescent with rage, accusing the French and British of treating the Russians as "nitwits and nincompoops." With a thinly veiled reference to Stalin, the British ambassador, Sir William Seeds, reported Molotov's words to Halifax: "If His Majesty's Government treated the Soviet Government as being naïve or foolish people, he himself could afford to smile, but he could not guarantee that everyone would take so calm a view."[9]

IN JUNE, THE Japanese Imperial Navy blockaded the British settlements at the North China port of Tientsin (modern-day Tianjin). By early July, Halifax remarked to Kennedy that the British must "start to withdraw" soon. In the same communication to Hull, Kennedy reported incredulously that "Halifax is of the belief that England appearing stronger all the time is having an effect on Germany."[10]

THAT JULY, KENNEDY knew he could not claim the Wohlthat connection as a personal triumph in view of the outrage expressed in the British press about returning the Czech gold to the Nazis. Kennedy's frustration boiled over, and he began to fulminate more than usual. Everywhere he went, regardless of who was there, the American ambassador advocated making peace and not "resisting Hitler." Lord Francis-Williams, editor of the *Daily Herald,* a newspaper that advocated the need for a national unity government to combat the deteriorating international situation, derided the stench of "peace in the air" that emanated from the American embassy in London. "Joseph Kennedy, a tycoon who seemed to me when I met him to combine all the disagreeable traits of all the very rich men I had ever met with hardly any of their virtues, had set flowing a constant stream of denigration of Britain backed by the assertion that we would have no chance against the superior power and discipline of Germany."[11]

Walter Lippmann revealed to both Harold Nicolson and Winston Churchill at a dinner during his June visit that his conversation with Kennedy had deeply depressed him. He had found it "shockingly undiplomatic," to say the least, and was alarmed by the Kennedy refrain: war was inevitable and Britain would be badly licked. Churchill rose from the dinner table. "It may be true, it may well be true, that this country will at the outset of this coming and to my mind inevitable war be exposed to dire peril and fierce ordeals. It may be true that steel and fire will rain down upon us day and night scattering death and destruction far and wide. It may be true that our sea communications will be imperiled and our food supplies placed in jeopardy," the great man growled, purple with anger. "Yet these trials and disasters, I ask you to believe me, Mr. Lippmann, will but serve to steel the resolution of the British people and to enhance our will for victory. . . . Yet supposing . . . that Mr. Kennedy were correct in that tragic utterance, then I for one would willingly lay down my life in combat, rather than in fear of defeat, surrender to the menaces of these most sinister men."[12]

As the London Season swung lightheartedly from tea parties to dinner parties to dinner dances and late suppers, it took no time for Joseph P. Kennedy's prognostications of defeat to make the rounds. The first secretary of the American desk at the Foreign Office, the mightily initialed J.V.T.W.T. Perowne, had the unenviable task of reporting on Kennedy's movements and actions to the Foreign Office.

In a minute to file, Perowne noted an informal conversation between a friend of his in the Coldstream Guards, Joe, and Jack Kennedy. The ambassador was pontificating about Germany's knowing precisely where all the British airplane factories were, while the British were ignorant of the position of the German ones. Then Joe waxed on about "the possibility of both Japan and Turkey joining the other side, which would have a disastrous effect on our sea power." Given the recent agreement with Turkey, "doubt was voiced about the mention of Turkey, but the informant insisted that Kennedy had said so." When Perowne asked his friend if Kennedy had said anything about the financial or economic strength of the Germans, he replied, "Come to think of it, Kennedy's son, Mr. Jack Kennedy, had interjected that even if the Neutrality Act was repealed it would not help us much as we had not got sufficient gold for large purchases."[13]

Somehow Kennedy was oblivious to the distinct frisson when he entered a room that July. Was he concentrating instead on saving Kick from a disastrous mistake in marrying Billy Hartington? He did complain he was in dire need of recharging his batteries, but that was hardly an excuse for his lack of diplomacy. On July 20, Kennedy wrote to Hull that the prime minister was looking forward to a long vacation, due to commence on August 5. Then, a few days later, Kennedy himself departed for the South of France.

ON AUGUST 22, Kennedy's chargé, Herschel Johnson, cabled the State Department that all the British Cabinet had returned to London, save Lord Maugham, the Chancellor, who was in Canada. News broke very late the night before "that both Berlin and Moscow have announced the intention to conclude a Russo-German non-aggression pact, and that Ribbentrop is to fly to Moscow to sign the agreement." Johnson admitted that it came as a "frank shock." Worse still, Maisky knew nothing. The *Daily Herald* was stunned, calling "the news so staggering as to hardly appear credible."[14] The British and French had been caught napping while the Germans successfully negotiated their way to war.

Kennedy flew back from Nice to London that same day. The King, on receiving the previous day's cabinet minutes from the prime minister, left Balmoral on the overnight train, arriving at Euston Station at eight A.M. on August 24. Two hours later, George VI held a meeting of the Privy Council at Buckingham Palace. The Queen joined him on August 29, leaving the princesses Elizabeth and Margaret Rose in Scotland. Ambassador Kennedy warned all Americans who had no essential business in the United Kingdom to make their way home. Billy Hartington, not wishing to be drafted, enlisted in the Coldstream Guards.[15]

KENNEDY WAS UNAWARE that his "loud talk" had been reported back to Harold Ickes in Washington. On July 15, 1939, Ickes wrote, "I discussed

Joe Kennedy fully with John [Cudahy].* He admits that Joe Kennedy does some pretty loud and inappropriate talking about the President. He does this before English servants, who are likely to spread the news. According to John," Ickes noted, "Kennedy is vulgar and coarse and highly critical in what he says about the President. And when John cautioned him on one occasion not to talk as he was doing before the servants, Joe said that he didn't give a damn."

Cudahy also said "if Joe couldn't be loyal to the President, he ought to resign." But Ickes would wait until August to share this tidbit with Roosevelt. "The President knows that Joe is not loyal," Ickes recorded, "but he had had a letter from him only a day or two previously protesting his great loyalty. The President said that Kennedy was as good as anyone in reporting carefully what was transpiring in England and in diplomatic circles and he gave no indication that he had an intention of removing him."[16] Ickes's revelation was hardly news to Roosevelt. Kennedy had never kept his unwanted opinions to himself, particularly if there was a newspaperman in the vicinity. These were treacherous days, and Kennedy's loose talk made his advice subject to daily scrutiny from the White House and State Department.

On August 23, Kennedy instructed Hull that "if the President is contemplating any action for peace it seems to me the place to work is on Beck [foreign minister] in Poland and to make this effective it must happen quickly." He said that Chamberlain was "very low" and feeling rather sorry for himself. "It seems as if all my work has come to naught," the prime minister lamented to Joe.[17] Then Kennedy suggested to Chamberlain "if the guarantee of the countries [Britain and France] might not be looked at in the same light as the guarantee to Czechoslovakia"—in other words, valueless. The prime minister replied that "he was afraid that it would," because Hitler would automatically believe Britain and France were bluffing. Kennedy hoped that they were.[18] Their frantic pursuit of peace was out of step with the British public's tacit acknowledgment that Hitler had to be stopped.

When the terms of the Molotov-Ribbentrop Pact became public

---

*   Cudahy served as the American ambassador to the Irish Free State until January 17, 1940, and afterward as ambassador to Belgium from January 17, 1940, to July 18, 1940. Previously he had served as ambassador to Poland.

after its signature on August 23, the British and French negotiating team packed their bags to leave Moscow.[19]* A worried Sir Horace Wilson suggested Kennedy ask Washington to pressure the Poles into negotiating with Germany. Joe phoned Washington twice on August 24, moving from the initial position "Sir Horace Wilson thought" to demanding that Washington force the Poles to "be more agreeable to the Nazi demands." Kennedy argued it was quite natural for Germany "to get back what she had before the world war, adding a little here and there" for her troubles. He followed up with a panic-stricken memorandum ordering Roosevelt what to do. Moffat recorded: "The president related this in an amused tone and said that the report was so unique that he had put it in his private files."[20]

Next, Kennedy spoke to Sumner Welles at the White House. He had the effrontery to ask if Welles "understood the import of my request for the President to get in touch with Poland." Welles said he had, but "it could not be done the way" Kennedy suggested. Joe shouted he "didn't care how it was done so long as something was done and quickly." In his diary, Joe recorded that Welles said, "Something will be done tonight 'whatever is going to be done.'" Years later, Kennedy wrote that the conversation was with Roosevelt, not Welles: "'Alright,' came the President's voice over the telephone. 'Something will be done tonight.'" That night Roosevelt sent a cable to the Polish president Ignacy Mościcki and Hitler to refrain from hostilities "for a reasonable and stipulated period" and "agree likewise by common accord to solve the controversies which have arisen between them."[21]

ON AUGUST 24, the British cabinet met to discuss a cable from Sir Percy Loraine,† the new British ambassador to Italy. When Loraine met Count Ciano, the Italian had made "insistent suggestions" that a possible solution might emerge if "a preliminary return of Danzig to the Reich"

---

* Article IV of the pact stated that should disputes or conflicts arise with other powers, neither party could become associated directly or indirectly with them. There were also four secret protocols dividing up Eastern Europe between Germany and the USSR.

† Loraine succeeded Lord Perth (Eric Drummond) as ambassador to Italy and was previously the British ambassador to Turkey. He was nicknamed "Pompous Percy" by his staff.

could be made. "Signor Mussolini wanted peace," but Ciano begged Loraine to understand Italy's difficult position with regard to Germany. Reading between the lines, Loraine deduced correctly that the Italians suspected an imminent invasion of Poland; and Mussolini did not want to be dragged into a war unprepared. Japan, too, Loraine wrote, had been "kept in the dark up to now."[22]

Friday, August 25, began badly for Kennedy. The British and French announced their guarantee for Poland. Joe was annoyed the president had ignored his advice when, after all, he was at the center of British decision-making. That said, Chamberlain wrote directly to Roosevelt that same day about the new American Norden air bombsight for precision bombing, without advising his friend Joe.* Then, too, Kennedy was furious when he learned the cabinet had raised the interest rate for sterling from 2 percent to 4 percent without warning him. How dare the Chancellor of the Exchequer, Sir John Simon, treat him like an outsider? Why hadn't Montagu Norman warned him? Joe had only to look in the mirror for his reply. There were "funny stories" circulating in The City about the ambassador and his investments. "The inference was that Kennedy's stock exchange activities," Perowne advised within the Foreign Office, "gave evidence of anti-British proclivities and a desire to make money without being too scrupulous as to the methods employed."[23] This explains Kennedy's violent reaction to the interest rate rise, which was intended to keep speculators from betting against the pound, and suggests he was doing just that through nominees.

Throughout the day, Joe prowled the corridors of British power to discover Hitler's response to the guarantee. It was ten P.M. before he was invited to Downing Street to read the day's dispatches. Afterward, according to Joe, he went to the cabinet room to join the prime minister, the foreign secretary, and Alec Cadogan. Sir Nevile Henderson had made a report of his meeting with Hitler. The führer's reply was "the most

---

* Chamberlain explained to Roosevelt that the British had gone through channels initially (British Air attaché in the United States to the U.S. Air Force) but had been flatly turned down. Although Chamberlain appreciated the reasons why, he was making a personal plea to the president to see if there might be a more beneficial outcome. FDR had to refuse the request on August 31 due to the Neutrality Acts as they stood (*Source:* FDRPL, PSFA 0322, Great Britain).

impudent document I have ever seen," Oliver Harvey wrote, "in that it is the old story. 'You leave us free in the East to deal with Poland and we will then guarantee you, but you must return our colonies.' Hitler very calm but absolutely immovable. Repeated again and again his intention to deal with Poles for their intolerable persecution of Germans!"[24]*

While Britain prepared, mobilizing its men, equipment, and emergency services, Kennedy wrote a dispatch to Sumner Welles on Saturday, August 26, forwarding a report from Joe Jr. based on his trip to Munich, Berlin, and Hamburg. "I am sure that the German people do not want a war and are pretty well convinced that there will be no war," young Joe's account began with pie-eyed optimism and no analysis of facts. In Hamburg, where British and Danish newspapers were widely available, the population was "fully conscious of the danger, but I did not meet one who believed that war would result. . . . The Russian pact has had a terrific psychological effect in that now they are confident that England and France can do nothing."[25] Joe Jr.'s report was barely more than a sophomoric travelogue, read against the background of Hitler's announcing his deadline of September 1 for the British and French to cave in.

Kennedy urged Chamberlain to make "your solution more attractive to Germany," then told him, time and again, how to do it. He said, "If [Hitler] accepted a reasonable Polish settlement perhaps he could get the U.S. and other countries to get together on an economic plan that certainly would be more important to Germany."[26]

Chamberlain, however, was a broken man, and never seriously considered Kennedy's advice. In his darker moments, the prime minister cursed the Poles for being unreasonable in not negotiating in earnest with Hitler, despite SIS intelligence that the Molotov-Ribbentrop Pact included a division of Poland between the signatories. Chamberlain was desperate to see the best in the Hitler "peace offer," calling Hitler's view of the Polish situation as "genuine idiosyncrasy rather than craftiness."[27]

Sir Nevile Henderson was cross-examined at the August 26 cabinet meeting, urging ministers to sign a nonaggression pact with Germany. When Halifax asked questions about Hitler's sincerity, Henderson answered,

---

* Only after the war was it learned that the invasion of Poland had been delayed by five days due to the guarantee.

"However little faith one might have in Herr Hitler's promises, one might at least test them out." Given that Henderson was viewed by the Foreign Office as an anti-Semite and more sympathetic to Germany than to Britain, it seems incongruous that the Chiefs of Staff agreed with him. But the chiefs knew they needed until August 31 to be fully prepared for a German attack on Britain—never mind assisting Poland. While the government was happy to delay, a nonaggression pact was out of the question. The British August 28 reply to Hitler was simple: negotiate directly with Poland for a reasonable solution. The White House received notice of the British guarantee to Poland from Lord Lothian in Washington the same day, forty-eight hours before Kennedy cabled Hull.

"I have a feeling that Englishmen are a little proud of themselves to-night," Edward R. Murrow broadcast over CBS Radio from London. "They believe that their government's reply was pretty tough; that the Lion has turned; and that the retreat from Manchukyo [Manchuria], Abyssinia, Spain and Czechoslovakia and Austria has stopped. They are amazingly calm; they still employ understatement; and they are inclined to discuss the prospects of war."[28]

THE NEXT DAY, August 29, Joe Kennedy waited nervously. He had met Halifax, but was not shown the German sixteen-point peace offer. Writing to Arthur Houghton, Joe felt the pulse of history surround him: "I am sitting at my desk waiting to hear what Mr. Hitler says to Sir Nevile and wondering whether it is to be peace or war."[29] The matter concerning Joe most, however, was his own reputation. "The children are all back in London, but I don't feel I should send them home until I have the rest of the Americans out of London," he told Houghton. "Another one of those great moral gestures that the American people expect you to make; that is, get your own family killed, but be sure and get Miss Smith of Peoria on the boat." Just the same, there was never any doubt that Kennedy's family would be in danger. Lord Derby had offered his country home as a safe refuge. On the same day Joe wrote to Houghton, J. P. Morgan offered the Kennedys his fully staffed and furnished Wall Hall in Hertfordshire as "a safe port in a storm." Without hesitation, Kennedy opted for Morgan's mansion.[30]

At midnight on August 29, Kennedy cabled Hull that the Germans agreed to direct negotiations with the Poles. The Polish ambassador, the sad-eyed Józef Lipski, returned to Berlin the following day. Kennedy thought this was a good sign, but his hopes were soon dashed when he met with Halifax. Hitler's demands for an agreement within twenty-four hours were both "impudent and impertinent," the Foreign Secretary said. The führer, however, thought his sixteen-point "magnanimous offer to Poland" particularly generous, given that Lipski had returned as a mere ambassador and not a plenipotentiary empowered to act on behalf of his government. So, Hitler refused to meet him, sending his sixteen points direct to Warsaw instead. "I needed an alibi, especially with the German Volk," Hitler later confided to his interpreter, Paul Schmidt, "to show them that I had done everything to maintain peace."[31] When Kennedy spoke to Roosevelt late that evening, the president did not tell him that Lothian in Washington had kept him abreast of the news as it happened.

On August 30, writing to Roosevelt about the British draft reply to Germany, Kennedy commented: "In its present form, I should say, a little too firm with Hitler and I have an idea that Halifax will tone it down before it is finally sent." Then Kennedy passed along his personal opinion as fact. "I think that Chamberlain, Halifax, Cadogan, and Butler realize that there is a great deal of negotiation still to be done," Kennedy said, "and that too firm a hand, which might preclude Hitler from finding any basis on which he could quit with honor, might be very disastrous." Then he affirmed "the rest of the cabinet . . . feel they have Hitler on the run and want to make it as tough as possible." Kennedy was wrong on all counts. In fact, Halifax brought in top diplomatic treaty wordsmiths to stiffen up the British response.[32]

A day later, Edward R. Murrow said in his "This Is London" broadcast at four P.M.: "It has been decided to start evacuation of school children and other priority classes as already arranged under the government scheme, tomorrow, Friday, September 1. . . . School children will be taken by their teachers to homes in safer districts, where they will be housed by people who have already offered to receive them," Murrow continued. "Posters are being distributed at the schools, showing the times, and mothers with children below school age should assemble at the school unless they have been notified in some other way."[33]

In Washington, Roosevelt told Jim Farley confidentially that Kennedy had taken tea with the King and Queen and found them "deeply disturbed." Apparently, America's ambassador added to the panic of those heady days, making the rounds of every "topside person" who would talk with him. Kennedy had no idea that much of their discomfiture was due to his Cassandra prophecies and his avowals as to how he possessed the magic bullet to avert war through "meaningful" concessions to Hitler. To Kennedy's mind, Poland—a country of 33 million souls—was just another commodity for trade. He told Tommy Corcoran, one of Roosevelt's closest advisers, that the British should just "let Hitler take over all of Europe since we could not possibly do business with the Russians but could always assassinate Hitler."[34]

In London, Parliament had concluded that "a great evil must be erased from the world," according to *The Times*. "That evil is the spirit of faithlessness, of intolerance, of bullying, and of senseless ambition. . . . The conviction overrides the horror of the thought that civilized man has had to tackle the same task twice in twenty-five years," and no matter what, "it will be done this time in a way which will ensure that our children will not have to repeat it."[35]

On August 31, Sir Horace Wilson greeted Joe Kennedy as "the stormy petrel." His use of the term "stormy petrel"—that harbinger of trouble to sailors—was significant. Kennedy's unremitting prognostications of a British defeat had, at long last, reached the highest circles.[36] That night, Hitler gave the order to begin *Fall Weiss* (Case White) with several dozen "false flag" incidents on the border between Germany and Poland.* At 4:45 A.M. on September 1, the German cruiser *Schleswig-Holstein* opened fire on the heavily fortified port of Danzig. At first, startled residents

---

* A false flag was often used by Hitler during the early days of the war. German commandos led incursions into Czechoslovakia, Poland, Rumania, and so forth, pretending to be soldiers from the other side. In the most notorious of these, the Gleiwitz incident, it became clear at the Nuremberg trial of the SS-Sturmbannführer Alfred Naujocks that the SS had murdered a German farmer sympathetic to the Poles as well as over a hundred concentration camp victims from Dachau, then claimed they were alleged victims of the Polish massacre.

thought it was a thunderstorm, relieving the oppressive heat. Instead, they were the first shots fired and the beginning of World War II.

CHAMBERLAIN DELIVERED HIS ultimatum to Hitler on September 1, telling the House of Commons, "His Majesty's Government will without hesitation fulfil their obligations to Poland" and that the Germans had until eleven A.M. British standard time to reply. Yet when Chamberlain addressed the House again on the evening of September 2, he had no news to report from Germany. Speculation arose that perhaps the Germans were considering "a proposal which had been put forward by the Italian Government," clinging to peace with the white knuckles of hope.

When Chamberlain sat down, a deadly hush descended. Then the dull, no-nonsense northerner Arthur Greenwood, deputy leader of the Labour opposition but never one to excite with his speeches, rose. Greenwood's Labour colleagues suddenly exploded with cheers, followed by a return salvo from the Conservatives. Greenwood was more than mildly surprised. "I am speaking under difficult circumstances," he began, ". . . and I speak what is in my heart at this moment."

From a seat at the far end of the government benches, an impassioned Leo Amery, the father of Kick Kennedy's friend Julian, stood up and shouted, "Speak for England, Arthur!" Chamberlain turned sharply toward his ally, Amery, in stunned silence. Greenwood continued: "An act of aggression took place thirty-eight hours ago. The moment that act of aggression took place one of the most important treaties in modern times came into operation. . . . Tomorrow we meet at 12. And I put this point to him. Every minute's delay now means the loss of life, imperilling our national interests . . . and honour."[37]

On September 3, after dithering for two days to discover if the French would honor their guarantee to Poland, a grave Chamberlain addressed the nation by radio from the cabinet room at 10 Downing Street at 11:15 A.M. to explain the situation.* He made no apology for the hiatus in declaring war, stating that despite calls to Herr Hitler to "suspend all

* The most notable change in the war cabinet reshuffle was the addition of Winston Churchill as First Lord of the Admiralty. Henceforth, he would *not* speak out against Chamberlain's policies, as he was now part of the government.

aggressive action against Poland and withdraw their forces from Polish territory" on September 1, no answer had been received. Then Chamberlain lamented gravely, "Consequently this country is at war with Germany."[38]

IMMEDIATELY AFTERWARD, CHAMBERLAIN asked Rab Butler how he liked his speech, when a loud wailing sound made it impossible to hear. It was exactly 11:27 A.M. when the first air raid siren of the war deafened all London. Mrs. Chamberlain "appeared in the doorway with a large basket containing books, thermos flasks, gas-masks and other aids to waiting" and they made their way to the basement of No. 10. Winston Churchill's wife, Clementine, joined her husband "braced for the crisis and commented favourably upon the German promptitude and precision." They climbed up to the rooftop to look, and seeing nothing, headed down to their shelter, "armed with a bottle of brandy and other appropriate medical comforts." Joe Kennedy directed the embassy staff to the shelter at the couturier's, Molyneux, across the square on Grosvenor Street, since the embassy had no air raid shelter to call its own.[39]

It was a false alarm—one of two that day. Once the all clear sounded, Kick Kennedy, flanked by her brothers Jack and Joe, were among the hundreds of spectators dashing into the Palace of Westminster to hear what would be said in the House of Commons. It was there at the Speaker's party for his granddaughters that Kick had first danced with Billy Hartington. Despite her fervent pleas to stay with her father in London, Kick had already been told that if it was war, she must return home with her mother and siblings.

In the Commons, tense MPs were "packed in like sardines. . . . All the stars—if there are any—were present," Ivan Maisky wrote in his diary. "The atmosphere was heavy, menacing and oppressive. The galleries of the Lords, the press and guests were jam-packed. . . . Lady Astor, as is her custom, seemed to be sitting on needles, and looked at me as if she meant to grab me by the hair." Amused, Maisky added, "Kennedy immediately leapt out of his seat when he saw that we would be neighbours, made a clumsy gesture, and took a seat in the second row (the 'envoys' row'), his great vanity as American ambassador notwithstanding."[40]

PART IV

INTO THE DARKNESS

It's the end of the world,
the end of everything.

—JOSEPH P. KENNEDY, SEPTEMBER 3, 1939

27

SINKING THE SS *ATHENIA*

This is the way the world ends
Not with a bang but with a whimper.
—T. S. ELIOT,
"THE HOLLOW MEN," 1925

All aboard the SS *Athenia* on September 3, 1939, listened intently to the radio broadcast as the prime minister's defeated voice crackled, "This morning the British Ambassador in Berlin handed the German Government a final note that, unless we heard from them by 11 o'clock . . . a state of war would exist between us. . . . It is the evil things that we shall be fighting against—brute force, bad faith, injustice, oppression and persecution—and against them I am certain that right will prevail."

When the broadcast finished, James Goodson, the eighteen-year-old American-born son of British parents who raised him in Toronto, recited aloud the concluding lines of T. S. Eliot's "The Hollow Men." Many in the third-class lounge of the *Athenia* bound for Montreal—especially the five hundred Jewish refugees aboard—thought they were "well out of it" and were right to "leave old Europe" to sink into the abyss.[1] Less than ten hours after the declaration of war, Goodson and his fellow passengers could hardly have known that they would become the war's first British, Canadian, and American civilian casualties.

By Goodson's estimate, there were around 1,300 passengers and crew on board.* In the third-class lounge, the younger Americans began a songfest, with the Irish and English joining in with their own favorite tunes. Everything was jolly until a young man, no older than Goodson, was persuaded to stand and sing solo. Small and slight with dark wavy hair and clear blue eyes, the boy sang in a high tenor that rang "as true as a bell." He began with "Oh where, tell me where, has my Highland laddie gone." Everyone stopped chatting, put down their glasses, and listened. When he finished, the boy moved on to "The Bonnie Banks o' Loch Lomond" and ended with "The Road to the Isles."

With each song, the feeling of yearning for what had been lost and what might have been increased. But most of all, the boy's singing reflected his "own sadness and touching the homesickness of all those who were leaving home and family, probably never to see them again. There were tears in their eyes, and the blue eyes of the singer, and even in the eyes of the Canadians and Americans as they shared the great sense of nostalgia for old places and beloved faces."[2]

BY EARLY EVENING on September 3, Joe Kennedy had finished his rounds of parliamentarians for the day and spoken to Missy LeHand and Hull. Missy was crying, wishing Joe well, and said "the President would try to talk" soon. There had been a second "false alarm" air raid, Kennedy told Hull, who responded like a "tired old man." After a long day's work, Joe headed back home for the safety of Wall Hall in Hertfordshire.[3]

AT 7:40 P.M., just off the Hebrides, as the *Athenia* pitched and rolled on the swells into a strong cold westerly, the ship "was struck by a powerful explosion quickly followed by a loud crack and whistle." At that moment, James Goodson was climbing the staircase to go to the dining room. The ship shuddered, and the lights went out. He could hear women screaming, and people running frantically, calling to one another in the dark. "We all knew the ship was mortally stricken; she was beginning to list." When the emergency lighting came on, Goodson returned to the

* There were 1,352 passengers and 315 crew members on board: 469 Canadians, 311 Americans, 72 British, and 500 Jewish refugees. Of these, 98 passengers and 19 crew were killed.

companionway and saw "a sort of Dante's Inferno; a gaping hole at the bottom of which was a churning mass of water on which there were broken bits of wooden stairway," and bodies swirling, "floundering in the water. Many screamed they couldn't swim." Goodson "slithered down the shattered stairway" and plunged in. "One by one I dragged them to the foot of the broken companionway, and left them to clamber up to the other rescuers above."[4]

WITH THE DECLARATION of war, Kennedy had ordered that the embassy provide twenty-four-hour staffing and demanded that the State Department fund better air raid protection for his people. Not only was the embassy responsible for repatriating thousands of Americans, but it had also become the official conduit between the British and the Germans, taking over the functions of the British consulate in Berlin to bring British citizens home. Kennedy had lost his temper with Hull, cabling that what he needed were ships, and that waiting for them would cost lives.

Shortly after going to bed, Kennedy was awakened by a call from the Foreign Office. The message read out to him from an unknown British clerk "with a clipped accent" said: "S.S. *Athenia,* Donaldson Line, torpedoed 200 Miles off Malin Head [the most northern point in Ireland], 1400 passengers aboard, S.O.S. received. Ship sinking fast."[5]

ABOARD THE SINKING *Athenia,* young Goodson worked to save children, then women, then men, who were marooned from the stairwell by the swirling sea. Some cowered in the corridors, waiting to drown. Goodson swam underwater to reach them, then explained that the stair could be reached after a short distance underwater, if only they would trust him. The children "left their mothers," Goodson recalled, "put their small arms around my neck and clung to me . . . as we slipped into the water; they clung as I swam to the foot of the dangling steps; they clung as I climbed the slippery wreckage; and they clung as I prized their little arms from around me and passed them to those at the top." One Glaswegian seaman climbed along the shattered stairwell to hasten Goodson's rescue efforts, passing many whom the young man had saved. When Goodson asked the seaman to help by joining him, the sailor replied that he couldn't swim.

Treading water, Goodson looked up at the other seamen. They all shook their heads. Not one of them could swim.*

Goodson, undaunted, called out repeatedly in the darkly lit, ghostly, listing gangways—one after another—"Anyone there? Anyone there?" While wading through the half-submerged corridors, he stumbled against what he thought at first was a bundle of clothing. When he turned it over, he saw—gashed and bloodied—those clear blue eyes and dark curly hair of the young man, his own age, who "would never weep again for the bonnie banks of Loch Lomond." The lower decks were now the property of the dead. With the ship listing even farther, Goodson headed up to the badly sloping boat deck. As he emerged, the last of the lifeboats was lowered into the surging sea.

He jumped to catch a dangling, disabled lifeboat, but slid from the ropes, falling into the water. After a tremendous struggle, Goodson was finally brought safely aboard another lifeboat—thanks in no small part to a young woman dressed only in a slip who knew how to land a sharp right punch onto the young man who was battering Goodson with an oar to keep him off the crowded dinghy. By the time the Foreign Office awakened Joe Kennedy at 2:30 A.M., the *Athenia* was beyond help. At 4:30 A.M., looming out of the gloaming, a Norwegian tanker out of Christiansand, the *Knute Nelson*, came to the rescue of Goodson's lifeboat.[6] Later, the *Knute Nelson* would save other lifeboats.

JUST DAYS BEFORE the sinking of the *Athenia,* Joe Jr. and Jack were put to work at the embassy. Their father had booked passage to New York for the family on the American ocean liner *Washington,* due to sail on September 9. It would be delayed until September 12. Jack was sensitive to the fact that it shouldn't be known that the Kennedy family were going home and deserting the proverbial sinking ship of Britannia; while others, less fortunate, had to wait their turn. When a reporter cornered Jack to ask when he would be leaving, Jack lied, saying, "Oh, we must get back to school, but we shan't go until all other American citizens have gone."[7]

Winston Churchill announced the *Athenia*'s sinking on the morning of September 4. The 13,500-ton vessel was heading *west* when it

---

* Goodson never said how many lives he saved.

was torpedoed twice and had sunk with "a loss of 112 lives, including twenty-eight Americans." The commander of the German U-boat 30, *Oberleutnant* Fritz-Julius Lemp, had been following the *Athenia* for three hours before he opened fire. He would later claim that it had been zig-zagging outside the normal shipping lanes, giving him to believe that it was carrying troops.* Of course, Churchill knew that no troop ship was ordered heading *away* from Europe, but the Germans tried to make the most of their blunder with a disinformation coup against him. After all, Winston was the man they feared the most. Propaganda Minister Joseph Goebbels announced that the First Sea Lord "personally had ordered a bomb to be placed on board this vessel in order by its destruction to prejudice German–American relations." The ruse fooled no one. Captain Alan Kirk, the American naval attaché in London, told the press that after speaking to the captain of the *Athenia* and its crew, it had definitely been hit twice "slightly abaft midships" between the bulkhead and the engine room.[8]

JOE KENNEDY DISPATCHED Jack and Eddie Moore to Scotland two days later. Some of the several hundred survivors were brought ashore in Ireland, including those aboard James Goodson's lifeboat, but the majority were returned by British ships and ferries to Scotland. The reason the ambassador gave for sending Jack and Eddie was simple: the embassy in London was swamped, and it seemed a "routine matter" to him, the newspapers reported. Nonetheless, these first American, Canadian, and British civilian casualties were anything but "routine." Kennedy never adequately explained his reasoning for sending Jack.

The *Daily Telegraph* reported that the ambassador's second "'eighteen-year-old son' [Jack was twenty-two] faced a determined audience of

---

* Lemp was in command of the most modern U-boat, the U-110, when it was captured on May 9, 1941. He was within sight of Greenland when the HMS *Bulldog,* HMS *Broadway,* and the corvette HMS *Aubrietia* saw it had not been scuttled. When Lemp saw the boarding party hauling up sheaves of signals, technical charts, handbooks, and his Enigma machine with its operating instructions, keying tables, and spare wheels, he realized that the charges he had set to sink the U-boat had failed. Rather than face the consequences, he committed suicide by drowning (*Source:* Anthony Cave Brown, *Bodyguard of Lies* [London: W. H. Allen & Co, 1977], 53–54).

fellow Americans who had survived the torpedoing of the British liner"
and who demanded a convoy to protect them. The *Evening News* added a
year to Jack's age, giving him the thumbs-up for displaying "wisdom and
sympathy of a man twice his age." With more tact and diplomacy than his
father possessed, Jack told the survivors an American vessel would be in
Britain to collect them within the week. There was no need of a convoy,
since President Roosevelt assured him personally that "American ships
would not be attacked," as they were neutral. "His boyish charm and
natural kindliness persuaded those whom he had come to comfort that
America was indeed keeping a benevolent and watchful eye on them."[9]

The ambassador's reaction to the *Athenia's* sinking was a strange combination of near hysteria and formality. Kennedy wrote to Hull on September 8 that "my son Jack went up to Glasgow to contact the people
rescued from the *Athenia*. He came back with the very definite impression that they are in a terrible state of nerves and that to put them on a
ship without a convoy . . . would land them back in New York in such
a state that the publicity and criticism of the Government would be
unbelievable." Joe then warned Hull: "Also remember that a great deal
of attention is being paid to these people and they are beginning to feel
terribly important and they are having an awful lot to say."[10]

DEEPLY SADDENED BY the *Athenia's* tragedy, on September 9, King
George VI wrote in his diary: "I paid a visit to the Central War Room, to
hear of the latest news on all fronts. Not much to report. The U.S. Ambassador Mr. Kennedy came to tea. He looked & was worried over the
international situation. He was very busy over the victims who were killed
in the 'Athenia' when she was sunk by the German U boat last Monday."

His Majesty described his conversation with Kennedy: "He [Kennedy]
looked at the War very much from the financial & material viewpoint.
He wondered why we did not let Hitler have S.E. Europe, as it was
no good to us from a monetary standpoint. He did not seem to realise
that this country was part of Europe, that it was essential for us to act as
policeman, & to uphold the rights of small nations, & that the Balkan
countries had a national spirit."[11] George VI was taken aback by Kennedy's prophecy that "'Britain will be thrashed' and there will be nothing
left of civilization to save after the war."

SINKING THE SS *ATHENIA* ❧ 263

The following day, George VI put pen to paper in a private and confidential letter on Buckingham Palace letterhead, thanking the ambassador for sharing his frank opinions; but he begged to differ. "On thinking over what you said, I would like to make clear to you one or two matters which are in my mind. When referring to the fact that England would be broke at the end of this war, & that in this statement you also inferred that your country, the United States of America, would be likewise broke, is it not possible for you to put this fact before the American Press." The King's words "not possible" meant "don't."

"As I see it," George VI wrote, "the U.S.A., France & the British Empire are the three really free peoples in the World, and two of these great democracies are now fighting against all that we three countries hate and detest, Hitler & his Nazi regime and all that it stands for." The use of the words "hate and detest" showed the strength of George VI's objections to Kennedy's rhetoric. "You were speaking about the loss of prestige of the British Empire under the changed conditions in which we live since the last war. England, my country, owing to its geographical position in the World, is part of Europe. She has been expected to act, & has had to act, as the policeman, and has always been the upholder of the rights of smaller nations." In conclusion, the King averred, "the British Empire has once again shown to the World an united front in this coming struggle."[12]

KENNEDY ISSUED A warning to all Americans still in Britain: "Ambassador Kennedy feels that in addition to the other statements he has made that it is his duty to warn American citizens taking passage on vessels of belligerent nations, that when such vessels are being convoyed, the opposing belligerent may claim the right to sink them without warning."[13]

Jack Kennedy flew back to the United States later that month on the Pan American clipper, the *Dixie,* to resume his final year of studies at Harvard. *The Boston Globe* reported he was "the general favorite with all" on board. He had been bloodied in his first encounter with irate Americans and had come out of the skirmish a winner, just for being himself, "bright and helpful and interesting."[14]

And James Goodson? Immediately after his return to Canada, he enlisted to become a fighter pilot. In fact, he joined the Royal Canadian Air Force; was then attached to the Royal Air Force (RAF) No. 43 Squadron;

followed by No. 416 Squadron in the RAF (the American Squadron); before joining the United States Army Air Forces, where he became the commanding officer of the 336th Fighter Squadron of the 4th Fighter Group; and finally the group deputy commander. During the war he was awarded more than twenty medals from five countries, including the American Distinguished Flying Cross nine times; the American Distinguished Service Cross; the American Silver Star; the Air Medal twenty-one times; the Purple Heart; the British Distinguished Flying Cross; the Order of Leopold and the Croix de Guerre from Belgium; and the Croix de Guerre and Knight of the Legion of Honor from France.

The sinking of the *Athenia* was the beginning of a long, arduous road for two war heroes with different destinies. It seems a pity that they did not quite meet, since Goodson returned to Glasgow only after Jack Kennedy had left.

28

"DEPRESSED BEYOND WORDS"

---

*You all think I'm licked. Well, I'm not licked. And I'm going
to stay right here and fight for this lost cause.*
—JIMMY STEWART AS JEFFERSON SMITH,
MR. SMITH GOES TO WASHINGTON

The London crowds are cool—cooler than they were in 1914—in
spite of the thundery weather which does its best to scare everybody by staging unofficial rehearsals for air raids at the end of breathlessly humid days," Mollie Panter-Downes wrote on September 3 for
her editor William Shawn at *The New Yorker*. "The eye has now become
accustomed to sandbags everywhere and to the balloon barrage, the trap
for enemy planes, which one morning spread over the sky like some
form of silvery dermatitis." The evacuation of London had begun on
September 2. All inward traffic was stopped and "all the principle routes
out of town were one-way streets" during the three-day evacuation.
London was blacked out at night, and in the interval of the Beethoven
promenade concert, the BBC broadcast to motorists "what to do in an
air-raid."[1] Soon enough, Londoners would get used to not seeing or
hearing any schoolchildren on the street.

   Two days after the sinking of the *Athenia,* the British lost the important
vessels *Bosnia, Royal Sceptre,* and *Rio Claro* off the coast of Spain.[2] British
planes flew over Germany dropping propaganda leaflets to "inform" the

German Volk of the truth. Although there were no air attacks on Britain, the German army was decimating Poland. The United States reacted by extending a security zone around North and South America to three hundred miles offshore and resolved to strengthen its ties with its South American neighbors. The only bright spot on the horizon was that Canada, as a Dominion of the British Empire, was left off the American list of belligerents.[3]

On September 10, Kennedy sent a lengthy "Triple Priority" encoded message to Roosevelt, giving him "my impressions as to what is taking place here." Describing "high Government officials" as "depressed beyond words" that the United States had reverted to "its old Neutrality Law" when all they wanted to do was to "buy equipment already on order or whatever other equipment which they may need, for which they are willing to pay cash and carry away," Kennedy was unaware the president had already opened his own direct channel of communication with Chamberlain specifically to allay his fears. The ambassador rambled on, giving several viewpoints about the hopelessness of the situation, without attributing ownership to anyone.[*]

Then Kennedy outlined how the British studied all economic and financial aspects of the war through a think tank of experts. "There the best brains in England have been concentrated. . . . At the moment there is a lot of hasty improvisation, but they have executive powers and the manpower." Sticking a knife into the presidential hide, he added: "There is no question that Mr. Hull's Trade Agreements program is completely out of the window. England is as much a totalitarian country tonight from an economic and trade point of view as any other country in Europe. The British have a line on every country in the world from which they can get the supplies they need and the Government controls the shipping to transport them." Kennedy advised that "we should make a careful survey of supplies of raw materials of which we have a surplus and

---

[*]   This message is dated September 11, 1939, but given that he also speaks of visiting the King and Queen, the original message was most likely drafted on September 10. It would have taken an incredibly long time to create the "Triple Priority" encoding for such a long message.

study our competitive position." This survey would lead on to the state of U.S. merchant shipping and how to avert the British fleet from taking over world trade. Kennedy clearly feared the repeal of the Neutrality Laws, warning Roosevelt to "exercise the greatest caution" in revising the legislation because it may do "untold harm." He then suggested that "if we are willing to accept" all the gold from "England and France" [an estimated $4.5 billion] "we are left with practically the whole world's supply." He concluded, "We should be on our guard to protect our own interests and bend our best brains to the problem."[4]

Although Kennedy couched all of his "must dos" and "should dos" politely, the cable was not well received. Nor was his message of the following day, where he stated: "It appears to me that this situation may resolve itself to a point where the President may play the role of savior of the world . . . there may [be] a situation when President Roosevelt himself may evolve world peace plans."[5]

"I want to tell you something, and don't pass it on to a living soul," Roosevelt told Jim Farley. "After his talks [with the King, the Queen, and government officials] Joe sat down and wrote the silliest message to me I have ever received. It urged me to do this, that, and the other thing in a frantic sort of way."[6] For a long time, Kennedy had been the metaphorical albatross hung around the presidential neck, weighing him down with his outspoken, unyielding opinions. Roosevelt did not want Kennedy back in Washington, giving hourly succor to the isolationists in Congress, particularly as the self-proclaimed expert in European affairs and avid publicity seeker. Yet if the president recalled Kennedy and did not reward him, Joe would become even more disloyal to the president's foreign policies and the prospect of winning a third term.

Roosevelt knew that the isolationist Senator Borah of Idaho had told Hull, "So far as the reports in your Department are concerned, I wouldn't be bound by them. . . . I have my own sources of information which I have provided for myself, and on several occasions I've found them more reliable than the State Department." Harold Ickes believed Kennedy was Borah's source.[7] Roosevelt recognized, too, that if Joe persisted in his prophecies he could continue as ambassador only so long as Chamberlain remained prime minister.

Next, Kennedy insisted to Treasury Secretary Henry Morgenthau that his "official status in London was at stake" and that as ambassador he "should be allowed to counsel the British government in its disposition of American securities." Joe had not considered that his reputation as a stock market speculator played against him; or that he had given Roosevelt and Morgenthau ample reason to believe that he should never be granted insider knowledge on such a scale. So FDR told Morgenthau that Joe's September 11 cable should be ignored. Predictably, Kennedy phoned Sumner Welles when he had no answer. Welles told Kennedy he was his own worst enemy and no reply would be forthcoming.[8]

ON SEPTEMBER 12, Kick, Eunice, and Bobby sailed home with their mother aboard the SS *Washington,* taking with them a clutch of other privileged American children, among them Condé Nast's younger daughter, Leslie. Although Leslie does not recall the melancholy Kick, she vividly remembers that the *Washington* had a fresh coat of paint of "stars and stripes all over and was brightly lit night and day." Nine-year-old Leslie was leaving her mother in Britain facing war with her two half brothers; while her stepfather, Rex Benson, aged fifty, served as the liaison officer to the French First Army. Although Leslie was returning to her beloved father in New York, she was fearful she might never see her mother, brothers, or Rex again.[9]

Kick wrote to her father just before docking that the crossing was smooth. The main purpose of the letter, however, was to say: "It can't be eighteen months since we were on this boat going in the other direction. It all seems like a beautiful dream. Thanks a lot Daddy for giving me one of the greatest experiences anyone could have had. I know it will have a great effect on everything I do from herein."

Joe Jr. left England on September 18 aboard the *Mauretania* to begin his studies at Harvard Law School. The younger Kennedys—Patricia, Jean, and Teddy—sailed on the *Manhattan,* with Jean writing to her father that their governess, Miss Hennessey, "was very sad to be leaving Roy [her English boyfriend] and was morning all the way over." Only Rosemary remained in England, since she had been so happy at the Montessori convent school, and Joe felt it would have been cruel to uproot her. It was convenient that the school had moved to Boxmoor, near to Kennedy's rented home, Wall Hall.[10]

EARLIER, THE WEEK published a damaging article on September 13 about "those in 'high places' in London who regard it as axiomatic that the war must not be conducted . . . as to lead to a total breakdown of the German regime." In the past, much of what *The Week* published included untrue and scurrilous rumors about the so-called Cliveden Set and Kennedy as their pawn. This time, however, both the United States and Britain sat up and took notice. In Washington, Harold Ickes read the lines: "These circles are certainly in direct touch with certain German military circles—and the intermediary is the American Embassy in London (after all, nobody can suspect Mr. Kennedy of being unduly prejudiced against fascist regimes and it is through Mr. Kennedy that the German Government hopes to maintain 'contacts')." When Ickes showed the article to the president, Roosevelt commented, "There's a lot of truth to that."[11] The Foreign Office in London concurred.

That same week, on every newsstand across America the ambassador's face smiled out from the cover of *Time* magazine's September 18 issue under the headline THE U.S. AND THE WAR. Though the purpose of the article was to "big up" Kennedy, both Washington and London were displeased. "Last week Joe Kennedy had already shuttered and barred the palatial Embassy house at No. 14 Prince's Gate . . . and moved to a country house away from the terror of bombs," the article began. Then enumerating Kennedy's new duties: "With 9,000 Americans to shepherd to England, with tangible U.S. business interests under his eye, with 150 Americans cabling from the U.S. daily for information on *Athenia* survivors, with British bigwigs to see, Franklin Roosevelt to keep informed, Joe Kennedy had a bigger job."[12] Not one bomb had dropped on London, of course, but Kennedy had decamped to Hertfordshire—without approval from the State Department—and sent his family home.

Joe was described by the assistant secretary of state and former ambassador to Italy, Samuel Breckinridge Long, as "terribly explosive" only four days into the war. Long had no time for Kennedy's "troublesome publicity seeking" and impossible demands. "Kennedy seems to think that the only people needing repatriation are in the lobby of the American Embassy in London. . . . Kennedy had been condemning everybody and criticizing everything and has antagonized most of the people in the Administration."[13] Cordell Hull actively sought other channels to avoid contact with Kennedy, usually opting to address questions or give information through the new British ambassador Philip Kerr, Lord Lothian. Henry Morgenthau had initiated possible payment for outstanding British war debts through Lothian by taking possession of the *Queen Mary,* which was at New York.* Rather than evaluating his position, Kennedy persisted, like Don Quixote, tilting at the elusive windmill of "peace."

On Sunday, September 17, Lord Beaverbrook, the diminutive Canadian-born newspaper baron and backstage political mover and shaker, allegedly telephoned Kennedy with the news that the Russians had crossed into Poland. It was the fourteenth day of the German onslaught. "Get your President to see what plans can be worked out to save this catastrophe," Joe quoted Beaverbrook as saying.[14] Even so, Beaverbrook knew better than to make such a call. When Kennedy complained to the prime minister a day later about the perfidious Russians, he couldn't understand why Chamberlain was so phlegmatic about Soviet military involvement. Halifax, too, was reluctant "to register anything more than a mild protest."[15] As Maisky tacitly knew, it was part of Halifax's strategy *not* to enter into a military conflict with Russia, noting in his diary on September 21: "History has played a cruel joke on the elite of the British bourgeoisie. Today they really do find themselves *between the devil and the deep [blue] sea.*"[16]

JOE KENNEDY WAS actively avoided on both sides of the Atlantic. He was closely monitored by the Foreign Office as a defeatist and a danger to Britain. In late September, Lothian was sent "specimens of reports" from the Kennedyiana file. Although Kennedy's attitude and pronouncements were deemed "regrettable," the conclusion passed on to the British ambassador was to do nothing, "for the time being at any rate."[17] Like Roosevelt, the consensus had been that any action taken against Kennedy could endanger Britain. His histrionics and habit of scolding his superiors were legend. His

* The SS *Normandie,* owned and operated by a French company, was also in an American port at the time, and similar discussions took place with the French through Ambassador Bullitt.

isolationism became more extreme daily, just as the German chargé d'affaires in Washington, Hans Thomsen, told Ribbentrop that *all* American
isolationists were Germany's friends. Any acts of sabotage against Americans would "cut the ground out from under the isolationists whose line is
that American interests are not involved in the European war."[18]

By the end of September, Kennedy was pouring vitriol against Britain
into Roosevelt's ear, paying no attention to the president's statement on
September 24 that "any peace achieved as a result of hostilities will be
meaningless."[19] Joe wrote to FDR that the fall of Poland "created a great
shock.... Of course, the real fact is that England is fighting for her possessions and place in the sun, just as she has done in the past." He then
pointed to *The Times* headlines of August 5, 1914, and September 4, 1939,
as identical, save for the words "Junker" and "Nazi." Despite the "God-
awful behavior of the Nazis, surely the fact is that the English people are
not fighting Hitler—they are fighting the German people, just as they
fought them twenty-five years ago," because the British and the Germans
"haven't learned to live together peacefully."

Kennedy declared, "There are signs of decay, if not decadence, here,
both in men and institutions." Not realizing he was lashing out at his
friend Chamberlain, Kennedy wrote: "No one in power over the past
dozen years has really told the English people where they stand politically, economically and financially—and they are reaping the result of
that now.... The Parliamentary machine is not operating to throw up
real, able leaders. Many people doubt, and I share those doubts, whether
the Chamberlain Government can survive a single serious reverse, and
who is to replace the Prime Minister?" Then he postulated that "for all
Halifax's mystical, Christian character and Churchill's prophesies in respect of Germany, I can't imagine them adequately leading the people
out of the valley of the shadow of death.... England passed her peak as a
world power some years ago and has been steadily in decline."[20] That was
Jack's view in 1938 when he came to England. A year later, Jack revised
his thinking while writing his senior thesis, which would become the
bestselling book *Why England Slept.**

---

* The thesis was reviewed by his father and several American and British statesmen for
their thoughts before finalized. Arthur Krock of *The New York Times* helped, too. That said,

Nonetheless, there was more than a grain of truth to Kennedy's diatribe. *The Times* leader on January 1, 1900, declared that the twentieth century would be the "century of Germany." The Great War—soon to be redesignated the First World War—had bankrupted the British Empire. The United States emerged onto the world stage as an international force in 1917. The rise of the first communist country, the Soviet Union, that same year was a massive event. The assassinations of the Russian royal family at Ipatiev House on July 18, 1918, by the Bolsheviks would leave an indelible scar on the world's aristocracy and ruling elite. The world was changing, but not for the reasons Kennedy outlined to Roosevelt.

OF COURSE KENNEDY was sore. Since the declaration of war, he was no longer privy to Chamberlain's or Halifax's innermost thoughts. Each one, in turn, dismissed Kennedy's peace initiatives without discussion. It was evident, even to Chamberlain, that Kennedy had not appreciated why Britain had been compelled to go to war.

Then, too, despite his private correspondence with Roosevelt, Chamberlain remained "actively hostile" to bringing the United States into the war. Armaments were one thing, American involvement another. To his mind, American influence at any ultimate peace conference would create a repetition of Versailles. While Poland suffered its grueling punishment during the blitzkrieg, each day that Britain and France remained unscathed meant another day of fruitful aircraft production to try to make up the deficit against Germany. Each day also brought German losses. Halifax deduced that after German troops entered Warsaw, another peace offer would be forthcoming—for the sole purpose of duping Britain and France into laying down their arms while Hitler planned his next conquest. In contrast to Kennedy, who believed bombs would be dropped on London at any moment that September, Halifax's cool head told him that Hitler would want to digest Poland first, then offer peace. [21]

In early October 1939, Billy Hartington's uncle, Robert "Bobbety" Cecil, wrote an article entitled "Americans Ask What Are Our War Aims" as the U.S. Senate began to debate the revising its neutrality legislation.

Jack Kennedy's thesis is still thought to be his own work. When Krock helped turn it into the bestselling book, it received more editorial input.

"Within the isolationist bloc such strange bedfellows as Vandenberg, Borah and Nye, Father Coughlin, Colonel Lindbergh and the American Communist Party—all in differing degrees—take the line that the issues in Europe are not between democracy and dictatorship but between rival imperialisms," Cecil stated.

While admittedly Nazi imperialism was "more unpleasant" than French or British imperialism, "there is not a moral stake involved but merely a sordid squabble about boundaries and trade rivalries ... which are definitely not worth the bones of one American 'doughboy' or one dollar spent in a foreign war."[22] Although Joe Kennedy is not listed by name among the "isolationist bloc," the sentiments expressed accurately represented his beliefs, too.

At the same time, the Archbishop of Canterbury, Cosmo Lang, wrote to Halifax, as he, too, was concerned about the significance of the Allies stating their war aims. Simultaneously, an approach was made to Pope Pius XII by the conspirators in a plot to overthrow Hitler. General Ludwig Beck* devised a plan to use the pope as their go-between. It would take a month to finally make contact.[23]

POLAND SUCCUMBED TO the brutality of the German and Soviet onslaught when the Germans entered Warsaw on September 27. The Belgians immediately declared their neutrality and the French army took its place behind the Maginot Line. The British Expeditionary Force (BEF) arrived on the Continent three days later. Churchill made an impassioned radio broadcast on October 1, saying that "Poland has again been overrun by two of the great Powers which held her in bondage for a hundred and fifty years but were unable to quench the spirit of the Polish nation. . . . How soon it [victory] will be gained depends upon how long Herr Hitler and his group of wicked men, whose hands are stained with blood and soiled with corruption, can keep their grip upon the docile, unhappy German people."[24]

The prime minister wrote to his sister that "I take the same view as Winston to whose excellent broadcast we have just been listening." Chamberlain was not surprised by the Soviets joining the attack on

---

* General Beck had resigned as the Wehrmacht's chief of staff out of principle in 1938 over Czechoslovakia.

Poland and reiterated: "I believe Russia will always act as she thinks her own interests demand, and I cannot believe she would think her interests served by a German victory."[25]

As Halifax predicted, Hitler convened the Reichstag on October 6 to silence its members with his new "generous offer of peace" to the people of Great Britain.* Poland no longer existed, Hitler declared, rambling on that there was no longer any reason for this "ludicrous state of war to exist between the Reich and England." He was prepared to forgive and forget. After all, the British had not even encountered the German armed forces on land or in the air. The war at sea had slowed to a trickle by the time Hitler made his peace offer.

Halifax felt that "Hitler's speech today makes negotiation not impossible, but the way to do so without causing a cry of 'appeasement again' is definitely difficult." Halifax was determined that Hitler should be "proved wrong and not the victor, he would have to give up a lot, thereby humiliating himself, retire partially from Poland, create an independent Czech State, give up half his air force . . . and lots more."[26]

That night, Kennedy was awakened by Churchill and discovered that the president had been communicating directly with the First Sea Lord. He was furious and deeply embarrassed, because it demonstrated Roosevelt's trust in Churchill and mistrust of him. It was just "another instance of Roosevelt's conniving mind which never indicates he knows how to handle any organization," Joe wrote in his diary. "It's a rotten way to treat his Ambassador and I think shows him up to the other people. I am disgusted." Kennedy never had time for the "warmongering" Churchhill. "I can't help feeling he's not on the level. He is just an actor and a politician," Kennedy wrote. "He always impressed me that he'd blow up the American Embassy and say it was the Germans if it would bring the U.S. in. Maybe I do him an injustice."[27]

Understandably, without family or close friends near, Kennedy was feeling sorry for himself. He couldn't see the point of the war, and aside from Rosemary, her companion, his golfing buddies Jim Seymour and

---

* The French did not make a separate declaration of war from the British, and it was Chamberlain who spoke for the "Allies" with one voice.

London Jack at the embassy, and the Moores, he increasingly spent more and more time at Wall Hall on his own, often listening to his favorite classical music. "I'm running true to form," he wrote Rose. "I'm sick of everybody and so I'm alone tonight by choice. . . . This job without you is comparable with a street cleaner's at home."[28]

By the middle of October, all the straggling Americans had gone home, and neither the British nor the Americans seemed to have any real use for Kennedy, other than to look after American business interests at the lowest level Joe could imagine. He busied himself mostly in an attempt to maintain a prewar level of American imports, particularly in motion pictures. But when Frank Capra's *Mr. Smith Goes to Washington*, starring Jimmy Stewart, was released in November, confronting widespread corruption, dishonesty, and criminality in Congress, Joe swung into action, writing a scathing cable to Will Hays. For him, the movie was "one of the most disgraceful things I have ever seen done to our country. To permit this film to be shown in foreign countries, and to give people the impression that anything like this could happen in the United States Senate is to me nothing short of criminal."[29]

On November 4, 1939, the Senate passed the repeal of arms embargo. Roosevelt's plea about the Neutrality Act being neither impartial nor in America's best interests had worked. "In such circumstances," Roosevelt concluded to Congress, "our policy must be to appreciate in the deepest sense the true American interest."[30] Four days later, Neville Chamberlain wrote a sealed private and personal letter to the president. "The repeal of the arms embargo, which has been so anxiously awaited in this country is not only an assurance that we and our French allies may draw on the great reservoir of American resources," the prime minister said, "it is also a profound moral encouragement to us in the struggle upon which we are engaged. . . . It will have a devastating effect on German morale; it will also, I am confident, have a great influence on world opinion."[31]

JOE KENNEDY WAS granted home leave on November 22, much to the relief of the British. He told everyone from Their Majesties to Chamberlain, Halifax, Churchill and even Sir Henry "Chips" Channon MP that "England is committing suicide." Nancy Astor was horrified and handed a sealed letter to Kennedy for her great friend Lord Lothian in

Washington. In the most discreet terms, she warned Lothian that Kennedy was telling everyone "that if the war did not stop soon, there would be no markets!!! It looks as though he may be a bit of a defeatist, so you had better watch out for this."[32]

Before leaving, Joe had made the difficult decision, without consulting Rose in advance, that Rosemary should remain at the Montessori school because she was so happy. Henceforth, too, he decided Rosemary would be separated from the rest of the family. "She must never be at home for her sake as well as everybody else's."[33]

Kennedy left London on November 29 for a meeting in Paris with the American ambassadors to France, Russia, and the Netherlands, before heading south to Lisbon to catch the Pan American *Dixie Clipper* across the Atlantic, carrying with him a secret message from Churchill for the president. While the ambassadors met in Paris on November 30, the Soviet Union invaded Finland.

29

"BEWARE THE BEAR"

K. is very bearish.

—JAY PIERREPONT MOFFAT,
DIARY, DECEMBER 8, 1939

S tepping off the *Dixie Clipper* at Port Washington, Long Island, Kennedy smiled broadly. Rose broke through the assembled news-papermen and -women firing questions at him and kissed her husband. It had been nearly two months since they had seen each other. When asked what the British thought about America's attitude to the war, Joe said that the British government hadn't the "slightest belief" that the United States would become involved in the war, but that America's attitude bemused them. When asked to clarify, Joe said, "It's like sticking your tongue out at a fellow, and yet not being ready to punch him on the nose." Then Joe called out and waved to the reporters he knew and answered a few more questions.

Someone must have called out *"What's next?"* since Joe answered this would be his last public job. He planned "to spend the next five years watching his children grow up" but had every intention of staying in the job until the end of the war.[1] Kennedy had been ruminating since leaving London if he *really* wanted the presidency for himself, particularly with the war. If he succeeded as an outsider for the Democratic nomination, then failed, he could ruin Joe Jr.'s chances—even in twenty years' time. Worse still, if he did not fight for America to stay out of the war, his two older sons would be—literally—in the firing line. There was no ducking that. Besides, he knew that if the war spread, as it seemed to be doing, Roosevelt would be unstoppable as a candidate.[2] Then there was the financial side, too. London had cost him a great deal, and there was good money to be made in the current climate by speculating on the markets and selling short.

JOE SPENT THE day with the youngest members of his family in Bronxville. He must have discussed his frustrations and feelings with Rose; and she would have reminded him that he mustn't appear disloyal to Roosevelt after all he had done for them. Rose had a point. Disloyalty would tarnish the Kennedy name irretrievably. So, when he took the overnight train south, his decision about what he should do had been made. In Washington, he checked into the Carlton Hotel, shaved, changed his clothes and had breakfast, before walking to the White House for a nine A.M. meeting with Roosevelt.

Pausing to chat with journalists before entering the executive mansion, Joe said little to reporters "either about the European war or prospects for peace." He did, however, endorse the president, citing the problems "growing out of the war as sufficient warrant to continue Mr. Roosevelt in office for another four years." When asked to give details for his decision, Kennedy said that it would take two years (which no one had) to educate another man into the job as the problems became greater each day. "First and foremost, we know from what we have seen and heard that President Roosevelt's policy is to keep us out of the war, and war at this time would bring this country chaos beyond anyone's dream." Kennedy concluded, "This, in my opinion, overshadows any possible objection to 'a third term.'"[3]

Minutes later, Roosevelt greeted Kennedy sitting up in bed making his morning coffee, unaware that Joe had given his endorsement for his controversial third term. Kennedy's first impression was that the president looked extremely tired, but soon enough, those feelings were swept aside by Roosevelt's most cordial reception. More than likely, Joe told him about his statement to the press minutes earlier. When Joe got down to advising on Great Britain, FDR was a dutiful "good listener." He gave the president both barrels of his bearishness, not forgetting to include his prediction that if the British sold their U.S. holdings en bloc it would break the stock market just as the campaign for the presidential election heated up in the fall of 1940. Then he handed over the list of "submarine sinkings" that Churchill had given him.[4]

Next, Kennedy delivered a secret oral message from Churchill. Drawing an imaginary map of neutral Norway with his finger on the president's armoire opposite the bed, Joe explained where the British hoped to lay their mines to prevent the Germans from shipping Swedish iron ore from the Norwegian port of Narvik, once the Baltic froze for winter. Roosevelt nodded. It was just where the U.S. had laid roughly 350,000 mines in the last war. Naturally, the Norwegians would protest, softly, meaninglessly. So, Kennedy resolved to cable Churchill that afternoon their prearranged positive response: EUNICE WOULD LIKE TO GO TO THE PARTY.[5]

The ambassador is the sole source of this "secret message," but Kennedy's version does not stand up to scrutiny. As late as December 15, 1939, the British cabinet had not decided if mining the waters around neutral Norway was a good idea. Churchill himself was of two minds on the issue at that cabinet meeting, saying, "It was imperative that every possible step should be taken to maintain the flow of trade, not only by building new ships and chartering neutral tonnage but also by making the most profitable use of every available ton of cargo space."[6] Mining Norwegian waters could backfire and create a further restraint on trade among all neutrals. Several neutral ships had been blown up, too, within Norway's three-mile limit.* The German navy, the Kriegsmarine, had mined these shallow waters with magnetic mines, and "as a result of Germany's ferocious threats," Churchill said, "many of the neutrals were reluctant to charter their shipping to us."

Consequently, it is more likely that Churchill's "secret message" asked Kennedy and Roosevelt to consider "a proposal for exchanging shipping routes with American companies," which the First Lord would report as

---

* At that point, most of the ships chartered by the British were either Norwegian or Danish vessels. The German Kriegsmarine had disabled four neutral ships (two trawlers and two tankers) in Norwegian waters on December 14, 1939. Only one of these was salvageable (*Source:* CAB 65/2/50, December 15, 1939).

"under examination" in the December 15 cabinet meeting.[7] That played to Kennedy's strengths, kept him happy that he was useful, and most important, kept him away from more sensitive issues. Kennedy inadvertently corroborated this when he confirmed that his discussion with Roosevelt was about "my shipping plan."[8]

Roosevelt was so welcoming that Joe relaxed and ventured to ask the president why he had initiated direct correspondence with Churchill outside of diplomatic channels. The president's reply served to reinforce Joe's prejudices. FDR said he had never liked Churchill, ever since the last war. Just the same, Roosevelt believed Churchill would be the next prime minister, so he was trying to develop a relationship with him now.[9] After their meeting, Kennedy was thrilled to be invited to attend the president's press conference. From the executive office, "the president told reporters of the plan to revive American shipping tied up by the restrictions of the Neutrality Act."

KENNEDY BEHAVED ADMIRABLY in public. In private meetings with Admiral Emery Land and his commissioner, Max Truitt, further preliminary discussions on the American shipping question continued. Ways to help expand British trade were also discussed. After all, the Kriegsmarine were chasing British merchant ships bringing meat from Argentina, as proven by the December encounters on and near the Río de la Plata in Argentina with the *Graf Spee*.* Before heading back to the White House for his last meeting of the day with the president, Kennedy popped in to see Jay Pierrepont Moffat, chief of the European Affairs Division.

The debonair Moffat was tolerant of Kennedy's foibles, but even he felt that the ambassador was like a bear with a sore head. Joe shot off his gripes like rapid machine-gun fire, concluding that he didn't trust Churchill, who "wants us there as soon as he can get us there. He is ruthless and scheming. He is also in touch with groups in America which

---

*   The German pocket battleship *Graf Spee* had been hunted to the Río de la Plata by two heavy and two light cruisers in December. The German vessel had been following British trade routes for some time, sinking some three merchantmen, before it was blockaded in the mouth of the river. The ship's captain was ordered by Berlin to scuttle her, rather than let her fall into British hands (*Source:* James Holland, *The War in the West: Germany Ascendant, 1939–1941* [London: Corgi Books, 2016], 176–77).

have the same idea, notably, certain strong Jewish leaders." If Moffat was shocked by this statement, he did not say. "K. is very bearish. . . . He says the British are a combination of cleverness and stupidity. . . . He says there is no question but that they have all our codes [secret codes for transmitting dispatches]*. . . . He said that his main work was now done, and that pretty soon the British would start trying to undermine him, as he was too much of a fighter."[10]

While it was reasonable for Kennedy to let off steam to Moffat, he made one mistake in an otherwise perfect day of being "Mr. Ambassador." On leaving the White House, Joe responded to a journalist that "if the newspaper men present had any work to do they had better stay in this country and do it."[11] Evidently, he did not relish the idea of returning to England. Afterward, Roosevelt told Ickes, "As might be expected, Joe Kennedy was utterly pessimistic. He believes that Germany and Russia will win the war and that the end of the world is just down the road." Ickes added, "I suspect that Joe has been worrying about his great fortune for a long time and the London atmosphere hasn't helped him any."[12]

THAT SAME DAY, Kennedy flew to Boston. At a reunion of parishioners at Our Lady of the Assumption Church in East Boston, he made a speech. As *The Times* of London reported, "Speaking extemporaneously at a parishioners' meeting in a church where he was once an altar boy he said, 'As you love America don't let anything that comes out of any country in the world make you believe that you can make a situation one whit better by getting into the war. There's no place in the fight for us.'"[13]

The following day Joe checked himself into the Lahey Clinic, where he always went for his medical checkups. He had complained about his stomach so much that on both sides of the Atlantic it had become a topic

---

* The American embassy codes had initially been broken in Italy, as Ambassador Bill Phillips had discovered when Kennedy was in Rome for the Coronation of Pope Pius XII. From October 5, 1939, an American cipher clerk suspected of trading secrets with the Soviets, Tyler Kent, began work at the American embassy in London. Security was very lax still within the American diplomatic corps. On March 18, the Foreign Office warned that "what they say in confidence to members of the United States embassy, may easily get around rather quickly" as their messages "may be no less accessible to the Germans than they are to us" (*Source:* FO371/24251/195).

of common jokiness. When Lord Beaverbrook replied to Frank Knox, publisher of the *Chicago Daily News*, that "Kennedy came home full of pessimism about the outcome," Beaverbrook's retort was dismissive. "As for Joe Kennedy, he has a pain in his belly. He is a fine ambassador here and everybody likes him. But a man who takes hydrochloric acid after every meal is apt to be pessimistic in his outlook."[14] Hopefully, Beaverbrook was a poor student of chemistry.

Nonetheless, this visit to the Lahey Clinic broke with tradition in that Joe asked his gastroenterologist to write to Roosevelt. Dr. Sara Jordan complied, declaring that his "chronic gastritis" had reached an "acute phase." Back then, that might have made some sense, as much as the treatment of "hospitalization, with rest and medication." However, Dr. Jordan concluded that Kennedy would be better resting at his "excellent facilities in Florida," where he could follow a "very careful routine, which to be effective should be of *at least two months duration*."[15]

Considering that *all* the Kennedy files have had every reference to medical conditions redacted or removed (including details of Rose's appendectomy in 1938), it is extraordinary that this letter should have been written and sent to the White House. The most reasonable explanation is that Kennedy was hedging his bets, and as in the Great War, was searching for a plausible exit route that would avoid the words "yellow" or "coward" being liberally applied to him.

That said, Joe was unaware that "treachery" and "cowardice" were just the words spoken aloud about him at the Foreign Office. Many felt Kennedy disrespected the special relationship of his office to the British people. So, it came as no surprise that the highly regarded weekly magazine, *The Spectator*, would write in its December 15 issue that "there would seem to be plenty of eminent persons in the United States to give isolationist advice without the ambassador to the Court of St. James's knowing all our anxieties and all our ordeal, finding it necessary to join himself to the number."[16] This was the first article where the British public were told who smiling Joe Kennedy really was.

NONETHELESS, KENNEDY'S "ACUTE" medical condition did not prevent him returning to Washington in December. Having come out for

Roosevelt's third term, he needed to embark on his next project while still in public office: keeping America out of the war. So, he contacted his newspaper buddies and gave some interviews. Joe knew that Arthur Krock, a Republican, could not garner Democratic support either for him or for Roosevelt.[17*] Instead, he turned to Alsop and Kintner, who bore a gruff admiration for Kennedy, describing him as "big, genial, overflowing with vitality, ostentatiously bespectacled, tough-talking and, at the same time, rather emotional." In their syndicated column on December 19, they called the ambassador a real "go-getter" and "no New Dealer," saying he "now believes that domestic policy is no longer worth the trouble of cursing at."

That said, the newspapermen also hung a sign around Kennedy's neck labeling him as a mercurial stock market manipulator whose only concern was to take a quick profit. Of course, "The blackout [in London] depresses him," the columnists write. "But depressing though he finds his task and dark though his views may be, he will certainly return to London to carry on. It is just as well, for a pessimist is always more useful than an optimist in international affairs."[18]

As part of the daily German embassy routine in Washington, copies of articles of special interest were sent to the Foreign Ministry in Berlin. *The New York Times* reported that Kennedy had returned to Washington on December 15 to meet with the State Department and "ranking admirals and generals at the War and Navy Departments." Kennedy lectured the naval men, to their great annoyance, for promoting war. The generals, too, had been reprimanded by him for "asking for absurdly large and quite unnecessary appropriations."[19] German intelligence in Washington passed the message on, giving Kennedy's star added luster in Berlin.

The German embassy also reported "adequate units of the Army and Air Force as the basis for military intervention are still not available;" and America's plan "is to obtain by military strength a basis for later peace mediation. The United States, however, will still enter the war if it considers that the Western Hemisphere is threatened."[20] Berlin was desperate

---

* The Foreign Office discounted Krock in its unofficial document *Record of Leading Personalities of the United States,* noting that he "combines a Jewish sense of social inferiority with social aspirations."

for good news out of America that December, since Fritz Kuhn, the leader of the German American Bund, had been convicted of misappropriating funds, and had alienated many Americans of German heritage from joining or renewing their membership.[21] Kennedy was a welcome antidote.

BACK IN LONDON, Kennedy's ill-timed and defeatist remarks were poorly received. Thomas North Whitehead, an Englishman who had been a professor at Harvard and taken a leave of absence to serve as an expert on American relations in the Foreign Office, tried to shed some light on why Roosevelt kept Kennedy in place.

"One of the most important problems which Mr. Roosevelt has had to face during his eventful tenure of office has been the inefficiency & even dishonesty of many American civil servants, executive officers & even politicians. This difficulty," North Whitehead revealed, "is augmented by the facts that the influence of an Administration is partly dependent upon a 'spoils system' of appointing senior civil servants . . . with whom the Administration wishes to stand well. The East Coast Irish are such a group & are of great importance to a Democratic Administration." In conclusion, North Whitehead stated, "Mr. Kennedy is, however, playing off his own bat in his stupid private conversations & uncalled for remarks to the press."[22]

While others commented fiercely on the circulated Foreign Office document that Mr. Kennedy should be taught a lesson in various ways, J. V. Perowne, that calm head in the storm, wrote: "I don't think anything will make Mr. Kennedy alter his views except a belief that it will pay him to do or to say so. I don't know how we can induce such a belief and I think we should leave him alone, except to remember not to trust him. He is quite unpopular enough with his own staff and the American press correspondents here. We can leave him to them."[23]

Ever since the Kennedy children were small, the expression "beware the bear" had become a family joke about their father. At the time the expression came about, the younger ones, of course, visualized their father as a live bear, not understanding that it referred to Joe's wary speculation on the stock market. In later life, it became a partial justification for a beloved father's and grandfather's inability to rise to the summit of his abilities in public life. Had Joe been better able to put his "bearish" tendencies into perspective and to keep his ideas to himself, his life would undoubtedly have been different. But then, he wouldn't have been Joe Kennedy.

30

SHADOWING WELLES

The minute hand is pointing at one minute to midnight.
—BENITO MUSSOLINI TO SUMNER WELLES,
MARCH 16, 1940

Kennedy would be gone from his post for sixteen weeks, which added to the understated British ire. For the first seven months of the war, neither France nor Britain were attacked. There had been no aerial bombing campaign either against Germany or the Allies. The British called it the Twilight War. For the French, it was the Drôle de Guerre. Germans called it the Sitzkrieg. Americans preferred the Phony War. Nonetheless, war thundered elsewhere. "There were never more than ten operational U-boats at sea," war historian James Holland wrote of the battle in the Atlantic, "but fifty-six Allied merchant ships were sunk along with three U-boats."[1] The war in the east raged, with Poland falling in twenty-seven days. The Soviets invaded Finland in what became known as the Winter War. Churchill watched darkly in early 1940, while Kennedy luxuriated in the warmth of the Palm Beach sun.

Nonetheless, Joe did not like being out of the limelight. So, he teased the press, not making a firm statement if he would run for the presidency or not. Vice President John Nance Garner had made his opposition to the possible third term clear, meaning Roosevelt would have to replace him if he won the nomination. If Joe played his cards right, maybe he could still become vice president?* The topic "would Kennedy or won't Kennedy run" could not be kept alive forever from Joe's Palm Beach idyll. Even so, he broke his silence only when he *knew* he must return to London. Decisions had been made there and in Washington, and if he did not go back, he would be replaced and forgotten. So on February 14, Kennedy declared through *The New York Times,* "I cannot forget that I now occupy a most important government post which at this particular time involves matters so precious to the American people that no private consideration should permit my energies or interests to be diverted."[2]

Kennedy's real reason for resuming his post was due to Roosevelt's early February announcements: the Welles mission to Europe and the appointment of "special presidential envoy" Myron C. Taylor to the Vatican. Kennedy's shock to both was palpable. Why was his "friend" Sumner Welles to be sent to Rome, Berlin, Paris, and London on a diplomatic mission? Cordell Hull said Roosevelt felt it would be "more satisfactory to have a report from one man after visiting various countries than to have four or five reports from as many men permanently stationed in as many capitals."[3] Evidently this mission had been at the back of the president's mind for some months, since it would not have been announced without prior agreement from the countries concerned.

DURING THE TWILIGHT War, the British had myriad peace plans laid before them, and treated Mr. Welles's mission as just one more of the unacceptable overtures from a well-wishing nonaligned country. The Foreign Office metaphorically rolled its eyes, even though Roosevelt assured Chamberlain that a lasting peace meant the end of Nazi aggression before any talks could be contemplated. At the Admiralty, Churchill was hounded by his "black dog"—a deep depression. Although he was initially uplifted by the American interest, he had been starved of answers from Roosevelt ever since Kennedy had returned. Hull's

---

* Roosevelt selected Henry Agard Wallace to be the thirty-third vice-president of the United States. He wanted the vice-presidency to be an additional set of eyes and ears to the president, and Wallace was the first vice president to attempt to fulfill this function by becoming more involved in foreign policy and administrative matters.

announcement that "Mr. Welles . . . will take no 'peace plan' with him and will not be authorized to make proposals or commitments in the name of the United States" left the British "considerably disturbed."[4]

The French, too, were bemused—not to mention bereft of their trusted friend Bullitt to interpret, as he had recently left Paris on home leave. The news was released on the very day that the French Chamber unanimously passed Daladier's resolution that there would be no peace until an Allied victory was achieved. The French press called the Welles mission nothing more than a *coup de théâtre* and a trip down that evil memory lane of Munich *à l'américain*.[5]

Many believed Roosevelt had been duped by Hitler and the earlier German wild offers of peace. The president's detractors thought he was playing into the führer's hands, since the Welles mission was regarded by the ordinary German with a "marked but muffled . . . torrent of voices and an avalanche of hopes." The official response in Berlin and Rome, however, remained muted.[6] Everyone believed—wrongly—that the American president was searching for some magic bullet to stop the war.

Perhaps as early as February, Roosevelt had heard about the planned German offensive in the west. His main goal in sending Welles to Europe was to delay an attack for as long as possible, and to attempt to keep Italy neutral. That was why Myron Taylor was dispatched to the Holy See. It was also why Hull simultaneously met to agree on a deal with the Allied military and U.S. aircraft engines manufacturers. While Welles sailed for Naples, Hull cabled Roosevelt that his meeting with the military and manufacturers was "historic" and that he hoped they had a breakthrough on "substantial progress" in speeding up deliveries to the French and British. Roosevelt was exercising his personal brand of realpolitik, knowing that each month the German offensive could be delayed, it would benefit the Allies. The invasion of Poland had cost Germany dearly in war matériel, particularly in ammunition. British intelligence had calculated that German iron ore stocks, so important to building of tanks, submarines, and ammunition, were running low.[7]

KENNEDY, HOWEVER, HAD not appreciated such things. Understandably, he was unhappy with the Welles mission and with not having been consulted on Taylor's appointment. Bullitt, who heartily disliked Sumner

Welles,* found out about the mission only when he arrived in New York on February 10, 1940. Bullitt was enraged and refused to return to Paris until after Welles left. Bill Phillips in Rome, however, made no such complaint.

Perhaps that was because Phillips knew he was getting an additional resource with the able Myron C. Taylor. Kennedy must have been unaware that Pius XII had written to Roosevelt on January 19 warning there were "slight probabilities of immediate success so long as the present state of opposing forces remains essentially unchanged."[8] But had Kennedy known about General Beck's plot to overthrow Hitler and the pope's role in it?

A Bavarian lawyer had been drafted in by the Beck plotters to make contact with one of Pius XII's oldest friends, Ludwig Kass,† who was in permanent exile at the Vatican and had assumed the role of Prefect of the Fabric of St. Peter's. Kass agreed to put the lawyer in touch with the pope's trusted adviser, the German Jesuit Robert Leiber. Beck's convoluted plan was for the pope to approach the British through Francis D'Arcy Osborne, the British minister to the Holy See, who reported to Halifax. Osborne would be empowered by the pope "to seek guarantees for an honorable peace between the democracies and Germany" once Beck's coup d'état succeeded.[9] In other words, Pius XII knew of a plot to overthrow Hitler, yet said nothing.

It was "among the most astounding events in the modern history of the papacy," historian Harold Deutsch wrote. Knowing what Hitler was like, Pius XII was playing a dangerous game with the standing of the Holy See. Leiber was shocked by the pope's agreement to become an

---

* In 1943, Bullitt was responsible for Welles's, and his own, downfall. Bullitt gave Roosevelt the confidential dossier he had compiled on the married assistant secretary of state, showing that Welles was an "uncontrollable" homosexual when he drank to excess, which was often. It was revealed that Welles had propositioned a Pullman porter, who refused his blandishments, and the incident was hushed up. Welles would often proposition men whom he had never met to have sex with him. Roosevelt would never forgive Bullitt when Welles was forced to resign.

† Kass was the German prelate who had worked with Pacelli for the Reichskonkordat and before that was the former head of the German Zentrumspartei (Central Party). Beck had gathered around him other disgruntled officers from the military intelligence unit, the Abwehr, including Admiral Canaris, who stopped the plot from being discovered.

intermediary, as was Kass. The pope did not tell Cardinal Maglione, his secretary of state, "that the Pope was prepared to do 'all he can.'"

In mid-January, Pius XII had summoned Osborne and betrayed the secret knowledge he had received from German army chiefs that "a violent offensive was planned" in the west in February. The offensive might not, however, occur if Britain could guarantee an "honorable peace" for Germany. The message was passed to Osborne without a papal endorsement or recommendation. During their conversation, Pius XII vacillated and changed his mind, telling Osborne to forget everything. Osborne replied, "I refused to have the responsibilities of his Holiness' conscience unloaded onto my own." Osborne knew Halifax had been bombarded by dozens of varying German overtures for a "just peace." In discussing it with Cadogan, they came to the only reasonable conclusion: "Let them get on with it, and I will then render my judgement!"[10] With the plethora of false information and false alarms, the British also discounted the intelligence passed on by the Vatican about the start date of the war in the west. Beck's group, fearing discovery, broke off all contact, and Pius XII receded into his stance of concerned neutrality.[11]

Still, Kennedy felt that he alone had ownership of the relationship with the Holy See. Given the extraordinary circumstances and the requirement to trust only those who were directly involved, there is little doubt that Kennedy knew nothing about the so-called putsch.* In fact, it seems that Pius XII, at this juncture, was plowing his own furrow, and even Galeazzi was unaware of the details of the coup.

AND SO, MYRON C. Taylor accompanied Sumner Welles aboard the Italian ocean liner *Rex,* arriving in Naples on February 25. Joe Kennedy never rated Taylor's negotiating skills and again was disappointed that the new position was merely designated as the "president's personal envoy." Evidently, Kennedy had forgotten the diplomatic imperatives of not offending Mussolini. Just the same, the Welles mission *and* Taylor's

---

* Just how realistic the putsch would have been is academic, as it was never carried out. Beck, however, was involved in the von Stauffenberg July 1944 plot (Operation Valkyrie) and was among the 4,980 people executed.

appointment meant that Kennedy had to either resign or return to work. He opted for the latter. A week after Welles and Taylor left, Joe Kennedy boarded the American ship *Manhattan,* docking at Genoa before sailing on to Naples. Italian ships were widely used to avoid attack by German U-boats and the British navy.

Joe wrote to Rose that "I went to bed before the ship left the dock and continued to run a temperature for about three days." So that his wife wouldn't worry, he added the caveat "not much at any time, but still enough to make me stay in bed." A few sentences later, Joe told his wife that "Clare Luce and Miss Case of *Vogue** were on the boat. Clare is writing a running story for *Life* but I don't know what news she got on the trip."[12]

Clare's marriage was on the proverbial rocks. She and Henry had begun arguing in public about his lack of libido, despite his deep love for his wife. Clare sought professional help. Henry complained of her "inconsistency": he had married a journalist who subsequently became a playwright and now wanted to become a war correspondent for Henry's publication, *Life*. Fellow playwright Alexander King visited them at Mepkin, their plantation home in South Carolina, for Christmas 1939, and described Henry as possessing "a great deal of dangerous integrity" and Clare as a woman of "relentless ambition." Long before their Christmas became a tawdry affair, Clare had made plans to go to Europe without her husband.[13] She *would* be a war correspondent.

Joe's "illness" and Clare's presence as explained to Rose were a charade. If Kennedy's sole purpose was to return to London to take up his post, he would have disembarked at Genoa. Instead, he sailed on to Naples in the company of the politically savvy Clare. He omitted to tell Rose that they went sightseeing at Pompeii together, pretending that his only company was his valet and London Jack. They took the same train to Rome, and both stayed at the Excelsior. Joe and Clare shared an unrelenting ambition and drive to overcome the slights,

---

* Margaret Case was the society editor of *Vogue* who took Clare Boothe Brokaw (as she was then known) under her wing and taught Clare how to dress for success. For more on Margaret and Clare, see *Condé Nast: The Man and His Empire* by the author (St. Martin's Press, 2019).

perceived or real, of their childhoods. Their sexual prowess was legendary. Despite her die-hard conservative Republican stance, they both wanted to keep America out of the war and Joe hoped she would help him put across his message. In Rome, Clare stayed in Sumner Welles's recently vacated room—still inhabited by his welcoming flowers. Joe stayed in a "first floor room, practically on the street." There was a fascist congress at the hotel and a bevy of Army officers wearing ill-fitting "musical comedy uniforms," Joe told Rose.[14]

At some point, Clare must have become wary about Joe's endless griping and how badly the British press were treating him. There was one man in London whose opinions she trusted, Raimund von Hofmannsthal, whom she had met and liked during her *Vanity Fair* days as its editor. Von Hofmannsthal was married to Lady Elizabeth Paget, the niece of Alfred Duff Cooper, the former First Lord of the Admiralty.[15] Clare resolved to write to Raimund for advice.

KENNEDY PROCEEDED AT a leisurely pace back to London. On the third day after landing, he was still in Rome where he saw both Bill Phillips and Myron Taylor in the morning before calling on Count Galeazzi in the afternoon. "He is terribly tired and working very hard," Joe wrote to Rose. "I didn't try to see the Pope, because my time was limited." After attending the opera that evening with Clare, he left Rome early the next day on the Simplon Express northward through Switzerland.

IN MILAN, JOE and London Jack alighted with the sole intention of seeing Leonardo da Vinci's *Last Supper* at Santa Maria della Grazie church. But it was closed, so a displeased Kennedy found out where the "head of the Museum" lived, tracked him down, and demanded that they be given a private showing. The church was dutifully opened, and they were given a private tour before both Kennedys and Joe's valet, Stephens, walked back to the central station and boarded the Paris Express. Joe claimed that only later he discovered Welles was on the same train, and by accident he "had the extreme good fortune of riding up to Paris with him."[16]

Had Welles told Kennedy the gist of his meetings in Rome with Mussolini and Ciano? If he hadn't, then Welles was exceptionally imperturbable. Always seen as fastidious and refined, Sumner Welles was highly intelligent, too. He was also known for having no sense of humor. In Rome, Welles had paid a courtesy visit to the king of Italy first, then Count Ciano at the Palazzo Chigi, the official residence of the minister of foreign affairs. Welles found Ciano quite agreeable, and not "filled with a sense of his own self-importance," as previously reported. Indeed, Ciano came across as sincere, intelligent, and more sympathetic to the Allies than he had expected.[17] Welles's encounter with Mussolini was equally frank, with Il Duce laying out what Hitler would accept by way of a peace settlement, telling Welles to listen specifically to Hitler's February 23 speech.

After speaking with Welles aboard the train, Kennedy suddenly increased his leisurely pace. Had Welles told him to return to his post by way of admonishment? Or had Kennedy learned that Welles had already made his London plans without consulting him? Whatever the reason, something had changed Kennedy's relaxed demeanor. He flew straight back to London, landing late on March 7, 1940. At Heston airport, he told reporters that Americans "understand the war less and less as they go along."[18] In all, Joe Kennedy had been away from London for ninety-nine days.

The March 7 edition of *The Spectator* was on newsstands everywhere. Harold Nicolson MP had written with a sarcastic pen that Mr. Kennedy would be "warmly welcomed" back at his post and that "we shall be glad to see his friendly face again." Then Nicolson qualified who the "we" were: "the influential and large Anglo-American community in London. . . . the unhyphenated rich, who hope that he may bring with him a little raft of appeasement on which they can float for a year or so longer." Then, too, "the bankers and isolationists" would roll out the red carpet. "He will be welcomed by the shiver-sisters of Mayfair and the wobble-boys of Whitehall," Nicolson wickedly wrote in his roll call of those against the war. "He will be welcomed by the Peace Pledge Union, the Christian Pacifists, the followers of Dr. Buchman, the friends of Herr von Ribbentrop, the Nürembergers, the Munichois, Lord Tavistock, and the *disjecta membra* of former pro-Nazi organisations.* A solemn gladness will even crown the brow of M. Maisky."[19]

IN BERLIN, WELLES'S relative optimism was dashed. After a series of meetings with Ribbentrop, Göring, and Hitler, he concluded that any notion of peace was illusory. "It was England and France who had insisted upon declaring war on Germany," Hitler told Welles. "Germany would not have declared war on England and France." Britain and France would therefore have to be crushed into submission.[20] Where Rome had been bathed in sunlight and Italian opulence, Welles found Berlin depressing, with its people obediently queueing for food amid a strong uniformed presence of the SS.

Ten days after Welles left, the Germans published their white paper containing damning records of interviews with the Polish ambassador to London and his commercial attaché in the summer of 1939. Germany was in possession of the Polish archives, and "it had incontrovertible proof that England had incited the Polish Government to refuse to sign the agreement" with Germany. In fact, the German white paper had more than a ring of authenticity about it, stating that Ambassador Kennedy said to the Polish ambassador "you won't believe to what extent my oldest son Joe [Jr.], who was recently in Poland, commands the ear of the President. I might almost say that maybe the President believes him more than me." Kennedy was also alleged to have offered British aid to Poland with cash. Fortunately, Welles had already left London when the "propaganda" broke. Kennedy of course denied the truth.[21]

Back in Paris briefly, the city most familiar to Welles in Europe, he remarked that it was no longer "the city of light." There was a dispirited atmosphere permeating all of his meetings with the French government

---

* The organizations mentioned were all antiwar. Dr. Frank Buchman was a Protestant Christian Evangelist and founder of the Oxford Group, who campaigned for "Moral Rearmament" and peace. The "Nurembergers" were those in favor of Hitler's stripping Jews of their rights to belong to German society and of their nationality as decided at Nuremberg on September 15, 1935. The Munichois were those who remained delighted with the result of Munich. Lord Tavistock was viewed as a significant Nazi sympathizer and founded the British People's Party in 1939. Even though the Soviets invaded Finland and had signed the nonaggression pact with Germany, the Soviet Union was not at war with Great Britain, meaning that Maisky remained in London.

officials. All the monuments tourists came to see were sandbagged, and shop windows were all crisscrossed with gummed paper to prevent shattering if and when bombing occurred. But it was his meeting with the former socialist prime minister and Jew, Léon Blum, which he found the most depressing. Blum was certain that France, too, would soon disappear.[22]

IN LONDON, THE Foreign Office was exceptionally worried about Kennedy's return. Nicolson's *Spectator* piece had just been published, but the mood was best summed up by J.V. Perowne in an earlier minute to his colleagues: "The views of any U.S. Ambassador in London on our war chances are a matter of considerable importance, and it must not be forgotten that Kennedy, rightly or wrongly is regarded as having achieved a very special position here." Mr. Kennedy is "on terms of intimacy with the Prime Minister and other members of the Government," which "only enhances the importance of any views he may express and their effect."[23]

Even the embassy staff had become wary of the ambassador. The American military attaché, the swashbuckling and handsome Colonel Raymond E. Lee, thought that Kennedy was deeply entombed in the gloom of defeatism. "Kennedy has the speculator's smartness but also his *sharpshooting* and *facile* insensitivity to the great forces which are now playing like heat lightning over the map of the world." Lee's predecessor, Lt.-Colonel Brad Chynoweth,* was so shocked by Kennedy's "lone wolf" approach, he felt obliged to report Kennedy to his superior. Apparently, the ambassador had been having conversations with the British Air Ministry about "a reciprocal release of our radio detection secrets," which Chynoweth found impossible to believe. When he asked Kennedy about it, "He said the matter was taken up with him as a secret, and he therefore hadn't told us. I argued that there should be no secrets between us in respect to military

---

* Chynoweth took up his post as military attaché to the embassy in London in March 1939. All the American embassies in Europe had military attachés, and they all reported to U.S. Military Intelligence G-2. From the outset, Chynoweth was frustrated by Kennedy's lack of cooperation. Kennedy had Chynoweth transferred out, and the onetime military attaché ended up as a brigadier general and commander of the Central Philippines Force. He was captured in 1942 and spent the rest of World War II as a prisoner of war.

information. He told me," an incredulous Chynoweth reported, "that I haven't earned his confidence and that he doesn't think I ever will."[24]

Welles knew all this and more. Like Roosevelt, he was aware that Kennedy had more than a passing admiration for the Nazis and respected how they had turned Germany around since Hitler came to power. Joe Jr. helped to hone his father's perceptions, too, as many of his letters from Berlin and elsewhere were full of admiration for the organization of the Third Reich.[25] Then, too, Welles was aware that Kennedy's pronouncements—the latest being that "Americans didn't understand the war"—would make diplomacy tricky.

Kennedy would not allow Welles to wander in and out of meetings with the government without his guiding hand, and unilaterally took over the presidential envoy's itinerary. From the initial press conference—where Welles's refrain was "no comment"—to the talks with leaders of the opposition benches (Attlee, Archibald Sinclair, and "all the others," including Eden), Kennedy was at Welles's elbow. Their first stop was at the Foreign Office to meet with Halifax. Although not part of his remit, Welles went so far as to outline a possible compromise that could lead to peace. He was taken aback by Halifax's "sincere" reply that "no lasting peace could be made in Europe so long as the Nazi regime dominated Germany, and controlled German policy."[26] When they visited the prime minister, Chamberlain commented afterward that "I got the strong impression that he appreciated our vital need for security. . . . The odd thing was that he seemed to think there was just a chance—1 in 10,000 he put it . . . for peace."[27]

Given that Kennedy made all the arrangements, it was irregular that he had been left off the invitation list to tea with the King and Queen at Buckingham Palace. Then again, Kennedy had crossed swords with the King the previous September. Only an official complaint to the Palace officials rectified the situation. George VI noted in his diary that on Monday March 11, "I saw Mr. Sumner Welles, who had arrived in London after visiting Rome, Berlin & Paris. It was difficult to tell him or ask him everything I wanted to, as Mr. Kennedy the U.S. Ambassador was present at Welles's request."[28]

WELLES HAD COME to London at the precise moment the Russian offer of peace—or ultimatum—was made to Finland. He left on March 14 and headed back to Rome for a second round of discussions with Mussolini and Ciano before sailing for the United States. Joe wrote to Rose that he had also "arranged for Eddie and Mary [Moore] to go to Rome on business for Welles."[29] It was a silly claim. Eddie Moore was expedited to Rome to keep an eagle eye on Welles and to deliver a message to Galeazzi and the pope.*

Welles had a shock. Mussolini's stance had hardened. It had been a long winter with the British fleet blockading all German exports and imports since November 21, 1939. Italy had almost no natural resources, and 70 percent of its coal came from Germany, mostly by sea. The laissez-passer granted to Ciano for Italy's coal had been a short-term solution. When Ciano negotiated a new deal for English coal, Mussolini cut off all talks with a resounding no in January 1940.[30] Nonetheless, Welles suggested—without foundation—that "the gap between the Allies and Axis suggested there was far more room for maneuver" according to London and Paris. Mussolini did not laugh in his face. Instead, he warned Welles that the German offensive in the west was near to hand. "The minute hand," Mussolini told Welles with sinister gravity, "is pointing to one minute before midnight." Il Duce was unimpressed with Welles. Ciano, tired of dealing with "the pack of conceited vulgarians that make up the German leadership," thought the presidential envoy was a gentleman.

Welles was nonplussed and telephoned the White House to ask permission to try to open the door through Mussolini to attempt some vague path toward peace. Roosevelt flatly refused. Later that day, the president made a speech to rule out anyone attempting such a move on his behalf. "It cannot be a moral peace," Roosevelt said, "if freedom from invasion is sold for tribute."[31] Welles was, of course, unaware that Ribbentrop had already made arrangements to meet Mussolini at the Brenner Pass after he sailed, on Monday, March 18. There, Mussolini and Hitler would agree the next phase of the war. Operation Weser-Exercise for the invasion of Denmark and Norway would begin three weeks later.

---

* Eddie and Mary Moore were accompanied by Rosemary Kennedy. They returned to New York from Rome after Eddie's "work" was completed.

31

KENNEDY AND THE "KING'S WEATHER"

"When the crocus blossoms," hiss the women in Berlin,
"He will press the button, and the battle will begin."

—A. P. HERBERT,
PUNCH, FEBRUARY 14, 1940

Clare Boothe Luce arrived at Joe Kennedy's rented Windsor home, St. Leonard's, on Good Friday, March 22.* Uppermost in Clare's mind was if she could turn Kennedy into a Republican supporter in the coming election and bring the 25 million strong Catholic vote with him. Enjoying Kennedy's company was an added thrill. They exchanged confidences about the upcoming election, including how and why Joe was "pretty sore" about the way he had been treated. "You would never believe the way public opinion in this country has turned anti-American," Joe wrote to Rose a few days before Clare arrived, "and incidentally anti-US Ambassador Kennedy."[1]

Joe had heard the rumors and read the articles but hadn't recognized that many of those who had been his friends before the war could no longer be seen entertaining him. Furious minutes of meetings at the

---

* Wall Hall in Hertfordshire was no longer made available to the ambassador alone (and free of charge) after his ninety-nine-day absence. Instead he rented St. Leonard's in Windsor, Surrey, which is now the site of Legoland.

Foreign Office accused Welles's ill-fated allusion to a compromise as indicative of Kennedy's malevolent influence.[2] Joe had not believed that the loss of the British navy would represent dire economic consequences to America—but he was certain that this war would cost the United States "a hundred percent" more than the last one. Clare was certainly no fan of Roosevelt, yet she had *seen* the preparations undertaken in Rome and Paris. Somehow, she resolved, she would have to shake Kennedy into action. Aware that a long weekend of lovemaking in Windsor would hardly suffice, Clare may have been behind the move for Joe to bring Rose over to London to stop the chattering against him.*

Clare had heard back from Raimund von Hofmannsthal, a man who never said anything remotely contentious about anyone. Raimund had previously given a great deal of information on Kennedy for the *Time* cover story the previous September, he told Clare. Just the same, he confirmed her worse fears. After Kennedy had bragged that he was the "Nine-Child Envoy" when he first came to London, none of those nine children were in the city now that war had been declared. Joe's defeatist speeches during his *long* absence in America had made everyone believe that he would not be returning to his post; and when he did, there was obvious consternation—particularly when his family did not join him. The final insult was that he had decamped to the Hertfordshire countryside. All this proved to the British that "he lacks the solidarity towards England which is expected of an ambassador."[3]

Worse, the smiling, likable Joe had been taken to their hearts, Raimund wrote. "People particularly resent the fact that he has been a popular figure in London and Court life, that they did overlook his childish—Prairie—County—Ohio mannerisms, and now feel that if they had been more severe with him from the beginning, he would not have let them

---

* Kennedy made arrangements shortly thereafter for Rose to travel from New York to Lisbon and arrive in London on May 7. He then had Herschel Johnson inquire on April 30, 1940, if Rose could board one of the "series of experimental flights" of Imperial Airways on May 10 from Lisbon to London. The Foreign Office was astounded at the request. The agreement with the Portuguese government had clearly stated that there should be no passengers on experimental flights, much less a woman. Also, they were "experimental" due to their dangerous nature. Permission was denied. In the end, Rose Kennedy stayed at home (*Source:* FO 371/24251/93).

down." In fact, the senior ambassador in London, the Brazilian Regis de Oliveira, professed some guilt in allowing Kennedy to keep breaking all the protocols and rules. And he was not alone. "All those who in the past must have worked for the best possible relationship between the Cabinet and the American Ambassador feel that Kennedy has let them down," Raimund concluded. Clare knew then that she could not help Joe in Europe, but he could help her and the Republicans in the United States. But how to get him back home without an utter loss of face? Their conversations, and lovemaking, would continue into April, when Clare entertained "JPK in bedroom all morning."[4]

APRIL WAS A golden month, with crystal clear skies and hardly a drop of rain. In London there was a cold snap, but by the end of the first week, the forsythia bloomed yellow, the azaleas blossomed early, and the people bought fleeting minutes in the sun on their two-penny deck chairs in the city's green parks. The trenches and barrage balloons had become a fact of life, just as those cardboard boxes with gas masks slung over everyone's shoulders had become invisible. The English called it the King's Weather—weather fit for a king. By dawn on April 9, in Berlin they called it *Hitlerwetter*, as the perfect spring heralded in the vicious invasion of Denmark and Norway.[5]

Short of warships for the invasion of Norway, the Germans imported their tanks, artillery, ammunition, and other war matériel on merchant vessels and had them stored in secure warehouses until needed. An embarrassing necessity for the Germans had become a clever ruse, since the Allies thought the vessels docking were for trade, not war.[6] Copenhagen, then all Denmark fell on April 10, with the king and government as a de facto protectorate under German military rule until 1943.*

When Kennedy called on Halifax that afternoon, the Foreign Secretary kept repeating it was "a very interesting situation" and that Churchill seemed "almost thrilled," even persuading the cabinet that Hitler had

---

* Churchill's earlier proposals to mine the Norwegian waters had twice been turned down in cabinet by Chamberlain and Halifax. It was only on April 8 that the decision to mine the seas around Norway was agreed. This would become the main reason for replacing Chamberlain. The de facto protectorate of Denmark lasted until August 29, 1943, when the German military took over until the country was liberated in May 1945.

made a major strategic blunder. The British were prepared, Churchill declared on April 11, and would repel the enemy. "I explained for the first time in public the disadvantage we had suffered since the beginning of the war by Germany's abuse of the Norwegian corridor," Churchill told the House of Commons. "It is not the slightest use in blaming the Allies for not being able to give substantial help and protection to neutral countries if we are held at arm's-length until these neutrals are actually attacked on a scientifically-prepared plan by Germany."[7]

BEFORE RETURNING TO London, Joe had intimated that he might be amenable to a family visit soon. Of course, it was meant to assuage Kick's desperate desire to return to her friends, and above all, Billy Hartington. Yet with all the negative press and the increased danger of bombs dropping on the country, he told Rose he did not want his children exposed to anti-American propaganda, and "the impact that such sentiment threatened to have on Kick." He preferred for her to live in blissful ignorance of any nasty political anti-American rhetoric and have happy memories. That didn't stop Joe, however, from delivering his own fatherly slap: "Tell Kick that Jakie [Astor] was there [at Cliveden] and said he was glad the Americans weren't doing anything, *because they really wanted to win this war without America taking credit for it.*"[8]

Jack wrote at Kick's behest during Easter vacation. He knew by appealing to his father's ego and his dependency on how the public perceived him, he could cast "Kick's London vacation" as benefiting the whole family. It would show the Kennedy tribe's support for the British, Jack reasoned. But Joe would not be dissuaded. With a broken heart, Kick wrote to Billy that she would not be able to come over in 1940 after all. She had no idea that he had already left England to join the British Expeditionary Force (BEF) on the Continent.[9]

Joe was desperate to feel useful but was kept at arm's length by the British cabinet, since it was feared he'd tell the press about their war strategy. As his idle days extended into weeks, he sent a cable to Roosevelt just as the guns blazed between the Allies and Germany in Scandinavia. Joe felt "the necessity to face up to this situation," despite its not being as urgent as the one in Scandinavia, but which remained "nevertheless real and soon may be the none-the-less urgent." Kennedy figuratively wrung his hands in a four-page missive that the British were selling gold in the United States at $35 an ounce, opting *not* to liquidate their American securities, as Kennedy thought they had previously agreed.

Morgenthau was asked to reply. He told his chief advisers, "It is one of these typical Joe Kennedy asinine letters." Everyone knew that Kennedy had been against the sale of American securities. So Morgenthau, like the British, deduced that Kennedy's volte-face must be because he wanted to depress stock prices to profit by selling short. "Every single move he has made is to depress our securities and our commodities," Morgenthau said.[10]

DESPITE CHURCHILL'S EBULLIENCE, the Norwegian campaign was going badly for the Allies. Kennedy cabled Hull that it was the latest in "a long, dismal picture of the state of unpreparedness and the lack of efficiency in the British Government." On May 2, Chamberlain addressed Parliament again. "If we had known that Denmark and Norway were to be victims, we could not have prevented what happened, without the co-operation of those countries," he said. "But, in the belief that their neutrality would save them, they took no precautions, and they gave us no warning of an attack, which, indeed, they never suspected."[11]

Five days later, the House of Commons held its main debate on the war. MPs were in a state of high dudgeon. Chamberlain was mocked for having told members that "Hitler had missed the bus" at the beginning of April, when now the Allies were in retreat in Norway. Opposition leaders Clement Attlee of Labour and Sir Archibald Sinclair of the Liberal Party tore into the government for its failures at Narvik, Trondheim, and Oslo; that is, until Brigadier-General Sir Henry Croft MP stood to speak. "Once the quarrel had been joined, all of us would have been pleased, I think, if we could have told the world that we were entering the war with an absolute elimination of old party divisions." It was a direct salvo aimed at Chamberlain for his continued mistrust of the Opposition. "It must be clear to all who have made a study of this question that it was weeks before the minefield was laid that soldiers were being hidden in cargo ships to be transported to Norway," the Brigadier-General-turned-MP rightly declared. Again, this was aimed at Chamberlain, who dithered over the mining of the waters around Narvik until April 8. Kennedy was not in the House to hear the May 7 evening debate.

Over the next twenty-four hours, the mood of the house changed from criticism of the government to a critique of Chamberlain's leadership. Sir Roger Keyes stood and told the Commons how the War Cabinet and the Admiralty would not allow him to take personal responsibility to lead the attack. Then the Conservative backbencher and stalwart friend of Churchill, Leo Amery, stood. "Somehow or other we must get into the government men who can match our enemies in fighting spirit, in daring, in resolution and in thirst for victory," Amery said. Then directing himself to Chamberlain, he added the words Oliver Cromwell used some three hundred years earlier to an unworthy Parliament: "You have sat too long here for any good you have been doing. Depart, I say, and let us have done with you. In the name of God, go!"[12]

These words uttered on May 8 were the fatal blows to the prime minister's leadership. Kennedy, seated in the diplomatic gallery, could scarcely believe his ears. The Opposition was out for blood, and a vote of no confidence was tabled. Chamberlain won by only a majority of eighty-one. The next day, Kennedy wired Washington that the "size of the majority . . . definitely indicates a failure." The Germans invaded Holland on May 9, and before dawn on May 10, Belgium, too, was at war. Finally, the prime minister saw Churchill's viewpoint: war meant a government of national unity. When Chamberlain approached the Labour leader, Clement Attlee, he refused to work under a Chamberlain premiership. This forced his resignation. Halifax refused the position and Churchill was asked by the King to form a new government.* The man Joe Kennedy trusted least was now prime minister.

---

* There were 615 MPs at the time, and the notional majority for the government was 213. The vote was 281 for Chamberlain's government and 200 against, with 41 voting for the Opposition and 60 abstaining. Halifax was Chamberlain's natural preference; however, his noble title prevented him from speaking in the House of Commons, requiring a surrogate. Halifax was not prepared to relinquish his title, despite George VI believing that it could be set aside for the duration of the war. He would remain Foreign Secretary during Churchill's first months in office. The Cromwell quote referred to the Long Parliament after it suffered defeat

The State Department noted that Kennedy refused to write to Churchill to congratulate him. After being prompted, however, he churlishly telephoned several days later to extend his good wishes. Enraged at his lack of power and position with Washington and in a Britain at war with Churchill as prime minister, Kennedy felt he was nothing more than "a $75 a week errand boy."[13] The burning question now was: How soon could he quit and leave London without the charges being leveled against him for cowardice and the abandonment of his post?

MAY 10, THE day Churchill became prime minister, was also when the battle of France began. The Netherlands and Luxembourg had surrendered five days earlier. As the Belgian army battled alongside the British and French, Churchill addressed the Commons on May 13. His new cabinet brought in the Opposition parties and thus was a government of national unity. Churchill's speech that day stands as one of his most famous: "If you ask what is our policy, it is to wage war by sea, land, and air with all our might. . . . I have nothing to offer but blood, toil, tears and sweat." The subsequent vote of confidence in the new government was 381–0, setting the tone for Churchill's historic leadership throughout the war.[14] "England will never give up so long as he remains a power in public life," a near-panicked Kennedy wrote in a "rush" message to Hull on May 15, "even if England is burnt to the ground. Why, said he, the government will move to Canada and take the fleet and fight on." Kennedy saw this as a direct threat to America's security.

The next day Churchill wrote to Roosevelt, "Although I have changed my office I am sure you would not wish me to discontinue our intimate, private correspondence." Then he warned that "the voice and force of the United States may count for nothing if they are withheld too long" and called upon the president to deliver on his promises of aid to Britain with "everything short of actually engaging armed forces" and the loan of "40 or 50 destroyers" as well as "aircraft, submarines, munitions and steel."[15] Churchill's May 15 encoded telegram, sent through the U.S. Embassy in London, and Roosevelt's May 16 reply that he would do his level best, received by Churchill on May 18, were both intercepted by a

---

after defeat in the English Civil War. For the gripping details of the "Churchill Conspiracy of 1940," read *Troublesome Young Men* by Lynne Olson.

spy. These highly confidential cables were in the hands of the Italians by May 23 and cabled on to Berlin *in their entirety* that same day.[16]

ON SATURDAY, MAY 18, Ambassador Kennedy received an official visit from Captain Maxwell Knight of MI5.* Apparently, a code room clerk with diplomatic status, the twenty-nine-year-old Tyler Gatewood Kent, whose distinguishing facial features were eyebrows that perpetually asked why, was suspected of espionage. This was not the first time Kent was considered a security risk. While he was stationed in Moscow, the State Department believed he might have been passing documents to the Soviets. So, defying reason, Kent was transferred to London, and began work at the American embassy on October 5, 1939. He became a "person of interest" to British military intelligence three days later. It was reported to Kennedy that the suave Kent was a rabid anti-Semite and apparently also a fascist sympathizer. But how was that possible given his earlier exploits in Moscow revealed he had spied for the Soviets? Simple. Kent's reputed "change of allegiance" mirrored the transformation in Soviet foreign policy when the Molotov-Ribbentrop Pact was signed the previous August. Kent's Soviet handlers ordered him not only to cooperate with the Nazis, but also keep an eye on the exiled White Russians, too.[17]

In early April, Kennedy was unaware Churchill had received a worrying report from a friend that "Germany was able to obtain in London information about the reports that were being made from the [British] Berlin embassy to the foreign office." When Dr. Heinrich Brüning, the former chancellor of a coalition German government in 1928, came to London later that month, he confirmed: "The Americans have the best intelligence from Germany" because they can be trusted not to reveal their sources. Churchill immediately shared the information with MI5. The investigation proved the allegation of leaks to be true. Moreover, it exposed that certain MPs were also colluding with the enemy.[18] The MI5 investigations revealed the long trail left by Tyler Kent and his accomplice society dressmaker,

---

* Kennedy's recollections in both his *Diplomatic Memoir* and diary are self-serving and unreliable. He was forced to admit to his biographer James M. Landis that he had "no detailed notes" about the incident that follows, and though he sought "clarification" from his former chargé Herschel Johnson ten years later, none was forthcoming (*Source:* LOC, Landis Papers).

Anna Wolkoff;* the flamboyant Italian military attaché at the Italian embassy in London, the Duke Francesco del Monte Marigliano; and Captain Archibald Maule Ramsay, MP, founder of fascist group the Right Club.

Kennedy understood the danger he ran as a scathing opponent of the war. If this incident was handled badly, not only would *his* diplomatic and political career end in dishonor and treachery; but Joe Jr.'s and Jack's would have been snuffed out before either had begun. The immediate problem, Kennedy was told, was that Kent as a diplomat would need to be stripped of that status for Special Branch to legally search his room.† Kennedy's mind raced. It was the eve of the nominating season for the presidential candidates in the United States. This scandal—if it could be attached to him— would ruin Joe Jr., a novice delegate with the Massachusetts representatives to the convention. It wouldn't help the Democrats or Roosevelt, either.

If Kennedy did not agree to strip Kent of his "extraterritorial" diplomatic status, enabling Kent to argue that his home was an extension of the embassy, then he could not be tried in Britain for possessing documents "useful to an enemy" under the Official Secrets Act. Kennedy's alternative was stark. If he chose to "hush it up" and retain Kent's diplomatic status, the young man would be publicly deported from Britain as a suspected spy, and with less than six months left until the presidential elections, his actions would become election manna for the Republicans. The quick-thinking Kennedy knew his only option would be to cooperate with the British and hope to keep it out of the press.[19] Kennedy agreed and withdrew Kent's diplomatic status, cabling the unsavory news to Washington immediately. Hull ordered that until they knew the extent of the security breach, only Herschel Johnson would be allowed to decrypt messages.

Kent's accomplice, the society dressmaker, Anna Wolkoff,‡ was arrested on May 19. Scotland Yard, accompanied by Franklin Gowen of the

---

* Anna Wolkoff was reportedly a local London dressmaker to Wallis Simpson in 1935.

† Special Branch is the term commonly used in the UK and the Commonwealth for the police forces concerned with national security.

‡ Wolkoff was the daughter of a White Russian admiral and loathed the Soviets and all Jews. Her father ran the Russian Tea Rooms near Whitehall. Del Monte was the cousin by marriage of Colonel Howard Kerr, the Duke of Gloucester's equerry. Kerr was warned not to fraternize with his cousin and dropped all contact with him until after the war (*Source:* TNA, KV2/1698).

embassy, attempted entry to Kent's rented room at 47 Gloucester Place, but they were forced to break down the door. Kent was standing there, in a state of undress. His mistress, Irene Danischewsky, was told to dress and allowed to leave. The search revealed well over two thousand secret and confidential embassy documents. These were confiscated, along with two sets of duplicate keys to the code and file rooms, a tin box, and a locked ledger. Kent was arrested by Special Branch and brought to the embassy.

The documents dated from early 1938 to the day of Kent's arrest—in other words, all of Kennedy's term as ambassador. Kent protested his innocence, asserting that the documents were for "his own private information." Yet the most damning was a pencil note Kent had made "of a highly secret confidential dispatch from the British Prime Minister to President Roosevelt" decoded in the early hours of the night of May 19–20. It was still in Kent's jacket pocket. He was due to hand across that message to his Italian accomplice, Del Monte, at dinner on the evening of his arrest.[20]

A young woman who worked at the Belgian embassy, Anne Van Lennep, revealed in her interrogation that there was a network of young women working with Anna Wolkoff. Van Lennep made a statement that she had already met several times with an older man, "Mr. Macaroni" (Del Monte), and that she knew Anna Wolkoff had previously conveyed messages to Macaroni at his home in Cadogan Square. Wolkoff had a key to Kent's room and could enter and leave at will. In fact, Van Lennep said, Wolkoff had taken some documents to Woolworth's to be copied and then returned them to Kent's Gloucester Place room. Through Van Lennep, Wolkoff passed messages into Belgium and onward to the British Nazi propagandist, William Joyce, "Lord Haw-Haw," in Berlin.[21]

Fortunately, Captain Knight had his own "young lady" working undercover as one of Wolkoff's "interesting friends." When he took Kent back to the embassy to interrogate him in front of Kennedy, Kent admitted nothing other than the locked leather-bound ledger belonged to Captain Ramsay of the Right Club and that they shared "certain views in common." (The ledger turned out to be their rather damning membership list and included Kent's name.) On May 21, Captain Knight delivered the official letter to Tyler Kent in prison from Ambassador Kennedy, advising he had been fired for Offences of the Official Secrets

Act, and that the U.S. government would not intervene on his behalf, as he had been stripped of his diplomatic status.[22]

MI5 had been onto the spy ring since Kent's arrival in London. Some of the documents ended up in Lord Haw-Haw's broadcasts aimed at undermining British morale over German radio. Others were sent via Rome to Berlin. Among the other cables Kent purloined were those between Roosevelt and Churchill when the prime minister was still "the naval person." British intelligence alone prevented a major spy ring operating through the American embassy in London from undermining the result of the 1940 election. The correspondence would have been deeply divisive and embarrassing if revealed at the time, given the strong isolationist movement in the United States, and could well have cost Roosevelt his third term in office.

Kennedy alleged that Churchill had given an undertaking that the trial would be set for some time after the American election on November 5, 1940.* On October 23, Tyler Kent was tried and convicted in camera at the Old Bailey on several counts of Offences under the Official Secrets Act and sentenced to seven years in prison. On November 7, two days after the U.S. presidential election returning Franklin D. Roosevelt to the White House for an historic third term, Anna Wolkoff was sentenced to ten years in prison for "attempting to assist the enemy." Captain Ramsay, like other active British fascists, was detained under Defence Regulation 18B on the Isle of Man.[23]

---

* Kennedy says this in his diary (JPK Papers, Box 100, August 15, 1940, handwritten and typed papers). As in the United States, the judiciary in the UK is separate from its executive and the government in power. If Kent had been British, the charges would have been treason, and so a trial without the press and the public attending was ordered. Thick brown paper was taped to the glass windows of the courtroom to prevent any journalists from seeing inside.

32

A TREACHEROUS FRIEND

The real defense of England will be
with courage and not with arms.

—JOSEPH P. KENNEDY,
JUNE 12, 1940

S uch unbounded heavenly weather over northern Europe prevailed
through most of May. Few doubted the King's Weather had become
Hitlerwetter. The first Canadian fighter pilots arrived in England, among
them James Goodson, the hero of the SS *Athenia.* These pilots, however,
would need to be trained on Spitfires and Hurricanes during the heroic
evacuation of 338,226 Allied soldiers cornered at Dunkirk, known as
Operation Dynamo. Soon enough, the Canadians would become a most
valued addition to those who fought in the ensuing Battle of Britain.

   In America, Kick Kennedy paid attention to Churchill's every speech
printed in the press, recognizing the value of honor and courage as
echoes of Billy Hartington's words. But she could hardly know that Billy's
Coldstream Guards battalion were part of the trapped Allied soldiers in
the Nazi-devised bag at Dunkirk. Kick half-jokingly wrote to her father
on May 21: "At the moment it looks as if the Germans will be in England
long before you receive this letter. In fact, from the reports here they
are just about taking over Claridge's now." Then she revealed that Billy
and Jean had written her gloomy letters—his from the Maginot Line.

Breathlessly, Kick asked, "Is Billy Alright? Hugh Fraser, the Astors, David Gore and the rest?"[1]

Joe couldn't respond properly. Gone were the days of a quasi-member of the prime minister's cabinet under Chamberlain. Kennedy seemed incapable of understanding that Britain was at war for its very existence. He persisted in his prewar polemic, exhausting the goodwill of the country to which he had been accredited.

"Mr. Roché of the French embassy telephoned to Mr. Balfour yesterday once more of the attitude of certain members of the U.S. embassy here in spreading alarmist rumours," J.V. Perowne wrote on May 22. "On May 17, Mr. Roché complained of remarks passed by Mr. Kennedy—he thinks and hopes that we shall be defeated—there is a considerable file in the Dept on the subject." On May 20, the British were told by Mr. Roché that Kennedy had told his government that "the less they had to do with the war, the better." The French complaint related to the American ambassador making "alarmist exaggerated tales of an air raid on Havre. Mons. Roché wanted to know if the F.O. cd not do something to restrain Mr. Kennedy and his satellites. . . . Mr. Bullitt has wholeheartedly espoused the French cause, which Mr. Kennedy is very far from having done."[2]

WHILE THE FRETTING over what to do with Kennedy continued, Anthony Eden, now Secretary of State for War, had ordered the creation of the Local Defence Volunteers—affectionately remembered as the Home Guard or "Dad's Army"—comprising men from the ages of seventeen to sixty to defend Britain's shores. Parliament passed the Emergency Powers (Defence) Act, giving the government unlimited powers to direct the nation's war effort. "We are free men fighting for our lives," Edward R. Murrow broadcast from London, "and in order that we may fight more effectively we must give up our freedom." Kennedy must have felt gratified. The war had created a fascist state.[3]

In mid-May, Churchill flew to Paris to give some backbone to the French government. According to an unnamed "unimpeachable source" of Kennedy's, "The French are not even fighting on the [Maginot] Line." Seemingly, the unnamed source neglected to tell Kennedy that the invasion of Belgium and France came through the Ardennes Forest far to the north. On May 16, Kennedy reported in his most secret message to the State Department that "Churchill said he will fight until England is burned to the ground."*

Four days later, Roosevelt requested his special assistant secretary, Samuel Breckinridge Long, warn all Americans to leave Europe and the Middle East. Once again, Kennedy assumed a role far outside his remit. Long sent a memo to Roosevelt the next day that he was in receipt of a cable from Kennedy of what "we should not do in our rearmament program if we want to avoid the mistakes which I have seen the British make." Kennedy's advice was: "The President might start considering, assuming that the French do not stiffen up what he can do to save an Allied debacle. . . . It is the view of my [unnamed friend] that nothing can save them from absolute defeat unless by some touch of genius and God's blessing the president can do it." Kennedy's sense of imminent defeat, mere days away, was further fueled by Joe Jr.'s letter from Harvard: "Some wonder what we are going to do with 50,000 planes, and suspect that it is Roosevelt's intention to get the country into war immediately after the election."[4]

The news that the French army south of the British Expeditionary Force (BEF) had melted away, creating a huge gap on their right flank, was initially withheld on May 21. Alfred Duff Cooper, the Minister for Information, broadcasted instead that "the news was grave but gave no cause for panic." There was little choice but to retreat to the sea at Dunkirk. Boulogne had fallen to the Germans, and the rescue of the garrison at Calais was impossible. Churchill sent the message to Brigadier Nicholson at Calais on May 26 around two P.M.: "Every hour you continue to exist is of the greatest help to the BEF. Government has therefore decided you must continue to fight." The men knew that their garrison was to be sacrificed to try to save the bulk of the 428,000 men gathered on the foreshore of Dunkirk beach.[5] Operation Dynamo began the following morning.

By June 4, when the Allied forces gave up the Dunkirk beachhead,

---

* This message was among those purloined by Tyler Kent. It would have given Mussolini great heart to learn that their misinformation to Kennedy, most likely through an unsuspecting Galeazzi to Eddie Moore, had been forwarded on to Hull and FDR.

338,226 men had been rescued in one of the most daring and successful operations involving military and civilian ships. The "Little Boats of
Dunkirk," over 700 of them, crewed by volunteers who owned cockle
boats, yachts, fishing smacks, a ferry, and small sailing barges joined the
military operation and answered the Royal Navy's call broadcast over the
radio to come to the aid of the troops.

In all, some 933 vessels were involved, including minesweepers and
destroyers among the "Big Ships" of Dunkirk—both naval and requi-
sitioned merchant ships. Heavy casualties were sustained, with the loss
of approximately 30,000 men, countless war matériel, and 236 ships.
Admiral Sir Bertram Home Ramsay masterminded the evacuation from
deep within the Napoleonic tunnels at Dover Castle in the room that
once held the castle's generator, or dynamo. But as Churchill warned the
nation afterward in its hour of relief, wars are not won by retreats. "We
shall fight in the seas and oceans, we shall fight with growing confidence
and growing strength in the air; we shall defend our Island, whatever the
cost may be," Churchill warned Parliament and the people. "We shall
fight on the beaches, we shall fight on the landing-grounds, we shall fight
in the fields and in the streets, we shall fight in the hills; we shall never
surrender."[6]

At the time, Kennedy did not comment on Dunkirk. Yet Dynamo
sealed Britain's resolve to fight on. It stopped dead the peace overture
from Mussolini. Chamberlain, still a member of Churchill's cabinet,
agreed with his prime minister. There could be no negotiated peace.
While the entire country celebrated the deliverance of the bulk of its
army on June 4, Joe Kennedy busied himself with the offer from Roosevelt to extend asylum in America to Queen Wilhelmina of the Netherlands.[7] As the United States remained neutral, it was not possible for
Wilhelmina to agree *and* take her government in exile with her. Instead,
London became her natural home, as it was to many European governments and foreign royalty.

In those early days of the fight, Joe mainly communicated with family
and friends. Two days after Churchill's stirring "We shall fight" speech,
Kennedy wrote to Joe Jr.: "If the French break—and the consensus here
is that they will—then I should think the finish may come quickly. . . .

With the French out of the way and the Germans in control of the ports I can see nothing but slaughter ahead. I am arranging to send everybody away except of about ten of us . . . who will stay and sleep at the Chancery."

In early June, Joe sent an upbeat cable to his Harvard friend and stockbroker, Arthur Goldsmith. Jack was graduating from Harvard with honors, the second Kennedy son to do so. THOUGHT YOU MIGHT DISCREETLY WHISPER TO WINCHELL . . . JACKS THESIS ON BRITISH APPEASEMENT TO BE PUBLISHED BY HARPERS NEXT WEEK RECEIVED MAGNA MAYBE YOU COULD WORK UP A LITTLE BOOST FOR HIM HE IS IN BRONXVILLE.[8]

Jack's senior thesis with the catchy title "Appeasement at Munich: The Inevitable Result of the Slowness of Conversion of the British Democracy to Change from a Disarmament Policy to a Rearmament Policy" had been transformed into *Why England Slept* through a great deal of hard graft from his father, those who felt obliged to read it (like Neville Chamberlain), and naturally Arthur Krock, as his editor. Before its completion as a thesis, Joe wrote to Jack that those who had seen it commented "no good purpose can be served by making scapegoats out of Chamberlain and Baldwin; on the other hand they feel you have gone too far in putting the blame on the British public." Jack changed his emphasis to reflect his father's viewpoint that "England slept. That means pretty much all Britain, leaders and people alike. You might point out the difficulties our own President has had in seeking to awaken the country to the dangers of aggression."[9]

This analytical Joe Kennedy was exceptionally short-lived. On the diplomatic scene, his near hysterics made him insufferable, particularly when compared to William Bullitt and Tony Biddle, who had escaped from Poland via Rumania and was now deputy ambassador to France. They were living through the horror of the German onslaught. Bullitt's diplomacy translated into action, too. René de Chambrun, the son-in-law of former prime minister Pierre Laval and a combatant at Dunkirk, landed safely in England on one of the English boats with the remnant of the French army. As soon as he flew back to Paris, Bullitt telephoned him.* The exhausted de Chambrun was asked to come to the embassy quickly so Roosevelt could hear directly from a reliable eyewitness what had happened. The next day de Chambrun was ordered by his government to be on the first available clipper flight to Washington from Lisbon to beg for help. His friend Clare Boothe Luce was on the same plane. On June 8, the French government fled westward, protected by their outriders, to Gien near Tours on the River Loire.

Kennedy, however, reported only that Britain's position was appallingly weak. At the same time, Count Ciano went to Berlin with the list of territories the Italians expected to receive if they joined the war.† Hitler promised to "unleash a storm of wrath and steel upon the English." There is no doubt the Vatican knew about these negotiations while Operation Dynamo was running. But had Kennedy known Mussolini's intentions from his good friend and avowed fascist at the Vatican, Galeazzi—the same man who had previously fed him Vatican disinformation?

By late May, Ciano warned the British ambassador that Italy was considering entering the war on Germany's side. Sir Percy Loraine replied then and there, "We shall answer war with war, but, notwithstanding this, my heart is filled with sadness to think that blood must flow between our countries." Ciano was sad, too; but on Monday, June 10, Italy officially entered as Germany's ally in arms.[10]

ON JUNE 12, Kennedy wrote in his diary: "No matter what action the United States takes towards this war it is only fair to say that short of a miracle this country after, and, if and when, France stops fighting, will hold on in the hope that the United States will come in." Churchill was adamant that the United States would enter the war immediately following the November 1940 election. Naturally, Kennedy worried that any sort of incident—manufactured or otherwise—might bring the United

---

* René de Chambrun, a lawyer by training, was an honorary American citizen by virtue of his direct descent from George Washington's loyal friend the Marquis de Lafayette. He had been a close personal friend of both Henry and Clare Luce, too. By the time the United States entered the war, he would be on *Time*'s blacklist of Americans not to be trusted.

† The list included the city of Nice and Corsica, Malta, Sudan, and Somalia.

States into the conflict. He hinted that Churchill might be desperate enough to consider this alternative.[11] Kennedy's lengthy entry continued:"The British only had their courage to fight with. The French were crumbling. It was 'fallacious' to believe anything else. There was no way the Allies could strike at the heart of German industry or its war effort. America should not get involved because these battles meant that "the United States will have plenty to worry about in their own country.""[12]

The day before, Roosevelt gave an important speech in Charlottesville, Virginia. "We will extend to the opponents of force the material resources of this nation," he told his audience, "and, at the same time, we will harness and speed up the use of those resources in order that we ourselves in the Americas may have equipment equal to the task of any emergency and every defense."[13] On June 13, Kennedy delivered to Churchill a copy of a cable sent in reply to the French leader Paul Reynaud's request for arms, airplanes, and tanks. Roosevelt echoed his Charlottesville speech in support of Britain and France stating that "this Government is doing everything in its power to make available to the Allied Governments the material they so urgently require, and our efforts to do still more are being redoubled."

According to Kennedy, Churchill asked him back to Downing Street to telephone the president from his secure line for permission to publish the telegram while the prime minister attended a late-night cabinet meeting. Even so, the cabinet minute makes it clear that Reynaud had already decided to publish Roosevelt's support in the hope it would halt Hitler's advance. When Churchill rejoined Kennedy, apparently "Mr. Kennedy was convinced that the president must have authorised publication of the message."[14] In fact, Roosevelt said he needed to take advice.

Kennedy returned to the embassy armed with the minutes of the meeting between Churchill and Reynaud earlier that day at Tours and cabled an outline to Roosevelt, advising France would fall within days. The next morning, the White House replied firmly: "My message of yesterday's date addressed to the French prime minister was in no sense intended to commit and did not commit the Government to military participation in support of Allied governments."[15] In the vain hope that France would keep fighting, Churchill knowingly exaggerated Roosevelt's meaning, cabling Reynaud that "If France on this message of President

Roosevelt's continues in the field and in the war, we feel that the United States is committed beyond recall to take the only remaining step, namely, becoming a belligerent in form as she has already constituted herself in fact."[16]

As Kennedy predicted, Paris fell on June 14, and she "died like a beautiful woman, in a coma, without a struggle, without knowing or even asking why," American journalist Eric Sevareid reported for CBS.[17] On June 16, the British agreed that the French could make their separate peace with Germany, "provided that the French fleet would sail to British ports and the British would fight on." An offer to unite France and Britain in a Declaration of Union was hastily drawn up, but Reynaud's government fell on June 17. He was replaced by collaborationist Maréchal Philippe Pétain as France's new president. Pétain, known as the "Hero of Verdun" in the last war, chose René de Chambrun's father-in-law, Pierre Laval, as his prime minister.

ON JUNE 18, Billy Hartington telephoned 10 Downing Street to speak to Churchill's Assistant Private Secretary, John "Jock" Colville, telling him where he thought Churchill's son, fighting with the BEF, might be. It was also the day Billy knocked on his cousin, Jean Ogilvy's, door.[18] According to Jean, Billy seemed "alright" at first sighting, all scrubbed up in his freshly pressed battle dress with his hair neatly combed. Internally, he was a mess. "They attacked and attacked," he cried out to Jean. "We ran away. We ran and we ran!"[19] Millions of Belgians and French had run ahead of them. They had already made their exodus to the south and the southern coasts, often with less than an hour to spare. Unfinished meals were left on kitchen tables, as cherished family photographs were scooped up in the rush to escape.

The Belgian gold treasury that had been sent to France for safekeeping was already on its way to Dakar, Senegal, while the French had shipped their gold to the United States. William Bullitt observed that the Nazis hoped "that France may become Germany's favorite province—a new Gau which will develop into a new Gaul."[20*] On June 21, René de

---

* Bullitt was designated to hand over the ceremonial keys to Paris in the absence of any French government official.

Chambrun met with Roosevelt and his trusted adviser, Harry Hopkins, at the White House. De Chambrun's intended request for U.S. arms and support had been superseded by events. The armistice signed at Compiègne on June 22, in the same railway carriage as the armistice of 1918, divided France into two zones, more or less diagonally across the country—the northern zone was Occupied France, the southern, Vichy France or "Free France." Pétain and Laval would form the French government at Vichy to oversee their slice of the country. The armistice came into effect at 1:35 A.M. on June 25.[21] Importantly for Hitler, Britain now stood alone.

33

"JITTERY JOE"

---

*Whilst we do not regard Mr. Kennedy as anti-British,
we consider that he is undoubtedly a coward.*

J. BALFOUR, FOREIGN OFFICE MINUTE,
MAY 23, 1940

Roosevelt worried about the anti-British French admiral, Jean-François Darlan, remaining in charge of most of the French fleet, still moored at Mers-el-Kébir and Oran on French Algeria's Mediterranean coast.[1] No one, save Pétain, believed the German fairy tale that they would not use the French fleet for its own operations, since much of their own navy was sunk or back in the dockyards for repairs. The president advised Churchill that should Darlan refuse to turn over the fleet to Britain as agreed by the previous French government, the United States would stand shoulder to shoulder with the prime minister, if it came to destroying it.

At 1:08 A.M. on July 2, a message was sent to Darlan: "It is impossible for us, your comrades up to now, to allow your fine ships to fall into the power of the German or Italian enemy. We are determined to fight to the end. . . . Should we conquer, we solemnly declare that we shall restore the greatness and territory of France. . . . In these circumstances, His Majesty's Government have instructed me to demand that the French Fleet" be immediately turned over to British control. Failing that, there were orders from His Majesty's Government "to sink your ships within six hours." Darlan did not reply, nor did he respond to the alternative for the French fleet to sail to the West Indies.

On the morning of July 3, all French vessels at Portsmouth and Plymouth in England were seized simultaneously along with ships at Alexandria in Egypt and taken under British control. Many of the captured French seamen in England joined the British Navy for the duration. The unenviable task of neutralizing the French fleet off Mers-el-Kébir and Oran was given to Vice-Admiral James Somerville. He issued a final ultimatum to Admiral Marcel-Bruno Gensoul to surrender or be blown out of the water. Gensoul was shocked, since he and many of his men wanted to continue the French fight alongside the Allies. Not believing that the British would actually open fire, he stalled for time. At 5:45 P.M., Somerville reluctantly gave the order. "Of the five French capital ships in harbor, all but one was immobilized; the battleship *Bretagne* was sunk with the loss of 977 of her crew."

After the vicious battles in French Algeria, where some 1,297 Frenchmen loss their lives and a further 351 were wounded, no one could doubt Britain's ruthless resolve to fight on. Although some smaller ships escaped back to Toulon on the French coast, and the *Richelieu* was chased to Dakar before its sinking, the rest of the French fleet was destroyed. Two days later the Pétain government broke off relations with Britain.[2]* And yet Hitler *still* hesitated to give the invasion order. It was Reichsmarschall Hermann Göring who took the decisive step, beginning the Luftwaffe's first wave of bombing attacks on July 10. Their targets were the RAF aerodromes, the Royal Navy defense installations, and south coast towns.

ON JULY 11, Hitler told his generals that Operation Sea Lion for the invasion of Britain would begin at once *if* Britain refused his final offer for a negotiated peace. That same day, the Republican Frank Knox, Lord Beaverbook's friend and publisher and part owner of the *Chicago Daily News*—who also didn't think much of Kennedy—became the new secretary of the navy. Henry L. Stimson, a former secretary of state under President Hoover, returned to the cabinet as Roosevelt's secretary of war.

The German War directive No. 16 was issued for Sea Lion on July

---

* Only the battle-cruiser *Strasbourg* survived.

16, stating, "Since England, despite her militarily hopeless situation, still shows no sign of willingness to come to terms, I have decided to prepare a landing operation against England, and if necessary, to carry it out. The aim of this operation is to eliminate the English homeland as a base for the carrying on of the war against Germany."[3]

KENNEDY'S SILENCE ON these momentous events may be explained by his preoccupation with the Democratic Convention and advising Joe Jr. as a delegate. It certainly came as a shock to him that Roosevelt was sending yet another observer to London—this time Colonel William J. "Wild Bill" Donovan. Furious, he called Sumner Welles and ranted that "Donovan cannot possibly get any information except thru our existing military and naval attachés and that his mission will simply result in creating confusion on the part of the British." Roosevelt told Welles to placate Kennedy but wrote to Knox that "somebody's nose is out of joint."[4] Again, Joe was oblivious that his prognostications about Britain's defeat were the cause of his own discomfort.

While a peptic Kennedy awaited Donovan, the Democratic Convention began. The fall of France had changed many minds about the "third-term question." "If times were normal," one senator told reporters, "I would not favor a third term for President Roosevelt, [but] I consider 1940 an abnormal year." Another congressman noted that "a speeding car simply cannot change drivers without losing control. No one in the United States is better informed on world affairs than President Roosevelt or so capably qualified to guide us through this critical period."[5]

Even so, Roosevelt wanted the convention to *draft* him in as its candidate. In other words, to paraphrase Shakespeare, he wanted greatness to be thrust upon him. But just to jolly along his leaderless supporters, a booming voice blared out from a hidden loudspeaker in the bowels of the convention hall, over and over again, "We want Roosevelt." Soon enough "California wants Roosevelt" was shouted out, with its banners waving. "New York wants Roosevelt" followed. And so on. "With state banners held aloft, the delegates formed a long parade which wound its way through the aisles, knocking down chairs, surging, singing, screaming. After a short struggle with the Farley contingent, the Massachusetts banner was seized . . . and carried into the parade."[6] Listening from the

White House, Roosevelt realized he had swept aside his contenders, Jim Farley and Vice President John Nance Garner.

As part of that Massachusetts delegation, Joe Jr. held for Farley—with a nudge from Arthur Krock. The eldest Kennedy son gave a summary of the pandemonium, too, emphasizing that Henry Agard Wallace's nomination for vice president was Roosevelt's choice as a running mate. He daren't vote twice against the administration, concluding, "I am not at all bullish on the Democratic chances."[7]

ROOSEVELT'S CHOSEN OBSERVER, Wild Bill Donovan, should have been a man after Joe Kennedy's heart. They were both ebullient, larger-than-life characters, serial womanizers, and American Irish Catholic. Their main differences were that the fearless Donovan was a lawyer, held an impressive and outstanding military record in the Great War, always evaluated any problem from various angles, and was utterly trustworthy. It was Frank Knox, a good friend of Donovan's, who suggested Wild Bill's mission, and Roosevelt heartily agreed. The president needed to understand how much of a gamble it would be to ramp up armaments production *during* a presidential campaign. Knox also asked Edgar Mowrer—the *Chicago Daily News*'s top foreign correspondent stationed in Lisbon—to join Donovan in London. Someone, Knox felt, had to provide an antidote to Kennedy's pessimistic voice.

Leaving nothing to chance, Knox involved British ambassador Lothian in the planning stages. It was Lothian who told the Foreign Office to fling open its doors in welcome, as Donovan "may exercise considerable influence" in Washington's ultimate decision to ship arms. From the moment he arrived in London on July 16, Donovan was offered unprecedented access to all the top brass, both military and political, even meeting with Churchill in the underground bunker off Whitehall, the Cabinet War Rooms. No secret dispatch or intercepted German document was held back. Indeed, Churchill divulged that he intended to also fight the Germans with his own network of fifth columnists in the countries Hitler had conquered.[8*]

---

* These are known today as "Churchill's War Rooms" and are now a fascinating museum. Churchill divulged the existence of the SOE (Special Operations Executive), which oversaw

Unlike the Welles mission, Kennedy was kept at arm's length. Donovan made his presence known at the embassy only on July 20, four days after his arrival. He did not meet with Kennedy, but hastened instead to talk to Colonel Raymond Lee, the embassy's London Observer. It was Lee's view that "the Germans cannot subdue this country without landing considerable armored forces" and that any landing would also require "attaining control of the air." When Donovan later convened with all the other American military attachés in London and asked, "Do you believe there is an even chance that Britain will remain unsubdued on September thirtieth?" Lee was delighted to hear "the unanimous verdict—'Yes.'" Of course, Kennedy disagreed, failing to see that the military men had the experience of war and knew that British courage and inventiveness (as already demonstrated at Dunkirk) counted for much more than the ambassador could imagine. "If we go in," Lee said, it must be "with eyes open and knowing everything."[9]

On July 31, Lee accompanied Donovan to meet Commander in Chief General Alan Brooke,* who was in charge of home defenses. Two days later, all the military attachés had breakfast with Donovan at Claridge's from 8:15 to 10:30 in what Lee termed as a "free and frank discussion." Since Wild Bill was leaving the next day on a British plane bound for New York via Foynes and Newfoundland the next morning, he asked for a list of the matters discussed "together with references to the cables and despatches in which these topics had been very fully treated."

What gave Donovan's breakfast companions great heart was that he had extraordinary access to everyone—"from the King and Churchill down"—and he gave the odds of 60/40 to the British to "beat off the Germans." When Donovan left on August 3, Lee told him that his role was independent of Kennedy, and that he had shared his conclusions with the ambassador only once. His analysis had been sent on to his military superiors, too. "Well," Donovan said, shaking his head, "I told him before I left that the American policy was to help in every way we can, and it

---

clandestine operations in occupied and neutral territories. This became the model for Donovan's own OSS (Office of Strategic Services), the precursor to the CIA.

* General Sir Alan Brooke was later appointed Chief of the Imperial General Staff (CIGS) and was promoted to Field Marshal in 1944. He was created Viscount Alanbrooke in 1946.

doesn't help these people any to keep telling them that they haven't got a chance."[10] Just the same, Donovan carried home letters to each of Kennedy's children, his wife, Clare Boothe Luce, Eddie Moore, John Burns, and other close friends.

Donovan dutifully reported back to Knox and Roosevelt. It came as no surprise that virtually all his advice contradicted Kennedy's. Still unable to reevaluate his position, Kennedy wrote to Hull: "If the British air force cannot be knocked out, then the war will drag out with the whole world continuously upset, with the final result the starvation of England and God knows what happening to the rest of Europe."

John Cudahy, the departing American ambassador to Belgium, announced that there would be a famine there by October. "Whatever the results of the issue raised by Mr. Cudahy," Mollie Panter-Downes wrote in *The New Yorker*, "Englishmen are sadly certain that bad blood between Britons and old friends must be one of them."[11] What Cudahy saw, however, were the Germans taking most of the food supplies for themselves, and shipping much of the stocks back to the Fatherland. It would be the same in all the conquered countries, creating a rampant black market and war profiteering.

When Cudahy was invited to lunch with Kennedy at Buckingham Palace on August 7, George VI was thankful that the former ambassador would report back home that his cousin, King Leopold of Belgium, really had no choice but to surrender. George VI recorded in his diary: "I was quite sure Leopold was no coward. He is now a prisoner & lives at Laeken with his mother very depressed." The King was surprised, however, that "Cudahy cannot understand the calm determination & cheerfulness of the people here. We told him we are waiting for what is coming if it does. We can only 'stay put' as we have nowhere to go," adding kindly, "Joe Kennedy was doing his best to get him back to normal."[12]

BY EARLY AUGUST, the airstrips of the RAF had taken a pounding. "Their losses had been heavy," James Goodson wrote, "not only in combat, but even more through bombing and strafing attacks on the ground, and, above all, accidents in training and as a result of bad weather." When Colonel Lee visited the RAF Fighter Command and met the melancholy Air Marshal Hugh Dowding, he was impressed, admitting that "I had no idea the British could evolve and operate so intricate, so scientific and rapid an organization, the tentacles of which reach out beyond the edges of the country." Kennedy, however, had had enough. He told Roosevelt in his August 2 telephone conversation that he was going home. The president charmed him into agreeing to stay another month.[13]

WHILE THE AIR bases and coastal towns were bombarded, life continued. The blackout was old hat—hardly anyone bumped into lampposts anymore. Sandbags were an accepted accoutrement garnishing buildings and monuments; gas masks in cardboard boxes slung over shoulders were the ubiquitous fashion. Men and women in uniform were the new normal. Waitresses replaced waiters. Women driving cars, buses, military vehicles, and ambulances abounded. Women "manned" the munitions factories, too. Newsprint was rationed—with only six pages allowed. So, too, were sugar and butter, meaning there were precious few cakes. The fall of France and entry of Italy on the Axis side made cheese a gourmet treat.

Theaters had been closed, but one by one were opening again to keep up morale, providing they could get electricity. Everyone read the polemic *Guilty Men,* which blamed Baldwin's and Chamberlain's governments for the country's unpreparedness.[14] Public works crews busily tore out iron railings and collected unwanted pots and pans to convert to scrap metal for military use. All radios had to be stripped from cars, and any car left empty had to have its windows and doors locked or the police would let the air out of its tires.

In the countryside, women became "land girls" to bring in the harvest. All road signs were uprooted, and the sale of maps made illegal. A strip of coastline all around Great Britain some twenty miles deep had all foreigners removed and any residents without essential business evacuated. Access to all beaches was forbidden, and the waters were mined. Barbed wire and derelict vehicles were strewn along many coastal stretches to prevent enemy aircraft from landing.

On August 13, the Luftwaffe mounted vicious coordinated attacks on airfields in southern England. The following day, an agreement in principle to swap destroyers for naval and air bases in the Americas was made. Roosevelt misleadingly told the press that "destroyers were . . . not involved in the prospective arrangements." The heaviest military losses reported by Fighter Command occurred on August 18—with thirty-three British planes lost and sixty-seven from the Luftwaffe. The Luftwaffe made the catastrophic error of shifting its bombardment from military installations and military targets to civilian targets, in what became known as the blitz.[15]

"The gratitude of every home in our Island, in our Empire, and indeed throughout the world, except in the abodes of the guilty, goes out to the British airmen," Churchill told Parliament on August 20, "who, undaunted by odds, unwearied in their constant challenge and mortal danger, are turning the tide of the World War by their prowess and their devotion. Never in the field of human conflict was so much owed by so many to so few."[16] By August 1940, the "British airmen" comprised Polish, Czech, Belgian, French, Danish, Dutch, Canadian, and American airmen, too. Kennedy never mentioned any of the young Americans who crossed the border into Canada to join the Royal Canadian Air Force to learn to fight and fly. Many went on to join the Royal Air Force as part of the three Eagle Squadrons. Kennedy never acknowledged these American boys putting their lives on the line to save Britain.

That August, Clare Boothe Luce was focused solely on the presidential election. Her concern was that Kennedy would support Roosevelt rather than the Republican candidate, Wendell Willkie, who was widely liked, tall, and handsome. No one questioned Willkie's ability. Even Harold Ickes called him "an attractive, colourful character, bold and resourceful." But Clare had understood that Willkie's support to rearm America and help Britain with armaments as announced in his Elwood, Indiana, nomination acceptance speech meant that Roosevelt was free without delay to implement measures for the nation's preparedness. Both candidates said they did not want the United States to send men into the European war. Willkie's stance knocked foreign policy out of any electoral debate.[17]

"If the British do hold on to September, you can—I'm sure, come home quite gracefully," Clare wrote to Joe on August 26. "And this would be a fine occasion for you to make a public speech in England before you leave—handing lots of bouquets to the British for their stamina and guts, and saying frankly, 'Boys, I didn't think you could do it—but you did. Thank God, I was wrong—!' And then say, 'I'll be seeing you later in the winter.'" But Joe did not venture out to see how the valiant British coped. Instead, he wrote about how he saw the blitz from the rooftop of the chancery with "my steel helmet;" how a bomb missed his rented home at Windsor by "250 yards;" and how "14 Princes Gate has just missed being hit." He also told Rose he had bought "quite a lot of French wine" and sent it to America.[18]*

The British impassiveness to the blitz unnerved Kennedy. But he had never understood his hosts. He did not tour any of the bombed areas as others did. He didn't see that the British weren't impassive, but instead, held on to an unostentatious bravado. People queued to get into the public shelters as if waiting to get a ticket to go see Greer Garson and Walter Pidgeon in *Mrs. Miniver* at the cinema. Barmaids in pubs continued to arrange sprigs of mint in some drinks to the sound of sirens, the shrieks of whistles, and the noise of footsteps outside. In the London Underground, a "Scotsman was holding twenty-five people enthralled with the story of the big fish that got away," Edward R. Murrow reported at three A.M. on August 26 after a night of unrelenting bombing in London. "I have seen a few pale faces, but very few. How long these people will stand up to this sort of thing I don't know, but to-night they're magnificent."[19]

As the British resolve grew, Kennedy's reputation plummeted to new lows. Not only were there bombs to fear, but he had acquired the cowardly label of "Jittery Joe." And it stuck. No amount of scripting by Clare could change Kennedy's dark outlook; nor could it change how negatively the British viewed him. When the latest military observers arrived, comprising General Carleton Emmons of the U.S. Air Force; General

---

* According to bombsight.org, bombing of Kensington, where Prince's Gate is located, did not begin until 1941. Kennedy lost 500 cases of fine French wine when the ship was sunk by the Germans.

George Strong, chief of the U.S. Army War Plans Division; and Admiral Robert Lee Ghormley, Kennedy suddenly discovered that he was cut out of all discussions on the bases for destroyers deal and told the president as much on August 27: "Frankly and honestly I do not enjoy being a dummy."[20] Joe Kennedy resolved he had been sidelined and censored long enough. It was time to let America know how he felt.

34

COME HELL OR HIGH WATER

There's hell to pay here tonight.

—JOSEPH P. KENNEDY TO FDR,
SEPTEMBER 6, 1940

K ennedy seethed over Roosevelt's decision to sign the bases for destroyers deal with the British without congressional approval. The
president had exercised his constitutional authority as commander in
chief to sign an agreement that strengthened America's defenses by getting the North American bases from the British. Congress could not
object.* "I am sure you must be aware of the very embarrassing situation
I feel myself in in this connection," Kennedy wrote in his "Triple Priority" cable, before enumerating how the British ambassador in Washington knew more than he did, and that Roosevelt's military missions
to London were humiliating, since he hadn't been told why they were
there. "Rarely, as a matter of fact, am I ever advised when important
conversations are held in Washington with the British Ambassador. . . . it
has been impossible for me to make any contribution to the destroyer-
bases discussion seeing as I do not know any of the facts, except second

---

* In exchange for fifty Caldwell, Wickes, and Clemson class outdated destroyers, the
United States was granted land in British possessions in North America for military purposes
in Newfoundland (with the agreement of the Canadian government), the eastern side of
the Bahamas, the southern coast of Jamaica, western St. Lucia, the Gulf of Paria in Trinidad,
Antigua, British Guiana (present-day Guyana), and two bases in Bermuda.

hand, but there was a possibility that I might have been able to make some contribution."[1]

The president's reply, drafted by Sumner Welles, stated: "There is no thought of embarrassing you and only the practical necessity for personal conversations makes it easier to handle details here."[2] Nonetheless, Joe knew that FDR did not want him back in the United States telling everyone "the truth" about the European war. Back in July, Roosevelt had offered Kennedy to direct his reelection campaign—alleging that it was against the wishes of the State Department, who thought he was doing a good job. The president knew if Joe had accepted the position as the bombs fell, he would face the charge of cowardice in the press. Kennedy understood that, too, and had remained. But from the third week in August, London, rather than military targets, was bombed. The Luftwaffe mistakenly believed that the RAF was finished.

Kennedy hosted the "Destroyer Dinner" on September 2 with Strong, Emmons, Ghormley, Beaverbrook, and Churchill, and learned that the deal would be signed the following day, on the one-year anniversary of Britain declaring war on Germany. Kennedy's blood boiled. He was fed up with these military experts. Wild Bill Donovan and Edgar Mowrer had written a series of four articles that Frank Knox shared with *The New York Times.* Indeed, Knox even wrote the foreword, stating the purpose of the articles: "They are designed to make every American fully conscious of methods used by the totalitarian powers, so that, if or when such methods are used here, they will instantly be recognized for what they are and their effect nullified. I regard defense against enemy propaganda," Knox concluded, "as second only to defense against enemy armaments."

Donovan and Mowrer gave credit to Hitler's military audacity. "Yet no amount of genius would have accomplished what Hitler accomplished in so short a time without two other elements. These were Germans abroad and sympathizers in the victim countries." Vidkun Quisling helped to defeat Norway. In Denmark, it was "fifth columnists" disguised as "newspaper men business men, and diplomats" *publicizing messages of defeat and surrender.*[3] Great Britain had Joe Kennedy.

In the second article, the authors turned their gaze briefly to Britain, stating that "the British police found it necessary to arrest a member of Parliament, Captain Ramsay on the charge of having transmitted to the German Legation in Dublin treasonable information given to him by Tyler Kent cipher clerk at the American Embassy in London, would seem to show that some of the many finely spun threads from Berlin to London remain."[4]

The New York Times called radio the latest weapon of warfare. It had been used effectively by the Germans and Italians in the Middle East and throughout the conquered countries of Europe. Now it was being used by those reporting from London against Germany. "Twelve months ago to-night we had a violent thunderstorm. As lightning streaked the sky and thunder rode down these crooked streets, I saw white-faced people running for air-raid shelters," Edward R. Murrow reminded his listeners of the anniversary in his *This Is London* broadcast made at 3:30 A.M. "If there should be a similar storm to-night, there would be no panic: nerves are much steadier; London is not as black to-night as it was on that first night when darkness settled over Europe." Cars drove with shaded head-lights, and the streets were lit by dimmed lampposts. Theaters and clubs were opened and doing good business. Sandbags had been renewed. The trenches that scarred London's parks had been shored up and roofed over to provide regular air raid shelters.[5] Four days later, the massive air attacks on London began in earnest.

JOE KENNEDY SPENT his fifty-second birthday in fear, writing to Roo-sevelt and Hull at midnight, "There's hell to pay here tonight." A day later, on September 7, nearly 1,000 German planes—348 bombers es-corted by 617 fighters—obscured London's skies. The first attack lasted two hours, followed by another, then another, and so on. The East End and its docks were the primary target, and as night gathered, the great plumes of noxious smoke gave way reluctantly to a fiery sky. Joe wrote to Rose, however, in a blatant falsehood, that "they are working against Kensington" and so he had "moved out of there completely."[6]

London was aflame. The Ministry of Home Security was hit, with some 430 people killed and 1,600 badly injured. From September 7, and for the next fifty-seven nights, Londoners could barely sleep, spending most evenings in air raid shelters listening and learning by sound how close the bombs were. The London docks would be virtually destroyed. St. Paul's Cathedral; eight churches built by Sir Christopher Wren in the seventeenth century; William the Conqueror's eleventh-century Tower of London; the BBC; Buckingham Palace; newspaper printing presses; the Houses of Parliament; Queen's Hall; the London Zoo; and countless residences were bombed. In Churchill's own words, "The whole fury and might of the enemy" were brought down upon England. "Of all the great cities in Europe," Eric Sevareid reported for CBS, "London alone behaves with pride, and battered but stubborn dignity."[7]

Nancy Astor's Plymouth and the naval base at Portsmouth were early targets, too, given their vast contingent of merchant and navy seamen. "These people are indeed the front line," Lady Astor wrote, "with pluck, patience and Providence as their only protection, and their poverty as the discipline which has prepared them to meet the direst danger with a demeanor as dogged as it is modest, and which touches the sublime."[8] It may not have been not too late for Kennedy to redeem what was left of his reputation; but he did not go out into the bombed areas or write to commiserate with the King and Queen.

INSTEAD, JOE KENNEDY made his displeasure increasingly known, both in England and in the United States. "A highly reliable member of the American Embassy who has now left London, said some months ago that Mr. Kennedy 'had lost his nerve,'" a Foreign Office Minute recorded. "We can only hope that this theory will get about in the U.S. and that Mr. Kennedy's remarks will be attributed to loss of nerve rather than to the actual state of affairs in England."[9]

On September 11, Kennedy wrote to fourteen-year-old Bobby, adapting his diatribe to a more suitable *Hardy Boys* or *Boy's Own* tone: "There is no question but that there is a very definite feeling that within the next forty-eight or seventy-two hours Germany will try an invasion." But then recognizing that Bobby was still a youngster, he added: "Of course, on the other hand, if he [Hitler] really plans an invasion, he will find it most difficult to hide ships in which he intends to move his troops in some dark alley, for the British reconnaissance 'planes are constantly looking for signs of any activity from the Germans." Joe sent a short letter to Rose in the same pouch as Bobby's, promising that he was "going to take care of myself in every way I can and still do my job," finishing with the lines, "Well, it won't be long now I'm sure."[10]

During the second week of the blitz, Kennedy telephoned Sumner Welles to let him know that "everybody was getting along well here." Welles was gratified but hadn't noted Kennedy's sarcastic tone. The next day Joe sent a long cable haranguing Welles with the real danger embassy staff were running. "For ten days now,* there has been continual day and night bombing. . . . It has been aggravated by an anti-aircraft barrage that has lasted all during the night . . . I have been living at St. Leonard's with about ten officers at weekends." He made it abundantly clear that he would continue to live out of town at Windsor "since 14 Prince's Gate is now considered in a danger zone." Oddly, despite Kennedy's letter to young Joe that 14 Prince's Gate was unsafe and that "there have been at least ten bombs dropped within 200 yards of the place and some every night," no bombs actually fell from September 7 to October 25, 1940, anywhere near that address in Knightsbridge.[11]

BEFORE WELLES COULD reply, the first peacetime draft in U.S. history became law on September 16, 1940.† All men aged between twenty-one and forty-five had to register, and like the Vietnam War draft, men were selected to serve by virtue of a lottery number designated for each day of birth in the year. If "your number was up," the draftee was obliged to serve in the U.S. military for one year. Kennedy knew that his son Joe Jr. was eligible but privately questioned that Jack, with his record of poor health, should serve.

Back then, there was no way a future presidential candidate like young Joe could dodge the draft *and* be elected. The ambassador had held several conversations with Ghormley, Strong, and Emmons about his sons and wrote to Joe Jr.: "Strong, who is really the topside man in the Army, feels that the chance for promotion and position is much better in the Air Force than anything else, principally because it is going to expand quickly and it isn't as hidebound as the regular army." Naturally, Kennedy would discuss it with Emmons, the Air Force man, "before he leaves and suggest that he gives you the benefit of his advice and suggestions as to

---

* It was seven days and nights. The cable is dated September 14.

† It was called the Selective Service and Training Act.

what you should do and I am also of the opinion that he may be able to give you a lift."

Jack, on the other hand, had been ordered by both the Lahey Clinic and the Mayo Clinic to take a year off before continuing on at Harvard Law due to his health. "As far as Jack goes, I don't know what to say," a forlorn Kennedy wrote to young Joe. "I don't see how he is going to be well enough to go into the army, but I am going to talk to Emmons and Ghormley about him, so that when you fellows talk your own situations over we will have somebody you can talk with to get good advice."[12]

ANGRY AND DISILLUSIONED at being frozen out from the "top table" conversations, Kennedy had been casting aspersions on the Roosevelt administration for a very long time. On October 7, Rose wrote to Joe from John J. Burns's office: "They think the Pres. Does not want you home before the election due to your explosive—defeatist, point of view, as you might so easily throw a bomb which would explode sufficiently to upset his chances. . . . You cannot tell about Father's or Archbishop Spellman's point of view as Johni [Burns] has influenced them all."[13]

On October 10, after meeting with Kennedy, Halifax felt compelled to write a warning cable to Lothian. "Mr. Kennedy seemed very much out of temper with the United States Government and with the President, his principal complaint being that they had not kept him adequately informed of their policy and doings during the last two or three months," Halifax wrote. "He told me he had sent an article to the United States to appear on November 1st, if by any accident he was not able to get there, which would be of considerable importance appearing five days before the Presidential election."

But there was more. "When I asked him what would be the main burden of his song," Halifax continued, "he gave me to understand that it would be an indictment of President Roosevelt's administration for having talked a lot and done very little. He is plainly a rather disappointed and embittered man." British sentiments were united in the potential for catastrophe that Kennedy represented. He was viewed as "dangerous to our forthcoming important discussions in Washington."[14]

In that October 10 fateful chat with Halifax, Kennedy had also asked for access to the Chancellor of the Exchequer, his advisers, and Montagu

334 +✤ THE AMBASSADOR

Norman at the Bank of England prior to his departure "as to the wisest way of handling the financial questions that must shortly arise between us and the United States." Joe boasted that he was better informed about what was happening in "Free France," too, and that the French "reported an improvement of feeling" between themselves and their German captors.* In what was tantamount to a fit of pique for Halifax, he disagreed, saying "that this was not at all our information" and that the French—now living in a divided country—had been sold a pack of lies about British resistance and German accommodation with the Vichy government.[15]

Of course, Halifax was quick to warn Lothian that in no circumstances should Kennedy be given any knowledge of the financial arrangements with the U.S. administration, as he may be tempted to pass this inside information along to his Wall Street friends. Lothian needed to be reminded of Kennedy's plan prior to his return to the United States, "which is only in line with many other indications which we have had throughout the last year of Mr. Kennedy's ultimate intentions."[16]

Then, too, Halifax warned Churchill about Kennedy. The prime minister would have felt compelled to telephone the president with the bombshell Kennedy had revealed about his damning article to appear in newspapers on November 1. A day later, on October 11, Kennedy had lunch with George VI to advise that he was returning home as "he thought that he could do more good there in telling his people what we are standing here from bombing, & what we need in the way of help from U.S.A.," the King wrote in his diary. Kennedy said that the Neutrality Acts would be difficult to repeal, but that the armaments and aircraft sent would demonstrate that "this country is their first line of defence," but then Kennedy embarked on "credit in connection with our financial assets for a loan towards paying for armaments."

Although Kennedy's remark was entirely out of order, George VI reflected that "I have always thought we should have sent a yearly token payment for our war debts of the last war instead of repudiating them." This led Kennedy to reveal that when he had come as ambassador, he had two burning questions he wanted answered: "(1) War Debts. (2) Why

---

* If Kennedy had such intelligence, it would certainly have come from Galeazzi again, as the Italians were nominally in charge of administration in the area surrounding Nice.

an American could not be Queen of England (in 1936 meaning Mrs. S. [Simpson]). He knows both answers now." Then the King wrote what he thought of Kennedy. "He is always the shrewd hard business man, & still thinks in terms of dollars as against the terms of human feelings. We are fighting for our lives & homes now, & if our houses are destroyed by Nazi bombing we are still alive & that is all that matters. Money & material things are of no account, in relation to life. The others can be replaced but not life."[17]

As EARLY AS mid-September, Kennedy told Halifax, Beaverbrook, and Montagu Norman he was going home and wrote: "They all nearly fainted," adding: "They give me the idea that the British people have come to respect me and have an affection for me and therefore it would be a great blow to them if I walked out." Kennedy hadn't realized that the British had been wondering why it was taking so long for him to go.

In a word, the answer was "Roosevelt." Apparently, Kennedy told Frank Murphy, the assistant justice of the Supreme Court—as well as Arthur Krock—that he'd warned Sumner Welles "he had written a full account of the facts to Edward Moore ... with instructions to release the story to the press if the Ambassador were not back in New York by a certain date." When Welles reported this to Roosevelt on October 11, the date by which Kennedy had to be back home was set for November 1, less than a week before the election.

Welles thought Kennedy should be recalled, but "the President did not want him to come. He looks upon him [Kennedy] as a trouble-maker and a person entirely out of hand and out of sympathy."[18] It was by all accounts a difficult discussion, but Welles prevailed. Roosevelt compromised, agreeing that Kennedy could come home in the latter part of October. The president would send Joe a letter, giving him clear instructions about his conversation and his conduct when he landed. Welles also told the president he was concerned Kennedy would "come out for Willkie."[19] Welles was not told that Roosevelt already knew what Kennedy had planned.

THE PRESIDENT DULY wrote to his ambassador on October 17: "I know what an increasingly severe strain you have been under during the past

336 + THE AMBASSADOR

weeks and I think it is altogether owing to you that you get a chance to get away and get some relief. The State Department has consequently telegraphed you by my desire to come back for consultation during the week commencing October 21. In your particular case the press will be very anxious to get some statements from you," the president continued, "and no matter how proper and appropriate your statements might be, every effort will be made to misinterpret and to distort what you say. I am, consequently, asking you specifically not to make any statement to the press on your way over nor when you arrive in New York until you and I have had a chance to agree upon what should be said."[20] It was cunning of Roosevelt *not* to recall Kennedy but to invite him back for consultation. If Joe came out for Willkie, Roosevelt could demand he return to his post. But FDR was not a man to take unnecessary chances with Joe as the wounded tiger and had already begun using Alsop and Kintner again. If Kennedy insisted on supporting Willkie, Roosevelt would reply with the full truth behind his treachery.

The British would certainly corroborate Kennedy's actions and verify that his explosive temper had taken hold of his senses. "In view of Mr. Kennedy's role in London throughout the war, and of his longstanding personal antagonism to the American Ambassador to France, Mr. Bullitt, his article if it duly appears will certainly be both sensational and influential," the secret memorandum on the retirement of Mr. Joseph Kennedy from the embassy of the United States in London declares. "Moreover, as Mr. Bullitt has openly supported Mr. Roosevelt since the latter recalled him from France, and Mr. Bullitt continues to enjoy the president's confidence, Mr. Kennedy's action, of which he made no secret to the Secretary of State [Halifax], can scarcely be taken as anything else than an attack upon the President's policy of preparing the American nation for war."[21] American desk expert Tom North Whitehead wrote: "I cannot imagine how Mr. Kennedy's recent behavior should improve his political position at Washington or in the country. It rather looks as though he was thoroughly frightened when in London, and has gone to pieces in consequence."[22]

On October 17, too, George VI read "Halifax's report to Lothian of Mr. Kennedy's parting interview with him at the F.O. last week." The King wrote: "The U.S. Ambassador was out of temper (he has always had a bad stomach) with his own Govt. & with the President, because he has not been kept informed by the State Dept. of their policy & doings during the last 3 months. Had he not been in London, he would not have known what was going on." That said, George VI was not surprised that Kennedy "was disgruntled & was going home to give up his job here." However, "He [Kennedy] told Halifax he had sent an article to the U.S. to appear in their Press on November 1st 5 days before the election, which would be an indictment of Roosevelt's administration for having talked a lot & done little. He must be a very disappointed & rather embittered man, to run down his own chief."[23]

By the time Kennedy met the King for tea on October 17 to say goodbye, Kennedy's reason had resurfaced. "He was in much better form I thought & talked much more sensibly. He had seen the P.M., Halifax again, & Kingsley Wood (over the loans question). . . . He knows, as well as we do, that we must have the armaments we need 'right now', & that Americans have got to realise that to them it is a kind of insurance policy against their future."[24]

AMBASSADOR JOSEPH P. Kennedy ended his stay in London in much the same way as it began, visiting other ambassadors, only this time he spread his doom-laden prophecies about Britain's demise as his parting gift. The Soviet ambassador, Ivan Maisky, remarked that "Kennedy is still a 'pessimist': of course, the threat of an invasion has passed," as indeed it had. But then, Maisky may well have known as early as September 17, Hitler had called off Operation Sea Lion for the invasion of England.[25]

In the cabinet meeting of October 18, Churchill reported: "Mr. Kennedy has decided to ally himself with Mr. Roosevelt's opponent, Mr. Willkie, on November 5th. The article which Mr. Kennedy has written is due to appear four days before the election in order to damage Mr. Roosevelt's cause. This confirms what we have heard at various times, namely that Mr. Kennedy's interests in Wall Street have been attracting him back into that sphere; and that as Wall Street is supporting Mr. Willkie, Mr. Kennedy has decided to go along with it."[26]

Three days later, Kennedy came to say his final goodbye to George VI. "He has had a series of Major-Generals & Admirals over here on a week's visit at a time, & he has had them shown round just to see what we are doing to counteract the invasion & the bombing from the air. I told Kennedy on Friday Oct 11th at lunch that my slogan was 'seeing is believing' & he has passed it on to them. He hopes Roosevelt will be reelected, as it will save time in getting things going now."[27] Of course, His Majesty did not comment on how these parting words contradicted his earlier talks or Halifax's report.

The last person Kennedy visited was his only surviving friend, the ailing former prime minister, Neville Chamberlain, who was undergoing treatment for colon cancer. It became obvious to Churchill that Neville would have to resign.[28] Chamberlain wrote his resignation letter on October 2, indicating that he was shoved out of office; however, he was persuaded to rewrite it "to make it appear that I was insisting on resignation instead."[29]

Joe Kennedy knew his friend was dying and found saying goodbye difficult. He wrote to Chamberlain just as he left London on October 22, saying: "I have met in my life two men whom I felt had dedicated their lives to the real good of humanity without any thought of themselves. The first one was the present Pope, the second was you." Then Kennedy declared: "You have retired but mark my words the world will yet see that your struggle was never in vain. My job from now on is to tell the world of our hopes."[30] In this, Joe Kennedy's loyalty was steady; he continued singing Chamberlain's praises and saying that Munich was a victory, not a defeat.

As Kennedy flew from Bournemouth to Lisbon on Tuesday, October 22, some two years and seven months after his arrival, he was blind to the fact that his own personal failures had led to the failure of his mission to London. He had been amply warned that he hadn't the temperament, training, or willpower to learn to become an ambassador, and frankly, he hadn't cared. He was absent from his post more than any other ambassador and had a whale of a time advancing the cause of Joe Kennedy and his nine "hostages to fortune." As for America, he had one last public chapter to star in: he must, at all costs, keep the United States out of the war.

35

THE DRAGON SLAYERS

Come not between the Dragon and his wrath.
—WILLIAM SHAKESPEARE,
KING LEAR, ACT I, SCENE I

On his five-day journey home, Joe Kennedy kept his own counsel, as Roosevelt had ordered, but was angry beyond imagining. He had been betrayed by the State Department and the White House and could prove it by the article they leaked to columnists Alsop and Kintner in early October. From the outset, "The president's lingering warmth toward him was finally chilled by unfortunately accurate reports of the language he used about the administration in the presence of important Englishmen. Nor has he been much loved of late in London."[1]

The macabre dance and charade that had been played between Kennedy and Roosevelt for over two years was correct in every detail. "In informed quarters, the London story has been taken as a sign that Kennedy is ready to lead his ace of trumps, by simply refusing to stay on any longer. . . . Generally speaking, even when right he has been too defeatist in tone to command an audience here."[2] It was the Alsop and Kintner article that spurred Kennedy to write his tell-all story to be published on November 1, should "by some accident" he had not returned to the United States. Even Kennedy's close friends, like Arthur Goldsmith, feared what he might do when he landed.[3]

Joe learned at his layover in Bermuda that Rose would be at LaGuardia

Field to meet him. The president had sent a wire asking for both of them to COME TO WASHINGTON IMMEDIATELY AFTER YOUR ARRIVAL IN NEW YORK TO SPEND SATURDAY NIGHT AT THE WHITE HOUSE. Since he was delayed by a day, he called Missy LeHand, and the president was put on the telephone. Sunday would be fine, too, Roosevelt assured him.[4]

As KENNEDY DESCENDED the airplane stairs clutching his bulging briefcase and homburg, Joe's former colleague from the Maritime Commission, Max Truitt, greeted him at the foot of the steps.[*] Truitt then handed Kennedy a letter from the president asking him to go to Washington at once.[5] Before Joe could respond, a veritable army of reporters and photographers swarmed around him, blocking his first view in seven months of his family. Rose, Kathleen (twenty), Eunice (nineteen), Patricia (sixteen), and Jean (twelve) rushed forward to smother the paterfamilias in a collective bear hug.[†] "Kennedy looked for all the world like a man bursting with things to say, but in the interval between his arrival and his departure by plane for the capital he limited himself to these words: 'I have nothing to say until I've seen the president.'" Then he grinned like the Cheshire cat and some observers noted: "He promised to 'talk a lot' when he had had his discussion with the president."[6]

Roosevelt wasn't the only person who needed to see Kennedy urgently. Other prominent Catholics like Jim Farley and Al Smith had not only abandoned the president but were actively campaigning for Willkie. The latest polls showed a worrying trend that the Catholic vote was abandoning FDR's bid for reelection. Newly appointed Jewish Supreme Court Justice Felix Frankfurter approached the other novice justice and Catholic, Frank Murphy, about how to correct the situation before Kennedy came home. Murphy was clear: have Joe Kennedy make a speech. So, a week before Kennedy's return to the United States, Justices Frankfurter, Murphy, and William O. Douglas went to the White House. They met with Harry Hopkins and Roosevelt to persuade the president to ask

[*] According to some reports, Kennedy also held a London air raid siren which he would later use to call the family to dinner.

[†] The car in which Teddy, aged nine, rode was held up in traffic.

Kennedy to endorse him publicly on radio. A reticent FDR agreed that it was a job he would have to handle himself.[7]

As suspected, Clare and Henry Luce had sent a car to pick up Kennedy at LaGuardia Field and were expecting him momentarily at their Manhattan apartment to go over his speech backing Willkie. They had even booked radio time. But Joe was a no-show. The Luces' intentions had been known, of course, to the White House and State Department since Henry Luce's wire to Kennedy back in July urging the ambassador's urgent resignation: "It is my personal judgment you should return to this country immediately and tell what you think about everything totally," Luce urged. That cable was also why Hull had refused Kennedy home leave in the summer of 1940.[8]

THE REPORTERS WERE left to interview the Kennedy daughters while Joe was shepherded into a private room in the terminal to meet with Rose, Judge John Burns, Eddie Moore, his politically wired Boston friend Cornelius "Connie" Fitzgerald, and Ted O'Leary.[*] They all went to work on him. Rose was left to do most of the running, as she was convinced her husband was about to undo years of hard work if he did not back Roosevelt. She reminded Joe that FDR had sent him, the first Irish Catholic ambassador to the Court of St. James's, for the *only* post he was prepared to take. Roosevelt had also made Kennedy his ambassador to the papal coronation.

Burns chimed in, agreeing with Rose that whatever happened since, these were two important and groundbreaking actions for Catholics. They told Joe he would be forever branded as ungrateful, and he could be sure Roosevelt was prepared for his betrayal. Burns went further. If Kennedy abandoned Roosevelt, he would become "a pariah. . . . None of his boys will be able to hold their heads up at a Democratic convention ever again. It will be destructive for all his dreams and hopes for his children."[9] His boys could never be Democratic candidates for public office, and the Republicans wouldn't have them with Kennedy's personal record. Burns made it clear that Joe had no choice other than to

---

* O'Leary was Joe's Mr. Fix-It, who drove Gloria Swanson to meet Cardinal O'Connell to end their affair.

back the president. Joe grudgingly agreed, but not before he upbraided Roosevelt yet again.

Joe and Rose Kennedy flew straight on to Washington, arriving shortly after seven P.M. To Joe's dismay, Senator James Byrnes of South Carolina and his wife had been asked to join them, too. Kennedy held his malevolent tongue, knowing that Byrnes was close to Roosevelt. Before they joined the president, Byrnes blurted out, "I've got a great idea, Joe. Why don't you make a radio speech on the lines of what you have said here tonight and urge the president's reelection?" Kennedy replied, shaking his head, that such a thing wasn't in his heart until he got "a few things off his chest."[10]

Joe, Rose, and the Byrneses joined the president and Missy LeHand in the upstairs Oval Study. Roosevelt, a masterful scene-setter, had especially chosen the location where he and Joe had first met. There they had often talked and joked during the early New Deal days when Kennedy sought to call the president his friend. That night, however, there was a tense atmosphere, as when a public engagement compels a warring couple to declare a temporary truce for the evening. The first thing Kennedy did was to show Roosevelt the scrawled letter from Chamberlain, written on October 19. Had the president noted the sentence "I should imagine there can have been few cases in our history in which the two men occupying our respective positions were so closely in touch with one another as you and I?" Nothing escaped Roosevelt's eye when he played the puppeteer.

At their dinner of scrambled eggs and sausages, toast, and rice pudding, Byrnes repeated his suggestion that Kennedy go on air to endorse Roosevelt. "He constantly referred to the President on this matter and he [FDR] agreed it was necessary. I didn't say, Yes, Aye, or No," Joe wrote in his diary. "The President worked very hard on Rose, whom I suspect he had come down because of her great influence on me. He talked to her about her father. All through dinner, Byrnes kept selling me the idea, but I made no comment, because I wanted to talk alone with the President before making any decision."

Joe waited, hoping to see FDR alone, but to no avail. Finally his temper flared. "Since it doesn't seem possible for me to see the President alone, I guess I'll just have to say what I am going to say in front of everybody," Kennedy blurted out. Without drawing breath, he launched into the most vitriolic tirade. "I am damn sore at the way I have been treated. . . . Mr. President, as you know, I have never said anything privately in my life that I didn't say to you personally, and I have never said anything in a public interview that ever caused you the slightest embarrassment." Did he really expect the president of the United States to swallow such a lie? Kennedy knew he had unbridled power at that moment—maybe for the last time—and he was going to spread his hurt around. Roosevelt and the State Department had actively worked against him, almost from the beginning, Kennedy claimed. All he got in return was "a bad deal."

"All these things were conducive to harming my influence in England, and if I had not gone to the British Government and said, 'If you don't let me know all about this, your country is going to find me most unfriendly toward the whole situation.' So I smashed my way through with no thanks from the American Government." Roosevelt attempted to deny that he was the source of any of Kennedy's personal complaints. It was the State Department, not he. It was the career men, not the White House. Still, Kennedy's high dudgeon would not be assuaged. What about all those leaks? That dreadful Alsop and Kintner story? Why did Breckinridge Long call Kennedy at two A.M. and put Alsop on the line to talk about the evacuation of British children to America?

Rose tried to lower the temperature while supporting Joe by interrupting to say how difficult it was to get the proper perspective on things from three thousand miles away. Somehow her intervention made the red mist clear.* Joe agreed to make the speech on the radio—on condition that he would write it himself and pay for it. He would not brook any interference. But he was still fuming. Kennedy refused to stay the night at the White House, and left Rose there. He was back in New York shortly after midnight.[11]

"I WANT ONLY for you to know, when you make that radio address tomorrow night, throwing as you will, all your prestige and reputation

---

* In Thomas Fleming's *The New Dealers' War: FDR and the War Within World War II* (Basic Books, 2001), on page 80, he states that in exchange for Kennedy's broadcast, Roosevelt agreed to back Joe Jr. for governor of Massachusetts in 1942, citing Michael Beschloss as his source on pages 218–21. Beschloss does not conclude this, positing instead that John Kennedy said later that Roosevelt had promised his backing for 1944. This is on page 218.

for wisdom, your experience abroad and into the scales for F.D.R. you'll probably help turn the trick for him," Clare wrote Joe. "And I want you also to know that I believe with all my heart and soul you will be doing America a terrible disservice."[12] She admonished herself for doubting his loyalty to Willkie, but she certainly knew her man. Joe hadn't told Clare what his speech contained. Missy LeHand made all the arrangements for him to speak to the country on CBS Radio over its 114 stations at nine P.M. EST the next day, Tuesday, October 29.

"On Sunday I returned from war-torn Europe, to the peaceful shores of our beloved country renewed in my conviction that this country must and will stay out of war," Kennedy began. "What counts in this hour of crisis is what we in the United States of America are prepared to do in order to make ourselves strong. . . . Even the most staid isolationist is now alive to the danger facing any nation in the modern world," he said. "The realization that oceans alone are not adequate barriers against revolutionary forces which now threaten a whole civilization has not come too late. We are rearming. . . . If we rearm fast enough, America will stay out of the war. It is today our guarantee of peace."

Kennedy went on to defend Chamberlain's stance at Munich. Then he stated that Roosevelt did not want to involve the country in war; that there had been no secret commitment to involve the United States in the war; and that "England is not now looking for manpower. She has not even called up all the men she has eligible. I repeat, this is a war, not of men, but of machines." He closed by saying, "My wife and I have given nine hostages to fortune. Our children and your children are more important than anything else in the world. The kind of America that they and their children will inherit is of grave concern to us all. In the light of those considerations, I believe that Franklin D. Roosevelt should be re-elected President of the United States."[13]

ON THE SATURDAY prior to election day, Joe Kennedy joined over seventy thousand fans at Yankee Stadium to watch Notre Dame defeat Army 7–0. Afterward, he paid a call to Frank Murphy, and for the next hour, gave vent to all his bitterness against Roosevelt. "He practically left no one uncursed but that is the style of this able and dynamic man so it ought not to be given too much emphasis," Murphy recalled in his contemporaneous diary notes. "That he was filled with wrath and possessed contempt for those who have tried to undo him was plain."[14]

The following Tuesday, Franklin D. Roosevelt became the first president to run successfully for a third term in office.* The next day, Joe Kennedy was back in Washington, tendering his resignation. Roosevelt asked Kennedy not to make his resignation public until he could find a replacement. Joe agreed. Next, he went to the State Department to disseminate his pessimism to Cordell Hull, Sumner Welles, and Samuel Breckinridge Long. Kennedy argued that the RAF had not turned back Hitler's Luftwaffe, but rather that the Germans had called off their invasion plans; that Spain had not entered the war on Germany's side because it was a spent force. Even Italy's invasion of Greece rather than the Middle East was down to German tactics and had nothing to do with Britain's fight.

"He sees a new philosophy, both political and economic, with the United States excluded from European markets and from Far Eastern markets and from South American markets," Long wrote. In many respects, Kennedy was right that a postwar world would attempt to do just that. But the fact that "he thinks we ought to take some steps to implement a realistic policy and make some approach to Germany and to Japan which would result in an economic collaboration" was an utter fantasy. "He does not believe in the continuing of democracy. He thinks that we will have to assume a Fascist form of government here or something similar to it if we are to survive in a world of concentrated and centralized power." Kennedy succeeded in making the normally lugubrious Long feel that "the end of everything" had finally come.

Despite Kennedy's doom-mongering, Long was shocked to hear that the former ambassador was about to embark on a tour to see Hearst and other publishers, like McCormick, in Chicago. Joe Kennedy was going to become a one-man band to educate the American people in foreign affairs, with the aim to keep America out of the war. Long warned

---

* Roosevelt won by a comfortable 5 million votes, with 54.8 percent of the total popular vote. He won the electoral college vote by a landslide 84.5 percent.

Kennedy in no uncertain terms that he should not talk to the press or "talk in a way that would scare the American people."

AFTER WASHINGTON, KENNEDY headed by plane for Boston and the Lahey Clinic for another checkup and to see young Joe and Bobby, who was now studying at the Priory School in Rhode Island. Four days later, on Sunday, November 10, in his suite at the Ritz-Carlton in Boston, Joe Kennedy entertained reporters Louis Lyons of *The Boston Daily Globe*, Charles Edmundson of the *St. Louis Post-Dispatch*, and Edmundson's editor, Ralph Coghlan, to whom he promised a background briefing. Kennedy was feeling grand, in his shirtsleeves, eating an apple pie. He was among old friends, forgetting that his interview with Lyons in December 1939 had landed him in hot water.

"I'm willing to spend all I've got to keep us out of the war," Kennedy flashed with vehemence. "There's no sense our getting in. We'd just be holding the bag." He revealed that he was starting a one-man crusade to "keep us out" because he knew "more about the European situation than anybody else, and it's up to me to see that the country gets it." Then came his zinger: "Democracy is finished in England and that national socialism will be the result." There's no democracy in England? one of them questioned. "Is there real opportunity there or does the aristocracy keep a rigid class structure that keeps the common man down?" Kennedy let loose a torrent of abuse about the class system. When asked what about America, Kennedy said, "If we get into the war it will be [finished] in this country too. . . . Everything we hold dear would be gone." In the words of Colonel Raymond Lee, Kennedy "used almost to get drunk on his own verbosity, and I am inclined to think that is what betrayed him on many occasions."[15]

Kennedy would later claim that their discussion was "off the record," but it was too late to save him from himself. Alsop and Kintner smelled blood, writing: "The history of American diplomacy is replete with fantastic incidents, but a good many State Department officials agree that the recent interview given by Joseph P. Kennedy comes near to winning the prize." The Associated Press picked up the original Kennedy interview and his denial that he was misquoted. It was never intended to be on the record.

A victim of his own "drunken verbosity," Kennedy dug himself a deeper hole, this time on the West Coast. He flew west to visit Jack, who was taking courses at Stanford University to see if he liked business any better than the law. The twenty-three-year-old didn't like either profession. After the fatherly visit, Joe headed for Hollywood to speak at a Warner Bros. studio luncheon. Among the glitterati present was Hitler's man in Los Angeles, Georg Gyssling, consul at the German embassy, who was one of the most influential men in Hollywood.*

Douglas Fairbanks Jr., who had been the target of German censorship, was not present but was so outraged by what he heard Kennedy had said that he couldn't restrain himself from writing to Roosevelt. "As you know, Mr. Kennedy was out here meeting with Mr. Hearst. . . . and he planned to meet with me on his return." Kennedy spoke for three hours, "and it was another 'off-the-record talk'. . . . the consensus was that he repeated more or less what he said in his now famous 'Interview' in Boston." Kennedy saw no reason to get into the war. "He suggested that the Lindberg [sic] appeasement groups are not so far off the mark when they suggest that this country can reconcile itself to whomever wins the war and adjust our trade and lives accordingly. He did maintain, however, that we should continue aiding Britain."

Kennedy also preached Jewish producers were "on the spot" and "they should stop making anti-Nazi pictures or using the film medium to promote or show sympathy to the cause of the 'democracies' versus the 'dictators.' He said that anti-Semiticism [sic] is growing in Britain and that Jews are being blamed for the war." Fairbanks was incandescent. "I *know* positively that there is not one half of one percent truth in such a statement, (on the other hand, I have had several reports from friends there that when the bombing started, the Ambassador was the most frightened man in the realm, and was the source of many private jokes)." Fairbanks continued, noting that Kennedy even suggested "clean ups" and "clean

---

* Gyssling worked under the San Francisco German consul, Hitler's former adjutant and trusted eyes and ears on the West Coast, Fritz Wiedemann. Together they would infiltrate the U.S. film, naval, and aeronautics industries from 1937. Gyssling had successfully banned Warner Bros. films in Germany until the studio agreed to German censorship (*Source:* Steven J. Ross, *Hitler in Los Angeles: How Jews Foiled Nazi Plots Against Hollywood and America* [New York: Bloomsbury, 2017], 114–17, 198, 214).

outs," which today would be tantamount to Nazi ethnic cleansing of the film industry. "He continued to underline the fact that the film business was using its power to influence the public dangerously, and that we all," Fairbanks added, "and the Jews in particular, would be in jeopardy if they continued to abuse that power."[16]

Kennedy's attack on Jewish producers was highly inflammatory. Many scratched their heads wondering if he wanted back in. If they had realized the power of Hitler in Hollywood at the time through his personal censors, counselors Georg Gyssling and Fritz Wiedemann, they might have wondered if Kennedy was imparting their message, too.

Doubtless ignorant of the poor impression he was making, Joe Kennedy flew east to New York in plenty of time for Thanksgiving, staying at the Waldorf Astoria Hotel. That same day, Winston Churchill congratulated the Home Secretary, Herbert Morrison, on his excellent remarks in the Commons, "both about Italy and in reply to Kennedy's vapourings. The points could not have been better made and I am sure they will strike home."[17]

At the Waldorf, Kennedy met with former President Herbert Hoover, Charles Lindbergh, and more newspapermen, confirming to all that the British situation was "hopeless" and advocated a negotiated peace. Kennedy kept them talking for an hour and a half, unstoppable about the hopeless conditions in Britain. "He said that war would stop if it were not for Churchill and the hope in England that America will come in.... Kennedy said that every major port in England had been either closed or seriously damaged, except Bristol, Liverpool, and Glasgow."[18]* Yet, when it came down to joining Lindbergh and America First or any other isolationist organization, despite being asked, Kennedy demurred.

Later in the Thanksgiving weekend, Joe was invited to spend the night at Hyde Park with President Roosevelt and the First Lady. Before he arrived, they discussed his Boston interview, his Hollywood debacle, and what they had learned of his meeting with William Randolph Hearst. Although Roosevelt never liked to show his temper, he was equally unwilling to allow a renegade to travel unconfronted "off the reservation."

---

* Of course, there had been extensive damage, particularly to Plymouth, Portsmouth, and Southampton, but the ports were still functioning.

Eleanor picked up Joe at Rhinecliff train station and drove him to see her husband. The two men remained sequestered in Roosevelt's tiny study at the front of the house, where Kennedy again became "drunk with his own verbosity."

What, if anything, had an unfettered, reelected Roosevelt replied to Kennedy? It remains their secret. But within ten minutes, Eleanor Roosevelt was called back to the Big House. Kennedy was asked to step out of the room. Eleanor noticed that her husband's face was drained. He oozed anger. Struggling to restrain his voice, Roosevelt said in a low, trembling growl, "I never want to see that son of a bitch again as long as I live. Take his resignation and get him out of here." At first Eleanor could not understand her husband's wrath. She reminded him that Kennedy had been invited for the weekend with other guests and that the next train didn't leave until two. Roosevelt replied, "Then you drive him around Hyde Park, give him a sandwich, and put him on that train!" After spending four hours in Kennedy's company, Eleanor recalled twenty years later, that these were "the most dreadful four hours of my life."[19]

UNBELIEVABLY, KENNEDY HAD hoped for a government position. Is that what angered Roosevelt? Did Joe tender his resignation and demand to be secretary of the treasury? We shall never know. What we do know is that, he popped in to see the president on December 1, to formally and finally submit his resignation. Although no replacement for Kennedy had as yet been named, a calmer Roosevelt accepted it.

Perhaps the president recalled the remarks of Douglas Fairbanks Jr.'s letter: "The general impression hereabout is that Joe has been violently influenced by strong Catholic appeasement groups, and is in favor of a negotiated peace."[20] At the end of the day, Roosevelt needn't do a thing to slay his dragon Kennedy. Joe had done it all by himself. Besides, the president knew better than to let his temper rule his head. Although it looked unlikely, there might come a time when Roosevelt still needed to call upon his former ambassador. And so the pair wished each other well, and Joe Kennedy exited from public life.

ON LEAVING THE White House, Kennedy announced his resignation: "Today the President was good enough to express regret over my decision, but to say that, not yet being prepared to appoint my successor, he wishes me to retain my designation as ambassador until he is prepared. But I shall not return to London in that capacity."[21]

Joe Kennedy would never serve the president again. His only role in public life would be as the man bankrolling the political careers of his three sons: John F. Kennedy, Robert F. Kennedy, and Edward M. Kennedy. He had failed as an ambassador; never ran for president or any public office himself; but succeeded in making the name of Kennedy as great to modern Americans as the name of Adams was to a nascent United States. In the words of President Kennedy, "He made it all possible."

EPILOGUE

On December 6, 1940, Jack Kennedy gave his father a few pointers about the article Joe planned to publish, entitled "As I See It." Jack's comments are reflective, supportive, and incisive. He knew his father but tried nonetheless to get Joe to tone down the unnecessary rhetoric.

A classic example was: "In giving your reasons why America should not go into the war I would not state that Britain does not want it as you did in your speech because I imagine that they will be asking for more direct aid in the near future." Jack suggested that his father ignore the ongoing war with "Alsop and Kintner, etc. . . . treating what they say as insignificant." Alsop and Kintner, like many Americans, "are guilty of throwing around the term *appeasement* when they never have stopped to think exactly what it meant"—or that it had a changing meaning over the years when Kennedy was ambassador.[1]

On December 17, 1940, Franklin D. Roosevelt revealed his plan to provide billions of dollars in war supplies to Great Britain in a press conference. The program would become known as Lend-Lease. Two days later, Joe Kennedy stated publicly his objections to the program. Roosevelt retaliated on December 29. "Never before since Jamestown and Plymouth Rock has our American civilization been in such danger as now," the president declared. "The experience of the past two years has proven beyond doubt that no nation can appease the Nazis."

American appeasers who demanded a "negotiated peace" were selling monkeyshines.

"Is it a negotiated peace if a gang of outlaws surrounds your community and on threat of extermination makes you pay tribute to save your own skins? . . . We must be the great arsenal of democracy. For us, this is an emergency as serious as war itself," Roosevelt said. When the House of Representatives scheduled the hearings for the Lend-Lease bill, Kennedy came forward as the opening witness for the opposition.[2]

On January 9, 1941, Harry Hopkins, Roosevelt's most trusted adviser, arrived in London. Before Hopkins's appearance, Herschel Johnson was "in a state of deep pessimism as to America's ability to appreciate the serious urgency of Britain's plight." Johnson had been through four months of the blitz, narrowly escaping death when bombs landed in Grosvenor Square. "I was immediately heartened by the sincerity and intensity of Harry Hopkins' determination to gain firsthand knowledge of Britain's needs and of finding a way to fill them." Where others were looking at ways to minimize American aid, "Harry wanted to find out if they were asking for *enough* to see them through."[3]

When Hopkins met Churchill and relayed that "there was a feeling in some quarters that he, Churchill did not like America, Americans or Roosevelt" the prime minister exploded, denying it vigorously, and embarking "on a bitter tho fairly constrained attack on Ambassador Kennedy who he believes is responsible for this impression." Hopkins saw the King, too, who had written in his diary that "Kennedy has not made a very kind speech (from his private point of view) & after his sojourn here as Ambassador he seems to be definitely anti-Roosevelt."[4]

Hopkins's report to Roosevelt concluded: "This island needs our help now Mr. President with everything we can give them."[5] Roosevelt replaced Kennedy with the Republican former governor of New Hampshire, John Gilbert Winant, who took up his post on March 1, 1941, and remained in office until April 10, 1946. He was a man worthy of the post, and was much loved by the British, Roosevelt, and Truman.

On March 11, 1941, the Lend-Lease Act was passed to lend or lease war supplies to any nation deemed "vital to the defense of the United States." Joe Kennedy continued his campaign for a "negotiated peace," and Joe Jr. at Harvard Law School was one of the founders of the Harvard Committee Against Military Intervention. But then young Joe was always a paler reflection of his father's opinions. The eldest Kennedy son could have joined the Naval Reserve and continued his law studies uninterrupted, but in June 1941, Joe Jr. enlisted as a naval aviation cadet to fulfill his role of one year's service in the U.S. military. He told his father, "I think in that Jack is not doing anything, and with your stand on the war, that people will wonder what the devil I am doing back at school [Harvard Law] with everyone else working for national defense. As far as the family is concerned, it seems that Jack is perfectly capable to do everything, if by chance anything happened to me."[6]

On Sunday, June 22, 1941, Hitler launched Operation Barbarossa and attacked his onetime ally, the Soviet Union. Great Britain and the USSR were now aligned, as Churchill had always wanted. It would prove to be the first turning point in the war.

THAT NOVEMBER, JOE Kennedy gave his approval for an "experimental operation" on his daughter Rosemary. According to her doctors, she had become violent and unmanageable and they believed "there were other factors at work besides retardation." A neurological disturbance of some unknown origin was diagnosed, and a lobotomy recommended. The operation would, so the surgeons told Kennedy, give Rosemary a 63 percent odds of being free of emotional distress afterward. They were right. Rosemary would never talk again. It would be years before she could walk. As if doing penance for his sin, Joe would be the only family member to visit Rosemary or consult with her doctors. Although she lived on and was moved to a facility in Jefferson, Wisconsin, Rosemary would not see her siblings again until after Joe's death in 1969. Thereafter, the Kennedy daughters especially visited her regularly until Rosemary's death in January 2005. Rose called her "the first of the tragedies that would befall us."

JOE KENNEDY WAS on vacation at Palm Beach when news of the Japanese attack on Pearl Harbor was announced on the radio. Like Roosevelt, December 7, 1941, was indeed a "date that would live in infamy" to Kennedy's mind. Like most Americans, Kennedy heard the news with anger and horror, and hopped off his appeasement bandwagon. America had been physically—rather than morally—attacked.

He shot off a wire to the president: "In this great crisis, all Americans are with you. Name the battle front. I'm yours to command." Roosevelt instructed the White House press secretary, Steve Early, to respond, and went on ignoring Kennedy. Young Joe was certified as able to fly solo two days after Pearl Harbor and was stationed in England. Kennedy offered his services to Lord Beaverbrook, now Churchill's minister of supply, in London. He was politely refused. On December 11, 1941, Hitler, bound by his pact with Japan, declared war on the United States. Joe's notoriously dodgy stomach acted up when in January 1942, a clutch of famous Hollywood directors like Frank Capra and William Wyler (both naturalized American citizens) went to Washington as "dollar-a-year men," joining John Huston to boost morale and make training films.[7]

JACK HAD BEEN turned down by the army, due to his health problems. So, Joe stepped in, and with help from Admiral Ghormley, lied about Jack's health. Jack had been working at naval intelligence headquarters in Washington when war broke out. Six weeks later, without any word of warning, he was transferred to the Charleston Navy Yard in South Carolina. The young man was "mystified," believing that his name had been pulled out of the hat. Jack did not know that his father—and inadvertently Walter Winchell—were behind the move.

Kick, aged twenty-one, had been working at the *Washington Times-Herald* and introduced Jack to the beautiful Danish blond, blue-eyed, married beauty Inga Arvad. On January 12, 1942, Winchell wrote in his column that Jack was the target of her affections based on a letter he had received from Drew Pearson that Inga was "casting eyes in the direction of ex-ambassador Joseph P. Kennedy's offspring [and that] Old Joe is reported to be very hot and bothered about it."[8]

Joe was forced to point out to Jack that not only was Inga four years older, but she was still married to some mysterious Hungarian film director. She had been pictured with Hitler at the 1936 Olympics and was suspected of spying by Joe's friend J. Edgar Hoover. By February 1942, Jack and Inga mutually agreed not to see each other again, although Jack did try to get Inga to meet him in Charleston in early March. The FBI was monitoring their call. By the summer of 1942, Jack was a graduate of the naval training school in Chicago and accepted into the elite PT (patrol torpedo) boat school at Melville, Rhode Island.

IN NOVEMBER 1942, Clare Boothe Luce won a Republican seat for Greenwich, Connecticut, in the House of Representatives and would serve two terms.* In January 1943, Joe Kennedy was offered a piffling government job handling the problems of small businesses in the war. He refused it. That March, another job was on offer, this time as an assistant to the assistant of the War Production Board. Kennedy informed Roosevelt he was "withdrawing myself from consideration" of any position going forward."[9]

KICK HAD BEEN keeping in touch as best she could with her wide circle of friends in England since her enforced departure in September 1939, thanks in no small part to her correspondence with Nancy Astor. She had been desperate to return to London for over three years, during which time, Billy had nearly married another girl, and Kick had been seeing several other men, the most serious of whom was John White, a features reporter on the *Washington Times-Herald*.

Now that both Billy and she were free of entanglements, and she was no longer a minor, she would not fail to go back to England in 1943. The Red Cross was recruiting young women to assist American military personnel overseas, so Kick quit her job. Although she knew what she wanted, she still tried to rely on her father to pull the necessary strings to be sure she made it back to England. Leaving nothing to chance, while she trained for the Red Cross in Washington, Kick set about making her own luck for her return. She contacted Lord Halifax, who had replaced Lord Lothian as the British ambassador on the latter's death in December 1940. In November 1942, Halifax's eldest son, Peter, was killed at the Battle of El Alamein. Eight

---

* She was instrumental in setting up the Atomic Energy Commission and campaigned vigorously against the spread of communism. Eisenhower named her ambassador to Italy (1953–1957). She resigned due to severe arsenic poisoning from flaking lead paint in her bedroom ceiling. In 1983, President Reagan awarded her the Presidential Medal of Freedom. She was the first congresswoman to be so honored.

weeks later, his younger son, Richard, was pinned under an unexploded bomb while serving in Libya and lost both his legs. He had come to Washington to recover and get himself a proper pair of prosthetics. Meeting Kick of the "fabulous Kennedys" was a godsend. She helped Richard recover, and his presence in Washington helped to make his rather solemn father much more popular.

On June 23, 1943, Kick, replete with tin helmet, first-aid kit, heavy backpack, and canteen fastened to her waist, sailed for Glasgow aboard the *Queen Mary*. From there she would catch the train to London along with the hundreds of other Red Cross recruits. She declared to her mother that the "pathetic" overcrowded living conditions were appalling.* "Mother, you wouldn't recognize this boat as the same one you made that comfortable cruise on in 1936." Kick would find Scotland and England "much altered" when she arrived.[10]

LIEUTENANT JACK KENNEDY was the commander of PT-109 in the Pacific when it was torn in half by the Japanese destroyer *Amagiri* on August 1, 1943. Kennedy survived and famously saved twelve members of his crew by swimming with non-swimmers lashed to a plank of the stricken vessel and towing another by his life vest belt clenched between his teeth. When they were rescued some six days later, Jack was awarded the Navy and Marine Corps Medal for his grit and determination, as well as a Purple Heart for him and his men. He was still recovering in the naval hospital when he heard of Kick's plans to marry.

KICK HAD MET up with her old friends and tried to re-create the world of 1939, but soon realized that a life lived with rations, coupons, shortages, and above all the death and serious injury of good friends had taken its toll. Despite their long separation, Kick and Billy were still deeply in love. However, Billy made it clear that no matter what, if they were to marry, their children must be raised in the Anglican faith. This was the most bitter pill for Kick to swallow and one that would take her months to resolve in her own mind. She had fallen in love with a man who represented a world of set traditions and values that were at odds with

---

* Some 18,000 soldiers crossed on the *Queen Mary* with Kick.

her Catholic upbringing. Kick begged her father to obtain a special dispensation from the Vatican—surely something Joe Kennedy could have done with his contacts there—so she wouldn't have to make the choice. Joe dutifully approached the issue through Rose's confessor, Archbishop Francis Spellman, but the verdict came back that there were no strings to be pulled. After all, both Rose and Joe were now a prominent Vatican "aristocratic" couple, having taken their ducal titles at last.

The Duchess of Devonshire had accepted Billy's choice of bride long before, but on Kick's twenty-fourth birthday that February, the duke gave her a lovely old volume of the Book of Common Prayer. She could still worship as she wished, but the children must be brought up as Anglicans. Nonetheless, this concession from the Duke of Devonshire did not resolve her very personal dilemma. In April, Kick wrote to her "Darling Daddy" that Joe Jr. had been helping her through her conundrum. Apparently, Joe Jr. had put her in touch with an Anglican bishop for advice. "The Bishop told me that it would put the Church in a very difficult position for us to get a dispensation," she wrote to her father. The proposed dispensation was for Kick as a practicing Catholic to marry a Protestant and raise their children as Protestants, without Kick's suffering excommunication. "It would be better if we went ahead and got married and then something might possibly be done afterwards." Kick had to wrestle with remaining a Catholic in good standing or becoming the Marchioness of Hartington. Later that month, while staying with Jean Ogilvy, now married to David Lloyd, Kick finally agreed to marry Billy in a registry office in London as soon as possible.

Joe Jr. would be the only family member to attend. Jack, who was probably closest to Kick, was still laid up with his back injury from the direct hit on PT-109. Rose was so distraught at the news that she made a highly publicized sojourn to the hospital. Joe, who had always indulged his daughter, told her that whatever she decided was fine by him. Kathleen Kennedy and William Cavendish, Marquess of Hartington, were married on May 6, 1944. She had become Kathleen Cavendish, Marchioness of Hartington, at long last. Very sadly, Billy was killed in action four months later. Kick would remain in England, and very close with Billy's mother. "I want you never, never to forget what complete happiness you gave him," the duchess wrote to Kick. "All your life you must think that you brought complete happiness to one person. He wrote that to me when he went to the front."[11]

THAT JUNE, JACK underwent back surgery at New England Baptist hospital. Joe Kennedy wrote a concerned letter to Joe Jr. that Jack was not recovering as quickly as he should have. But Jack, at least, was safe. Kennedy should have realized that his sons remained highly competitive and failed to see that Jack's heroic endeavor ate away at Joe Jr.

"I am working on something different," young Joe wrote home on August 4, 1944. "It is terribly interesting, and by the time you receive this letter, it will probably be released, but at this point is quite secret. Per usual I have done nothing, but it is far more interesting than patrolling over the bay. Don't get worried about it, as there is practically no danger."

Joe Jr. should have been back home on furlough after flying thirty missions. Instead, he volunteered to become one of the first drone pilots, as part of the Aphrodite drone program taking off from the airfield in East Anglia. On August 12, the plan had been for Joe Jr. and his copilot to bail out once they had set the plane's heading after takeoff for Moyecques, France. But the plane blew up within the first minute. Joe Jr. and his copilot were killed, their bodies never recovered. Joe Jr. was awarded the Navy Cross (posthumously) and died a hero. In Jack's own words, "his death seems to have cut the natural order of things." Although he heard the news in the hospital, Jack knew that his future course was set for him—Joe Jr. had been born to become president—and now it fell to him.

Joe Kennedy, on hearing the news at his Cape Cod home, shut himself up in his bedroom. His eldest son's death was never discussed among the family, even though they would set up a charitable foundation in his name.

MORE TRAGEDIES WOULD befall the Kennedy children and grandchildren in the years to come. After three and a half years of widowhood, Kick fell in love with multimillionaire coal magnate Peter Wentworth-Fitzwilliam, Viscount Milton, who was in the process of divorcing his wife. The war had been the making of Fitzwilliam, and he had been awarded the most coveted Distinguished Service Order for courage. Like

Billy, he was mad about Kick. Still, Peter was married, and their affair scandalized postwar London society. Kick's old friends thought that Peter was too wild for her. As Kick told Jack, he was her "Rhett Butler."[12] Peter's closest friend was Prince Aly Khan, the billionaire leader of 15 million Ismaili Muslims in Asia and Africa. As soon as Peter's divorce was final, Kick had resolved to marry him.

In May 1948, Kick wanted Joe to meet Peter so he could make up his mind for himself. As luck would have it, Joe would be in Paris on business, and it was agreed that Peter and Kick would fly there on their way back from the Riviera. Their private pilot, Captain Peter Townshend, was highly experienced, with over 2,000 hours in civil aviation and an additional 550 hours as chief pilot in an RAF bomber squadron. From Paris, the couple were due to fly on to the French Riviera. Townshend was already extremely familiar with the route, its weather patterns, and above all his aircraft, a De Havilland Dove. He knew, too, that a violent thunderstorm would brew up in the late afternoon over the Rhône Valley. When Peter and Kick arrived at Croydon Airport an hour and a half late, Townshend warned them that they could not linger at Le Bourget in Paris.

But Peter and Kick had to meet their friends in the center of Paris and were hopelessly late returning to the airport. It was agreed, nonetheless, that they would be back by two o'clock. Townshend set his takeoff time with air traffic control for 14.20. When they didn't show, he amended it to 15.00, then 15.30, then resolved that they shouldn't fly. By the time they arrived, all commercial flights to the south had been canceled. Peter Fitzwilliam argued, cajoled, and possibly bribed Townshend to fly on to Nice, and Townshend sadly agreed. At 17.03, air traffic control at Lyon lost contact with their plane. It had crashed near Saint-Bauzile, France, killing all on board.

The telephone rang in the early hours of the morning of May 13, 1948, in Joe Kennedy's suite at the George V. It was a reporter asking him to confirm reports that "Lady Hartington" was dead. At first Kennedy wondered if the reporter meant Debo Cavendish (formerly Mitford), who had married Andrew, Billy's younger brother. Then he realized it was Kick. On a scrap of George V notepaper, Joe Kennedy wrote: "No one who ever knew her didn't feel that life was much better that minute.

And we know so little about the next world that we must think that they wanted just such a wonderful girl for themselves. We must not feel sorry for her but for ourselves."[13]

Joe was the only Kennedy family member present at Kick's funeral. Too grief-stricken to make arrangements, he expected Jack or Rose to handle the repatriation of Kick's body to the United States. But neither lifted a finger. Kick's biographer, Barbara Leaming, paints a shocking portrait of Rose's actions just two weeks before Kick's death: pursuing Kick to her London home from New York in an argument that lasted four days about Kick's planned marriage to Peter Fitzwilliam; threatening expulsion from the Kennedy family; and demanding that Kick come "home" and give up her married lover.* Rose was undoubtedly behind the silence from the family congregating around her at Hyannis after Kick died. Rose refused to attend Kick's funeral. In fact, none of Kick's siblings went, either. The Duchess of Devonshire valiantly stepped in to relieve the shocked and grieving Joe. And so Joe Kennedy stood at Kick's graveside, diminished in power, silent, and thankful to the Devonshires for burying his "favorite daughter" in full accordance with the rites of the Roman Catholic Church.[14]

Kick's funeral service took place at London's Catholic Farm Street Church. Mourners boarded a special train to Chatsworth in Derbyshire, where she was buried in the sheltered graveyard behind Edensor Church. Yet days before the funeral, Rose finally sprang into action. She prepared a memorial mass card and sent it to all Kick's friends. "The prayer printed on it was a plea for plenary indulgence, applicable to souls in purgatory. . . . Those who had loved and now mourned Kick could not forgive Rose." Somerset Maugham believed that "Kick's mother had put a curse on her daughter."[15] Rose Kennedy would lie to herself and the world about her destructive reaction to Kick's marriage to Billy Hartington; damning her daughter over the relationship with Peter Wentworth-Fitzwilliam; and ultimately ignoring Kick's death in her autobiography

---

* On hearing the devastating news, Andrew Cavendish, now Marquess of Hartington, made sure that the British press did not write anything about Kick's relationship with Fitzwilliam, a married man.

Times to Remember until the day she died on January 22, 1995. Rose was 104 years old.[16]

Eugenio Pacelli, later Pope Pius XII, lived until 1958, long enough to know that his legacy would not remain unblemished from his actions in World War II. In 2014, Pope Francis said that he would not allow his beatification to proceed, because Pius XII had not performed enough miracles. Count Galeazzi would live on until 1986, remaining friends with the Kennedy family. The Kennedys' Vatican ennoblement was passed on to their children.

JOE KENNEDY WOULD, of course, go on to make many more millions in real estate and the stock market, and would bankroll his sons' campaigns for the presidency. He suffered a massive stroke on December 19, 1961, nearly eleven months to the day after his dream came true when Jack, now President John F. Kennedy, was sworn in as president of the United States. Then came Jack's assassination on November 22, 1963.

Then Bobby's on June 5, 1968. Then Teddy's disgrace as Senator Edward M. Kennedy at Chappaquiddick on July 19, 1969, when he tried to cover up the accident that killed campaign worker Mary Jo Kopechne. Three sons dead. His first daughter, Rosemary, as good as dead; and his beloved Kick killed in a plane crash. His fourth son disgraced.

Joe Kennedy finally died on November 18, 1969, after eight long years of powerlessness, unable to speak and yet fully aware of everything around him. He died wealthy, but without the knowledge that his other dream—the one where he would create a political dynasty far more enduring than that of John and John Quincy Adams—might have come true. The Adams fixation was passed on to John F. Kennedy, who believed that the "story of the son is not wholly separable from the story of the father."[17] John F. Kennedy, for better and worse, remained a Kennedy.

AUTHOR'S NOTE
AND ACKNOWLEDGMENTS

I OFTEN WONDERED while writing Joseph P. Kennedy's story as U.S. Ambassador to the Court of St. James's why he did not try to understand the British better. Certainly his undiplomatic language and "plain-spoken" thoughts did nothing to advance his cause, and eventually would be his undoing. That he labored so long in semi-retirement on his unpublished—and absolutely unpublishable—*Diplomatic Memoir* with James M. Landis and others for over a decade showed how much his success in London mattered to him. Indeed, he always insisted afterward on being called "Mr. Ambassador."

Joe Kennedy thought that the British would love his frankness, and never once glanced at himself in the mirror. He was a fascist sympathizer and an anti-Semite. But the driving forces behind these seemingly united ideologies were not the same in origin. He was a fascist sympathizer because he was bedazzled by the Vatican, which sympathized with Franco and Mussolini for religious and venal reasons; and sought to placate Hitler before he turned on Catholics once the Jews had been exterminated. Kennedy rightly believed that war economies take away all civil liberties, without understanding that in democracies these are temporary measures for the survival of a nation. Separately, Joe Kennedy was an anti-Semite through his own ignorance and prejudices, accepting Jews only if they would benefit his personal interests. Jack, Bobby, and Ted Kennedy were not anti-Semitic and fought hard to overcome their father's image; all three were friends of Israel.

Joe Kennedy placed prosperity above human life and liberty, above democracies being crushed, above loss of life for those who opposed the Nazis in Europe or who were unfortunate enough to be Jewish, and ultimately above right and wrong. Such was his epitaph in the United Kingdom. Sadly, he never understood by broadcasting his biased opinions and phony facts, in an era when radio propaganda was first used with great aplomb, that he was acting against the British and U.S. administrations. Hitler certainly viewed Kennedy's treachery in the years leading up to and including the first year of the war in Europe as a weapon to use in any invasion of Britain and North America. That Roosevelt never forgave Joe or used him again in his administration speaks volumes.

Joe was a philandering husband, a great father, grandfather, and provider. His children and grandchildren adored him. That John F. Kennedy credited Joe for making "it all possible" is the best testament a father who valued money above all could receive from his son in later life.

MYTHS AND LEGENDS have an odd and truthful place in writing nonfiction. The Kennedy "curse" is laid bare here by simple facts. Joe's dreams bred a familial recklessness and competitiveness which killed one son and led to the death of two others. His lust for riches and keeping an eye firmly fixed on *the* goal—having his son become the first Catholic president of the United States—shows how money and a charismatic candidate in Jack, eventually, brought him the first important dream come true. But it also drove Bobby and Ted Kennedy to make the "Kennedy political dynasty" a reality. If Joe Jr. had survived and became president, I shudder to think how that may have made McCarthyism in America even more unbearable than it was. Conversely, if Bobby—the smartest son—had survived the assassin's bullet, he might have made America a more tolerant nation sooner. I often wonder if Joe Kennedy had known the price he would have to pay, would it have still been worth it all?

WHILE WRITING IS a solitary business, there are many dozens of people who have helped me through the process. First and foremost, my husband and historian, Dr. D.A.B. Ronald, for his unstinting and selfless support, improved cooking skills, relentless good humor even through our self-isolation for COVID-19, and especially his outstanding research assistance. Research trips alone are tedious and a trial, but he made them sheer joy. A very special thank-you to my editor at St. Martin's Press, Charles Spicer, who continues to believe in me and my writing projects, for which I am forever grateful. In fact, from publisher Sally Richardson to assistant editor Sarah Grill, the entire team at SMP have been fabulous. But I would say that, since this is my fifth book with them.

Others who gave their expertise and energy unselfishly were Robin Benson, Lady Leslie Bonham Carter, Ramrattie Constantine, John Cornwell, Sophie Cox, Helen Fry, Tom Geoffino, Pam Head, James Holland, Alexander C. Hoyt, Fredrik Logevall, Helen Rappaport, Charlotte and Steven Sass, Julie Summers, Phil Tomaselli, Gadi Warsha, Christopher Warwick, Paul Willetts, and American Ambassador to the Court of St. James's, Robert W. Johnson. To Her Majesty Queen Elizabeth II, my thanks for allowing me to make use of the material at the Royal Archives. To her staff at the Royal Archives at Windsor, my gratitude for your assistance. For the staff at Bodleian Library at the University of Oxford; the University of Birmingham Archive; the British Library; the Churchill Library University of Cambridge; the Houghton Library at Harvard University; the London Library; the Met Office Archives; the National Archives at Kew, England; the National Archives at College Park, Maryland; the Library of Congress; the FDR Presidential Library; and the John F. Kennedy Library, my humble thanks for all the invaluable assistance you provided.

And above all, to you, the reader, I hope you enjoyed the book.

SUSAN RONALD, DEVON, ENGLAND

DRAMATIS PERSONAE

Note: The names and titles of people listed herein are in alphabetical order except the Kennedy family. The Kennedy daughters are listed by their names during the period covered in the book, but an additional very brief biography is included for them.

Only the main characters are listed.

THE KENNEDY FAMILY *[In birth date order]*

Joseph Patrick Kennedy (1888-1969), husband, father of nine children, his "hostages to fortune," celebrity businessman, movie producer and distributor, chairman of the SEC, chairman of the Maritime Commission, Ambassador Plenipotentiary to the Court of St. James's (1938-1941).

Rose Fitzgerald Kennedy (1890-1995), daughter of Boston mayor John "Honey Fitz" Fitzgerald and wife of Joseph P. Kennedy.

Joseph Patrick Kennedy, Jr. (1915-1944), eldest child of Joe and Rose Kennedy, private secretary to his father and served as a naval pilot. After his death, a charitable foundation was established in his name.

John Fitzgerald "Jack" Kennedy (1917-1963), second son of Joe and Rose Kennedy, congressman, senator, then 35th president of the United States (1961-1963). He was the first Catholic president of the United States.

Rose Marie "Rosemary" Kennedy (1918-2005), eldest daughter of Joe and Rose Kennedy. She suffered from a lack of oxygen at birth and had special needs.

Kathleen "Kick" Kennedy, Marchioness Hartington (1920-1948), second daughter of Joe and Rose Kennedy, who married William "Billy" Devonshire, Marquess of Hartington in 1943. She was killed in a plane crash.

Eunice Kennedy (1921-2009), third daughter of Joe and Rose Kennedy, who married Sargent Shriver and founded the Special Olympics.

Robert Francis "Bobby" Kennedy (1925-1968), attorney general of the United States in JFK's term as president, then senator for New York State. He was assassinated during his run for the presidency in 1968.

Patricia "Pat" Kennedy (1924-2006) was the seventh child of Joe and Rose Kennedy. She married British actor Peter Lawford in 1954. They had four children and divorced in 1965.

Jean Kennedy (1928-2020), youngest daughter and eighth child of Joe and Rose Kennedy. Jean married JFK's campaign manager Steve Smith and they had four children. She was the founder of Very Special Arts, a charity for children with special needs encouraging their involvement with the arts, and was the U.S. ambassador to Ireland.

Edward Moore "Ted" Kennedy (1932-2009), youngest Kennedy child. He served as a U.S. senator for nearly forty-seven years. His bid to run for president after Bobby's assassination was stopped when he covered up the car accident at Chappaquiddick, killing campaign worker Mary Jo Kopechne.

Patrick J. "P.J." Kennedy (1858-1929), Ward Two politician in Boston and beloved father of Joe Kennedy.

John F. "Honey Fitz" Fitzgerald (1863-1950), two-time Boston mayor and congressman, and father of Rose Kennedy.

THE AMERICANS

Allen, Robert, powerful syndicated columnist writing the "Washington Merry-Go-Round" with Drew Pearson.

Alsop, Joseph, syndicated columnist writing with Robert E. Kintner. They also wrote *The White Paper* together about American foreign policy and amending the Neutrality Acts.

Baruch, Bernard M., financier, stock market investor, philanthropist, and economic adviser to presidents Wilson and Roosevelt.

Bullitt, William C., a wealthy Philadelphian, Bullitt was the first U.S. ambassador to the Soviet Union (1933-1936); U.S. ambassador to France (1936-1940).

Burns, John J., the first Catholic faculty member at Harvard Law School, and a Massachusetts superior court judge at the age of thirty. He left the bench to become legal counsel to Kennedy's SEC, and remained a trusted friend of Joe Kennedy.

Carter, Harold Boake, columnist at the *Philadelphia Daily News* and radio commentator on WCAU Philadelphia, and broadcast on syndicated CBS radio stations. He was a friend of Joe Kennedy.

Coughlin, Father Charles E., also known as the "radio priest," was the most powerful Catholic voice in the United States in the 1930s. He admired Kennedy but broke with Roosevelt during the 1936 election campaign, backing William F. Lemke as his candidate for the presidency instead.

Cudahy, John, American ambassador to Poland (1933-1937); Belgium (January–July 1940) and Free State of Ireland (1937-1940).

Dietrich, Marlene, actress and lover of Joe Kennedy. She became a naturalized U.S. citizen during the Nazi era.

Dodd, William E., professor and U.S. ambassador to Berlin from 1933-1937.

Garner, John Nance "Cactus Jack," former speaker of the House of Representatives from Texas, and Roosevelt's first and second term vice president. He was opposed to Roosevelt's bid for a third term and was replaced by Henry A. Wallace in the 1940 election.

Hays, Will, the former postmaster general of the United States who became the president of the Motion Picture Association of America (MPAA) from 1922-1945. The MPAA set the Motion Picture Production Code for morality guidelines for studios and what could and could not be seen on screen from 1934-1968.

Hopkins, Harry, an architect of the New Deal, Hopkins held several important positions in Roosevelt's New Deal hierarchy. During Kennedy's term as ambassador, he was Roosevelt's chief diplomatic troubleshooter and liaison with both Churchill and Stalin. He also served as secretary of commerce 1938-1940.

Houghton, Arthur, Houghton was the manager of the song-and-dance man Fred Stone, meeting Joe during his Fore River Days. It was Houghton who advised Kennedy to go to Hollywood. Houghton was seconded from Will Hays's office in Hollywood when Kennedy went to London. He was on Kennedy's private payroll.

Howard, Roy, publisher of Scripps-Howard newspapers and opponent of Joe Kennedy's.

Hull, Cordell, secretary of state during Kennedy's term as U.S. ambassador to London. Hull, as U.S. secretary of state 1933-1944, was the longest serving secretary of state in history. Hull suffered remitting-relapsing sarcoidosis, frequently mistaken for tuberculosis, compelling him to take frequent "vacations" for his health. He received the Nobel Peace Prize for his role in setting up the United Nations in 1945.

Johnson, Herschel V., chargé d'affaires at the U.S. Embassy in London during Robert Worth Bingham's and Kennedy's terms in office.

Kennedy, Jack "Ding Dong" (aka "London Jack"), originally a publicist with RKO in Europe, London Jack was the man Kennedy called upon to "fix" things generally for him. He was on Kennedy's private payroll.

Knox, Frank, publisher and editor of the *Chicago Daily News* and secretary of the navy 1940-1944. He was the Republican vice-presidential candidate on the 1936 ticket with Alf Landon for president.

Krock, Arthur, *New York Times* bureau chief in Washington. Close confidant and friend of Joe Kennedy, and on Kennedy's payroll during his years working for *The New York Times*.

Land, Vice-Admiral Emery Scott "Jerry," successor to Kennedy as chairman of the Federal Maritime Commission in the United States and cousin of aviator Charles A. Lindbergh.

Lee, Col. Raymond, was the military London observer in 1938, then again in 1940-41, and was an opponent of Kennedy's.

LeHand, Missy, secretary and mistress of President Roosevelt.

Lindbergh, Charles A., the first man to fly solo across the Atlantic and aviation expert. He was an admirer of the German Luftwaffe and a spokesperson of the America First Committee, a right-wing organization to keep America out of the war.

Luce, Clare Boothe, journalist, editor, playwright, author, wife of Henry R. Luce and lover of Joe Kennedy.

Luce, Henry R., powerful publisher of *Time, Fortune,* and *Life.* Husband of Clare Boothe Luce.

Messersmith, George S., career diplomat, the U.S. assistant secretary of state (1937-1940), and former ambassador to Austria (1934-1937).

Moffat, Jay Pierrepont, career diplomat and chief of the Division of European Affairs at the State Department during Kennedy's ambassadorship.

Moore, Edward E. "Eddie," former secretary of "Honey Fitz" and closest business confidant and close personal friend of Joe and Rose Kennedy.

Morgenthau, Henry, secretary of the treasury 1934–1945 and opponent of Kennedy's.

Murphy, Paul, long-serving administrator in Joe Kennedy's business based at 30 Rockefeller Center in New York City.

O'Brien, William "Bill," JPK's personal adviser and head of Pathé News stationed in Paris.

O'Connell, Cardinal William Henry, Boston's cardinal who married Rose and Joe Kennedy and remained a close family friend. O'Connell intervened to try to stop Joe's affair with Gloria Swanson.

O'Leary, Ted, Kennedy associate from Joe's Fore River days. He was one of the men running Gloria Productions on a daily basis for Joe and remained involved in Kennedy's business affairs after the ambassador stepped down.

Pearson, Drew, syndicated columnist with Robert Allen best known for the "Washington Merry-Go-Round." He had been briefly married to Felicia Gizyscka, daughter of Cissy Patterson.

Phillips, William, seasoned U.S. ambassador to Italy 1936–1941.

Roosevelt, Eleanor, wife of FDR and social campaigner.

Roosevelt, Franklin Delano, U.S. president from 1933–1945. The only president to be elected to four terms in office.

Roosevelt, James "Jimmy," eldest son of Franklin D. and Eleanor Roosevelt and "foster son" of Kennedy. After his insurance business failed to take off, he became his father's secretary but was forced to resign in November 1938, after allegations of using his position for financial gain. He then became Sam Goldwyn's administrative assistant in Hollywood.

Roosevelt, Sarah Delano, the president's domineering mother.

Rublee, George, the Washington lawyer who served as the director of the Intergovernmental Committee on Refugees on Roosevelt's personal recommendation after the Évian Conference of July 1938.

Seymour, James "Jim," an old friend of Kennedy's from his Hollywood days, who owed Kennedy money for bailing him out of debt. He worked on Kennedy's private payroll in London.

Spellman, Cardinal Francis, Rose and Joe Kennedy's confessor and cardinal of New York from 1939. He was very close to Count Enrico Galeazzi and Cardinal Eugenio Pacelli, later Pope Pius XII.

Swanson, Gloria, Hollywood's top actress and producer, lover of Joe Kennedy.

Taylor, Myron C., former chairman of U.S. Steel who represented the United States at the Évian Conference on Refugees. Later, from 1939 to 1950, he was the presidential envoy to the Holy See.

Welles, Sumner, undersecretary of state (1937-1943) who often covered for Cordell Hull.

Willkie, Wendell, lawyer and 1940 Republican candidate for the presidency.

THE BRITISH

Aitken, Max, Lord Beaverbrook, Canadian-born British press baron and backstage politician. Owner of the *Daily Express* and *Evening Standard*. He was minister of Aircraft Supply in Churchill's government 1940-1941.

Astor, Lady Nancy, outspoken American-born British Member of Parliament who was the first woman to sit in the House of Commons. Married to Waldorf Astor.

Astor, Lord Waldorf, American-born British politician. On the death of his father, he sat in the House of Lords and was chairman of the Royal Institute of International Affairs (RIIA).

Baldwin, Stanley, Member of Parliament for Bewdley, Worcestershire 1908-1937, Prime Minister from May 1923–January 1924; November 1924–June 1929; June 1935–May 1937.

Ball, Sir Joseph, owner of the magazine *Truth* and media expert serving Neville Chamberlain. He worked in tandem with Sir Horace Wilson to control the press and unruly Members of Parliament.

Brand, Robert, partner at Lazard Brothers investment bank in London and brother-in-law of Nancy and Waldorf Astor.

Cadogan, Sir Alexander, succeeded Sir Robert Vansittart as Permanent Secretary of State for Foreign Affairs (1938-1946).

Cavendish, Edward William Spencer, 10th Duke of Devonshire, father of Billy Hartington and initially opposed to his son's marriage with Kick Kennedy.

Cavendish, William "Billy," Marquess of Hartington, eldest son of the 10th Duke of Devonshire and heir to the title. He married Kick Kennedy in 1943 and was killed in action four months later.

Chamberlain, Neville, Prime Minister May 1937-May 1940, and co-architect of appeasement with Lord Edward Halifax.

Channon, Sir Henry "Chips," American-born Member of Parliament, Parliamentary Private Secretary and Undersecretary of State for Foreign Affairs, 1938–1941.

Churchill, Winston Spencer, Britain's wartime prime minister from May 10, 1940. He was First Lord of the Admiralty during the Great War, then out of government from 1929–1939. Chamberlain made him First Lord of the Admiralty in September 1939.

Colville, Sir Jock, prime minister's Personal Private Secretary.

Cranborne, Viscount, Robert Arthur James Gascoyne Cecil, became the 5th Marquess of Salisbury on his father's death in 1947. He was known to all his friends as Bobbety.

Dawson, Geoffrey, editor of *The Times* in London. Its owner was John Jacob Astor V, younger brother of Waldorf Astor.

Duff Cooper, Alfred, First Lord of the Admiralty 1937–1938 and staunch supporter of Churchill. After the war, he was British Ambassador to France.

Eden, Anthony, resigned as Foreign Secretary February 1938. Reinstated by Churchill as Colonies Secretary in May 1940. Then when Halifax became ambassador to Washington in the fall of 1940, Eden took up his post again as Churchill's Foreign Secretary.

Halifax, Lord Edward Wood, British politician and coauthor of the appeasement policy. He replaced Anthony Eden as Foreign Secretary in February 1938. In 1940, he became British Ambassador to the United States.

Hardinge, Sir Alexander, Private Secretary to the Sovereign during the Abdication Crisis of Edward VIII (after Duke of Windsor) and throughout World War II.

Harvey, Oliver, Permanent Private Secretary to Lord Halifax at the Foreign Office.

Henderson, Sir Nevile, British ambassador to Germany (1937–1939).

Hoare, Sir Samuel, Foreign Minister 1935, First Lord of the Admiralty 1936–1937.

Inskip, Sir Thomas, Minister for the Coordination of Defence (1937–1939), Secretary of State for Dominion Affairs (1939), Lord Chancellor (1939–1940), Leader of the House of Lords (1940), and Lord Chief Justice of England (1940–1946).

374 ·:· DRAMATIS PERSONAE

Jones, Tom "T.J.," the former deputy cabinet secretary to four prime ministers (Lloyd George, Bonar Law, Ramsay MacDonald, and Stanley Baldwin), and reputedly "the keeper of a thousand secrets."

Kerr, Philip, Marquess of Lothian, was Britain's ambassador to the United States succeeding Lindsay on his retirement in June 1939. Lothian died of kidney failure while in office in December 1940. He was succeeded by Lord Halifax.

Lindsay, Sir Ronald, British ambassador to Washington (1930–1939) and old friend of Roosevelt's.

Loraine, Sir Percy, British ambassador to Italy (1939–1940), replacing Lord Perth.

Phipps, Sir Eric, British ambassador to Germany (1933–1937), then ambassador to France (1937–1940).

Stanley, Sir Oliver, president of the Board of Trade (1937–1940) negotiated with Kennedy and then Hull. He became secretary of state for war (1940).

Vansittart, Robert, known as "Van," Permanent Secretary of State for foreign affairs 1930–1938, who opposed appeasement. He was succeeded by Alec Cadogan in 1938 when he became the Chief Diplomatic Adviser to the Foreign Office.

Wilson, Sir Horace J., Chief Industrial Adviser and close confidant of Chamberlain who worked in tandem with Sir Joseph Ball to control public opinion.

Wood, Kingsley, Secretary of State for Air (1938–1940), then Lord Privy Seal (1940) and Chancellor of the Exchequer (1940–1943).

THE FRENCH

Blum, Léon, Socialist French premier, 1936–1937, 1938.

Bonnet, Georges-Étienne, French foreign minister 1938–1939 and advocate of appeasement.

Chautemps, Camille, three-time prime minister of France (1930, 1933–1934, and 1937–1938). He was also the deputy premier in the governments of Daladier and Reynaud.

Corbin, André Charles, French ambassador in London, 1933–40.

Daladier, Édouard, French prime minister 1933, 1934, 1938–40.

Darlan, Admiral Jean-François, admiral of the French fleet. When France surrendered, he was in charge of most of the French fleet and refused to surrender it to the British, forcing them to capture or destroy most of it.

de La Falaise, Henri, Marquis de La Coudraye, third husband of Gloria Swanson. He divorced her because of her affair with Joe Kennedy and later married actress Constance Bennett.

Laval, Pierre, French prime minister 1931–1932 and 1935–1936. In 1940–41, he dismantled the French Third Republic's democracy and took up the cause of National Socialism. He returned to government in 1942–1944 as chief of the Vichy Government. In 1943–1945, Laval headed up the hated Milice, a paramilitary organization of Frenchmen and women who fought against the French Résistance.

Pétain, Maréchal Philippe, hero of Verdun in the First World War. Appointed prime minister of Vichy "Free" France after the surrender of France in June 1940–April 1942. Thereafter, he was known as chief of the French State until the liberation of France in August 1944.

Reynaud, Paul, French minister of finance 1938–1940. In 1940, he held several other ministerial positions, including minister for national defence and war, minister of foreign affairs, and prime minister when France surrendered.

THE GERMANS

Dirksen, Herbert von, German ambassador to Great Britain 1938–1939, after Ribbentrop.

Göring, Hermann, Reichsmarschall of the Third Reich and effectively second in command. It was Göring who masterminded much of the industrial output and the Luftwaffe.

Hitler, Adolf, leader of the National Socialists German Workers' Party (NSDAP) or Nazi Party and German chancellor of the Third Reich 1933–1945.

Kordt, Theodor, German chargé d'affaires to Great Britain 1938–1939. With his brother Erich, he was involved with the Oster Conspiracy to overthrow Hitler in 1938.

Ribbentrop, Joachim von, German ambassador to Great Britain 1936–1938, foreign secretary 1938–1945.

Schacht, Hjalmar, head of the German Reichsbank (1933–1939) and German economics minister (1934–1937).

von Weizsäcker, Ernst, German secretary of state for foreign affairs, and later ambassador to the Vatican during the Nazi era.

Wohlthat, Helmuth, one of Göring's main economic advisers on the Four-Year Plan, and the man behind the repatriation of the Czech gold to the Nazis.

THE ITALIANS

Ciano, Count Galeazzo, politician and nobleman son-in-law of Benito Mussolini and Italian foreign minister (1936–1943). He was executed by the Nazis in 1943.

Galeazzi, Count Enrico, confidant of Cardinal Eugenio Pacelli and architect at the Vatican. He became a lifelong friend of Joseph P. Kennedy.

Mussolini, Benito, Il Duce, fascist leader of Italy 1922–1943.

Pacelli, Eugenio (later Pius XII), Cardinal Secretary of State of the Vatican (1930–1939), then Pope Pius XII (1939–1958). Friend of Joseph P. Kennedy.

THE SOVIETS (RUSSIANS)

Litvinov, Maxim Maximovich, Soviet foreign minister 1930–1939, Soviet ambassador to the United States 1941–1943.

Maisky, Ivan Mikhailovich, Soviet ambassador to the Court of St. James's 1932–1943.

Molotov, Vyacheslav, Soviet foreign minister 1939–1949.

Stalin, Joseph Vissarionovich, general secretary of the Soviet Union 1922–1953.

OTHER FRIENDS AND FOES

Henlein, Konrad, leader of the Nazi Sudeten-German Party in 1938.

Masaryk, Jan, Czech minister to Great Britain who remained in London after Czechoslovakia was absorbed into the Reich.

Schuschnigg, Kurt von, Austrian chancellor ousted by Hitler's Anschluss in March 1938.

NOTES

ABBREVIATIONS:

AA	Lord and Lady Astor Archive, Reading University, Reading, England
BL	British Library, London
BOD	Bodleian Library, University of Oxford
CA	Churchill Archive, University of Cambridge
CAB	British Cabinet Minutes at National Archives UK
CBL	Clare Boothe Luce papers at the Library of Congress
DBFP	E. L. Woodward and Rohan Butler, eds., *Documents on British Foreign Policy*, Third Series, Vol. 1 (London: HMSO, 1949)
DGFP	Documents on German Foreign Policy 1918–1945, Series C and D, Vols. 3–8 (London: HMSO, 1955)
DM	Final Draft of Joseph P. Kennedy's unpublished *Diplomatic Memoir* at the JFK Library
FDRPL	Franklin D. Roosevelt Presidential Library
FRUS	Foreign Relations of the United States Diplomatic Papers: Office of the Historian, Bureau of Public Affairs, United States Department of State. The British Commonwealth, Europe, Near East, and Africa (Foreign Relations of the United States Diplomatic Papers, 1938, Volume II)." E-book: Apple Books.

HTF	Amanda Smith, ed., *Hostage to Fortune—The Letters of Joseph P. Kennedy* (New York: Viking, 2001)
JFKL	John F. Kennedy Presidential Library (unless otherwise stated all references are from the Joseph P. Kennedy Archive)
JSTOR	Online Academic Journals
LOC	Library of Congress, Washington, D.C.
MO	Met Office Library and Archive, Exeter, England
MOFFAT	Moffat Diary, Jay Pierrepont Moffat Papers, Houghton Library, Harvard University, Cambridge, Massachusetts
NA	National Archives, College Park, Maryland
NCP	Neville Chamberlain Papers, University of Birmingham, England
NYT	*New York Times*
ODNB	Oxford Dictionary of National Biography (online)
OMP	Oswald Mosley Papers, University of Birmingham, England
PAR	Parliamentary Papers, House of Lords, London
RA	Royal Archives, Windsor Castle, Windsor
TNA	The National Archives, Kew, London

ENDNOTES

PROLOGUE

1 David E. Koskoff, *Joseph P. Kennedy: A Life and Times* (New Jersey: Prentice-Hall, 1974), 297. This remark was overheard by journalist George Bilainkin.

2 George Bilainkin, *Diary of a Diplomatic Correspondent* (London: George Allen & Unwin Ltd, 1942), 252, 242.

3 MO, DWR_1940_10, weather report for October 22, 1940.

4 *HTF*, 474–75.

1. THE PRESIDENT'S MAN

1 Charles Fanning, *The Irish Voice in America: 250 Years of Irish-American Fiction,* 2nd ed. (Lexington: University of Kentucky Press, 2000), 317.

2 For a fascinating profile of how ward politics worked in P. J. Kennedy's day, see Doris Kearns Goodwin's *The Fitzgeralds and the Kennedys* (New York: St. Martin's Press, 1987), 80–89.

3 David E. Koskoff, *Joseph P. Kennedy: A Life and Times* (New Jersey: Prentice-Hall, 1974), 17.

4 Ralph F. de Bedts, *Ambassador Joseph Kennedy 1938–1940: An Anatomy of Appeasement* (New York: Peter Lang, 1985), 2.

5 Ibid., 3.

6 David Palmer, Ph.D. dissertation, *Organizing the Shipyards: Unionization at New York Ship, Federal Ship, and Fore River 1898–1945*, vol. 1 of 2 (Boston, MA: Brandeis University, 1990), 164.

7 Ibid., 162.

8 Ibid., 168–72. Palmer's research is, as one would expect from a Ph.D. thesis, groundbreaking. It demonstrates clearly that Kennedy was not a good "man manager" when he did not directly employ them.

9 Betty Lasky, *RKO: The Biggest Little Major of Them All* (Santa Monica, CA: Roundtable Publishing, 1989), 13.

10 Ibid., 55.

11 Swanson, *Swanson on Swanson* (London: Michael Joseph, 1981), 329, 327.

12 Ibid., 339.

13 *HTF*, 77.

14 Swanson, *Swanson on Swanson*, 390.

15 Lasky, *RKO: The Biggest Little Major of Them All*, 55.

16 Swanson, *Swanson on Swanson*, 393–95.

17 https://www.youtube.com/watch?v=uQwKI4xvuC0. Rose Kennedy, *Times to Remember* (New York: Doubleday & Co., 1974), 190–91.

18 Lasky, *RKO: The Biggest Little Major of Them All*, 57–59.

19 Michael R. Beschloss, *Kennedy and Roosevelt: The Uneasy Alliance* (New York: W. W. Norton, 1980), 70–73.

20 Ibid., 74. "Warwick" the kingmaker refers to Richard Neville, 16th Earl of Warwick, who made Edward of York Edward IV in 1461, theoretically ending the Wars of the Roses.

21 Koskoff, *Joseph P. Kennedy: A Life and Times*, 74. See also *Ickes Diary*, entry of October 9, 1936; Arthur M. Schlesinger Jr., *The Coming of the New Deal* (Boston: Houghton Mifflin, 1958), 542.

22 Beschloss, *Kennedy and Roosevelt: The Uneasy Alliance*, 79.

23 David Nasaw, *The Patriarch: The Remarkable Life and Turbulent Times of Joseph P. Kennedy* (New York: Penguin Books, 2013), 193.

24 JFKL, JPK Papers, Box 40, Box 47. See also Box 126, accounts of Rose Fitzgerald Kennedy. Numerous references are made to such loans, for example $233,948.98 to Edward E. Moore, Trustee, on December 26, 1930, due on June 26, 1931; $33,000 from the trust funds in 1948; payment to the State Liquor Authority in New York City, dated January 1948, with funds borrowed from the trust funds; a loan to Rose from her trust fund on April 24, 1937; borrowing from Jean and Teddy's trust fund and so on.

25 Beschloss, *Kennedy and Roosevelt: The Uneasy Alliance*, 86; David E. Koskoff, *Joseph P. Kennedy: A Life and Times*, 54–56.

26 Beschloss, *Kennedy and Roosevelt: The Uneasy Alliance*, 86.

27 Raymond Moley, *The First New Deal* (New York: Harcourt, 1966), 288.

28 https://www.newspapers.com/image/261015415/

2. AN IMPERFECT FAMILY PORTRAIT

1 *HTF*, 160.

2 *DM*, I, 1. Throughout the *DM* Kennedy uses quotes for *all* his conversations, yet there is no evidence anywhere in the documents held at the JFK Library or at the Library of Congress that Kennedy had either made copious notes or systematic recordings of *all* of his conversations. James M. Landis, who wrote much of the memoir on behalf of Kennedy, drew Joe's attention to this fact and that the ubiquitous use of quotation marks made him uncomfortable. LOC, Landis Papers.

3 JFKL, JPK Papers, Box 70, letters addressed to U.S. ambassadors in London, Berlin, Paris, Rome, and the Hague dated September 23, 1935.

4 CA, CHAR 2/237/58.

5 JFKL, JPK Papers, Box 70, letter from Bishop Spellman dated September 22, 1935 [translation by Dr. D. Ronald].

6 Rose Kennedy (with Robert Coughlan), *Times to Remember* (New York: Doubleday & Co., 1974), 200.

7 Nigel Hamilton, *J.F.K.: Reckless Youth*, vol. 1 (London: Random House UK, 1992), 42–45.

8 Rose Kennedy (with Robert Coughlan), *Times to Remember*, 81.

9 https://archiveblog.jfklibrary.org/2015/02/newly-opened-collection-ace-of-clubs -records/

10 Victor Lasky, *J.F.K.: The Man and the Myth* (New York: Macmillan, 1963), 25.

11 Ibid.

12 *HTF*, 161.

13 Doris Kearns Goodwin, *The Fitzgeralds and the Kennedys* (New York: St. Martin's Press, 1987), 409.

14 John Baxter, *Chronicles of Old Paris: Exploring the Historic City of Light* (New York: Museyon, 2011), 268.

3. THE PRESIDENTIAL ENVOY

1 Tim Bouverie, *Appeasing Hitler: Chamberlain, Churchill, and the Road to War* (London: Vintage, 2019), e-book, 40–41. See also CAB 16/111. DC (M) (32) Paper 120, "Note by the Chancellor of the Exchequer on the Report of the DRC," June 20, 1934.

2 Robert Rhodes James, ed., *Chips: The Diaries of Sir Henry Channon* (London: Weidenfeld & Nicolson, 1967), 35–36.

3 JFKL, JPK Papers, Box 75, Radio Address of JPK October 24, 1936.

4 ODNB, Arthur Neville Chamberlain, https://doi.org/10.1093/ref:odnb/32347.

5 Keith Feiling, *The Life of Neville Chamberlain* (Hamden, CT: Archon Books, 1970), 245–47.

6 Winston S. Churchill, *The Second World War*, vol. 1, *The Gathering Storm* (London: The Reprint Society, 1948), 107–109.

7 Rose Kennedy (with Robert Coughlan), *Times to Remember* (New York: Doubleday & Co., 1974), 201.

8 BL, *The Graphic* magazine, C. Patrick Thompson, "Governor of the Bank" (published in London: Illustrated News Group), August 1930, 352. See also Rose Kennedy (with Robert Coughlan), *Times to Remember*, 201.

9 Erik Larson, *In the Garden of Beasts: Love, Terror, and an American Family in Hitler's Berlin* (New York: Crown Publishing Group, 2011), e-book, locations 5563 and 5552.

10 Ibid. See also William Phillips Diaries (Boston: Houghton Library, Harvard University, Cambridge), no date, 1219.

11 Nicholas Wapshott, *The Sphinx: Franklin Roosevelt, the Isolationists, and the Road to World War II* (New York: W. W. Norton, 2014), 32.

12 Ibid., 8.

13 Ralph McInery, *The Defamation of Pius XII* (South Bend, IN: Saint Augustine's Press, 2001), 31.

14 Nigel Hamilton, *J.F.K.: Reckless Youth*, vol. 1 (London: Random House UK, 1992), 141.

4. THE IMPORTANCE OF BEING CATHOLIC

1 *HTF*, 164.

2 Ibid.

3 *NYT*, TimesMachine, November 15, 1935.

4 Ibid., December 4, 1935.

5 David Nasaw, *The Patriarch: The Remarkable and Turbulent Times of Joseph P. Kennedy* (New York: Penguin Books, 2013), 240.

6 *HTF*, 172–73.

7 Ibid., 181–82.

8 Ibid., 182.

9 Wallace Stegner, "The Radio Priest and His Flock," *The Aspirin Age*, Isabel Leighton, ed. (London: Penguin Books, 1964), 241–53.

10 Susan Ronald, *A Dangerous Woman: American Beauty, Noted Philanthropist, Nazi Collaborator—The Life of Florence Gould* (New York: St. Martin's Press, 2018), 251. See also Susan Ronald, "Hitler's Americans," https://historynewsnetwork.org/article/168206, February 2018.

11 Michael R. Beschloss, *Kennedy and Roosevelt: The Uneasy Alliance* (New York: W. W. Norton, 1980), 117–18.

12 Robert I. Gannon, *The Cardinal Spellman Story* (London: Robert Hale Limited, 1963), 92.

13 Ibid., 98.

14 Ibid., 107.

15 Joseph P. Kennedy, *I'm for Roosevelt* (New York: Reynal & Hitchcock, 1936), 5.

16 Beschloss, *Kennedy and Roosevelt: The Uneasy Alliance*, 126.

17 Ibid, 127. See also *HTF*, 187.

18 Gannon, *The Cardinal Spellman Story*, 111.

19 Nasaw, *The Patriarch*, 253.

20 Gannon, *The Cardinal Spellman Story*, 115.

21 Rose Kennedy (with Robert Coughlan), *Times to Remember* (New York: Doubleday & Co., 1974), 205.

5. PROJECT KENNEDY

1   *HTF,* 191.

2   Doris Kearns Goodwin, *The Fitzgeralds and the Kennedys* (New York: St. Martin's Press, 1987), 577, 576.

3   *HTF,* 190.

4   Michael R. Beschloss, *Kennedy and Roosevelt: The Uneasy Alliance* (New York: W. W. Norton, 1980), 128.

5   Rose Kennedy (with Robert Coughlan), *Times to Remember* (New York: Doubleday & Co., 1974), 212.

6   *HTF,* 210.

7   JFKL, JPK Papers, Box 70, March 21, 1936 letter from Krock to JPK asking for money. See also Arthur Krock, *Memoirs: Sixty Years on the Firing Line* (New York: Funk & Wagnalls, 1968), 331. Nigel Hamilton *J.F.K.: Reckless Youth,* vol. 1 (London: Random House UK, 1992), 211–12, testimony of Charles Houghton, a friend of John F. Kennedy, who said, "the old man hired Arthur Krock for $25,000 to keep the Kennedy name in the papers." John F. Kennedy was Houghton's source.

8   David Nasaw, *The Patriarch: The Remarkable and Turbulent Times of Joseph P. Kennedy* (New York: Penguin Books, 2013), 256.

9   Goodwin, *The Fitzgeralds and the Kennedys,* 580, quoted from the Arthur J. Krock Papers, Princeton University.

10 JFKL, JPK Papers, Box 96, Looker article for *Fortune*; *HTF,* 199–210.

11 *HTF,* 211–12.

6. "THE LOADED PAUSE"

1   Nigel Hamilton, *J.F.K.: Reckless Youth,* vol. 1 (London: Random House UK, 1992), 175.

2   JFKL, JFK Archive, JFKPP-001-016, School Report on Jean-Jacques Rousseau, undated.

3   Hamilton, *J.F.K.: Reckless Youth,* 165.

4   Ibid., 177. See also JFKL, JFK to JPK in JPK Papers, n.d., Family Correspondence, Box 1.

5   JFKL, Diary European Trip, JFKPP-001-012.

6   Hamilton, *J.F.K.: Reckless Youth,* 179–80, based on Hamilton interviews with Lem Billings; JFKPP-001-012, entry for July 13.

7   Ibid., 182, based on Hamilton interviews with Lem Billings; JFK Library, Diary European Trip, JFKPP-001-012, entry for July 24.

8   JFKL, JFK Archive, Diary European Trip, JFKPP-001-012, entries for August 1–9, 1937.

9   Ibid., entries for August 18, 1937.

10 Susan Ronald, *Hitler's Art Thief: Hildebrand Gurlitt, the Nazis, and the Looting of Europe's Treasures* (New York: St. Martin's Press, 2015), 178–79.

11 John Cornwell, *Hitler's Pope: The Secret History of Pius XII* (New York: Viking, 1999), 175.

12 JFKL, JPK Papers, Box 71, Sept. 8, 1937 letter to James Roosevelt.

13 *HTF,* 188.

14 Susan Ronald, *Condé Nast: The Man and His Empire—A Biography* (New York: St. Martin's Press, 2019), 308.

15 PAR, BBK/G/6/20, undated memo regarding advice given to Edward VIII, 6.

16 http://www.fdrlibrary.marist.edu/_resources/images/msf/msf01127.

17 *HTF,* 213. The italics are mine.

18 Very little of JPK's correspondence with Galeazzi is in the JFK Library Archive. JPK's letters are, I understand, at the Vatican's Secret Archive, where access is very difficult to obtain unless you are affiliated with a university.

19 Cornwell, *Hitler's Pope,* 182. See also Ernst Christian Helmreich, *The German Churches Under Hitler: Background, Struggle, and Epilogue* (Detroit: Wayne State University Press, 1979), 281.

20 DGFP, Series C, vol. VI, 20, 83, 220.

21 Hamilton *J.F.K.: Reckless Youth,* 215.

22 JFKL, JPK Papers, Box 94, O'Brien letter of January 22, 1937 to JPK.

23 Michael R. Beschloss, *Kennedy and Roosevelt: The Uneasy Alliance,* (New York: W.W. Norton, 1980), 153.

24 Elliott Roosevelt, ed., *The Roosevelt Letters: Being the Personal Correspondence of Franklin Delano Roosevelt* (London: George G. Harrap & Co. Ltd, 1952), 201.

25 *HTF,* 213 (letter to William Reid dated August 31, 1937); ODNB, https://www-oxforddnb-com.ezproxy2.londonlibrary.co.uk/view/10.1093/ref:odnb/9780198614128.001.0001/odnb-9780198614128-e-35252?rskey=FuEAGo&result=2.

26 Ronald, *Hitler's Art Thief,* 188–90.

27 Ibid., 180.

7. THE MOVIE MOGUL AND THE TRADE DEAL

1 FDRPL, PSFA 0497, letter to FDR dated October 18, 1937.

2 John Cornwell, *Hitler's Scientists: Science, War, and the Devil's Pact* (New York: Viking Books, 2003), 287–288.

3 JSTOR, John Sedgwick and Michael Pokorny, "The Film Business in the United States and Great Britain During the 1930s," *Economic History Review,* New Series, vol. 58, no. 1 (February 2005), 79.

4 Ibid., 80.

5 FRUS, 611.4131/383, Document 46, September 22, 1937, Butterworth (Second Secretary to the U.S. embassy in London) Memorandum.

6 Ibid., 611.4131/399, Document 50, October 28, 1937, Bingham to U.S. Secretary of State Hull.

7 Ibid.

8   Michael R. Beschloss, *Kennedy and Roosevelt: The Uneasy Alliance* (New York: W. W. Norton, 1980), 155.

9   JFKL, Oral History Project, Arthur Krock. See also Nigel Hamilton, *J.F.K.: Reckless Youth*, vol. 1 (London: Random House UK, 1992), 212.

10 JFKL, Series 7.2. Box 93, December 8, 1937 letter from Arthur Krock to JPK.

11 Beschloss, *Kennedy and Roosevelt: The Uneasy Alliance*, 155.

12 *The Times* (London, England), Friday, December 10, 1937, 16.

8. THE LAST FAMILY CHRISTMAS

1   LOC, Henry Morgenthau Diary, Microfilm 18,195, December 8, 1937. See also as quoted in David E. Koskoff, *Joseph P. Kennedy: A Life and Times* (Englewood Cliffs, NJ: Prentice-Hall, 1974), 116–17.

2   Ralph F. De Bedts, *Ambassador Joseph Kennedy 1938–1940: An Anatomy of Appeasement* (New York: Peter Lang, 1985), 18.

3   LOC, Henry Morgenthau Diary, Microfilm 18, 195, December 8, 1937.

4   Boake Carter syndicated column, "Kennedy No Diplomat. Too Hardhitting. Needed in America." December 11, 1937; https://www.newspapers.com/image/14687747/?terms=%22Joseph%2BP.%2BKennedy%22.

5   Nigel Hamilton, *J.F.K.: Reckless Youth*, vol. 1 (London: Random House UK, 1992), 213.

6   JFKL, Rose Kennedy Archive, Box 1.

7   Rose Kennedy (with Robert Coughlan), *Times to Remember* (New York: Doubleday & Co., 1974), 216.

8   Ibid., 212–14.

9   JFKL, Rose Kennedy Archive, Box 19.

10 Rose Kennedy (with Robert Coughlan), *Times to Remember,* 214.

11 W. N. Medlicott and Douglas Dakin, eds., *DBFP*, Series II, vol. 21, no. 204, August 26, 1937; FO 5728/5727/10.

12 Hamilton, *J.F.K.: Reckless Youth*, 216.

13 Ibid.

14 *DM*, chapter 1, 3.

15 TNA, FO 371/21524/160.

16 RA PS/PSO/GVI/PS/MAIN/2650.

17 TNA, FO 371/21524/162.

18 FDRPL, PFSA 0302, 2–3.

19 *HTF*, 235.

20 *DM*, chapter 1, 4.

21 FDRPL, PFSA 0321, Neville Chamberlain to President Roosevelt, January 14, 1938. See also Keith Feiling, *The Life of Neville Chamberlain* (Hamden, CT: Archon Books, 1970), 336.

22 FRUS, 841.4061 Motion Pictures/70 telegram, Document 64, November 20, 1937, Cuthbertson Memorandum.

23 Ibid., 841.4061 Motion Pictures/70 telegram, Document 65, November 29, 1937, Hull to Johnson.

24 Ibid., 841.4061 Motion Pictures/70 telegram, Document 68, December 10, 1937, noon, Hull to Johnson; FRUS 841.4061 Motion Pictures/70 telegram, Document 69, December 11, 1937, Johnson to Hull.

25 Ibid., 841.4061 Motion Pictures/81 telegram, Document 70, December 13, 1937, Hull to Johnson.

26 https://www.newspapers.com/image/133086007/?terms=Joseph%2BP.%2BKennedy, *Oakland Tribune,* January 7, 1938.

27 *Oakland Tribune,* January 26, 1938. The Kennedys were scheduled to sail for London at the end of the first week in February, with Admiral Land taking over at the Federal Maritime Commission on February 18.

28 *HTF,* 235–36.

29 FRUS, 841.4061 Motion Pictures/91: Telegram January 12, 1938; Telegram 94: January 13, 1938; Telegram 96: January 18, 1938.

30 Ibid., 841.4061 Motion Pictures/107: Telegram February 9, 1938.

31 Ibid., 841.4061 Motion Pictures/107: Telegram February 9, 1938.

32 Ibid., 841.4061 Motion Pictures/106b: Telegram February 15, 1938.

9. THE CELEBRITY AMBASSADOR

1 MOFFAT, vol. 39, November 24, 1937.

2 MOFFAT, vol. 40, January 27, 1938.

3 LOC, James M. Landis Papers, MS 29348, letters to JPK dated July 2, 1948, August 2, 1948, and September 23, 1948. Landis specifically queries Kennedy's quoting Chamberlain's alleged use of "jitters" in the letter of September 23, as he knew that it was hardly a word the staid British politician was likely to use. *HTF,* 225; *DM,* chapter 1, 11.

4 *DM,* chapter 1, 11–12.

5 Nigel Nicolson, ed., *The Harold Nicolson Diaries and Letters 1907–1964* (London: Weidenfeld & Nicolson, 2004), 332.

6 https://hansard.parliament.uk/Commons/1938-02-21/debates/907e082d-62b8-4a5d-adb3-2cb0c25c7d08/PersonalExplanations, 21 February 1938.

7 NCP, NC/1/17/1-26, letter dated December 16, 1937.

8 Count Galeazzo Ciano, *Diary 1937–1943: The Complete, Unabridged Diaries of Count Galeazzo Ciano, Italian Minister for Foreign Affairs, 1936–1943* (London: Phoenix Press, 2002), entry dated 1 February 1938, 52.

9 Ibid., 29.

10 JFKL, JPK Papers, Diary, Box 100, February 22, 1938.

11 *HTF*, 236.

12 Nicholas Wapshott, *The Sphinx: Franklin Roosevelt, the Isolationists, and the Road to World War II* (New York: W. W. Norton, 2015), 1.

13 JFKL, JPK Papers, Diary, Box 100, February 23, 1938.

14 Ibid., February 22, 1938.

15 David E. Koskoff, *Joseph P. Kennedy: A Life and Times* (Englewood Cliffs, NJ: Prentice-Hall, 1974), 119; quoted from *Time* magazine, March 7, 1938.

16 JFKL, JPK Papers, Diary, Box 100, February 28, 1938.

17 MO: https://digital.nmla.metoffice.gov.uk/IO_b514b289-5d69-45e3-9db0 -553d3bbc87ba/, DWR 1938_03.

10. HITTING THE GROUND RUNNING

1 *NYT*, TimesMachine, March 2, 1938.

2 JFKL, JPK Papers, Box 147, voluminous correspondence; TNA: T 3501, T 3709/276/373.

3 JFKL, JPK Papers, Diary, Box 100, March 2, 1938.

4 JFKL, Series 7.2., Maritime Commission Correspondence, Jim Seymour to JPK, Box 100, letter dated May 19, 1937. Seymour owed Kennedy a substantial sum of money that he had not as yet been able to pay back.

5 JFKL, JPK Papers, Diary, Box 100, March 2, 1938.

6 *HTF*, 239.

7 JFKL, JPK Papers, Box 114, JPK Correspondence with Offie, May 13, 1938. This box contains numerous references to champagne and orchids sent to London; Series 8.2.5, Box 147 for numerous other references.

8 Rose Kennedy (with Robert Coughlan), *Times to Remember* (New York: Doubleday & Co., 1974), 219–20.

9 Andrew Roberts, *The Holy Fox: The Life of Lord Halifax* (London: Weidenfeld & Nicolson, 1991), 6.

10 https://history.blog.gov.uk/2013/04/24/prime-ministers-in-the-house-of-lords/.

11 JFKL, JPK Papers, Diary, Box 100, diary entry, March 2, 1938.

12 TNA, FO371/22829/A1385/1292/45.

13 Roberts, *The Holy Fox*, 49.

14 Ibid., 47, 48.

15 JFKL, JPK Papers, Diary, Box 100, March 4, 1938.

16 Tim Bouverie, *Appeasing Hitler: Chamberlain, Churchill, and the Road to War* (London: Vintage, 2019), e-book, 121; quoted from the *Daily Telegraph*, May 26, 1937.

17 JFKL, JPK Papers, Diary, Box 100, diary entry, March 4, 1938.

18 FRUS, 611.4131Motion Pictures/Telegram: 183, March 4, 1938, 3 p.m.

19 *NYT*, TimesMachine, March 5, 1938.

20 Andrew Boyle, *Montagu Norman: A Biography* (New York: Weybright and Talley, 1968), 315.

21 David E. Koskoff, *Joseph P. Kennedy: A Life and Times* (Englewood Cliffs, NJ: Prentice-Hall, 1974), 123. Quoted from Leonard Mosley, *Backs to the Wall: The Heroic Story of the People of London During World War II* (New York: Random House, 1971), 36n; *The Secret Diary of Harold L. Ickes*, vol. II: *The Inside Struggle, 1936–1939* (New York: Simon & Schuster, 1954), diary entry for April 17, 1938, 370.

22 N. A. Rose, ed., *Baffy: The Diaries of Blanche Dugdale 1936–1947* (London: Vallentine Mitchell, 1973), 87.

23 FDRPL, PSA0355, letter from Wise dated March 4, 1938. See also Saul Friedländer, *Nazi Germany and the Jews: The Years of Persecution, 1933–1939* (New York: HarperCollins, 1997), 1:168.

11. "SPRING MANOEUVRES"

1 *NYT*, TimesMachine, March 6, 1938; JFK Library, JPK Diary, Series 8.1, Box 100, March 7, 1938.

2 *HTF*, 239–40.

3 FDRPL, PSFA 0321, Bingham to FDR, letter dated January 5, 1937.

4 *HTF*, 240.

5 JFKL, JPK Papers, Diary, Box 100, diary entry, March 8, 1938.

6 Ibid., March 10, 1938.

7 Andrew Roberts, *The Holy Fox: The Life of Lord Halifax* (London: Weidenfeld & Nicolson, 1991), 87–88.

8 American writers Nasaw and Swift place this event as taking place on March 11 at No. 10 Downing Street, as does Winston Churchill in his *The Gathering Storm*. After verifying with direct correspondence and the DBFP, I believe that this is incorrect and agree with Andrew Roberts, *The Holy Fox*, 91, that this event took place at No. 11 Downing Street on March 10. It is the only way that the DBFP makes any sense in the reading of subsequent telegrams.

9 NCP, NC 18/1/1045, Chamberlain to Hilda, March 13, 1938.

10 Tim Bouverie, *Appeasing Hitler: Chamberlain, Churchill, and the Road to War* (London: Vintage, 2019), e-book, 127.

11 *HTF*, 240–41.

12 FDRPL, PSFC000190, George S. Messersmith memo to Cordell Hull and Sumner Welles of February 18, 1938.

13 *HTF*, 241.

14 NCP, NC 18/1/1045, Chamberlain to Hilda, March 13, 1938.

15 DBFP, telegrams no. 70 and 71, Halifax to Henderson, 5–6.

389 ENDNOTES ✦ 389

16 JFKL, JPK Papers, Diary, Box 100, entry, March 9, 1938.

17 C. L. Sulzberger, *The Last of the Giants* (New York: Macmillan, 1971), 629.

18 British Newspaper Archive, *Evening Standard*, March 9, 1938.

19 *DM*, chapter 2, 8–9.

20 *HTF*, 241.

21 Ibid., 241–42.

22 Robert Rhodes James, ed., *Chips: The Diaries of Sir Henry Channon* (London: Weidenfeld & Nicolson, 1967), 150.

23 British Newspaper Archive, *Tatler*, March 16, 1938.

24 Helen Fry, *Spymaster: The Secret Life of Kendrick* (London: Marranos Press, 2014), 100–104.

25 JFKL, JPK Papers, Diary, entry, March 12, 1938.

26 FRUS, 863.00/1744: Telegram. Cardinal Pacelli to JPK, March 15, 1938.

27 JFKL, JPK Papers, Box 100, entry, April 15, 1938.

12. THE PILGRIMS

1 JFKL, JPK Papers, Diary, Box 100, entry, March 15, 1938.

2 David Nasaw, *The Patriarch: The Remarkable and Turbulent Times of Joseph P. Kennedy* (New York: Penguin Books, 2013), 293. See also LOC, Hull Papers, cables Moffat to JPK, JPK to Moffat dated March 15, box 66, reel 35.

3 MOFFAT, Diary, March 15, 1938.

4 Rose Kennedy (with Robert Coughlan), *Times to Remember* (New York: Doubleday & Co., 1974), 220.

5 JFKL, JPK Papers, Diary, Box 100, entry, March 15, 1938; Speeches, Box 155.

6 British Newspaper Archive, *Leeds Mercury*, March 19, 1938.

7 Ibid.

8 Tom Jones, *Diary with Letters 1931–1950* (London: Oxford University Press, 1954), 398.

9 Peter Neville, *Appeasing Hitler: The Diplomacy of Sir Nevile Henderson, 1937–1939* (Basingstoke, UK: Macmillan, 2000), 38.

10 Andrew Roberts, *The Holy Fox: The Life of Lord Halifax* (London: Weidenfeld & Nicolson, 1991), 64–65. See also TNA A4/410/3/2.

11 Neville, *Appeasing Hitler*, 52.

12 https://teachingamericanhistory.org/library/document/addess-delivered-by-the-secretary-of-state/. British Newspaper Archive, *Leeds Mercury*, March 19, 1938.

13 *HTF*, 246.

14 FO 371/22321. A special thanks to Dr. Helen Fry for sharing her original research about this and other incidents with me in a conversation November 10, 2019.

15 Helen Fry, *Spymaster: The Secret Life of Kendrick* (London: Marranos Press, 2018), 136.

16 https://hansard.parliament.uk/Commons/1938-03-24/debates/64f1b994-a007-4e92
-af8d-ce51f175116a/ForeignAffairsAndRearmament?highlight=czechoslovakia#
contribution-53a7f123-c0b6-4ef6-b88e-556e5f8e8758.

17 *NYT*, TimesMachine, March 25, 1938. See also *HTF*, 248–49.s

13. THE ENGLISH SWANS

1 *HTF*, 245.

2 Ibid.

3 Barbara Leaming, *Kick Kennedy: The Charmed Life and Tragic Death of the Favorite Kennedy Daughter* (New York: Thomas Dunne Books, 2016), 4.

4 Contrary to Barbara Leaming's wonderful portrait of Kick, Eights Week took place on April 2, 1938, not in June as stated on page 20. Confirmation is at the LOC, James Landis Papers, Box 26, containing JPK's handwritten diary. This means that Kick's visit to Oxford took place prior to her going to Cliveden.

5 http://thames.me.uk/s00231j.htm; MO, https://digital.nmla.metoffice.gov.uk/IO
_0aab99fe-6697-4515-960b-2bf5e88d923c/.

6 AA, MS1416/1/4/109, JPK to Nancy Astor, January 5, 1929.

7 https://www.clivedenhouse.co.uk/media/5327/cliveden-history.pdf.

8 Leaming, *Kick Kennedy*, 8.

9 Ibid., 11.

10 Ibid., 14.

11 Rose Kennedy (with Robert Coughlan), *Times to Remember* (New York: Doubleday & Co., 1974), 221. See also JFKL, JPK Papers, Box 99, entry April 2, 1938.

12 Ibid., 222.

13 Ibid., 222–23.

14 Ibid., 224.

15 *HTF*, 251.

16 Ibid.

17 ODNB, https://www-oxforddnb-com.ezproxy2.londonlibrary.co.uk/view/10
.1093/ref:odnb/9780198614128.001.0001/odnb-9780198614128-e-32902?rskey
=VT7t1Y&result=9.

18 *HTF*, 252–53.

19 Ibid., 253.

20 Ibid., 254.

21 *NYT*, TimesMachine, April 12, 1938.

22 JFKL, JPK Papers, Box 99, entries for March 24–26, March 30, April 1, 1938.

23 Rose Kennedy (with Robert Coughlan), *Times to Remember*, 226–29.

24 Will Swift, *The Kennedys Amidst the Gathering Storm: A Thousand Days in London, 1938–1940* (New York: Smithsonian Books, 2008), 49, quoted from Kick Kennedy's diary, May 11, 1938.

14. TRADING INSULTS

1 *HTF*, 248.

2 FDRPL, PSFA 0355, April 15, 1938.

3 FRUS, JPK to Hull, April 6, 1938.

4 NCP, NC 18/1/1046/1070, Chamberlain to Ida, May 1, 1938.

5 http://www.aboutnorthgeorgia.com/ang/FDR%27s_Brother%27s_Keeper_Speech.

6 FRUS, 741.65/541b: Telegram: Welles to JPK, April 19, 1938.

7 Ralph F. De Bedts, *Ambassador Joseph Kennedy 1938–1940: An Anatomy of Appeasement* (New York: Peter Lang, 1985), 58.

8 Winston S. Churchill, *The Second World War: The Gathering Storm* (London: The Reprint Society, 1950), 237.

9 JFKL, JPK Papers, diary entry, Allen to JPK April 5, 1938.

10 https://www.newspapers.com/image/260215203/?terms=%22Washington%2BMerry -Go-Round%22, March 22, 1938.

11 https://www.newspapers.com/image/259988416/?terms=%22Washington%2BMerry -Go-Round%22, April 29, 1938.

12 Jane Karoline Vieth, *Joseph P. Kennedy: Ambassador to the Court of St. James's 1938–1940,* vols. 1 and 2. Ohio State University, PhD dissertation., ProQuest Dissertations Publishing, 1975, 89.

13 https://www.newspapers.com/image/259978517/?terms=%22Washington%2BMerry -Go-Round%22, April 22, 1938.

14 Claud Cockburn, *I, Claud* (London: Penguin Books, 1967), 180.

15 *HTF*, 255.

16 Tim Bouverie, *Appeasing Hitler: Chamberlain, Churchill, and the Road to War* (London: Vintage, 2019), e-book, 58.

17 DBFP, vol. 1, 97, telegram no. 286, Henderson to Halifax, March 24, 1938.

18 De Bedts, *Ambassador Joseph Kennedy 1938–1940*, 60. See also MOFFAT, vol. 13, May 3, 1938.

19 Harold Ickes, *The Secret Diary of Harold L. Ickes: The Inside Struggle*, vol. 2 (London: Weidenfeld & Nicolson, 1955), 337. Canton Island is spelled "Kanton" today.

20 JFKL, JPK Papers, Box 99, entry for April 6, 1938.

21 FRUS, 841.4061Motion Pictures/117: Telegram. JPK to Hull, April 9, 1938. On March 28, the House of Commons restored the renters' quota to 15 percent for the first year of the act and restored the triple quota and reciprocity credit provisions put into the bill by the House of Lords.

22 FRUS, 841.4061Motion Pictures/139: Telegram, JPK to Hull, April 26, 1938.

23 FRUS, 841.4061Motion Pictures/139: Telegram, Hull to JPK, May 3, 1938.

24 Irwin F. Gellman, *Secret Affairs: FDR, Cordell Hull, and Sumner Welles* (Baltimore, MD: The Johns Hopkins University Press, 1995), 30, 156, 160–61.

25 FRUS, 841.4061Motion Picture/129a: Telegram, Welles to JPK April 25, 1938; 841.4061Motion Pictures/140: Telegram, JPK to Hull May 5, 1938; FRUS, 841.4061Motion Pictures/142: Telegram, JPK to Hull June 2, 1938; https://www .newspapers.com/image/259977016/?terms=%22Washington%2BMerry-Go -Round%22, April 22, 1938.

26 Vieth, *Joseph P. Kennedy: Ambassador to the Court of St. James's 1938–1940*, 89.

27 FRUS, 611.4131.15481/2: Telegram. British Trade Delegation to the Department of State Memorandum, undated, presumably April 1938.

28 J.C.W. Reith, *Into the Wind* (London: Hodder & Stoughton, 1949), 306.

15. THE EMERALD ISLE AND "CASE GREEN"

1 NCP, NC 18/1/1046/1070, Chamberlain to Ida, May 1, 1938.

2 Winston S. Churchill, *The Second World War: The Gathering Storm* (London: The Reprint Society, 1950), 231.

3 FO371/21496/A3834/1145, Lindsay to Halifax, May 9, 1938.

4 Harold Ickes, *The Secret Diary of Harold L. Ickes: The Inside Struggle*, vol. 2 (London: Weidenfeld & Nicolson, 1955), 416.

5 Author interview with Helen Fry, author of *Spymaster: The Secret Life of Kendrick* (London: Marranos Press, 2018), November 8, 2019.

6 FRUS, 863.00/1515: Telegram, Chargé d'Affaires Wiley to Hull, March 16, 1938.

7 FRUS, 741.51./284: Telegram, JPK to Secretary of State, May 5, 1938.

8 NCP, NC 18/1/1046/1070, Chamberlain to Ida, April 16, 1938.

9 Andrew Roberts, *The Holy Fox: The Life of Lord Halifax* (London: Weidenfeld & Nicolson, 1991), 106.

10 CAB 27/623/30, Chamberlain's remarks in Cabinet, June 1, 1938.

11 FRUS, 741.51./284: Telegram, JPK to Secretary of State, May 5, 1938; FRUS, 741.62/270: Telegram, JPK to Secretary of State, May 16, 1938.

12 Max Domarus, *Hitler—Speeches and Proclamations 1932–1945: The Chronicle of a Dictatorship*, vol. 2 (London: I. B. Tauris & Co., 1992), 991.

13 Roberts, *The Holy Fox*, 105.

14 NCP, NC 18/1/1046/1070, Chamberlain to Ida, May 1, 1938.

15 Tim Bouverie, *Appeasing Hitler: Chamberlain, Churchill, and the Road to War* (London: Vintage, 2019), e-book, 220.

16 Roberts, *The Holy Fox,* 104–105.

17 CA, CHAR 2/329/90, May 10, 1938.

18 CA, CHAR 2/329/95 and CHAR 2/329/98, May 13 and 15, 1938, respectively.

19 Gabriel Gorodetsky, ed., *The Maisky Diaries: The Wartime Revelations of Stalin's Ambassador in London* (New Haven, CT: Yale University Press, 2015), 114–15.

20 TNA, FO/800/269/90-91, Henderson to Halifax, April 7, 1938.

21 FRUS, 460F.62/262: Telegram, JPK to Hull May 14, 1938.

22 *HTF*, 256.

23 DBFP, vol. 1, 341, telegram no. 174, May 22, 1938.

24 Charles A. Lindbergh, *The Wartime Journals of Charles A. Lindbergh* (New York: Harcourt Brace Jovanovich, 1970), 26.

25 Silvia Jukes Morris, *Rage for Fame: The Ascent of Clare Boothe Luce* (New York: Random House, 2014), 318. See also Will Swift, *The Kennedys Amidst the Gathering Storm: A Thousand Days in London, 1938–1940* (New York: Smithsonian Books, 2008), 51.

26 Jane Karoline Vieth, *Joseph P. Kennedy: Ambassador to the Court of St. James's 1938–1940*, vols. 1 and 2. Ohio State University, PhD dissertation, ProQuest Dissertations Publishing, 1975, 101.

16. TO BE OR NOT TO BE—PRESIDENT

1 JFKL, JPK Papers, Box 110, JPK to Krock May 24, 1938, and Krock to JPK June 1, 1938.

2 Silvia Jukes Morris, *Rage for Fame: The Ascent of Clare Boothe Luce* (New York: Random House, 2014), 322.

3 NYT, TimesMachine, June 15, 1938.

4 Ibid., June 21, 1938.

5 David Nasaw, *The Patriarch: The Remarkable and Turbulent Times of Joseph P. Kennedy* (New York: Penguin Books, 2013), 315. The original Ickes quote is not cited.

6 Doris Kearns Goodwin, *No Ordinary Time: Franklin and Eleanor Roosevelt: The Home Front in World War II* (New York: Touchstone, 1995), 106.

7 Nasaw, *The Patriarch*, 317–18. See also Ralph F. De Bedts, *Ambassador Joseph Kennedy 1938–1940: An Anatomy of Appeasement* (New York: Peter Lang, 1985), 64.

8 Andrew Roberts, *The Holy Fox: The Life of Lord Halifax* (London: Weidenfeld & Nicolson, 1991), 106–107.

9 Ibid., 105–106.

10 Nasaw, *The Patriarch*, 310.

11 DGFP, Series D (1937–1945), vol. 9. *The War Years, March 18, 1940–June 22, 1940* (London: HMSO, 1956), 716.

12 Nasaw, *The Patriarch*, 316–17. See also Joseph P. Lash, *Eleanor: The Years Alone* (New York: W. W. Norton, 1972), 287.

13 https://www.newspapers.com/image/369837441/?terms=Kennedy *Chicago Tribune*, Trohan article, 1; https://www.newspapers.com/image/369837441/?terms=Kennedy, *Chicago Tribune*, David Darrah article, 8.

14 https://www.newspapers.com/image/171110637/?terms=Kennedy, *Philadelphia Inquirer*, 1.

15 https://www.newspapers.com/image/431721312/?terms=%22honorary%2Bdegree%2B Harvard%22, *The Boston Globe*, 14.

16 https://www.britishnewspaperarchive.co.uk/viewer/bl/0001898/19380630/014/0001, June 30, 1938.

17 Nasaw, *The Patriarch*, 316–17. See also Lash, *Eleanor: The Years Alone*, 320–21.

17. RETURN TO ALBION

1 JFKL, JPK Papers, Box 101, JPK to Baruch, May 2, 1938.

2 https://auislandora.wrlc.org/islandora/object/pearson%3A29482#page/2/mode/1up.

3 Ibid.

4 Will Swift, *The Kennedys Amidst the Gathering Storm: A Thousand Days in London 1938–1940* (New York: Smithsonian Books, 2008), 65.

5 NCP, NC 18/01/1059, Chamberlain to Hilda, July 9, 1938.

6 *The Times*, July 7, 1938.

7 Harold Ickes, *The Secret Diary of Harold L. Ickes: The Inside Struggle*, vol. 2 (London: Weidenfeld & Nicolson, 1955), 415.

8 FRUS, 611.4131/1668: Telegram, Document 33, JPK to Hull, July 14, 1938.

9 FRUS, 611.4131/1668: Telegram, Document 34, Hull to JPK, July 18, 1938.

10 FRUS, 611.4131/1681: Telegram, Document 35, Hull to JPK, July 22, 1938.

11 JFKL, JPK Papers, Box 100, Appointments for July 26, 1938; FRUS, 611.003/3822a [undated, but sometime in July 1938]; LOC, Morgenthau Diary, Microfilm, Morgenthau, August 30, 1938.

12 TNA, FO 371/21502/3-6, Stanley to Lindsay, July 27, 1938.

13 Tim Bouverie, *Appeasing Hitler: Chamberlain, Churchill, and the Road to War* (London: Vintage, 2019), e-book, 224.

14 Ibid., 225.

15 Andrew Morton, *17 Carnations: The Royals, The Nazis, and the Biggest Cover-Up in History* (New York: Grand Central Publishing, 2015), 180–81.

16 JFKL, JPK papers, Box 100, diary entry July 20, 1938.

17 *NYT*, TimesMachine, July 22, 1938.

18 Ibid., July 30, 1938.

19 DGFP, D, 1, 721. Dirksen to Weizsäcker, July 20, 1938.

20 DGFP, D, 1, 721–22. Dirksen to Weizsäcker, July 21, 1938.

21 Ibid.

22 FRUS, 741.62/280: Telegram, Kennedy to Hull, July 20, 1938.

23 N. A. Rose, ed., *Baffy: The Diaries of Blanche Dugdale 1936–1947* (London: Vallentine Mitchell, 1973), 93.

24 FRUS, 760F.62/528: Telegram, JPK to Hull, July 29, 1938.

25 Andrew Roberts, *The Holy Fox: The Life of Lord Halifax* (London: Weidenfeld & Nicolson, 1991), 103–104.

26 For an insightful depiction of how Kick fitted in, see chapters 1–3 of Barbara Leaming's bestselling book *Kick Kennedy: The Charmed Life and Tragic Death of the Favorite Kennedy Daughter* (New York: Thomas Dunne Books, 2016).

27 Ibid., 24–25.

28 Ibid., 26.

29 Ibid., 27.

30 Ibid., 30–31.

18. A FRENCH INTERLUDE

1 Mary S. Lovell, *The Riviera Set* (London: Abacus, 2016), 176–77.

2 Susan Ronald, *A Dangerous Woman: American Beauty, Noted Philanthropist, Nazi Collaborator—The Life of Florence Gould* (New York: St. Martin's Press, 2018), 137.

3 Maria Riva, *Marlene Dietrich: The Life* (New York: Pegasus Books, 1992), 467.

4 Ibid., 468–69.

5 Ibid., 469.

6 Ibid.

7 Mary S. Lovell, *The Riviera Set*, 177; Maria Riva, *Marlene Dietrich: The Life*, 471–72.

8 FRUS, 760F.62/542, Memorandum of Conversation between Welles and François-Poncet, August 2, 1938.

9 Ibid., 760.00/446: Telegram, Bullitt to Hull, August 12, 1938.

10 Gabriel Gorodetsky, ed., *The Maisky Diaries: The Wartime Revelations of Stalin's Ambassador in London* (New Haven, CT: Yale University Press, 2015), 115.

11 FRUS, 760F.62/580: Telegram, Johnson to Hull, August 18, 1938.

12 Tim Bouverie, *Appeasing Hitler: Chamberlain, Churchill, and the Road to War* (London: Vintage, 2019), e-book, 228.

13 DBFP, vol. 2, 41, telegram no. 574, Chamberlain to von Dirksen, August 3, 1938.

14 Max Domarus, *Hitler: Speeches and Proclamations 1932–1945: The Chronicle of a Dictatorship*, vol. 2 (London: I. B. Tauris & Co., 1992), 1137.

15 Andrew Roberts, *The Holy Fox: The Life of Lord Halifax* (London: Weidenfeld & Nicolson, 1991), 108. See also FO/800/309 for detailed correspondence.

16 Domarus, *Hitler: Speeches and Proclamations 1932–1945*, 991.

17 Winston S. Churchill, *The Second World War: The Gathering Storm* (London: The Reprint Society, 1950), 243.

19. THE "FARAWAY COUNTRY"

1 DBFP, vol. 2, 149, telegram no. 679, Halifax to Lindsay [Washington], August 24, 1938.

2 NCP, NC 7/11/31/1066, Chamberlain to Ida, September 3, 1938.

3 DBFP, vol. 2, 149–66, 179, telegrams nos. 679, 689, 694, 695,709 various correspondents, August 24–August 29, 1938.

4 FRUS, 840.48 Refugees/699: Telegram, Hull to Johnson, August 30, 1938.

5 NCP, NC 7/11/31/1066, Chamberlain to Ida, September 3, 1938.

6 David Nasaw, *The Patriarch: The Remarkable and Turbulent Times of Joseph P. Kennedy* (New York: Penguin Books, 2013), 330. See also JPK to Hull, FRUS 1938, 1:560–61.

7 Gabriel Gorodetsky, ed., *The Maisky Diaries: The Wartime Revelations of Stalin's Ambassador in London* (New Haven, CT: Yale University Press, 2015), 122.

8 https://www.newspapers.com/image/421925519/?terms=Ambassador%2BKennedy, August 31, 1938; https://www.newspapers.com/image/370317838/?terms=Kennedy, September 3, 1938.

9 MOFFAT, September 1, 1938.

10 MOFFAT, August 31, 1938.

11 Morgenthau Diaries, vol. 138, September 1, 1938.

12 NCP, NC 7/11/31/1067, Chamberlain to Ida, September 6, 1938.

13 NCP, NC 7/11/31/1068, Chamberlain to Ida, September 11, 1938.

14 FRUS, 760F.62/723: Telegram, Kennedy to Hull, September 10, 1938.

15 Ibid.

16 DBFP, Series III, vol. 2, 296.

17 FRUS, 760F.62/732: Telegram, Kennedy to Hull, September 11, 1938.

18 TNA, FO 371/21736, Halifax to Lindsay, September 11, 1938.

19 DGFP, Series D, II, 743–44.

20 Ibid.

21 Max Domarus, *Hitler: Speeches and Proclamations 1932–1945: The Chronicle of a Dictatorship*, vol. 2 (London: I. B. Tauris & Co., 1992), 1153–54, 1159.

22 NCP, NC 7/11/31/1069, Chamberlain to Ida, September 19, 1938.

23 Winston S. Churchill, *The Second World War: The Gathering Storm* (London: The Reprint Society, 1950), 249.

24 Ibid., 251.

25 FRUS, 760F.62/1018: Statement issued by the State Department, September 15, 1938.

26 FRUS, 760F.62/866: Telegram, Kennedy to Hull, September 17, 1938.

27 NCP, NC 7/11/31/1069, Chamberlain to Ida, September 19, 1938.

28 *HTF*, 276.

29 Ibid., 279.

30 FRUS, 760F.62/973: Telegram, Kennedy to Hull, September 21, 1938.

31 Charles A. Lindbergh, *The Wartime Journals of Charles A. Lindbergh* (New York: Harcourt Brace Jovanovich, 1970), 72.

32 Ibid., 73.

33 Ibid., 73–75.

34 *HTF*, 281–82.

35 Andrew Roberts, *The Holy Fox: The Life of Lord Halifax* (London: Weidenfeld & Nicolson, 1991), 115.

36 FRUS, 760F.62/1147a: Telegram, Franklin D. Roosevelt to Adolf Hitler, September 26, 1938.

37 https://www.bbc.co.uk/archive/chamberlain-addresses-the-nation-on-his-negotiations -for-peace/zjrjgwx.

38 Keith Feiling, *The Life of Neville Chamberlain* (Hamden, CT: Archon Books, 1970), 372.

39 Alexander Kendrick, *Prime Time: The Life of Edward R. Murrow* (New York: Avon Books, 1969), 220; *HTF*, 288. See also Ralph F. De Bedts, *Ambassador Joseph Kennedy 1938–1940: An Anatomy of Appeasement* (New York: Peter Lang, 1985), 103. Cummings was also quoted in the *Chicago Daily Tribune*, November 24, 1938.

40 Feiling, *The Life of Neville Chamberlain*, 381.

20. TRAFALGAR DAY

1 *HTF*, 292.

2 Charles A. Lindbergh, *The Wartime Journals of Charles A. Lindbergh* (New York: Harcourt Brace Jovanovich, 1970), 79.

3 *DM*, chapter 17, 2–3.

4 William L. Shirer, *The Rise and Fall of the Third Reich* (London: Mandarin Paperbacks, 1991), 424.

5 Ibid.

6 Max Domarus, *Hitler—Speeches and Proclamations 1932–1945: The Chronicle of a Dictatorship*, vol. 2 (London: I. B. Tauris & Co., 1992), 1217–20.

7 *HTF*, 292.

8 CA, CHAR 2/606.

9 https://api.parliament.uk/historic-hansard/commons/1938/oct/03/prime-ministers -statement, Hansard October 3, 1938.

10 FRUS, 840.48 Refugees/756: Telegram, Welles to JPK, October 5, 1938.

11 Winston S. Churchill, *The Second World War: The Gathering Storm* (London: The Reprint Society, 1950), 272.

12 Tim Bouverie, *Appeasing Hitler: Chamberlain, Churchill, and the Road to War* (London: Vintage, 2019), e-book, 296.

13 https://www.globalsecurity.org/military/world/europe/skoda-cz.htm.

14 Churchill, *The Second World War: The Gathering Storm*, 273.

15 Bouverie, *Appeasing Hitler*, e-book, 296–97. See also Hugh D. Phillips, *Between the Revolution and the West: A Political Biography of Maxim M. Litvinov* (Boulder, CO: Westview Press, 1992), 164.

16 Harold Ickes, *The Secret Diary of Harold L. Ickes: The Inside Struggle*, vol. 2 (London: Weidenfeld & Nicolson, 1955), 468–69.

17 Churchill, *The Second World War: The Gathering Storm*, 80.

18 Ibid., 269. See also CA, CHAR2/604.

19 Ibid., 267.

20 Keith Feiling, *The Life of Neville Chamberlain* (Hamden, CT: Archon Books, 1970), 383.

21 Andrew Roberts, *The Holy Fox: The Life of Lord Halifax* (London: Weidenfeld & Nicolson, 1991), 126.

22 Ibid., 123.

23 Ibid., 114.

24 Ibid., 124.

25 *HTF*, 295.

26 *The Times*, "Incentive to Peace—The Navy's Task—American Ambassador on Common Sense," October 20, 1938.

27 Ibid.

28 Ralph F. De Bedts, *Ambassador Joseph Kennedy 1938–1940: An Anatomy of Appeasement* (New York: Peter Lang, 1985), 101.

29 https://www.newspapers.com/image/171425425/?terms=Ambassador%2BKennedy, October 22, 1938.

30 BL, Samuel I. Rosenman, *The Public Papers and Addresses of Franklin D. Roosevelt*, vol. 7 (New York: Random House, 1941), 564.

31 MOFFAT, October 22–23, 1938.

21. THE AMBASSADOR AND THE JEWS

1 MOFFAT, October 21, 1938.

2 N.A. Rose, ed., *Baffy: The Diaries of Blanche Dugdale 1936–1947* (London: Vallentine, Mitchell, 1973), 110.

3 Ibid.

4 Ibid., 111.

5 Susan Ronald, *Hitler's Art Thief: Hildebrand Gurlitt, the Nazis, and the Looting of Europe's Treasures* (New York: St. Martin's Press, 2015), 71.

6 Dore Gold, "The Historical Significance of the Balfour Declaration," *Jewish Political Studies Review* 28, no. 1–2 (2017), 8.

7   Ibid., 9.

8   Klaus Polkehn, "The Secret Contacts: Zionism and Nazi Germany, 1933–1941," *Journal of Palestine Studies* 5, no. 3–4 (1976), 55. See also *Das Leben der Juden in Deutschland in Jahre 1933* for original statistics.

9   DGFP, D, V, 904–905; Polkehn, "The Secret Contacts: Zionism and Nazi Germany, 1933–1941," 61. See also https://encyclopedia.ushmm.org/content/en/article/berlin.

10 Polkehn, "The Secret Contacts: Zionism and Nazi Germany, 1933–1941," 64–65.

11 FRUS, 840.48 Refugees/659: Telegram, Johnson to Hull, August 15, 1938.

12 https://www.haaretz.com/jewish/.premium-1939-hitler-makes-first-call-for-jews-annihilation-1.531.6931.

13 Ibid., 840.48 Refugees/315: Telegram, JPK to Hull, June 1, 1938.

14 Ibid., 840.48 Refugees/374a: Circular telegram to all pertinent ambassadors, June 14, 1938.

15 DBFP, Series D, vol. 5, 894–95, circular telegram from Weizsäcker to all Reich ambassadors, July 8, 1938.

16 FRUS, 840.48 Refugees/513: Telegram, Taylor to Hull, July 14, 1938.

17 Hugh Gibson and Count Galeazzo Ciano, *The Ciano Diaries 1939–1943: The Complete, Unabridged Diaries of Count Galeazzo Ciano, Italian Minister for Foreign Affairs, 1936–1943* (Simon Publications, 1945), 113.

18 *DM*, chapter 18, 4.

19 JFKL, JPK, Series 1.1, Box 1, no date, JFK to parents.

20 FRUS, 840.48 Refugees/Telegrams: 739, 756, 759, 759a. Rublee, Taylor, Hull signatories.

21 Ibid., 840.48 Refugees/798 ½ Telegram Enclosure: Chamberlain to Roosevelt, October 7, 1938.

22 Ibid., 840.48 Refugees/805: Memorandum of telephone conversation between Rublee and Welles, October 10, 1938.

23 David Nasaw, *The Patriarch: The Remarkable and Turbulent Times of Joseph P. Kennedy* (New York: Penguin Books, 2013), 358–59.

24 Ronald, *Hitler's Art Thief*, 191.

25 Ralph F. De Bedts, *Ambassador Joseph Kennedy 1938–1940: An Anatomy of Appeasement* (New York: Peter Lang, 1985), 115.

26 DGFP, D, V, 639–40.

27 MOFFAT, November 14, 1938.

28 Peter Neville, *Appeasing Hitler: The Diplomacy of Sir Nevile Henderson 1937–1939* (London: Macmillan, 2000), 119.

29 *NYT*, TimesMachine, November 10, 1938; Nasaw, *The Patriarch*, 361 (italics are mine); JFKL, REFK Diary, Series 1, Box 1, November 13, 1938 entry.

30 JFKL, Rose Kennedy archive, Box 1, November 13, 1938.

31 FRUS, 840.48 Refugees/659: Telegram from Taylor [under Johnson] to Hull, August 15, 1938.

32 John Cornwell, *Hitler's Pope: The Secret History of Pius XII* (New York: Viking, 1999), 197.

33 FRUS, 840.48 Refugees/657: Telegram personal from Taylor to Hull, August 12, 1938.

34 https://www.newspapers.com/image/422073232/?terms=Kennedy; https://www.newspapers.com/image/456487225/?terms=Kennedy.

35 *The Times*, November 16, 1938.

36 MOFFAT, November 16, 1938; *NYT*, TimesMachine, November 16, 1938.

37 JFKL, JPK Papers, Box 163, Telegram, Boothe Luce to JPK, November 18, 1938.

38 De Bedts, *Ambassador Joseph Kennedy 1938–1940: An Anatomy of Appeasement*, 118.

39 TNA, FO 371/21637.

40 FRUS, 840.48 Refugees/911½: Memorandum of conversation between Lindsay and Welles, November 17, 1938.

41 John Harvey, ed., *The Diplomatic Diaries of Oliver Harvey 1937–1940* (London: Collins, 1970), 219–20.

22. A WELTER OF RUFFLED FEATHERS

1 FRUS, 611.4131/1855a: Telegram, Hull to Kennedy, November 3, 1938.

2 https://auislandora.wrlc.org/islandora/object/pearson%3A46158?solr_nav%5Bid%5D=42b6044629e69ca60376&solr_nav%5Bpage%5D=0&solr_nav%5Boffset%5D=7#page/1/mode/1up/search/Kennedy.

3 FRUS, 611.4131/1855b: Telegram, Hull to Kennedy, November 3, 1938.

4 *HTF*, 305.

5 https://auislandora.wrlc.org/islandora/object/pearson%3A44538#page/1/mode/1up/search/Kennedy.

6 https://www.newspapers.com/image/247758140/?terms=%22Kennedy%22.

7 *NYT*, TimesMachine, December 13, 1938. An article appeared on December 8, 1938, incorrectly stating that Kennedy was returning with his son John and the rest of the family would spend Christmas at St. Moritz. He was returning with Joe Jr., and John would join them in Palm Beach. The rest of the family, less Joe Jr. and Jack, would spend Christmas at St. Moritz.

8 FDRPL, PFSA 0355, December 19, 1938.

9 Ibid.

10 JFKL, JPK Papers, Box 101, JPK to Galeazzi November 25, 1938.

11 John Cornwell, *Hitler's Pope: The Secret History of Pius XII* (New York: Viking, 1999), 190.

12 Ibid.

13 JFKL, Rose Kennedy papers, Box 1, entries for December 1–6, 1938.

14 Ibid., entries for December 1 and December 3, 1938; *HTF*, 304–305.

15 https://www.britishnewspaperarchive.co.uk/viewer/bl/0001542/19381207/144/0008.

16 Thomas Jones, *A Diary with Letters 1931–1950* (London: Oxford University Press, 1954), 421–22.

17 Nick Smart, ed., *The Diaries and Letters of Robert Bernays, 1932–1939: An Insider's Account of the House of Commons* (Lampeter, Wales: The Edwin Mellen Press, 1996), 389.

18 Winston S. Churchill, *The Second World War: The Gathering Storm* (London: The Reprint Society, 1950), 278–79.

19 Tim Bouverie, *Appeasing Hitler: Chamberlain, Churchill, and the Road to War* (London: Vintage, 2019), e-book, 309–10.

20 https://www.infoplease.com/primary-sources/government/presidential-speeches/state-union-address-franklin-d-roosevelt-january-4-1939.

21 https://www.newspapers.com/image/431837134/?terms=Kennedy.

22 *NYT*, TimesMachine, January 10, 1939.

23 Ibid., January 14, 1939.

24 Andrew Roberts, *The Holy Fox: The Life of Lord Halifax* (London: Weidenfeld & Nicolson, 1991), 131; John Harvey, ed., *The Diplomatic Diaries of Oliver Harvey 1937–1940* (London: Collins, 1970), 235.

25 Roberts, *The Holy Fox*, 138.

26 Ibid.

23. A CORONATION TO REMEMBER

1 FDRPL, PSFA 0322, Halifax to Roosevelt, February 7, 1939; John Harvey, ed., *The Diplomatic Diaries of Oliver Harvey 1937–1940* (London: Collins, 1970), 248.

2 FDRPL, PSFA 0322, Lindsay to Roosevelt, February 28, 1939.

3 Keith Feiling, *The Life of Neville Chamberlain* (Hamden, CT: Archon Books, 1970), 396.

4 Harvey, ed., *The Diplomatic Diaries of Oliver Harvey 1937–1940*, 253–58.

5 FDRPL, PSFA 0355, Kennedy to Roosevelt, February 1939 [no exact date].

6 JFKL, JPK Papers, Series 8.2.1, Box 101, JPK to Galeazzi, February 25, 1939.

7 Ibid.

8 John Cornwell, *Hitler's Pope: The Secret History of Pius XII* (New York: Viking, 1999), 189–90.

9 Ibid.

10 FDRPL, PSFC 000192 Diplomatic/Confidential File: Phillips to State Department, February 24, 1939.

11 JFKL, JPK Papers, Box 130, memo of telephone conversation JPK and FDR, March 5, 1939; cable, JPK to Welles, March 6, 1939; cable, Hull to JPK, confirming status and further cables, March 6, 1939.

12 Rose Kennedy (with Robert Coughlan), *Times to Remember* (New York: Doubleday & Co., 1974), 244.

13 JFKL, JPK Papers, Box 130, Hull to JPK, March 6, 1939.

14 JFKL, Box 130, Jim Seymour to JPK, March 7, 1939.

15 JFKL, JPKOHP, Pope Paul VI, oral history, 1964.

16 *HTF*, 317; JFKL, JPK Papers, Box 130, Byrnes to JPK, March 7, 1939.

17 Nigel Hamilton, *J.F.K.: Reckless Youth*, vol. 1 (London: Random House UK, 1992), 256; *HTF*, 317.

18 *HTF*, 318.

19 Ibid., 257.

20 JFKL, JPK Papers, Box 130, JPK press release March 13, 1939; DGFP, D, IV, 600–601.

21 Harvey, ed., *The Diplomatic Diaries of Oliver Harvey 1937–1940*, 261–62.

22 JFKL, JPK Papers, Box 130, journal entry March 14, 1939.

23 Ibid., journal entry March 15, 1939.

24. "A WAVE OF PERVERSE OPTIMISM"

1 JFKL, JPK Papers, Box 130, journal entry March 17, 1939.

2 BOD, MS Dawson 43, February 25, 1939.

3 David Nasaw, *The Patriarch: The Remarkable and Turbulent Times of Joseph P. Kennedy* (New York: Penguin Books, 2013), 377; BOD, MS Dawson 43, February 28, 1939.

4 Orville H. Bullitt, ed., *For the President Personal & Secret: Correspondence Between Franklin D. Roosevelt and William C. Bullitt* (Boston, MA: Houghton Mifflin, 1972), 319.

5 Winston S. Churchill, *The Second World War: The Gathering Storm* (London: The Reprint Society, 1950), 281.

6 Harvey, ed., *The Diplomatic Diaries of Oliver Harvey 1937–1940*, 260; BOD, MS Dawson 43, March 7–10, 1939.

7 Richard Crockett, *Twilight of Truth: Chamberlain, Appeasement and the Manipulation of the Press* (London: Weidenfeld & Nicolson, 1989), 102.

8 Gabriel Gorodetsky, ed., *The Maisky Diaries: The Wartime Revelations of Stalin's Ambassador in London* (New Haven, CT: Yale University Press, 2016), 158–63.

9 NCP, NC17/11/32/11, Halifax to Chamberlain, March 11, 1939.

10 John Harvey, ed., *The Diplomatic Diaries of Oliver Harvey 1937–1940*, 262.

11 https://avalon.law.yale.edu/wwii/blbk09.asp, from DBFP, Third Series, IV, fn. 291, Chamberlain speech March 17, 1939; Churchill, *The Second World War: The Gathering Storm*, 286.

12 DBFP, Third Series, IV, 380, Halifax to Lindsay, March 18, 1939.

13 Bullitt, ed., *For the President Personal & Secret: Correspondence Between Franklin D. Roosevelt and William C. Bullitt*, 332.

14 Churchill, *The Second World War: The Gathering Storm*, 286–87.

15 Keith Feiling, *The Life of Neville Chamberlain* (Hamden, CT, Archon Books, 1970), 403; DGFP, D, IV, 631–32, Schulenburg to Ribbentrop, March 13, 1939.

16 FRUS, 641.6231/178 Telegram: Kennedy to Hull, March 18, 1939; and reply Hull to Kennedy, March 20, 1939.

17 https://hansard.parliament.uk/Commons/1939-03-31/debates/1524fe0b-019d-48fd -982d-99547a359ec6/EuropeanSituation?highlight=%22european%20situation%22#- contribution-f99b74f1-0fd5-4a83-a8d1-227a261c6a0e.

18 *HTF*, 324–25.

19 Nigel Hamilton, *J.F.K.: Reckless Youth*, vol. 1 (London: Random House UK, 1992), 255.

20 Ibid., 257.

21 Bullitt, ed., *For the President Personal & Secret: Correspondence between Franklin D. Roosevelt and William C. Bullitt*, 273.

22 Hamilton, *J.F.K.: Reckless Youth*, vol. 1, 258–59.

23 Ibid., 265.

24 https://avalon.law.yale.edu/20th_century/angap04.asp.

25 Hamilton, *J.F.K.: Reckless Youth*, vol. 1, 265.

26 https://avalon.law.yale.edu/20th_century/brwh1939.asp.

27 N. A. Rose, ed., *Baffy: The Diaries of Blanche Dugdale 1936–1947* (London: Vallentine, Mitchell, 1973), 138–39.

28 Sabri Jiryis, "Secrets of State: An Analysis of the Diaries of Moshe Sharett," *Journal of Palestine Studies* 10, no. 1 (1980), 35–57.

25. THE LAST SEASON

1 Gabriel Gorodetsky, ed., *The Maisky Diaries: The Wartime Revelations of Stalin's Ambassador in London* (New Haven, CT: Yale University Press, 2016), 172.

2 FRUS, 740.00/817a: Telegram from FDR to Hitler. Telegram 740.00/817b was addressed to Mussolini; Max Domarus, *Hitler—Speeches and Proclamations 1932–1945: The Chronicle of a Dictatorship*, vol. 3 (London: I. B. Tauris & Co., 1997), 1548–51.

3 JFKL, JPK Papers, Box 117, JPK to Welles, April 5, 1939.

4 *HTF*, 330.

5 Andrew Morton, *17 Carnations: The Royals, the Nazis, and the Biggest Cover-Up in History* (New York: Grand Central Publishing, 2015), 202–203; Messersmith (Havana) to Hull, Messersmith Papers, MSS 109, Box 12 F90.

6 *HTF*, 330–32; JFKL, JPK Papers, Box 174, Welles to JPK, May 4, 1939.

7 David Nasaw, *The Patriarch: The Remarkable and Turbulent Times of Joseph P. Kennedy* (New York: Penguin Books, 2013), 383–85; Morton, *17 Carnations*, 203–204.

8 John Harvey, ed., *The Diplomatic Diaries of Oliver Harvey 1937–1940* (London: Collins, 1970), 303; https://www.britishnewspaperarchive.co.uk/viewer/bl/0000560/19390722 /002/0001.

9 Anne de Courcy, *1939: The Last Season* (London: Phoenix, 2003), 46.

10 Ibid., 47, 48n.

11 Barbara Leaming, *Kick Kennedy: The Charmed Life and Tragic Death of the Favorite Kennedy Daughter* (New York: Thomas Dunne Books, 2016), 54–56.

12 https://www.parliament.uk/about/living-heritage/transformingsociety/private-lives /yourcountry/overview/conscriptionww2/.

13 RA, PS/PSO/GVI/C/352/1939: 4 May 1939.

14 FDRPL, PSFA 0322; Elliott Roosevelt, *The Roosevelt Letters: Being the Personal Correspondence of Franklin Delano Roosevelt*, vol. 3, 1928–1945 (London: George G. Harrap & Co.), 239.

15 RA, PS/PSO/GVI/PS/VISCOM/03400/003/001, FDR letter to George VI, September 17, 1938.

16 RA, PS/PSO/GVI/C/352/1939.

17 Anne de Courcy, *1939: The Last Season*, 103–105.

18 Tim Bouverie, *Appeasing Hitler: Chamberlain, Churchill and the Road to War* (London: Vintage, 2019), e-book, 347. See also Ronald Cartland, *Headway*, summer 1939.

19 Sylvia Jukes Morris, *Rage for Fame: The Ascent of Clare Boothe Luce* (New York: Random House, 2014), 341–42; LOC, CBL Papers, Box 91, folder 4.

20 Robert Rhodes James, ed., *"Chips": The Diaries of Sir Henry Channon* (London: Weidenfeld & Nicolson, 1967), 205.

21 Leaming, *Kick Kennedy*, 58.

22 Nasaw, *The Patriarch: The Remarkable and Turbulent Times of Joseph P. Kennedy*, 394.

23 *NYT*, TimesMachine, July 18, 1939.

24 Maria Riva, *Marlene Dietrich: The Life* (New York: Pegasus Books, 1992), 487.

25 JFKL, JPK Papers, Box 109, JPK to Houghton, August 31, 1939.

26. "THIS COUNTRY IS AT WAR WITH GERMANY"

1 Nigel Hamilton, *J.F.K.: Reckless Youth*, vol. 1 (London: Random House UK, 1992), 262.

2 John Harvey, ed., *The Diplomatic Diaries of Oliver Harvey 1937–1940* (London: Collins, 1970), 286; *The Times*, May 3, 1939.

3 Ralph F. De Bedts, *Ambassador Joseph Kennedy 1938–1940: An Anatomy of Appeasement* (New York: Peter Lang, 1985), 138–39. See also Joseph E. Davies, *Mission to Moscow: A record of confidential dispatches to the State Department, official and personal correspondence, current diary and journal entries up to October 1941* (London: Victor Gollancz, 1942).

4 Gabriel Gorodetsky, ed., *The Maisky Diaries: The Wartime Revelations of Stalin's Ambassador in London* (New Haven, CT: Yale University Press, 2016), 182–83.

5 Ibid., 184.

6 FRUS, 741.61/644: Telegram, JPK to Hull, May 25, 1939.

7 Keith Feiling, *The Life of Neville Chamberlain* (Hamden, CT: Archon Books, 1970), 409.

8 Robert Self, ed., *The Neville Chamberlain Diary Letters*, vol. 4, *The Downing Street Years, 1934–1940* (London: Ashgate, 2005), 415.

9 Tim Bouverie, *Appeasing Hitler: Chamberlain, Churchill, and the Road to War* (London: Vintage, 2019), e-book, 352, 353. See also DBFP, Third Series, vol. 6, Seeds to Halifax, June 17, 1939, no. 73.

10 FRUS, 741.61/756: Telegram, JPK to Hull, July 5, 1939.

11 De Bedts, *Ambassador Joseph Kennedy 1938–1940: An Anatomy of Appeasement*, 141.

12 Leonard Mosley, *On Borrowed Time: How World War II Began* (New York: Random House, 1969), 257–58.

13 TNA, FO 371/22827/1090/154.

14 FRUS, 761.6211/61: Telegram, Johnson to Hull, August 22, 1939.

15 Harvey, ed., *The Diplomatic Diaries of Oliver Harvey 1937–1940*, 304; Barbara Leaming, *Kick Kennedy: The Charmed Life and Tragic Death of the Favorite Kennedy Daughter* (New York: Thomas Dunne Books, 2016), 59.

16 Harold Ickes, *The Secret Diary of Harold L. Ickes: The Inside Struggle*, vol. 2 (London: Weidenfeld & Nicolson, 1955), 685, 707.

17 FRUS, 760C.62/942: Telegram, JPK to Hull, August 23, 1939.

18 CAB 23/100/10, August 22, 1939.

19 CAB 23/100/11, August 24, 1939.

20 MOFFAT, August 24, 1939; Harold Ickes, *The Secret Diary of Harold L. Ickes: The Inside Struggle*, vol. 2, 707.

21 *HTF*, 357; *DM*, chapter 23, 5; FRUS, 760C.62/990b: Telegram, FDR to Hitler and Mościcki, August 24, 1939.

22 CAB 23/100/11, August 24, 1939; Count Galeazzo Ciano, *Diary: 1937–1943: The Complete, Unabridged Diaries of Count Galeazzo Ciano* (London: Phoenix Press, 2002), 263.

23 TNA, FO 371/22827/1090.

24 Harvey, ed., *The Diplomatic Diaries of Oliver Harvey 1937–1940*, 306.

25 *HTF*, 362–63.

26 *DM*, chapter 23, 7–8; *HTF*, 362–63.

27 *DM*, chapter 23, 7–8; CAB 23/100/12.

28 Elmer Davis, ed., Edward R. Murrow, *This Is London* (London: Cassel and Company, 1941), 4.

29 Peter Neville, *Appeasing Hitler: The Diplomacy of Sir Nevile Henderson, 1937–1939* (London: Macmillan, 1999), 162–63.

30 JFKL, JPK Papers, Series 8.2.2, Box 108, JPK to Houghton, August 29, 1939; Box 112, JP Morgan to JPK.

31 Max Domarus, *Hitler: Speeches and Proclamations 1932–1945: The Chronicle of a Dictatorship*, vol. 3 (London: I.B. Tauris & Co., 1997), 1730–31.

32 Harvey, ed., *The Diplomatic Diaries of Oliver Harvey 1937–1940*, 306.

33 Murrow, *This Is London*, 6, 8.

34 De Bedts, *Ambassador Joseph Kennedy 1938–1940: An Anatomy of Appeasement* 144–45. See also Studs Terkel, *The Good War: An Oral History of World War Two* (London: Hamish Hamilton, 1985), 318; James A. Farley, *Jim Farley's Story* (New York: Greenwood Press, 1948), 198–99.

35 *The Times*, August 31, 1939.

36 David Nasaw, *The Patriarch: The Remarkable and Turbulent Times of Joseph P. Kennedy* (New York: Penguin Books, 2013), 404. See also *DM,* chapter 23, 14–15; JFKL, JPK Papers, Box 100, Diary August 30, 1939.

37 Lynne Olson, *Troublesome Young Men: The Churchill Conspiracy of 1940* (London: Bloomsbury Publishing, 2008), 209–10; https://hansard.parliament.uk/Commons/1939-09-02/debates /621e8d90-8e86-4856-b0b8-a2b5bd2ea776/GermanyAndPolandItalianProposals.

38 https://hansard.parliament.uk/Commons/1939-09-03/debates/18ec98fb-8576-4573 -8a82-9f97d7585074/PrimeMinisterSAnnouncement?highlight=prime%20minister#- contribution-6c5783c9-29ec-4e85-b106-7105dc9da9d3; https://www.theguardian.com /world/2009/sep/06/second-world-war-declaration-chamberlain.

39 R.A. Butler, *The Art of the Possible: The Memoirs of Lord Butler* (London: Hamish Hamilton, 1991), 80; Winston S. Churchill, *The Second World War: The Gathering Storm* (London: The Reprint Society, 1950), 329; JFKL, JPK Papers, Series 8.1.1. Box 100, JPK diary September 3, 1939.

40 Barbara Leaming, *Kick Kennedy*, 59; Gorodetsky, ed., *The Maisky Diaries*, 222.

27. SINKING THE SS *ATHENIA*

1 James Goodson, *Tumult in the Clouds: The Classic Story of War in the Air* (London: Penguin Books, 2003), 13.

2 Ibid., 14.

3 Nigel Hamilton, *J.F.K.: Reckless Youth*, vol. 1 (London: Random House UK, 1992), 282; *HTF*, 367.

4 Goodson, *Tumult in the Clouds*, 15.

5 Hamilton, *J.F.K.: Reckless Youth*, vol. 1, 283.

6 Goodson, *Tumult in the Clouds*, 17–22.

7 Hamilton, *J.F.K.: Reckless Youth*, vol. 1, 283.

8 Winston S. Churchill, *The Second World War: The Gathering Storm* (London: The Reprint Society, 1950), 340–41; https://www.britishnewspaperarchive.co.uk/viewer/bl/0000329 /19390909/021/0005, September 9, 1939;

9 https://www.britishnewspaperarchive.co.uk/viewer/bl/0000337/19390907/063/0003; Hamilton, *J.F.K.: Reckless Youth*, vol. 1, 285–86.

10 *HTF*, 370–71.

11 RA, GVI/PRIV/DIARY/ P 7 Saturday, September 9 [1939].

12 RA, GVI/PRIV/03/K/3, letter from George VI to JPK, September 11, 1939.

13 FRUS, 740.00.111A Passenger Travel/4: Telegram: JPK to Hull and reply Hull to JPK, September 8, 1939.

14 *Boston Globe*, September 21, 1939.

28. "DEPRESSED BEYOND WORDS"

1 William Shawn, ed., Mollie Panter-Downes, *London War Notes: 1939–1945* (London: Longman Group Limited, 1972), 3–4.

2 Winston S. Churchill, *The Second World War: The Gathering Storm* (London: The Reprint Society, 1950), 341.

3 Joseph Alsop and Robert Kintner, *American White Paper: The Story of American Diplomacy and the Second World War* (London: Michael Joseph Ltd., 1940), 93.

4 *HTF*, 374–76.

5 Ibid., 376.

6 Ralph F. De Bedts, *Ambassador Joseph Kennedy 1930–1940: An Anatomy of Appeasement* (New York: Peter Lang, 1985), 144–45. See also Studs Terkel, *The Good War: An Oral History of World War Two* (London: Hamish Hamilton, 1985), 318; James A. Farley, *Jim Farley's Story* (New York: Greenwood Press, 1948), 198–99.

7 Alsop and Kintner, *American White Paper*, 63–64; Harold Ickes, *The Secret Diary of Harold L. Ickes: The Inside Struggle 1936–1939* (London: Weidenfeld & Nicolson, 1955), 712.

8 LOC, Morgenthau diaries, Microfilm, September 7, 1939; September 11, 1939.

9 Email correspondence with Lady Leslie Bonham Carter and Robin Benson, January 29, 2019; https://www-oxforddnb-com.ezproxy2.londonlibrary.co.uk/view/10.1093/ref:odnb/9780198614128.001.0001/odnb-9780198614128-e-30716?rskey=ngqzfV&result=1.

10 JFKL, JPK Papers, Box 2, KK letter September 18, 1939; JPK letter dated October 3, 1939.

11 Harold Ickes, *The Secret Diary of Harold L. Ickes: The Lowering Clouds 1939–1941*, vol. 3 (London: Weidenfeld & Nicolson, 1955), 22–23.

12 *Time* magazine, September 18, 1939.

13 David Nasaw, *The Patriarch: The Remarkable and Turbulent Times of Joseph P. Kennedy* (New York: Penguin Books, 2013), 410. See also LOC, Breckinridge Long Papers, diary entry September 7, 1939, box 5.

14 JFKL, JPK Papers, Box 100, September 17, 1939.

15 Andrew Roberts, *The Holy Fox: A Biography of Lord Halifax* (London: Weidenfeld & Nicolson, 1991), 176.

16 Ibid., 178; Gabriel Gorodetsky, ed., *The Maisky Diaries: The Wartime Revelations of Stalin's Ambassador in London* (New Haven, CT: Yale University Press, 2016), 226.

17 TNA, FO 22827/1090.

18 DGFP, VII, Thomsen to Ribbentrop, September 18, 1939.

19 Alsop and Kintner, *American White Paper*, 21.

20 *HTF*, 385–86.

21 Roberts, *The Holy Fox*, 176–77.

22 FO 800/325, October 2, 1939.

23 John Cornwell, *Hitler's Pope: The Secret History of Pius XII* (New York: Viking, 1999), 235.

24 Max Domarus, *Hitler: Speeches and Proclamations 1932–1945: The Chronicle of a Dictatorship*, vol. 3 (London: I. B. Tauris & Co., 1997), 1828–29; Churchill, *The Second World War: The Gathering Storm*, 363.

25 Keith Feiling, *The Life of Neville Chamberlain* (Hamden, CT: Archon Books, 1970), 425.

26 Roberts, *The Holy Fox,* 177.

27 JFKL, JPK Papers, Box 100, October 6, 1939.

28 *HTF,* 391–92.

29 Ibid., 400.

30 Alsop and Kintner, *American White Paper*, 102.

31 FDRPL, PSFA 0322, Chamberlain to Roosevelt, November 4, 1939.

32 Robert Rhodes James, ed., *Chips: The Diaries of Sir Henry Channon* (London: Weidenfeld & Nicolson, 1967), 225; AA, MS 1416/1/1/1449, Nancy Astor to Lothian, November 27, 1939.

33 *HTF*, 394.

29. "BEWARE THE BEAR"

1 https://www.newspapers.com/image/168051201/?terms=%22Joseph%2BP .%2BKennedy%22, December 7, 1939.

2 FO 371/24251/145, January.

3 *NYT*, TimesMachine, December 8, 1939.

4 *DM*, chapter 38, 4–5.

5 *DM*, chapter 37, 18; chapter 38, 4–5.

6 CAB 65/2/50, December 15, 1939.

7 Ibid.

8 *DM,* chapter 38, 4.

9 *DM,* chapter 38, 9–10.

10 MOFFAT, vol. 43, December 8, 1939.

11 *NYT*, TimesMachine, December 8, 1939.

12 Harold Ickes, *The Secret Diary of Harold L. Ickes: The Lowering Clouds 1939–1941*, vol. 3 (London: Weidenfeld & Nicolson, 1955), 85.

13 *The Times*, December 12, 1939.

14 PAR, Beaverbrook, BBK/D/399-404, Knox to Beaverbrook, January 5, 1940; Beaverbrook to Knox, March 4, 1940.

15 FDRPL, PPF 207, Jordan to FDR, December 13, 1939. The italics are mine.

16 *The Spectator*, December 15, 1939.

17 Ralph F. De Bedts, *Ambassador Joseph Kennedy 1930–1940: An Anatomy of Appeasement* (New York: Peter Lang, 1985), 184–85n.

18 https://www.newspapers.com/image/332898305/?terms=%22Alsop%22%2BAND%2B%22Kintner%22, December 19, 1939.

19 *NYT*, TimesMachine, December 15, 1939; MOFFAT, vol. 43, December 15, 1939.

20 DGFP, Series D, vol. 3, 470–71.

21 Ibid., 504.

22 FO 371/24251/65-66r, undated.

23 FO 371/24251/85r-86, March 2, 1939.

30. SHADOWING WELLES

1 James Holland, *The War in the West: Germany Ascendant 1939–1941* (London: Corgi Books, 2016), 183.

2 *NYT*, TimesMachine, February 14, 1940.

3 Ibid., February 10, 1940.

4 Ibid., February 10, 1940; Stanley E. Hilton, "The Welles Mission to Europe, February–March 1940," *Journal of American History* 56, no. 1 (1971), 94.

5 Hilton, "The Welles Mission to Europe, February–March 1940," 96.

6 Ibid., 98.

7 Ibid., 105–107; Holland, *The War in the West: Germany Ascendant 1939-1941*, 217.

8 *NYT*, TimesMachine, February 10, 1940; FRUS 811.001Roosevelt, F.D./1-1940.

9 John Cornwell, *Hitler's Pope: The Secret History of Pius XII* (New York: Viking, 1999), 235; Roger Collins, *Keepers of the Keys of Heaven: A History of the Papacy* (London: Phoenix, 2010), 476.

10 Cornwell, *Hitler's Pope: The Secret History of Pius XII*, 236–37; FO, 800/318/6; Andrew Roberts, *The Holy Fox: A Biography of Lord Halifax* (London: Weidenfeld & Nicolson, 1991), 182–83.

11 Collins, *Keepers of the Keys of Heaven*, 476.

12 *HTF*, 406–407, JPK to Rose, March 14, 1939.

13 Sylvia Jukes Morris, *Rage for Fame: The Ascent of Clare Boothe Luce* (New York: Random House, 2014), 361.

14 Ibid., 369; *HTF*, 407, JPK to Rose March 14, 1939.

15 LOC, CBL Papers, Box 96, Raimund von Hofmannsthal reply to CBL, March 27, 1940.

16 *HTF*, 407–408, JPK to Rose, March 14, 1939.

17 FDRPL, PSFA 0355, Welles Mission, Part I.

18 *NYT*, TimesMachine, March 8, 1940.

19 FO 371/24251/202, March 8, 1939.

20 FDRPL, PSFA 0355, Welles Mission, Part I; Holland, *The War in the West: Germany Ascendant 1939–1941*, 209.

21 *NYT*, TimesMachine, March 17, 1940; Ralph F. De Bedts, *Ambassador Joseph Kennedy 1938–1940: An Anatomy of Appeasement* (New York: Peter Lang, 1985), 193–94.

22 FDRPL, PSFA 0355, Welles Mission, Part I.

23 FO 371/24248/A825, January 29, 1940.

24 James Leutze, ed., *The London Observer: The Journal of General Raymond E. Lee, 1940–1941* (London: Hutchinson of London, 1971), x.

25 JFKL, JPK Jr. various correspondence, Boxes 18–19.

26 *HTF*, 408; *NYT*, TimesMachine, March 8, 1940; FDRPL, PSFA 0355, Welles Mission, Part I; Holland, *The War in the West: Germany Ascendant 1939–1941*, 209.

27 Keith Feiling, *The Life of Neville Chamberlain* (Hamden, CT: Archon Books, 1970), 428.

28 RA GVI/PRIV/DIARY/ P 7, vol. 2, 7-3-40-19.7.40, March 11, 1940.

29 *HTF*, 409.

30 Holland, *The War in the West: Germany Ascendant 1939–1941*, 212.

31 FDRPL, PSFA 0355, Welles Mission, Part II; James Holland, *The War in the West: Germany Ascendant 1939–1941*, 210; Galeazzo Ciano, *Diary 1937–1943: The Complete, Unabridged Diaries of Count Galeazzo Ciano* (London: Phoenix Press, 2002), 320, 329.

31. KENNEDY AND THE "KING'S WEATHER"

1 *HTF*, 410.

2 FO 371/24238/45, various remarks from ministers and civil servants.

3 LOC, CBL Papers, Box 96, letter from von Hofmannsthal to CBL, March 27, 1940. According to John Julius Norwich (https://www.youtube.com/watch?v=l _AivTGsCbU), son of Alfred Duff Cooper, Raimund never said anything against anyone, and yet he wrote at the top of this memo to Clare that what he had to say was "controversial."

4 LOC, CBL Papers, Box 96, letter from von Hofmannsthal to CBL, March 27, 1940; CBL diary, April 2, 1940, as quoted in Sylvia Jukes Morris, *Rage for Fame: The Ascent of Clare Boothe Luce* (New York: Random House, 2014), 372.

5 Clare Boothe Luce, *European Spring* (London: Hamish Hamilton, 1941), 141; MO, DWR_1940_4, weather report for April 1940.

6 I am grateful to war historian James Holland for this information in our email correspondence of January 27, 2020.

7 JFKL, JPK Papers, Diary Box 100, April 9, 1940; Winston S. Churchill, *The Second World War: The Gathering Storm* (London: The Reprint Society, 1950), 480.

8 Barbara Leaming, *Kick Kennedy: The Charmed Life and Tragic Death of the Favorite Kennedy Daughter* (New York: Thomas Dunne Books, 2016), 68–69 (italics are mine); *HTF*, 408–409.

9 Leaming, *Kick Kennedy*, 69.

10 FDRPL, OF 229, JPK to FDR, April 11, 1940; LOC, Morgenthau Diaries, Microfilm, April 29, 1940.

11 https://hansard.parliament.uk/Commons/1940-05-02/debates/99b16f05-a580-4bfd -b169-c503d6e13b8a/Norway(Situation)?highlight=%22narvik%22#contribution-e98d c3a6-3239-4a26-b984-9737bf1719a4.

12 https://hansard.parliament.uk/Commons/1940-05-07/debates/ee7fb681-43ae-4a17 -a06f-cdf0a62e1ce2/ConductOfTheWar?highlight=narvik#contribution-d6179dd8 -9f3a-4037-8e4e-b180643a0073; Churchill, *The Second World War: The Gathering Storm*, 525.

13 Leaming, *Kick Kennedy*, 80.

14 https://time.com/3848735/churchill-best-speeches-blood-toil-tears-sweat/. *Time* also voted it as part of the "80 Days that Changed the World" Series in 2003.

15 *HTF*, 424 and 424n.

16 TNA, KV2/1698 del Monte; *The Spectator*, October 26, 1956. The "Golden Egg" article coincides with the first publication in English of vol. 9, Series D, of the *DGFP (Documents on German Foreign Policy)*, proving the efficiency of the spy network.

17 TNA, KV 2/543/1 Tyler Kent. Paul Willetts, *Rendezvous at the Russian Tea Rooms* (London: Constable, 2015). Also, I thank Paul Willetts for his generous time in private correspondence helping me to unpick Tyler Kent's complicated tale.

18 CHAR 2/371A-B/126-127, marked "very secret." An undated report from April 1940 to Churchill.

19 TNA, LO 2/330 (FOI Request granted) on significance of Kent's loss of diplomatic status. The attorney general clearly sets out what any foreign government should do in cases where a crime is committed against Great Britain on British soil within a foreign embassy (deemed "foreign" soil) and once that crime is carried out of the building onto British soil.

20 TNA, KV2/1698 del Monte; KV2/543, Tyler Kent.

21 TNA, KV2/543, Tyler Kent.

22 Ibid.

23 Ibid., KV2/843, Anna Wolkoff; KV2/1698 del Monte.

32. A TREACHEROUS FRIEND

1 MO, DWR_1940_5; James Goodson, *Tumult in the Clouds: The Classic Story of War in the Air* (London: Penguin Books, 2003), 51-52; FRUS, 740.0011 European War/1939/3358 Telegram: Bullitt to Hull, May 28, 1940; JFKL, JPK Papers, Box 7, KK letter to JPK May 21, 1940; Doris Kearns Goodwin, *The Fitzgeralds and the Kennedys* (New York: St.

Martin's Press, 1987), 704. For some bizarre reason, Joseph P. Kennedy published a book cowritten with James M. Landis in March 1950 entitled *The Surrender of King Leopold,* which alleges that he had no choice than to sacrifice the armies of the Allies. It is not a straightforward polemic; but it has as its main purpose to repudiate Winston Churchill's history *The Second World War: Their Finest Hour,* vol. 2 (London: The Reprint Society, 1956), 75–85.

2   FO 371/24251/79-80/82, May 20–22, 1940.

3   Elmer Davis, ed., Edward R. Murrow, *This Is London* (London: Cassell and Co., 1941), 102, 111, 113.

4   FDRPL, PFSA 0357, Breckinridge Long to FDR, May 21, 1940; *HTF,* 428–429.

5   Winston S. Churchill, *The Second World War: Their Finest Hour,* vol. 2 (London: The Reprint Society, 1956), 83; Davis, ed., Edward R. Murrow, *This Is London,* 113.

6   https://www.english-heritage.org.uk/visit/places/dover-castle/history-and-stories /operation-dynamo-things-you-need-to-know/; Churchill, *The Second World War: Their Finest Hour,* vol. 2, 109.

7   FRUS, 856.001W64/53, 1–5, Telegrams: May 20–28, 1940.

8   *HTF,* 436; JFKL, JPK Papers, Box 2, JPK to JPK Jr., June 6, 1940.

9   JFKL, JPK Papers, Box 1, JPK to JFK letter May 20, 1940.

10 James Holland, *The War in the West: Germany Ascendant 1939–1941* (London: Corgi Books, 2016), 360–62.

11 *HTF,* 439.

12 Ibid.

13 Holland, *The War in the West: Germany Ascendant 1939–1941,* 408.

14 TNA, CAB 65/7/60.

15 *HTF,* 443n.

16 FDRPL, PSFA 0038, JPK to Hull, June 12, 1940; Churchill, *The Second World War: Their Finest Hour,* vol. 2, 161; TNA, CAB 65/7/60.

17 https://winstonchurchill.org/publications/finest-hour/finest-hour-153/citizens-of-london/.

18 FDRPL, PSFA 0038, JPK to Hull, June 16, 1940; John Colville, *The Fringes of Power: The Downing Street Years 1939–1955* (London: Weidenfeld & Nicolson, 2004), 90.

19 Barbara Leaming, *Kick Kennedy: The Charmed Life and Tragic Death of the Favorite Kennedy Daughter* (New York: Thomas Dunne Books, 2016), 75.

20 Susan Ronald, *A Dangerous Woman: American Beauty, Noted Philanthropist, Nazi Collaborator: The Life of Florence Gould* (New York: St. Martin's Press, 2018), 205–207.

21 https://avalon.law.yale.edu/wwii/frgearm.asp.

33. "JITTERY JOE"

1   FRUS, 740.0011 European War 1939:4228 Telegram Biddle to Hull, June 27, 1940.

2   James Holland, *The War in the West: Germany Ascendant 1939–1941,* vol. 1 (London: Corgi Books, 2015), 380, 405; Winston S. Churchill, *The Second World War: Their Finest Hour,*

vol. 2 (London: The Reprint Society, 1956), 198–203; Warren Kimball, *Forged in War: Churchill, Roosevelt and the Second World War* (New York: HarperCollins, 1997), 56; Max Domarus, *Hitler: Speeches and Proclamations 1932–1945: The Chronicle of a Dictatorship*, vol. 3 (London: I. B. Tauris & Co., 1997), 2036.

3   Domarus, *Hitler: Speeches and Proclamations 1932–1945*, 2037–40.

4   FDRPL, PSFA 0357, July 12, 1940, cross-referenced with July 13 memo to Frank Knox; James Leutze, ed., *The London Observer: The Journal of General Raymond E. Lee 1940–1941*, (London: Hutchinson of London, 1971), 19.

5   Doris Kearns Goodwin, *No Ordinary Time: Franklin & Eleanor Roosevelt: The Home Front in World War II* (New York: Touchstone, 1995), 108.

6   Ibid., 126.

7   *HTF*, 449–451.

8   Douglas Waller, *Wild Bill Donovan: The Spymaster Who Created the OSS and Modern American Espionage* (New York: Free Press, 2011), 59.

9   Leutze, ed., *The London Observer: The Journal of General Raymond E. Lee 1940–1941*, 20–21.

10 Ibid., 26–28.

11 NA, RG 59, 740.0011, Telegram, JPK to Hull, August 2, 1940; William Shawn, ed., Mollie Panter-Downes, *London War Notes 1939–1945* (London: Longman, 1972), 88.

12 RA, vol. 3. 20.7.40 31.12.40, Wednesday, August 7 [1940].

13 James Goodson, *Tumult in the Clouds: The Classic Story of War in the Air* (London: Penguin Books, 2003), 53; Leutze, ed., *The London Observer: The Journal of General Raymond E. Lee 1940–1941*, 30; *HTF*, 455.

14 *Guilty Men* was written by Michael Foot (*Evening Standard*), Frank Owen (the *Standard* editor), and Peter Howard (*Daily Express*) and published under the pen name "Cato." Foot went on to become a Labour MP, and leader of the Labour Party from 1980–1983.

15 Leutze, ed., *The London Observer: The Journal of General Raymond E. Lee 1940–1941*, 24–25; Churchill, *The Second World War: Their Finest Hour*, vol. 2, 330–31.

16 http://www.churchill-society-london.org.uk/thefew.html.

17 Goodwin, *No Ordinary Time: Franklin & Eleanor Roosevelt: The Home Front in World War II*, 141–48.

18 *HTF*, 466.

19 Panter-Downes, *London War Notes 1939–1945*, 89–90; Elmer Davis, ed., Edward R. Murrow, *This Is London* (London: Cassell and Co., 1941), 164–65.

20 *HTF*, 463.

34. COME HELL OR HIGH WATER

1   *HTF*, 463.

2   FDRL, PSFA 0357, August 28, 1940.

3   *NYT*, TimesMachine, August 20, 1940 (my italics).

4   Ibid., August 22, 1940.

5   Elmer Davis, ed., Edward R. Murrow, *This Is London* (London: Cassell and Co., 1941), 165.

6   *HTF*, 465, 466. Several statements he made in the letter to Rose are contradicted elsewhere. The only sighting of the bomb "250 yards" from his home at Windsor was by Kennedy. Herschel Johnson was at the same club as Raymond Lee and was not "almost killed" at the time Kennedy stated. Also, the bombing at the beginning of September was aimed at the East End and the docks, not Kensington.

7   *Front Line 1940–1941: The Official Story of the Civil Defence of Britain* [S.I.] (London: HMSO, 1941), 12; https://winstonchurchill.org/publications/finest-hour/finest-hour -153/citizens-of-london/.

8   AA, MS 1416/1/1/1643.

9   FO 371/24251/94–94r, October 19, 1940.

10   *HTF*, 469, 471.

11   JFKL, JPK Papers, Box 100, Diary, September 15, 1940; Box 176, JPK cable to Welles, September 16, 1940; JPK Papers, Box 1, JPK to JPK Jr. letter, September 10, 1940; http://bombsight.org/?#.

12   JFKL, JPK Papers, Box 1, JPK to JPK Jr. letter, September 10, 1940.

13   *HTF*, 474–75.

14   FO 371/24251/96, October 10, 1940.

15   Ibid.

16   FO 371/24251/97, October 18, 1940.

17   RA, GVI/PRIV/DIARY/ P 7, vol. 3, October 11, 1940.

18   JFKL, JPK Papers, diary, Box 100, October 11, 1940.

19   David Nasaw, *The Patriarch: The Remarkable and Turbulent Times of Joseph P. Kennedy* (New York: Penguin Books, 2013), 482; see also Breckinridge Long Diaries, October 11, 1940 entry.

20   *HTF*, 475.

21   FO 371/24251/97, October 18, 1940.

22   FO 371/24251/96, November 15, 1940.

23   RA, GVI/PRIV/DIARY/P 7, vol. 3, October 17, 1940.

24   Ibid., Thursday Oct. 17, Sunday Oct. 20, 1940.

25   Gabriel Gorodetsky, ed., *The Maisky Diaries: The Wartime Revelations of Stalin's Ambassador in London* (New Haven, CT: Yale University Press, 2016), 321.

26   FO 371/24251/97, October 18, 1940.

27   RA, GVI/PRIV/DIARY/P 7, vol. 3, October 20, 1940.

28   CHAR 8/211/51. Chamberlain's doctors reported he "should" recover, but given the severity of his cancer, Churchill remained unconvinced.

29 NCP, NC 2/24 Journal, October 2, 1940.

30 *HTF*, 477.

35. THE DRAGON SLAYERS

1 https://www.newspapers.com/image/298560088/?terms=Alsop%2Band%2BKintner, October 8, 1940.

2 Ibid.

3 FDRPL, PSFA 0357, memo from Missy LeHand concerning Goldsmith's call to Jerome Frank, current chairman of the SEC, about the White House taking Kennedy in hand when landing.

4 *HTF*, 479.

5 Ibid., 480.

6 *NYT*, TimesMachine, October 28, 1940.

7 Michael R. Beschloss, *Kennedy and Roosevelt: An Uneasy Alliance* (New York: W. W. Norton, 1980), 213–14.

8 Ibid., 213.

9 David Nasaw, *The Patriarch: The Remarkable and Turbulent Times of Joseph P. Kennedy* (New York: Penguin Books, 2013), 491.

10 Michael R. Beschloss, *Kennedy and Roosevelt: An Uneasy Alliance*, 216–17.

11 *HTF*, 480–82.

12 CBLP, Box 96, CBL to JPK, October 28, 1940.

13 *HTF*, 482–87; Rose Kennedy (with Robert Coughlan), *Times to Remember* (New York: Doubleday & Co., 1974), 274–75.

14 Nasaw, *The Patriarch*, 497. For Murphy's diary of November 2, 1940, consult box 1 in the Eugene Gressman Papers, Bentley Historical Library, the University of Michigan, Ann Arbor, MI. I am thankful to David Nasaw for this original reference.

15 https://www.newspapers.com/image/139754732/?terms=Kennedy, November 10, 1940; James Leutze, ed., *The London Observer: The Journal of General Raymond E. Lee 1940–1941* (London: Hutchinson of London, 1971), 219–20.

16 FDRPL, PSFA 0357, Douglas Fairbanks Jr. to FDR, November 19, 1940.

17 CHAR 20/2 B.

18 Charles A. Lindbergh, *The Wartime Journals of Charles A. Lindbergh* (New York: Harcourt Brace Jovanovich, 1970), 419–21.

19 Beschloss, *Kennedy and Roosevelt: An Uneasy Alliance*, 229.

20 FDRPL, PSFA 0357, Douglas Fairbanks Jr. to FDR, November 19, 1940.

21 *HTF*, 497–98.

EPILOGUE

1 JFKL, JPK Papers, Box 7, JFK to JPK, December 6, 1940.

2 Michael R. Beschloss, *Kennedy and Roosevelt: An Uneasy Alliance* (New York: W.W. Norton, 1980), 232–33.

3 Robert E. Sherwood, *Roosevelt and Hopkins: An Intimate History* (New York: Harper & Brothers, 1948), 235–36.

4 Ibid., 238; RA, GVI/PRIV/DIARY/P 7, vol. 4, Monday, January 20–Saturday, January 25, 1941.

5 Robert E. Sherwood, *Roosevelt and Hopkins: An Intimate History*, 243.

6 Cari Beauchamp, "Two Sons, One Destiny." *Vanity Fair*, January 4, 2012; Charles River, ed., *Joseph P. Kennedy, Jr.: The Life and Legacy of the Eldest Kennedy Brother* (Boston: Charles River Editors, 2017), e-book, location 478–79.

7 https://auislandora.wrlc.org/islandora/object/pearson%3A7814?solr_nav%5Bid%5D =074d5736a390a43e7ff5&solr_nav%5Bpage%5D=0&solr_nav%5Boffset%5D=4#page /2/mode/1up/search/Washington+Merry-Go-Round+January+6%2C+1942.

8 David Nasaw, *The Patriarch: The Remarkable and Turbulent Times of Joseph P. Kennedy* (New York: Penguin Books, 2013), 540, based on the letter dated January 6, 1942, from Pearson to Winchell.

9 JFKL, JPK Papers, Box 101, diary entry March 12, 1943.

10 Barbara Leaming, *Kick Kennedy: The Charmed Life and Tragic Death of the Favorite Kennedy Daughter* (New York: Thomas Dunne Books, 2016), 95, 110, 114–15; Andrew Roberts, *The Holy Fox: A Biography of Lord Halifax* (London: Weidenfeld & Nicolson, 1991), 289.

11 JFKL, https://www.jfklibrary.org/learn/about-jfk/jfk-in-history/john-f-kennedy-and -pt-109; Charles River, ed., *Joseph P. Kennedy, Jr.: The Life and Legacy of the Eldest Kennedy Brother,* e-book, location 526; *HTF,* 582; Leaming, *Kick Kennedy,* 95, 110, 114–15; Roberts, *The Holy Fox,* 176.

12 Catherine Bailey, *Black Diamonds: The Rise and Fall of an English Dynasty* (London: Viking, 2007), 405.

13 Ibid., 332, 421–30.

14 Barbara Leaming, *Kick Kennedy,* 241–45.

15 Ibid., 332, 421–29.

16 Rose Kennedy (with Robert Coughlan), *Times to Remember* (New York: Doubleday & Co., 1974), 287–302. Rose specifically does not mention the circumstances of Kick's liaison with Peter Wentworth-Fitzwilliam, Viscount Milton, or Kick's untimely and tragic death.

17 Victor Lasky, *J.F.K.: The Man and the Myth* (New York: Macmillan, 1963), 24.

SELECTED BIBLIOGRAPHY

MANUSCRIPTS AND ARCHIVAL DOCUMENTS

ASTOR ARCHIVE

MS1416/1/4/109, MS 1416/1/1/1643.

BRITISH LIBRARY

Add. MS 74132.

The Graphic, C. Patrick Thompson "Governor of the Bank" (London: Illustrated News Group), August 1930.

BODLEIAN LIBRARY, UNIVERSITY OF OXFORD

Bjerk, Roger, *Kennedy at the Court of St. James: The Diplomatic Career of Joseph P. Kennedy, 1938–1940.* PhD dissertation, Washington State University, ProQuest Dissertations Publishing, 1971. 7207633.

Vieth, Jane Karoline, *Joseph P. Kennedy: Ambassador to the Court of St. James's 1938–1940,* vols. 1 and 2. Ohio State University, PhD dissertation, ProQuest Dissertations Publishing, 1975. MS 7519497.

MS Dawson 38–45.

MS. Eng. C. 6656.

CHURCHILL ARCHIVE

CHAR 2/235; CHAR 2/237; CHAR 2/238; CHAR 2/329; CHAR 2/332; CHAR 2/359; CHAR 2/606; CHAR 8/211/51; CHAR 8/610; CHAR 9/130; CHAR 20/2B.

CHAMBERLAIN PAPERS

NC/1/17/1–26; NC/2/24; NC 18/1/1045; NC 18/1/1046/1070; NC 7/11/31/1066; NC 7/11/31/1067; NC 7/11/31/1068; NC17/11/32/11.

HARVARD UNIVERSITY

Moffat Diary, Jay Pierrepont Moffat Papers, Houghton Library, Harvard University.

William Phillips Diaries, Houghton Library, Harvard University.

LIBRARY OF CONGRESS

The Diaries of Henry J. Morgenthau (Microfilm 18,915).

The Clare Boothe Luce Papers, Boxes 91–96.

The James M. Landis Papers, MS 29348.

Breckenridge Long Papers, Box 5.

THE NATIONAL ARCHIVES, KEW, ENGLAND

A 60; A 108460/45; A 5134/45; A 2144/1/45; A 666/60/45—German attitude to JPK;

A 8046/45; A 1089/45; A 3142/1089/45; A 1386/A; A 6561/1090/45; A 6501/9—1938.

T 2592; T 2833; T 3107; T 5214/22/383; T 5488; T 589322/383; T 13865/22/383;

T 15438/169/373; T 1477/1025/383; T 8003; T 8957; T 10198; T 11308;
    T 15646/22/383;

T 3501; T 3709/276/373; T 273/403-409; T 13306; T 13076/1025/383.

LO2/330; HO 262/14, HO 139/45-A 471/47145; R 1177/153/37; KV 4/447;
    KV2/678;

KV 4/318; KV 4/331; HO 262/9; HO 262/5; HO 262/7; HO 262/10.

FO 372/3245; FO/800/269; FO371/22829/A1385/1292; FO 371/391; FO 371/22491;

FO 21502; FO 371/21524; FO 371/21542; FO 371/26217; FO 371/21637; FO
    371/22321;

FO 371/22827/1090; FO 371/24217/339; FO 371/24962; FO 5728/5727/10; FO
    371/24248.

FO 371/24251; FO 372/6173; FO 372/3310; FO 372/3319; FO 800/309; FO 800/309-328;

FO 800/322; FO 800/325.

CAB 16/111; CAB 27/623/30; CAB 23/100/10; CAB 23/100/11; CAB 65/2/50.

THE NATIONAL ARCHIVES, COLLEGE PARK, MARYLAND

RG 266/12044568, RG 59.

FDR PRESIDENTIAL LIBRARY

PSFA 0010, 0023, 0028, 0036, 0038, 0052, 0071, 0072, 0117, 0181, 0191–0195, 0207, 0211–
    0214, 0216–0218, 0299–0306, 0312–0314, 0320–0324, 0333, 0334, 0336, 0355–0357,
    0384, 0392, 0360, 0402, 0427, 0491, 0497, 0498.

PPF 0207.

PSFC 0015, 000190, 0205, 0206, 0208.

OF 229.

OXFORD DICTIONARY OF NATIONAL BIOGRAPHY

Chamberlain, Neville, https://doi.org/10.1093/ref:odnb/32347.

Norman, Montagu, https://www-oxforddnb-com.9780198614128-e-
    35252?rskey=FuEAGo&result=2.

JSTOR

(Academic Journal Website)

https://www-jstor-org.ezproxy2.londonlibrary.co.uk/stable/pdf/24447868.pdf?refreqid=exc elsior%3A36e665d9b4780dbd257c05d08af5f3f7.

Blaazer, David, "Finance and the End of Appeasement: The Bank of England, the National Government and the Czech Gold." *Journal of Contemporary History* 40, no. 1 (2005).

Gold, Dore, "The Historical Significance of the Balfour Declaration." *Jewish Political Studies Review* 28, no. 1–2 (2017).

Hilton, Stanley E., "The Welles Mission to Europe, February–March 1940." *Journal of American History* 56, no. 1 (1971).

Jiryis, Sabri, "Secrets of State: An Analysis of the Diaries of Moshe Sharett." *Journal of Palestine Studies* 10, no. 1 (1980).

Polkehn, Klaus, "Secret Contacts: Zionism and Nazi Germany, 1933–1941." *Journal of Palestine Studies* 5, no. 3–4 (1976).

Sedgwick, John, and Michael Pokorny, "The Film Business in the United States and Great Britain in the 1930s." *Economic History Review* New Series 58, no. 1 (2005).

OTHER ONLINE RESOURCES/LIBRARIES

https://auislandora.wrlc.org.

https://avalon.law.yale.edu/wwii/blbk09.asp.

Boston Globe online.

Britishnewspaperarchive.co.uk.

Fortune web archive.

www.haaretz.com.

hansard.parliament.uk.

The Met Office: https://digital.nmla.metoffice.gov.uk/IO_b514b289-5d69-45e3-9db0 -553d3bbc87ba/.

Newspapers.com.

New York Times TimesMachine.

https://www.proimdb.com.

The Times online.

https://www.jpost.com/Opinion/When-FDR-wanted-to-silence-the-Jews-561877.

https://archive.org/details/isbn_9781402200267.

https://history.state.gov.

https://www.storiesfrom1916.com/1916-easter-rising/irish-american-connection.

https://www.youtube.com/watch?v=uQwKI4xvuC0.

https://www.gov.uk/government/news/chancellor-to-repay-the-nations-first-world-war-debt.

http://thames.me.uk/s00231j.htm.

https://www.sis.gov.uk/our-history.html.

www.thespectator.com.

House of Lords, Parliament Archive

BBK/G/6/20, BBK/D/400, BBK/D/399-404, BBK/G/6/19-24.

Royal Archives:

GVI/PRIV/PAL/K/3–6

QM/PRIV/CC/47/1885

QM/PRIV/CC49/144–145

GVI/PRIV/DIARY: 9 Sep, 28 Nov 1939, 11 Mar, 30 May, 7 Aug 11, 13, 17, 20 Oct, 3 Dec 1940, 20–25 Jan 1941

PS/PSO/GVI/PS/MAIN/2650: Letters dated 1 Jan 1938–23 Oct 1940

PS/PSO/GVI/C/100/8

PS/PS/PSO/GVI/C/190/4

PS/PSO/GVI/C/243/6–7, 10–11, 13, 18

PS/PSO/GVI/C/352/1938: 8 Mar

PS/PSO/GVI/C/352/1939: 4 May

PS/PSO/GVI/PS/VISCOM/03400/003/001/001–054

GDKH/ENGT/A/06

JFK Presidential Library:

JFKL/JPKPP-100-015-p0001 (Joseph P. Kennedy Diary April–May 1940).

JFKL/JPKPP-152-003-p0001 (Joseph P. Kennedy Research files May 1940).

JFKL/ JPKPP-071-007-p0001(Joseph P. Kennedy Private Papers, Franklin D. Roosevelt 1933–1944).

https://archiveblog.jfklibrary.org/2015/02/newly-opened-collection-ace-of-clubs-records.

JFKPL/JFKPP-004-097-p0002 (Joseph P. Kennedy Private Papers, letter to Jack Kennedy from James Seymour, press attaché to JPK July 1, 1940).

JFKL, JFK Archive, JFKPP-001-016, School Report on Jean-Jacques Rousseau, undated.

JFKPP-001-012 (JFK Diary European Trip Summer 1937).

Oral History Project, Arthur Krock, Pope Paul VI.

JFKL, Joseph P. Kennedy Private Papers (not available online):

Boxes: Series 1: 1, 2, 3, 7, 18, 19, 26, 40, 47, Series 7: 69–71, 75, 100, Series 8: 90–118, 119, 124, 126, 130–133, 140, 145–147, 154–161, 165, 166, 176, 331.

BOOKS

KENNEDY BIOGRAPHIES

Beschloss, Michael R., *Kennedy and Roosevelt: The Uneasy Alliance*. New York: W. W. Norton, 1980.

De Bedts, Ralph F., *Ambassador Joseph Kennedy 1938–1940: An Anatomy of Appeasement*. New York: Peter Lang, American University Studies, Series IX, vol. 12, 1985.

Goodwin, Doris Kearns, *The Fitzgeralds and the Kennedys: An American Saga*. New York: St. Martin's Press, 1987.

Hamilton, Nigel, *J.F.K.: Reckless Youth*, vol. 1. London: Random House UK, 1992.

Kennedy, Joseph P., ed., *The Story of Films*. New York: A. W. Shaw Company, 1927.

———, *Diplomatic Memoir*. Unpublished.

———, *I'm for Roosevelt*. New York: Reynal & Hitchcock, 1936.

Kennedy, Rose Fitzgerald (with Robert Coughlan), *Times to Remember*. Garden City, NY: Doubleday, 1974.

Kessler, Ronald, *Sins of the Father: Joseph P. Kennedy and the Dynasty He Founded*. New York: Warner Books, 1996.

Lasky, Victor, *J.F.K.: The Man and the Myth*. New York: Macmillan, 1963.

Leaming, Barbara, *Kick Kennedy: The Charmed Life and Tragic Death of the Favorite Kennedy Daughter*. New York: Thomas Dunne Books, 2016.

Nasaw, David, *The Patriarch: The Remarkable Life and Turbulent Times of Joseph P. Kennedy*. New York: Penguin Group (USA) LLC, 2013.

Smith, Amanda, ed., *Hostage to Fortune: The Letters of Joseph P. Kennedy*. New York: Viking, 2001.

Swift, Will, *The Kennedys Amidst the Gathering Storm: A Thousand Days in London, 1938–1940*. New York: Smithsonian Books, 2008.

Whalen, Richard J., *The Founding Father: The Story of Joseph P. Kennedy*. Washington, D.C.: Regnery Gateway, 1993.

GENERAL BOOKS

Alsop, Joseph, and Robert Kintner, *American White Paper: The Story of American Diplomacy and the Second World War*. London: Michael Joseph Ltd., 1940.

Bailey, Catherine, *Black Diamonds: The Rise and Fall of an English Dynasty*. London: Viking, 2007.

Barnes, John, and David Nicolson, eds., *The Empire at Bay: The Leo Amery Diaries 1929–1945*. London: Hutchinson & Co. Ltd, 1988.

Baxter, John, *Chronicles of Old Paris: Exploring the Historic City of Light*. New York: Museyon, 2011.

Bilainkin, George, *Diary of a Diplomatic Correspondent*. London: George Allen & Unwin Ltd, 1942.

Bonham Carter, Violet, *The Impact of Personality in Politics*. Oxford: Clarendon Press, 1963.

Bouverie, Tim, *Appeasing Hitler: Chamberlain, Churchill, and the Road to War*. London: Vintage e-book, 2019.

Boyle, Andrew, *Montagu Norman*. New York: Weybright and Talley, 1967.

Breitman, Richard, Norman J.W. Goda, Timothy Naftali, and Robert Wolfe, *U.S. Intelligence and the Nazis*. New York: Cambridge University Press, 2005.

Bullitt, Orville H., ed., *For the President Personal & Secret: Correspondence between Franklin D. Roosevelt and William C. Bullitt*. Boston: Houghton Mifflin, 1972.

Butler, R.A., *The Art of the Possible: The Memoirs of Lord Butler*. London: Hamish Hamilton, 1971.

Cave Brown, Anthony, *Bodyguard of Lies*. London: W. H. Allen & Co., Ltd., 1977.

Chamberlain, Neville, *Struggle for Peace*. London: Hutchinson & Co., 1939.

Chisholm, Anne, and Michael Davie, *Beaverbrook: A Life*. London: Hutchinson Publishing Co., 1992.

Churchill, Winston S., *The Second World War*, vol. 1. *The Gathering Storm*. London: The Reprint Society, 1956.

———, *The Second World War*, vol. 2. *Their Finest Hour*. London: The Reprint Society, 1956.

Ciano, Count Galeazzo, *Ciano's Diary 1937–1943*. London: Phoenix Publishing, 2002.

Cockburn, Claud, *I, Claud*. London: Penguin Books Ltd, 1967.

Cole, W. S., *Roosevelt and The Isolationists: 1932–1945*. Lincoln: University of Nebraska Press, 1983.

Collins, Roger, *Keepers of the Keys of Heaven: A History of the Papacy*. London: Phoenix, 2010.

Colville, John, *The Fringes of Power: Downing Street Diaries 1939–1945*. London: Weidenfeld & Nicolson, 2004.

Colvin, Ian, *The Chamberlain Cabinet*. London: Victor Gollancz Ltd, 1971.

Cornwell, John, *Hitler's Pope: The Secret History of Pius XII*. New York: Viking, 1999.

———, *Hitler's Scientists: Science, War, and the Devil's Pact*. New York: Viking Books, 2003.

Crockett, Richard, *Twilight of Truth: Chamberlain, Appeasement and the Manipulation of the Press*. London: Weidenfeld & Nicolson, 1989.

Davis, Elmer, ed., Edward R. Murrow, *This Is London*. London: Cassell and Company Ltd, 1941.

De Courcy, Anne, *1939: The Last Season*. London: Phoenix Books, 1989.

Dilks, David, ed., *The Diaries of Sir Alexander Cadogan O.M. 1938–1945*. London: Cassell, 1971.

Documents on German Foreign Policy 1918–1945, Series C (1937–1945), vol. 5. The Third Reich First Phase, March 5, 1936–October 31, 1936. London: HMSO, 1966.

Documents on German Foreign Policy 1918–1945, Series C (1937–1945), vol. 6. The Third Reich First Phase, November 1, 1936–November 14, 1937. London: HMSO, 1983.

Documents on German Foreign Policy 1918–1945, Series D (1937–1945), vol. 7. The Last Days of Peace, August 9–September 3, 1939. London: HMSO, 1956.

Documents on German Foreign Policy 1918–1945, Series D (1937–1945), vol. 8. The War Years, September 4, 1939–March 18, 1940. London: HMSO, 1954.

Documents on German Foreign Policy 1918-1945, Series D (1937–1945), vol. 9. The War Years, March 18, 1940–June 22, 1940. London: HMSO, 1956.

Domarus, Max, *Hitler: Speeches and Proclamations 1932–1938*, vol. 2: The Years 1935 to 1938. London: I. B. Tauris & Co.

———, *Hitler: Speeches and Proclamations 1932–1945*, vol. 3: The Years 1939 to 1940. London: I. B. Tauris & Co.

Fanning, Charles, *The Irish Voice in America: 250 Years of Irish-American Fiction*, 2nd ed. Lexington: University of Kentucky Press, 2000.

Farley, James A., *Jim Farley's Story: The Roosevelt Years*. New York: McGraw-Hill, 1948.

Feiling, Keith, *The Life of Neville Chamberlain*. Hamden, CT: Archon Books, 1970

Foreign Relations of the United States Diplomatic Papers, 1937, Vol. II, The British Commonwealth, Europe, Near East and Africa. Washington, D.C.: Department of State Office of the Historian, ebook, 2018.

Foreign Relations of the United States Diplomatic Papers, 1938, Vol. I, General. Washington, D.C.: Department of State Office of the Historian, ebook, 2018.

Foreign Relations of the United States Diplomatic Papers, 1938, Vol. II, The British Commonwealth, Europe, Near East and Africa. Washington, D.C.: Department of State Office of the Historian, ebook, 2018.

Foreign Relations of the United States Diplomatic Papers, 1939, Vol. I, General. Washington, D.C.: Department of State Office of the Historian, ebook, 2018.

Foreign Relations of the United States Diplomatic Papers, 1939, Vol. II, The British Commonwealth, Europe, Near East and Africa. Washington, D.C.: Department of State Office of the Historian, ebook, 2018.

Foreign Relations of the United States Diplomatic Papers, 1940, Vol. I, General. Washington, D.C.: Department of State Office of the Historian, ebook, 2018.

Foreign Relations of the United States Diplomatic Papers, 1940, Vol. III, The British Commonwealth, Europe, Near East and Africa. Washington, D.C.: Department of State Office of the Historian, ebook, 2018.

Fry, Helen, *Spymaster: The Secret Life of Kendrick*. London: Marranos Press, 2018.

Gannon, Robert I., *The Cardinal Spellman Story*. London: Robert Hale Limited, 1963.

Gellman, Irwin F., *Secret Affairs: Franklin Roosevelt, Cordell Hull, and Sumner Welles*. New York: 1995.

Goodson, James, *Tumult in the Clouds: The Classic Story of War in the Air*. London: Penguin Books, 2003.

Gorodetsky, Gabriel, ed., *The Maisky Diaries: The Wartime Revelations of Stalin's Ambassador in London*. New Haven, CT: Yale University Press, 2016.

Hart-Davis, Duff, ed., *King's Counsellor: Abdication and War: The Diaries of Sir Alan Lascelles*. London: Weidenfeld & Nicolson, 2006.

Helmreich, Christian, *The German Churches Under Hitler: Background, Struggle, and Epilogue*. Detroit: Wayne State University Press, 1979.

Holland, James, *The War in the West: Germany Ascendant 1939–1941*. London: Corgi Books, 2016.

Holmes, Colin, *Anti-Semitism in British Society 1876–1939*. London: Edward Arnold (Publishers), 1979.

Hooker, Nancy Harvison, ed., *The Moffat Papers: Selections from the Diplomatic Journals of Jay Pierrepont Moffat 1919–1943*. Cambridge: Harvard University Press, 1956.

Ickes, Harold L., *The Secret Diary of Harold L. Ickes: The Inside Struggle 1936–1939*, vol. 1. London: Weidenfeld & Nicolson, 1955.

———, *The Secret Diary of Harold L. Ickes: The Lowering Clouds 1939–1941*, vol. 3. London: Weidenfeld & Nicolson, 1955.

Jones, Tom, *Diary with Letters 1931–1950*. London: Oxford University Press, 1954.

Kendrick, Alexander, *Prime Time: The Life of Edward R. Murrow*. New York: Avon Books, 1970.

Kennedy, John F., *Why England Slept*. Westport, CT: Greenwood Press Publishers, 1961.

Kennedy, Joseph P., and James M. Landis, *The Surrender of King Leopold*. New York: Joseph P. Kennedy Memorial Foundation, 1950.

Kimball, Warren, *Forged in War: Churchill, Roosevelt and the Second World War*. New York: Harper-Collins, 1997.

Krock, Arthur, *Memoirs: Sixty Years on the Firing Line*. New York: Funk & Wagnalls, 1968.

Larson, Erik, *In the Garden of Beasts: Love, Terror, and an American Family in Hitler's Berlin*. New York: Crown Publishing ebook, 2011.

Lasky, Betty, *RKO: The Biggest Little Major of Them All*. Santa Monica, CA: Roundtable Publishing, 1989.

Leutze, James, ed., *The London Observer: The Journal of General Raymond E. Lee 1940–1941*. London: Hutchinson of London, 1971.

Lindbergh, Charles A., *The Wartime Journals of Charles A. Lindbergh*. New York: Harcourt Brace Jovanovich, 1970.

Lovell, Mary S., *The Riviera Set*. London: Abacus, 2016.

Luce, Clare Boothe, *European Spring*. London: Hamish Hamilton, 1941. (Note: the U.S. edition is entitled *Europe in the Spring*. New York: Alfred A. Knopf, 1940.)

McInery, Ralph, *The Defamation of Pius XII*. South Bend, IN: Saint Augustine's Press, 2000.

Moley, Raymond, *The First New Deal*. New York: Harcourt, 1966.

Morris, Silvia Jukes, *Rage for Fame: The Ascent of Clare Boothe Luce*. New York: Random House, 2014.

Mosley, Leonard, *On Borrowed Time: How World War II Began*. New York: Random House, 1969.

Neville, Peter, *Appeasing Hitler: The Diplomacy of Sir Nevile Henderson*. Basingstoke, UK: Macmillan Press, 2000.

Nicolson, Harold, *Diaries and Letters 1930–1939*, vol. 1. London: William Collins Sons & Co., 1966.

Nicolson, Harold, *Diaries and Letters 1939–1945*, vol. 2. London: William Collins Sons & Co., 1967.

Nixon, Edward B., ed., *Franklin D. Roosevelt and Foreign Affairs*, vol. 3, September 1935–December 1937. New York: Belknap Press, 1969.

Offner, Arnold A., *American Appeasement: United States Foreign Policy and Germany 1933–1938*. Cambridge: Harvard University Press, 1969.

Olson, Lynne, *Troublesome Young Men: The Churchill Conspiracy of 1940*. London: Bloomsbury Publishing, 2008.

Palmer, David, *Organizing the Shipyards: Unionization at New York Ship, Federal Ship, and Fore River 1898–1945*, vol. 1 of 2. Boston, MA: Brandeis University, 1990 (Ph.D. dissertation).

Panter-Downes, Mollie, *London War Notes 1939–1945*. London: Longman Group Limited, 1972.

Reith, J.C.W., *Into the Wind*. London: Hodder & Stoughton, 1949.

Reston, James, *Deadline*. New York: Random House, 1991.

Rhodes James, Robert, ed., *Chips: The Diaries of Sir Henry Channon*. London: Weidenfeld & Nicolson, 1967.

Riva, Maria, *Marlene Dietrich: The Life*. New York: Pegasus Books, 1992.

Roberts, Andrew, *Hitler and Churchill: Secrets of Leadership*. London: Weidenfeld & Nicolson, 2003.

———, *The Holy Fox: The Life of Lord Halifax*. London: Weidenfeld & Nicolson, 1991.

Ronald, Susan, *A Dangerous Woman: American Beauty, Noted Philanthropist, Nazi Collaborator—The Life of Florence Gould*. New York: St. Martin's Press, 2018.

———, *Hitler's Art Thief: Hildebrand Gurlitt, the Nazis and the Looting of Europe's Treasures*. New York, St. Martin's Press, 2015.

———, *Condé Nast: The Man and His Empire—A Biography*. New York: St. Martin's Press, 2019.

Roosevelt, Elliott, ed., *The Roosevelt Letters: Being the Personal Correspondence of Franklin Delano Roosevelt*. London: George G. Harrap & Co., 1952.

Rose, N.A., ed., *Baffy: The Diaries of Blanche Dugdale 1936–1947*. London: Vallentine, Mitchell, 1973.

Rosenman, Samuel I., *The Public Papers and Addresses of Franklin D. Roosevelt*, vol. 7. New York: Random House, 1941.

Ross, Stephen J., *Hitler in Los Angeles: How Jews Foiled Nazi Plots Against Hollywood and America*. New York: Bloomsbury, 2017.

Sebba, Anne, *That Woman: The Life of Wallis Simpson Duchess of Windsor*. London: Weidenfeld & Nicolson, 2011.

Seib, Philip, *Broadcasts from the Blitz: How Edward R. Murrow Helped Lead America into War*. Washington, D.C.: Potomac Books, 2006.

Self, Robert, ed., *The Neville Chamberlain Diary Letters, vol. 4. The Downing Street Years, 1934–1940*. London: Ashgate, 2005.

Self, Robert C., ed., *The Austen Chamberlain Diary Letters*. Cambridge, UK: Cambridge University Press, 1995.

Shakespeare, Nicholas, *Six Minutes in May: How Churchill Unexpectedly Became Prime Minister*. London: Harvill Secker, 2017.

Sherwood, Robert E., *Roosevelt and Hopkins: An Intimate History*. New York: Harper & Brothers, 1948.

Smart, Nick, ed., *The Diaries and Letters of Robert Bernays, 1932–1939: An Insider's Account of the House of Commons*. Lewiston, NY: The Edward Mellen Press, 1996.

Stegner, Wallace, "The Radio Priest and His Flock," in *The Aspirin Age*, Isabel Leighton, ed. London: Penguin Books, 1964.

Sulzberger, C. L., *The Last of the Giants*. New York: Macmillan, 1971.

Swanson, Gloria, *Swanson on Swanson*. London: Michael Joseph, 1981.

Vansittart, Lord R.G.V., *The Mist Procession: The Autobiography of Lord Vansittart*. London: Hutchinson of London, 1958.

Waller, Douglas, *Wild Bill Donovan: The Spymaster Who Created the OSS and Modern American Espionage*. New York: Free Press, 2011.

Wapshott, Nicholas, *The Sphinx: Franklin Roosevelt, the Isolationists, and the Road to World War II*. New York: W. W. Norton, 2015.

INDEX